S0-ASQ-558

Analyzing
English Grammar

Fifth Edition

THOMAS P. KLAMMER
California State University, Fullerton

MURIEL R. SCHULZ

ANGELA DELLA VOLPE
California State University, Fullerton

PEARSON
Longman

New York San Francisco Boston
London Toronto Sydney Tokyo Singapore Madrid
Mexico City Munich Paris Cape Town Hong Kong Montreal

Publisher: Joseph Opiela
Senior Supplements Editor: Donna Campion
Media Supplements Editor: Jenna Egan
Senior Marketing Manager: Sandra McGuire
Production Manager: Eric Jorgensen
Project Coordination, Text Design, and Electronic Page Makeup: Electronic Publishing Services Inc., NYC
Cover Design Manager: John Callahan
Manufacturing Manager: Mary Fischer
Printer and Binder: RR Donnelley & Sons Company
Cover Printer: Coral Graphics Services

Selected headlines (pp. 65, 151, 372, 392–393, 408) reprinted from *Columbia Journalism Review* ©1989, 1996, 2000, 2001, 2002, 2003, 2004, 2005 by *Columbia Journalism Review*.

Library of Congress Cataloging-in-Publication Data

Klammer, Thomas P., 1944-
 Analyzing English grammar / Thomas P. Klammer, Muriel R. Schulz, Angela Della Volpe—5th ed.
  p. cm.
 Includes index.
 ISBN 0-321-42618-5
 1. English language—Grammar. I. Schulz, Muriel. II. Della Volpe, Angela. III. Title.
PE1106.K5 2006
428.2--dc22

                          2006014074

Copyright © 2007 by Pearson Education, Inc.

All rights reserved. No part of this publication may be reproduced, stored in a retrieval system, or transmitted, in any form or by any means, electronic, mechanical, photocopying, recording, or otherwise, without the prior written permission or the publisher. Printed in the United States.

Visit us at www.ablongman.com

ISBN 0-321-42618-5

  3 4 5 6 7 8 9 10—DOH—09 08 07

━━Contents━━

━━━━━ CHAPTER 3 ━━━━━━━━━━━━━━━━━━

THE MORPHOLOGY OF ENGLISH   37

━━━━━ CHAPTER 4 ━━━━━━━━━━━━━━━━━━

FORM-CLASS WORDS   63

CHAPTER 7

FIVE BASIC SENTENCE TYPES   197

CHAPTER 8

BASIC SENTENCE TRANSFORMATIONS   239

CHAPTER 9

FINITE VERB CLAUSES, PART I:
Adverbial and Adjectival Clauses   285

CHAPTER 10

FINITE VERB CLAUSES, PART II:
Nominal Clauses   323

▬▬▬ CHAPTER 11 ▬▬▬

NONFINITE VERB PHRASES, PART I:
Infinitive Phrases   353

▬▬▬ CHAPTER 12 ▬▬▬

NONFINITE VERB PHRASES, PART II:
Participle and Gerund Phrases   377

Preface

In preparing the fifth edition of *Analyzing English Grammar*, we have benefited from questions, corrections, and suggestions sent to us by students and teachers who have used earlier editions of the book. They have urged us to retain our analytical approach, which is based on our underlying premise that grammar instruction at the college level should provide students with the tools to deduce for themselves how language works and how grammars have been made. The grammar of English that students are asked to master is the construct of linguists who sat down and analyzed spoken and written English, dividing it into words and groups of words that they interpreted as being alike in some way, then classifying those groups into meaningful categories, and, finally, labeling the categories. In *Analyzing English Grammar*, we show students how those categories were arrived at and why it is that language does not always fit the description that linguists have imposed upon it. Retracing the logical, step-by-step reasoning used in language description and showing the peripheral examples that resist neat classification provide keys to understanding English grammar and diminishing students' fears of new terminology.

This revised fifth edition evolved in a number of ways as we addressed the requests of students and professors who have used earlier editions.

- To help students master the material, we have added brief *Chapter Previews* alerting students to what they are about to study and encouraging them to recall what they already know about those topics. We have retained *Chapter Goals,* which are intended to help students focus on core concepts as they read through the material.

- In most of the exercises in the current edition, we embed the structures to be reviewed within paragraphs of ordinary prose, either written as paragraphs or as a series of numbered questions forming a related paragraph. The exercises continue to emphasize the development of skills of independent analysis and inductive reasoning, but they also ask students to recognize and manipulate grammatical constructions within extended discourse.

- We have always striven to increase students' awareness of the linguistic diversity that is present around them. It has also been our wish to explain diversity in a way that leads our readers to respect nonstandard dialects and their speakers. In this edition, in order to show how Standard American English differs systematically from one of several dialects of American English, we have expanded our discussion of African-American Vernacular English variants of some of the grammatical structures presented here. Although our text deals with the grammatical rules of Standard American English, we remind students that all dialects of English are rule-governed; that is, speakers of all dialects share a set of common rules of grammar that may differ from, but are not linguistically inferior to any other. Social considerations have made Standard English the dialect taught in our schools.

- Although we have tried to keep linguistic jargon to a minimum throughout the text, a core set of terms used to describe grammar is inevitable in a book like this. In order to provide students with a resource for rapidly looking up grammatical terms, we have expanded the glossary, elaborating some of the definitions already there and adding many terms not previously included. All glossary terms also appear in the Index, with entries that will lead students to a more detailed discussion of the concept named.

- To help students understand the language processes evident in their own lives, we have broadened our discussion of everyday language and have expanded our discussion of word formation and semantics.

- Readers have asked us to demonstrate how *Analyzing English Grammar* relates to the language and linguistic requirements for students seeking a teacher certification credential in English. In many states, the passing of a comprehensive exam in English grammatical structure (the subject of our text) is a step in the certification process, but a wider understanding of language is expected, as well. We discuss this question in more detail below.

TEACHER CERTIFICATION REQUIREMENTS

In an ever-changing world, the diversity of our student population requires that candidates for a teaching credential in English understand something about the nature of human language, the principles of language acquisition and development, the manner of language variation, and the historical and cultural influences on the development of English. Specific credential requirements vary from state to state, but the requirements set forth by the California Commission on Teacher Credentialing for English Subject Matter are typical and straightforward. California expects candidates for the credential to have a broad knowledge of language and of grammar, as well as of English literature.

The language requirements state that students should be able to do the following:

a. Recognize the nature of human language, the kinds of differences that exist among languages, the universality of linguistic structures, and the kinds of change that occur in different languages across time.

b. Demonstrate a knowledge of the structure of words, including sound patterns (phonology), word formation (derivation, compounding, roots, and affixes), and inflection (morphology).

c. Demonstrate knowledge of sentence structure (syntax), word and sentence meanings (semantics), and language function in communicative context (pragmatics).

d. Use appropriate print and electronic sources to research etymologies; recognize conventions of English orthography; and perceive changes in the meaning and pronunciation of words.

In addition, students must have a thorough knowledge of the grammatical structures of English, including the ability to do the following:

a. Identify methods of sentence construction (that is, sentence combining involving coordinators and subordinators; sentence embedding and expanding using clausal and phrasal modifiers).

b. Analyze parts of speech and their distinctive structures and functions (nouns, including count and non-count nouns, and noun phrases involving the determiner system; prepositions and prepositional phrases; adjectives and adverbs).

c. Describe the forms and functions of the English verb system (tenses, modals, verb modifiers, objects and complements, verbal phrases).

In *Analyzing English Grammar,* Fifth Edition, we have added material that is particularly suitable for preparing students who will seek a teaching credential in English. Such students, by studying this book, will acquire the knowledge required for the double domain of language and linguistics. Our book presents them with a broad and a deep conceptual knowledge of the subject matter, preparing them to teach grammatical structures to learners coming from a variety of linguistic and sociocultural backgrounds.

ASSUMPTIONS AND GOALS

Students can use *Analyzing English Grammar,* Fifth Edition, without having previously studied grammar or linguistics. While the book draws on traditional, structural, and transformational grammatical theory, its primary concern is to be a sound pedagogical grammar, not a treatise on linguistic theory. It takes an eclectic approach, aiming to be an effective tool that will support and assist students in learning about English.

Grammar instruction—at the primary, secondary, or university level—has traditionally relied heavily on rote learning. The charts and exercises favored by writers of textbooks and workbooks encourage students to memorize large chunks of information about the syntactic structure of English. Such memorization might be successful if the language were organized clearly into neat categories, but it is not. In fact, modern linguistic theory—with its recognition of the existence of a substantial segment of "fuzzy grammar," consisting of items that do not fit neatly into any of the existing taxonomies—demonstrates that we cannot hope to memorize a body of materials that will enable us to analyze any but the most prototypical exemplars of grammatical categories.

Even more important, studies of cognition demonstrate that, in general, the memorization process distracts attention from and interferes with the ability to comprehend the information at hand. As a result, many students fail to master the material in grammar courses, and others who perform adequately on tests are hopelessly confused six months or a year later when asked to identify or explain even a common grammatical form.

Analyzing English Grammar, Fifth Edition, differs in several ways from texts aimed at a similar audience. First, it directly addresses the needs of its readers, a diverse group of students who may have limited knowledge of traditional grammatical terminology and concepts. Second, it is enlightened by the work of Piaget, Bloom, and many other researchers into the modes of human cognition and learning, who suggest a variety of instructional strategies that prompt students not just to memorize but to analyze and think critically. Third, because it recognizes that language categories are not all neatly delineated and differentiated, the text presents and organizes material to involve students in analytical thinking throughout; numerous exercises are arranged to lead students from mastery of prototypical cases toward exploration and analysis of the exceptions and inconsistencies that characterize actual language. The intended result is that students achieve a permanent ability to think critically and analytically about the English language, not just a temporary and partial mastery of a few grammatical terms and categories through rote learning of simple examples.

ORGANIZATION OF THE BOOK

The first two chapters introduce students to the study of grammar, distinguish descriptive and prescriptive grammar, introduce the key concept of grammatical *prototype*, explain the role of diagrams in analyzing syntax, and suggest how students can most effectively approach learning about grammar. We give particular prominence in these opening chapters to the variable nature of language, placing standard English in a context of regional, social, and stylistic variation and relating the study of grammar to the language acquisition process.

Chapters 3, 4, and 5 present word-level grammar, from derivational and inflectional morphology through form-class words and structure-class words. Chapter 6 focuses on the nature of phrases, with particular attention to the regular patterns of the English verb phrase.

Chapter 7 teaches students to analyze sentences in terms of five prototypes that underlie the sentences that actually occur in speech and writing. Chapter 8 introduces basic sentence transformations that help students to understand negative, interrogative, imperative, and passive sentences as well as those with indirect objects.

In Chapters 9 and 10, students analyze finite verb clauses (subordinate, relative, *that*, and interrogative clauses) and achieve a thorough understanding of the complex sentence. Chapters 11 and 12 extend this understanding to nonfinite verb phrases (infinitives, participles, and gerunds) that are derived from clauses.

The appendix on phonology gives students a basic grounding in the sound system of English. An understanding of the phonemic principles covered in the appendix is important to elementary school teachers today, as an essential part of phonics instruction is concerned with fostering phonemic awareness in students learning to read and write. The appendix fits well between the second and third chapters; however, the discussion of the morphological structure of English words in Chapters 3, 4, and 5 is self-contained and does not require that students study the appendix. A glossary, giving succinct explanations of key terms, follows the appendix. A comprehensive index is provided as well.

Special Features

- Students learn to move from clear, prototypical cases to more complex, borderline, "fuzzy" examples.

- Chapter Previews and Goals alert students to what they are about to study and encourage them to recall what they already know about those topics. Chapter Summaries allow for quick review.

- Within chapters, critically important concepts and processes are briefly restated in Summary figures. Figures outlining Rules of Thumb recapitulate step-by-step analytical methods and verification procedures in simple language.

- Phrase marker tree diagrams, adapted from transformational grammar, and traditional Reed-Kellogg diagrams serve as alternative visual tools for analyzing sentence structure graphically. Students who are planning to become teachers may eventually be given a textbook that requires them to teach others how to draw Reed-Kellogg diagrams. For that reason, we have included enough information throughout the text to enable students to understand and practice the principles of sentence diagramming.

- Structural sentence formulas supplement diagrams to represent the five prototypical patterns underlying English sentences.

- "What's the Usage?" sections and "Practical Applications" exercises show how grammatical concepts apply in current written and spoken language.

- Frequent exercises lead students to use and master the information and techniques of analysis that they are learning.

- The concepts of *form* and *function* continue to constitute a unifying theme of the fifth edition. Attaining a solid understanding of their relationship in English grammar is, we believe, essential to successful student learning in the courses for which our text is intended.

- Supplementing the book is an instructor's manual, which includes suggestions for teaching each chapter, quiz questions, and reproducible study guides and answer keys for the exercises. Please ask your Longman sales representative for a copy: ISBN 0-321-44751-4.

Support for Real Student Learning

Analyzing English Grammar, Fifth Edition, is consistently concerned with developing student thinking skills and genuine understanding, not just the rote learning and memorization that have characterized English grammar textbooks and classes since their inception more than a century ago. In its discussion, description, and explanation, the text speaks directly to students in understandable language, modeling throughout the techniques of step-by-step reasoning that we teach in our own classes. The text discusses in the first chapter (and wherever appropriate in later chapters) the various kinds of learning that are involved in studying grammar (or any other subject), helping students to recognize which matters are properly learned by memorization (some terminology, for example) and which are better approached with higher-level thinking skills.

Because a few students in grammar classes can almost always guess the "correct" answers to simple exercises, our text takes special care to diminish the rewards for correctness that make "right" answers an end in themselves. Instead of focusing its attention on filling in the blank correctly, *Analyzing English Grammar,* Fifth Edition, models inquiry and verification procedures, repeatedly demonstrating and eliciting critical thinking and analysis from students. The arrangement of discussion and exercises is particularly helpful for slow learners, who need time to digest the solutions to problems while they are being discussed. Throughout, the book emphasizes verifying and explaining answers to exercises and solutions to problems rather than simply coming up with the "right" answer without knowing why. Even as it speaks to students without sophisticated background in the subject, the book remains faithful to the complexity of real language by recognizing the role of ambiguity in the structure of English and frequently evaluating alternative answers to exercises.

Some students have remarked that in spite of being good writers, they have difficulty reading and understanding the material in grammar texts. The following are study tips our students have found useful. **Preview** the text material that will be covered in the lecture by quickly reading the introductory and summary pages, the section headings, and the examples and diagrams; look over the exercises at the end of each section and familiarize yourself with the list of terms at the end of the chapter. During the lecture, **take notes** on the concepts, procedures, or examples that the instructor emphasizes. After class, and as soon as possible, **summarize**, **review,** and **edit** your notes. Lastly, set aside time to **study** your text so that you understand the material thoroughly. Pause periodically to recall what you have read, and compare your recollection with your notes.

We hope that this new edition of *Analyzing English Grammar* will be as helpful to the instructors and students who use it as it has been to us and our students. We will be grateful for comments and criticisms.

ACKNOWLEDGMENTS

Students and teachers who use the text will benefit from the help we have received from our students and colleagues in the Department of English and Comparative Literature and in the Linguistics Program at California State University, Fullerton, in particular Mary Kay Crouch, Ane Ipsen, Franz Müller-Gotama, Sherri Sawicki, and Heping Zhao. We are deeply grateful to them. We owe special thanks to students in English 303, the Structure of Modern English, who have used progressively revised versions of this book in our classes over several years. They have been the kindest (and most honest) critics we have ever had.

We are grateful to Fred Field, of the California State University, Northridge, Christine Rauchfuss Gray, of the Community College of Baltimore County, Maryland, and Xiaozhao Huang, of the University of North Dakota. Their thoughtful responses to the earlier editions helped us to clarify our thinking as we began the revision. We appreciate, as well, the careful and attentive reading of the completed text, by Sherri Sawicki, of the California State University, Fullerton.

We want to thank the reviewers selected by Pearson Longman Publishers, who provided careful critiques that were extremely helpful to us: Garry Molholt, West Chester University; Marshall Myers, Eastern Kentucky University; Teresa Dalle, University of Memphis; Mary B. Zeigler, Georgia State University; Tometro Hopkins, Florida International University; Linda Mitchell, San Jose State University.

Working with the staff of Pearson Longman Publishers has been a real pleasure. As in the preparation of the earlier editions, we have benefited enormously from the wisdom and advice of Senior Vice President and Editor in Chief Joseph Opiela. We thank him for his patience and wise counsel.

Finally, we thank Joan Klammer, Max Schulz, and Ronald Hughes, whose patient love, support, and good humor have not wavered through years of what must seem an inexplicable fascination with the pedagogy of grammatical analysis.

THOMAS P. KLAMMER

MURIEL R. SCHULZ

ANGELA DELLA VOLPE

Introduction 1

As a speaker of English, whether as your first language or as a language you have learned or are still learning later in life, you already know much of the grammar that we present in this book. However, there are different ways of knowing. Our goal is to change your way of knowing grammar.

When you are able to list the steps to be followed in order to produce a result, you are said to have _focal knowledge_ of a process. When your information about how to produce a result is at an unconscious level, it is said to be _tacit knowledge._ You can probably describe precisely to someone else the steps you follow to turn on a light switch, light an oven, or start an automobile. Your knowledge of these actions is both tacit (you can perform them without thinking about them) and focal (you can describe to someone else how to do them).

Although much of the knowledge you possess is controlled both at a tacit and at a focal level, some is not. For example, if you drive a car, you have acquired an unconscious knowledge of how to steer an automobile. If the wind blows your car to the right when you are driving at a high speed, you must make rapid and precise calculations of how much to move the steering wheel to the left and how rapidly to make that move in order to maintain your forward motion as steadily as possible. If you move the wheel too little or too late, you may be carried off the road before you can correct your error. If you move the wheel too much or too suddenly, the result could be equally catastrophic. Although you make such adjustments continuously as you drive, you would find it difficult to explain to someone else how you do it.

What you have now is mostly an unconscious knowledge of English grammar. If you have been speaking English all your life, you are able to communicate quite efficiently without thinking much about what you are doing. You know, for example, that English speakers say _She is a girl_ but not _She girl a is._ Your ability as a speaker of English enables you to distinguish English sentences from non-English sentences. If you learned English as an adult, you may still think consciously of some of the rules of English, whether to use an article before _girl,_ for example, and, perhaps surprisingly to you, you may have more focal, or conscious, knowledge of some aspects of English than your native-English-speaking classmates, even though they may possess a more effective ability to communicate.

Our purpose in this book is to improve your *focal* knowledge of English grammar, to enable you to explain exactly what it is that you do to produce grammatical spoken or written English and how you do it. Furthermore, we want to assist you to become less dependent on language "authorities," like English teachers, grammar handbooks, usage guides, and textbooks such as this one by enabling you to analyze English grammar for yourself, to find your own answers independently. Focal knowledge requires a knowledge of the terminology used to think about and to talk about language use. Having it will enable you to explain to others why one form is acceptable in standard English and another is not—to explain, for example, that *She is girl* does not occur in English because it violates the English rule that specifies that a singular common noun must be preceded by an article or some other kind of determiner. If you have any difficulty writing standard American English, then you must learn to edit your own writing. To do so requires a conscious knowledge of the rules governing standard usage. If you try to edit by feel, you will find that you cannot rely on your intuition. In fact, students often intuitively change what was originally a correct answer on a grammar test or a grammatical structure in a piece of writing, only to discover that they have substituted a wrong choice for the right one.

Even if you are able to write standard English without difficulty and to do well on objective tests of English grammar, you may find it necessary to have a focal knowledge of English grammar. If you wish to become a teacher, you will find that you cannot teach your intuitive knowledge to others. You will need to be able not only to tell your students which of two competing forms is better but also to explain to them why it is preferable. Most important, however, focal knowledge adds a dimension to your understanding of grammar, enabling you to evaluate the rules and advice given in grammar handbooks and to make wise stylistic choices between alternatives in your own use of language.

WHAT IS GRAMMAR?

Many linguists assume that the form human languages take is determined by the nature of the human mind. Because human memory is limited, for example, we must group words into small phrases and these into larger ones in order to communicate information. To see why this is so, try to repeat, after reading once, each of the following:

(1)   *Stands corner little the on house old of and 12th that Vine the* belongs to me.

(2)   *The little old house that stands on the corner of 12th and Vine* belongs to me.

The second set of words is easier to understand and remember because it is made up of meaningful groupings of words called *phrases,* groupings specified by the grammar of English. Example (2) is a sentence, whereas (1) is not. We find it difficult to keep 13 unrelated words in memory while we are processing new information; putting the same words into a standard pattern considerably simplifies the operation for us. Those patterns differ somewhat from language to language, and linguists speak of them as being determined by the rules that constitute any given language. A rule of English specifies, for example, that subjects usually precede predicates. This is not true of all languages, but it is characteristic of English that the subject usually appears at the beginning of the sentence.

It is, perhaps, because language structure reflects some aspects of the human mind that children mastering language typically form a remarkably uniform set of patterns for using language, a set far more complex than any that grammarians have been able to describe. Children seem to form those patterns by generating and testing hypotheses about how language works. By the time they enter school, most children have mastered the most essential parts of the system and are able to form quite complicated sentences.

When linguists write a grammar of a language, they attempt to describe the rules that govern the grouping of the words of that language into meaningful patterns. But the grammarian's rules are not necessarily laws that the language obeys. They are merely hypotheses, imperfect and incomplete at best, about how the language system operates. For example, grammarians agree that the rules of English specify not only that *the little old house* constitutes a noun phrase (a sequence of words that can stand in place of a single noun) but also that *little* must precede *old*. They specify more, as well, including how such a phrase shall be pronounced (*phonology*), where it can occur in a sentence (*syntax*), what it means (*semantics*), and the influence of social context on the way it is interpreted (*pragmatics*). In fact, the grammar of English specifies more than has ever been described by any grammarian of English. All grammatical descriptions, including the ones followed in this book, are partial because all languages have proven far too complex for any grammarian to describe completely.

The word for the subject of our study, **grammar,** has a number of distinct meanings. Grammar can refer to the linguistic system that presumably exists in the mind of a speaker[1] of a language, the knowledge to which we refer when we say that someone "knows" a language. Grammar can also mean a description of the language system (*They are writing a grammar of English*). Furthermore, grammar can refer to an ideal set of rules (*He always uses good grammar*), sometimes taught with a righteous tone as so-called correct or proper grammar. Or grammar may refer to a handbook containing the prescriptive rules (*Look it up in your grammar*). You must see the word in context before being able to judge the meaning intended.

We are concerned in this text with two kinds of grammatical description. The first involves **descriptive rules,** which describe how our grammatical system operates, rules that are the same for all speakers of English (e.g., subjects precede verbs in most sentences). The second involves **prescriptive rules** (such as whether to use *who* or *whom* in a given context), which govern the version of English considered appropriate for use by educated speakers, the version designated as **Standard American English.**

An emphasis on prescriptive rules has characterized American elementary ("grammar") schools and high schools for a long time. American schools of the eighteenth and nineteenth centuries inherited from England an approach to teaching grammar that was rooted in the Latin-centered curriculum of

Elizabethan schools. When Latin was the language of instruction, Latin grammar had to be taught as a tool to help students learn to read and write in a foreign language. When English replaced Latin, instruction in English grammar
aimed to make students better writers in English, just as the teaching of Latin
grammar had helped them become better writers in Latin.

Defining *grammar* as the art of speaking and writing correctly, late eigh-
teenth- and nineteenth-century textbooks helped to nurture a popular convic-
tion that still persists today as a characteristic of the **prescriptive grammar**
tradition, namely, the belief in an absolute standard of correctness. According
to this view, language use is either correct or incorrect, and any educated person should be able to understand at once and follow faithfully the norms of
correctness (the prescriptive rules), which are thought to be preserved in
authoritative reference works such as dictionaries and handbooks. The rules of
grammar, according to this tradition, remind us, for example, that *ain't I* is
wrong, but they may leave us wondering about our options if we find the "correct" alternative, *am I not,* pedantic and pretentious.

However, prescriptive rules are not based on logic. They occur because
there is a prejudice in our society against people who speak some dialects of
American English, and that prejudice extends to a negative evaluation of the
speakers themselves.

■ *EXERCISE 1.1*

A *tag question* comes at the end of a statement (as in example A.1 below)
and usually seeks the listener's agreement with the statement. In forming
tag questions for the sentences in A, B, and C, you will be following
descriptive rules of English: rules that simply describe how we make tag
questions in English. To see what those rules are, list the steps you follow
in creating the tags.

A. Complete sentences 2–4 by providing a tag question at the end.
   1. Our garden is beautiful at this time of year, __isn't it__?
   2. We should have dinner outdoors tonight, *shouldn't we*?
   3. Barbara and Jim are going to cook, *aren't they*?
   4. You have strung some lights outdoors, *haven't you*?

B. How would you describe the sequence of rules you followed in creating the tag
   questions in Part A? How did you decide what pronoun to use? How did you decide
   what part of the verb to use in the tag and what form it should take?
   5. Barbara ordered an ice cream cake, *didn't she*?
   6. We have enough food for twelve people, *don't we*?

C. For some kinds of tags, the rules are complex. Although it becomes more difficult to
   state what the rules are, speakers of English can easily produce the proper tags.
   7. It may rain, _____?
   8. You ought to check the weather report, _____?

passive aggressive

9. If it rains, we will eat inside, <u>right? </u>?

[handwritten: won't we? right?]

D. What possibilities are there for creating a tag question for the following sentence?

10. I am expected to bring a large salad, <u>aren't I</u>?

Creating a tag for part D involves *prescriptive* as well as *descriptive* rules. A number of possibilities are available to you in forming the tag, but not all of them are equally acceptable to speakers of standard English. Compare your results with those of your classmates.

Although we often hear prescriptive grammar referred to as *traditional grammar,* there is another tradition of grammar, the roots of which go considerably further back in history than the prescriptive tradition. This other tradition does not look at grammar only as a utilitarian means of learning to use a language correctly but rather as philosophical inquiry into the nature of language. This scholarly tradition is descriptive rather than prescriptive. It aims at recording facts, at describing the actual language (its descriptive rules) as comprehensively as possible, and it avoids the law-giving tone of schoolroom traditional grammars.

Much that was good in scholarly traditional grammars became part of the **descriptive grammars** of modern theoretical linguistics, a scientific field that developed in the twentieth century. The most significant contributions from linguistics to the study of English grammar have come from two schools of thought, American structural linguistics, from the 1920s through the 1950s, and **transformational generative grammar,** since the 1960s. Both of these approaches are rigorously descriptive and, like other scientific disciplines, are concerned with analyzing data, formulating hypotheses, and then verifying those hypotheses through reference once again to data. Although the two orientations differ strongly in a number of their fundamental assumptions, we draw on the insights of both structural and transformational linguists, as well as on those of scholarly traditional grammarians, in this textbook, which might best be described as a **pedagogical grammar**—one concerned first of all with the needs of students and teachers.

Educated people of all kinds need to be able to think clearly and analytically about language. When young children acquire language, they gain the ability to participate in the social community around them, first with their immediate family and then, progressively, with a broader and broader section of humanity. As college students, you participate through written and spoken language in a worldwide community in which your linguistic skills are central to your ability as an effective communicator. In using language, you must constantly make decisions that determine how well you will communicate, and most of the time, you have only yourself to rely on; you don't have time to consult an "authority" (a handbook or dictionary or acquaintance who knows well the rules of standard English). Often, in fact, you must evaluate the advice of competing authorities; you will find that different handbooks give contradictory rules, or a dictionary will disagree with the analysis given in a handbook. In addition, you may be called on to assist others in analyzing linguistic alternatives, either informally as a friend or colleague or more formally as a peer tutor, classroom teacher, or editor. Whether your goal is to acquire for its own sake the kind of knowledge about the structure of the English language that educated members of our society share, to improve your skills as a speaker and writer, or to master the vocabulary and analytical skills that are part of the professional competence of classroom teachers, *Analyzing English Grammar* will help you reach your goal.

GRAMMAR VERSUS USAGE

Before you begin to study grammar, you should be aware that every living language, including English, is in a constant state of change. In fact, a language stops changing only when it is no longer used by a group of speakers in everyday communication—in other words, when it is dead. As long as people continue to use a language, they will change and shape it to their needs. Attempts by regulatory groups to control that change have failed everywhere.

As a result of the diverse needs it must serve, there are as many varieties of English as there are groups of speakers. Each group follows a slightly different subset of the rules by which the language operates, and each bends the rules a bit to meet specific needs. Over time, the adaptations or creations of one group of speakers or another may enter the language and become acceptable to all, that is, become **standard.**

To take a simple example of how this works, consider the word *contact*. It began as a noun referring to "the state in which two things touch one another." Its meaning eventually extended to refer to "the state of people being in touch (or *in contact*) with one another." Relatively recently, people in need of a verb meaning "to bring about a contact with another person" converted the noun *contact* into the verb *to contact*, meaning "to get in touch with someone." Is *contact* an acceptable verb in this sense? Some people think so, and some do not.

Editors of dictionaries and usage handbooks (which attempt to describe how English is used by standard speakers) decide such questions by consulting a panel of experts, people of distinction who have a special interest in language (teachers, writers, and editors, for example). In 1969, when *The American Heritage Dictionary* was published, 66 percent of its Usage Panel voted that, despite the widespread popular use of *contact* as a verb, a sentence like *I'll contact you next week* was not acceptable in writing produced for formal occasions. Notice, first of all, that the experts did not fully agree that the sentence was unacceptable. Presumably, the 34 percent of the Panel who judged *contact* to be acceptable as a verb had observed the form in the speech and writing of a substantial number of people whom they considered to be members of the elite group whose language use sets the standards for others. When enough of the elite adopt any form, it becomes a part of Standard American English.

The history of *contact* illustrates how quickly a word may move in status from nonstandard to standard. Before the fourth edition of *The American Heritage Dictionary* was printed in 2000, a survey of the Usage Panel found that the numbers had reversed. Only 35 percent of them considered the use of *contact* as a verb unacceptable in formal writing; 65 percent approved.[2]

You may wonder how people who use language deemed unacceptable by 66 percent of the panel of experts can be considered by others to be members of an elite whose changing preferences in language cause language norms to change. However, few writers and even fewer speakers have mastered all the rules of standard English. We consider people standard speakers so long as they do not use any strongly stigmatized forms (like *I seen it,* for instance) and their speech contains *relatively few* minor violations of speech etiquette (like *I'll contact you next week*). We seem to have internalized a threshold of tolerance for secondary grammatical "errors." Speakers who remain below that threshold in the production of minor stigmatized items are heard as standard speakers, despite infelicities that occur in their speech. Minor items include pronunciation, such as inserting a *k* sound in *schism* or a *t* in *often*; grammatical forms, such as saying *different than* instead of *different from;* or even vocabulary choice, like the substitution of *enormity* for *enormousness*. Dominant social groups more or less unconsciously use language to mark themselves off from others, tolerating only a small amount of deviation from the norms established for their group, fighting against any relaxation of their standards, and believing that their own version of English is the purest, the most correct, or the best. They overlook momentary lapses in fellow members' speech and remain generally unaware that some of the currently acceptable forms they use were once considered incorrect.

Throughout the text we include "What's the Usage?" sections, in which we discuss attitudes toward the use of a variety of grammatical options available in everyday speech and writing (the choice between *who* and *whom* for instance). You may wonder who it is that enforces the conformity to standards of what is thought to be acceptable and what is not. Most schools see acquainting students with accepted English grammar as part of their educational mission. The command of Standard American English will enable their students to feel confident and to be accepted in almost any business or social setting. You should remember, however, that different social groups have different language norms. Some speakers, for instance, consider themselves to be members of a language elite: those who understand and always use what they consider to be the "correct" forms of English. They may be intolerant of any deviation from their own norms and unaware of lapses in their own speech and writing. As you work your way through this textbook, think about your own attitudes toward language varieties other than your own and about where those attitudes have come from. Did your family, or your teachers, or people you admired stigmatize some speakers of nonstandard English? Or, on the other hand, did they ever stigmatize speakers who adhered too closely to the standard in informal group settings (using *He didn't* in a group where *He don't* was the norm, for instance)?

▪ *EXERCISE 1.2* _____

This exercise draws your attention to *prescriptive* rules. The *American Heritage Dictionary of English* created a Usage Panel to vote on whether certain usages are considered acceptable or unacceptable among educated, prestigious American speakers. How would you vote on the sentences below if you were a member of the panel? You can compare your answers with those of the Usage Panel by looking up the italicized words in a recent copy of *The American Heritage Dictionary* or by searching for them online at *http://education.scd.yahoo.com/reference/dictionary/*.

1. The "Tour de France" *transpires* every year in July.
2. The race *is comprised of* many stages, some on the flat, some in the mountains.
3. Lance Armstrong's racing style is nearly *unique*.
4. Simply by pedaling fast, he is able *to rapidly accelerate* away from his competitors, who use higher gears and pedal more slowly in climbing hills.
5. *Equally as* important is his ability to maintain a high speed for long distances, without having to taper off.
6. No one but *I* seemed to fear that he might lose in 2005.
7. He has won so many times that some *individuals* have renamed the race the "Tour de Lance."
8. His success has also *impacted* the popularity of biking in the United States.

DESCRIPTIVE GRAMMARS

The variations in usage occurring in the language used by speakers of Standard American English create problems for linguists who wish to describe the rules of modern English. Whose version shall they use as a model? Which style of speech should be followed? At what point does a form become acceptable? What shall the grammarian say about borderline cases?

Describing how the system works is even more complex. Should a grammatical description point out how *snoring* differs from *boring* in *the snoring professor* and *the boring professor*? Are both words participles, derived from the verbs *snore* and *bore*? Or have they both become adjectives? If they have, why is it possible to say *the very boring professor* but not **the very snoring professor*?[3] Because all speakers of standard English seem to know that the first is permissible and the second is not, is it really desirable to describe how the system operates without accounting for such differences?

Linguists do, in fact, try to describe the difference between these two phrases, with an argument that runs more or less as follows. It is possible in English to convert the participle in a sentence like *The professor is snoring* (or *arguing, sleeping, fighting*) into *the snoring/arguing/sleeping/fighting professor*. Each of the words tells something about the professor (that is, each modifies the word *professor*). We can say that the words have acquired privileges somewhat like adjectives (*the tall/young/intelligent professor*). However, adjectives can be compared

(*She is taller/younger/more intelligent than he is*) and qualified (*the quite tall/rather young/very intelligent professor*); participles cannot (**She is more snoring than he is, *the very arguing couple*). Another set of participles (*The professor is charming his students/boring his students*) behaves more like adjectives. As noun modifiers, they can be qualified (*the very charming professor*), and they can be compared (*This professor is more boring than that one*).

■ EXERCISE 1.3

One aspect of your competence as a speaker of English is to be able to distinguish English sentences from utterances that are not English sentences. In addition, however, you are able to make even finer distinctions. Examine the following sequences of words and try sorting them into groups according to the following general classifications:

A. Sentences that no speaker of English would ever use—that is, sentences that violate the descriptive rules of English.

B. Sentences that have the sentence patterns of English, even though they contain nonsense words.

C. Sentences that obey the grammatical rules of English, but that use words in strange, illogical ways.

D. Sentences that native speakers of English do use, but that some people disapprove of in formal usage.

E. Fully acceptable sentences of English.

1. The crunkolating gruzzles slished rumilously through the skrunk.
2. Me and Henry are going to the movies tonight.
3. Cell phones are invading our society.
4. My neighbor elderly on the sidewalk slipped yesterday.
5. We'll stay right here until you tell me who drank the piano.
6. Lisa and Bill sure aced the midterm!
7. Did you see the grinkelnaphs congruding near the gnams?
8. Joey knows who done it, but he ain't talking.
9. My hairbrush is attacking my comb.
10. There was no reason for you to stay home yesterday.
11. To forgive all is ice cream.
12. Never we can go to the movies on weekdays.

The variations within Standard American English sometimes force linguists to provide alternative descriptions to account for competing forms. However, the repeated discovery that language data (like *snoring* and *boring*) do not always fall neatly into a simple grammatical system has resulted in an approach involving **prototype theory** that we believe you will find useful in understanding the nature of grammatical relationships.

GRAMMATICAL PROTOTYPES

Your first job in studying grammatical analysis will be to learn how forms are categorized so that you can classify new forms as you encounter them. You already know the names of most of the categories used in language study—nouns, verbs, adjectives, and adverbs, for instances. Sorting words into the proper group would be simple if membership in each category were an either-or proposition—if a word could belong to only one part of speech, for example, and if it behaved like all other members of that group. Unfortunately for students of language, this is not the case. Words can belong to more than one group: We can *down* (verb) a drink, look *down* (adverb), walk *down* (preposition) a corridor, and talk about the fourth *down* (noun) in football, for example. We can also feel *down* (adjective) on a bad day. And not all members of a given group behave identically; most nouns in English can be made plural (*cats, houses, references*), but many cannot (*hay, honesty, happiness*) in ordinary usage.

Recent research into the nature of cognition and the process by which very young children form concepts may help students of language grasp the nature of and the reason for the so-called exceptions to grammatical rules that have traditionally plagued their attempts to understand grammatical theory. Concepts are general ideas we have formed about objects and actions in the world around us based on our grouping together of similar things under a single label (which names the concept). Current prototype theory suggests that concepts are not clear-cut categories to which members belong on an all-or-none basis. Some members are better examples of the class than others.

For example, we have a concept of what is named by the word *cup*, and if asked to draw an example, most of us would produce as a prototype a bowl-like object with a handle. But not all cups have handles, and not all are shaped like bowls; some are cylindrical, and some are even cubes. Our decision about whether something is a cup is based not only on its form but also on its function: We drink beverages from cups. When we begin to try to distinguish between cups and glasses or cups and mugs, we begin to see that the concept named by *cup* is really quite complex. A prototypical cup exists, which most of us associate with the label, and we encounter thousands of varieties that are very much like that prototype. But we also have, as part of our knowledge of cups, a set of *peripheral* objects, which differ in some marked degree from the prototype but which we accept as belonging to the class. It is generally the case that a concept or class will have not only a clearly defined center, where members (**prototypical cases**) exhibit all the characteristics associated with the prototype, but also fuzzy borders, where other members (**peripheral cases**) seem to belong, even though they exhibit only a few of the characteristics associated with the category. Membership in a class can be described as a matter of degree rather than as an either-or proposition. Thus, a bowl might, in some situations, be considered a cup.

In the course of our education, we are initiated into the nature and limits of the concepts accepted by our culture. Their vague borders generally present few problems to us. We accept arbitrary labeling of peripheral examples of things like cups and desks, and in school we memorize, when necessary, the infrequent exceptions to generalized ideas of what constitutes a class or category. Many of us, for example, have learned the striking facts that a whale is a mammal, that a bat is not a bird, and that a tomato is a fruit. We can learn exceptions such as these as long as we need to memorize only a few for each category. But if we were specializing in zoology or botany, we would be unable to memorize all the examples of mammals, or birds, or fruits. We would need to learn the criteria that determine whether something belongs to one of those classes. Once we had mastered the criteria, we would be able to examine a new example, note its structure or habits (or both), and decide how to classify it.

That is exactly the task the student of language faces. Yet traditionally, students have hoped to master the *list* of grammatical categories, expecting symmetry and consistency not to be found elsewhere in life. The fact is that language—like nature—presents us with a fair set of prototypes of any category we can establish, along with a substantial number of peripheral examples: items that finally seem to belong to the category partly on the basis of shared characteristics (family resemblance) and partly because they do not fit as well into any other category. In other instances, the same linguistic example may belong to more than one category, depending on the context in which it occurs.

The student of language, then, must learn the criteria used to classify various linguistic forms. The criteria, because they are relatively few in number, can be memorized, and because the prototype of the class exhibits the largest number of the defining criteria for that class, the most efficient way to learn the criteria is *to associate them with a prototype*. For example, when we come to the classification of parts of speech, you will see that the word *happy* is a prototypical adjective. It exhibits the following characteristics, which are typical of (though not necessarily always required of) adjectives:

1. It ends in *-y*, a suffix added to many words to create adjectives: *grumpy, funny, grody, funky, cheesy*.

2. It can be made comparative and superlative: *happier, happiest*.

3. It can be intensified with words like *very, rather*, and *quite*.

4. It can be a predicate adjective: *I feel happy*.

5. When it modifies a noun, as in *happy child*, its meaning can be paraphrased by a sentence in which its noun is the subject and it is the predicate adjective following a form of the verb *to be*: *The child is happy*.

6. It can function as an object complement: *The new doll made her happy*.

It is safe to say that any word that has all of these characteristics is an adjective, and if all adjectives shared all of these traits, learning to classify them would be simple. One test would enable us to sort out all of the members of the category. Unfortunately, our language is much more complicated than that—so much so, in fact, that there seems to be no single attribute that all adjectives share. When speakers want to modify a noun, they can use adjectives *or* nouns *or* verb participles *or* even adverbs to do the job. When any of these are used over a long period, they may begin to acquire the characteristics associated with adjectives. The question then becomes, How many of these traits and which ones must a word exhibit in order for us to classify it as an adjective? If you try to rely on memorizing examples of adjectives, you will lack a strategy for dealing with exceptions and unusual cases or with words you have never encountered before. If, on the other hand, you understand the principles of word classification, you will be prepared to deal with borderline examples.

Another situation that occurs frequently as we try to decide what to call the different kinds of words we use to make even the simplest of sentences is illustrated in the following examples:

(3)   A *rock* wall surrounded the field.

(4)   A *rocky* path surrounded the field.

Both *rock* and *rocky* describe the nouns that follow them, *wall* and *path*. Are both *rock* and *rocky* therefore adjectives, like *happy?* Many traditional schoolroom grammars would call both words adjectives because both words modify nouns. Descriptive linguists, however, distinguish between a word's **form** (what kind of word it is) and its **function** (what it is doing in a particular phrase or sentence). They would agree that both *rock* and *rocky* are functioning as adjectival modifiers—that is, both are being used the way adjectives frequently are: to describe nouns. But only *rocky* is an adjective in form; *rock* remains a noun, even though it is being used in a typical adjectival function. The descriptive linguist looks at the actual characteristics of each word to determine the class to which it belongs. *Rocky* has all of the most important traits of an adjective; for example, it ends in the common adjective suffix *-y* (like *happy*), it can be made comparative and superlative (*rockier, rockiest*), and it can be intensified (*very rocky, rather rocky*). *Rock*, on the other hand, not only has no adjective suffix (which isn't *required* of adjectives—*red, tall, rich* are adjectives without adjective suffixes), but in addition, it can't be made comparative and superlative (**rocker, *rockest*) nor can it be intensified (**very rock, *rather rock*). Furthermore, it easily functions as a noun (*a heavy rock, on the rock*), which *rocky* can't do (**a hard rocky, *on the rocky*).

The fact that a word's form and function often contrast is another reason that understanding English grammar requires learning to think critically and analytically about language rather than simply memorizing rules and lists. (We will return to the distinction between form and function repeatedly in this book because understanding it is essential for comprehending how English works.)

The grammar of sentences—their **syntax**—also presents barriers to any approach based on rote learning. Because even linguists do not fully understand all of the syntactic rules that account for the structure of English sentences, they have described only the most regular of those rules. It is not possible, therefore, simply to memorize all of the rules. A more practical and useful approach is to learn how linguists arrive at the rules, so that you can deal with grammatical structures you have already studied and with peripheral and borderline cases.

We will assist you in learning to understand the principles that can enable you to do grammatical analysis independently, with confidence. As we discuss the classifications of linguistic forms, the structure of English sentences, and the other topics that this text deals with, we will remind you—in learning these concepts—to pay close attention to prototypes. Researchers have discovered that prototypical members of any concept are easier to understand and to remember than are peripheral members and that information about the prototype is more readily generalized to peripheral members than the reverse. In other words, prototypes can help us to identify both other prototypes and exceptions more certainly than can exceptions help us to recognize prototypes or other exceptions.

In each case we present the prototype and the defining attributes first, highlighting the attributes that should be mastered, before working with the peripheral instances. It is, of course, those peripheral examples that are the difficult cases in grammar study. Students sometimes think they understand a grammatical concept when they are able to recognize and produce isolated prototypical examples, but when they must work with peripheral examples set into a distracting natural language background, they can't tap their knowledge of the material. In fact, they often become so disoriented that they cannot identify even the prototypical examples with any reliability.

Each of the following chapters is interspersed with exercises to help you grasp essential concepts, practice independent analysis, and extend your thinking beyond prototypical cases. As you read the chapters, you should complete the exercises as you come to them. *In every exercise, it is more important for you to be able to explain how you arrived at an answer and to verify through your own analysis whether it is right or wrong than it is to get the correct answer without understanding how you did it.*

LEARNING ABOUT GRAMMAR

One of our purposes in this book is to train you to think about language using the same methods that linguists use: namely, analysis, hypothesis, and verification. None of these techniques is particularly difficult or complicated once you understand how it operates; what *is* difficult is breaking away from your traditional methods of dealing with grammar: memorizing and guessing.

There is nothing intrinsically wrong with memorizing or guessing; in fact, every academic and professional discipline requires both. Memorization furnishes the mind with some of the tools and information necessary at higher levels of thinking, and educated guesses, based on intuition, often provide a fruitful way to begin work, one that will become more systematic as it proceeds.

Mathematicians, for example, memorize a body of tables, terms, and formulas to be used in complex reckoning, and quick estimates are an essential part of their way of working. Training in medicine requires future doctors to commit to memory innumerable facts about the human body and the symptoms of disease, and before experienced physicians reach a diagnosis or make a prescription, they may follow intuitive hunches that sometimes turn out to be right and sometimes wrong. Many examples like these offer parallels to support the legitimate roles of memorization and guessing in the learning process. Yet in no field of learning do these two processes constitute the sole or even the most important means of achieving mastery.

Some of the material in this book should be memorized, and we will point out what it is as we go along. However, we want to discourage you from believing that you can master English grammar by using rote memory. Students who come to the study of grammar with the hope of memorizing a set of rules that will enable them to differentiate between right and wrong soon find themselves overloaded with information, much of it contradictory. When students bog down, they complain, understandably, about all the exceptions to the rules, as well as the exceptions to the exceptions. Frustrated, students may blame their instructors, their books, or both and wonder why the rules of the language cannot be more consistent and orderly.

Guessing, like memorizing, has an important role to play in scientific (including linguistic) inquiry; however, the expert's guess is quite different from the novice's. Scientists begin with a guess called a *hypothesis,* which is a proposition they expect to test and prove. More important than the guess itself is the development of proof. Evidence may prove a guess wrong, but if supporting evidence is found, the hypothesis develops into a *theory* of how a given system operates, and after it has been tested and verified, the theory is stated as a *rule* or set of rules.

The beginning student usually bypasses all of the speculative steps the linguist has taken and instead tries to guess what the rule is.

There are two major difficulties with the student's guess. First, verification must come from an outside authority. The student hazards an answer and awaits verification from the instructor or the book. Unfortunately, inquiry ends for the student if a guess is confirmed by someone else. The important step of hypothesis testing is bypassed, and as a result, a second difficulty follows: Students are often at a loss when no one is available to verify their guesses. In a testing situation, for example, where verification is delayed, students are forced to decide for themselves whether a guess is correct. Ironically, their judgments are likely to be based on intuition rather than reasoning, and the more unsure the students are, the less they trust their intuitions. As a result, they often change what would have been a correct answer and provide an incorrect one.

Successful students—in linguistics, as in math or physics or psychology—rely less on memorization and guessing than do less successful ones. In studying and during an examination, successful students behave more like experts in their fields, constantly checking their work by reviewing the steps followed in arriving at answers. We will model for you throughout this book the procedures by which you can test your hypotheses—or your guesses—about language. You should not assume that you have mastered the material until you can verify your analysis of a grammatical item. Developing the ability to formulate and verify a hypothesis is more important than having the ability (or good luck) to guess correctly. Many people reading this book can already guess correctly often enough to write acceptable standard English or to pass a multiple-choice grammar test. However, few can explain to others why any given answer is the best one.

So much emphasis is usually placed on "correct" answers that students are sometimes reluctant to risk forming a hypothesis that may have to be revised or rejected. Yet there is often more to be learned from a "wrong" answer or a hypothesis that needs revision than from a lucky guess, if only because the mind continues to explore a concept as long as there is an unresolved problem associated with it. *It is, in the long run, more useful to understand why an answer is wrong (or right) than never to be guilty of guessing incorrectly.*

AIDS TO LEARNING ABOUT LANGUAGE

Using language to learn about language provides little assistance for visual learners, people for whom a picture or diagram clarifies abstract concepts better than a verbal explanation does. Each of the grammatical systems from which we draw our material—traditional, structural, and transformational—has developed one or more systems of visual mapping to supplement verbal description. The following are very brief examples of the three most important graphic systems for representing sentence structure.

Diagramming

Reed-Kellogg diagrams are visual maps commonly used in traditional schoolroom grammar to display the structure of sentences. During the nineteenth century, a number of styles of diagramming evolved, but the system still used in many schools today is that developed by Alonzo Reed and Brainerd Kellogg. Because no competing systems have survived, Reed-Kellogg diagramming is usually referred to simply as *diagramming*. Figure 1.1 is a Reed-Kellogg diagram of the sentence *Those tall trees framed our lovely view nicely.*

In Reed-Kellogg diagrams, the main horizontal line represents the core of the sentence. A vertical line intersects the horizontal between the main words of the subject, *those tall trees*, and the main words of the predicate, *framed our*

Figure 1.1   A Sample Reed-Kellogg Diagram

lovely view nicely. A vertical line following the verb, *framed*, separates it on the horizontal plane from the main word of its direct object, *view*. Diagonal lines point toward words they modify. Notice that the noun modifiers *those* and *tall* are on diagonals below *trees*; the adverb *nicely* is on a diagonal below the verb *framed*; and the modifiers *our* and *lovely* are on diagonals below the noun *view*. We will use Reed-Kellogg diagrams throughout the book where we think they help clarify a grammatical concept for visual learners. As we do so, we will explain the logic underlying the diagrams as a guide for those of you who may eventually find yourselves in classrooms where you will be expected to teach Reed-Kellogg diagrams to your own students.

IC Analysis

Immediate constituent (IC) analysis, a system of analyzing the hierarchical structure of sentences and their parts, is a tool developed by Leonard Bloomfield and other American structural linguists. They employed several graphic devices to represent the results of IC analysis. The version in Figure 1.2 uses arrows to show what words and phrases modify. *Those*, for example, modifies *tall trees*, and *tall* modifies *trees*. The vertical line between *trees* and *framed* divides the subject from the predicate, and the vertical between *framed* and *our lovely view* divides the verb from its object.

Working upward from the bottom, you can see how phrases contained within the sentence form its parts. The first vertical divides the entire subject, *those tall trees*, from the entire predicate, *framed our lovely view nicely*. Each of these, in turn, is divided into the parts that constitute it—parts considered to be its *constituents*. The subject, for instance, has two major constituents: *those* and *tall trees*. *Tall trees* has two: *tall* and *trees*. The predicate is analyzed first into two components: *framed our lovely view* and *nicely*. Then *framed* is separated from its direct object: *our lovely view*. The direct object has two components: *our* and *lovely view*; and *lovely view* has two: *lovely* and *view*. An advantage of IC analysis is that it can show how there is a hierarchy in modifiers, with one modifying another that modifies yet another. For example, Figure 1.2 makes clear that *tall* forms a unit with *trees* that is, in turn, modified by *those*.

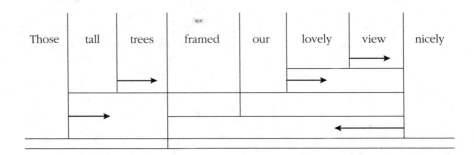

Figure 1.2   A Sample IC Analysis Diagram

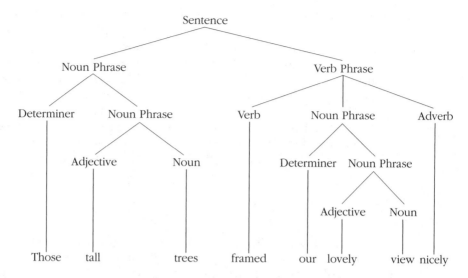

Figure 1.3   A Sample Phrase Structure Tree Diagram (Phrase Marker)

Phrase Structure Trees

The **phrase structure tree diagrams** (also called **phrase markers**) used in transformational generative grammar, created by Zellig Harris and Noam Chomsky, show some relationships more clearly than is possible through Reed-Kellogg diagramming or immediate constituent analysis boxes. In later chapters, we explain exactly how you can use tree diagrams with grammatical labels to analyze syntactic structure.

The lines in Figure 1.3 are considered the branches of an upsidedown tree. The sentence branches into two parts: a subject and a predicate. These branches then subdivide into other constituents of the sentence and finally into its individual words. Phrase structure trees can show the same hierarchy of relationships IC analysis can. Thus, the tree branching divides *those* from the phrase it modifies, *tall trees*. Similarly, it shows that *trees* is a unit modified by *tall*. Tree diagrams have an additional advantage in that they can efficiently represent visually how one sentence is placed inside another. They are also easier to read than are the boxes used in IC analysis. Consequently, we have chosen phrase structure tree diagrams, as well as Reed-Kellogg diagrams, as important analytical tools in this textbook.

▬▬▬ *SUGGESTIONS FOR READING THIS BOOK* ▬▬▬

You will find most of the chapters of this kind of book too complex for reading at a single sitting. We suggest that, before you begin reading each chapter, you look at the Table of Contents to get an idea of what the chapter contains and consider, for a moment, what you already know about the topics covered.

To get a sense of the material, read the Chapter Goals and browse through the chapter before reading. Note how the material has been divided; skim the first and last sentences of each paragraph; study the diagrams; read the Chapter Summary; try to orient yourself as fully as possible. When you begin to read the material carefully, don't try to do it all in one sitting. Stop partway through, and give your mind time to absorb new material before going on.

If you are not accustomed to preparing for reading in this way, you may fear that you are wasting valuable time. You are not. You are creating a framework of knowledge that will make your close reading of the chapter more coherent and meaningful. The technique is one that is useful with any complicated new material you have to study.

KEY TERMS

We use a minimum of jargon in this text, but you should understand that part of knowing any academic discipline, whether it is in the sciences or the humanities, is comprehending the language used to talk about the concepts within the area of study. We include as **Key Terms** words involved in major topics covered in a chapter, as well as terms that are basic to an understanding of our discussion of grammatical concepts. Before you go on to the next chapter, you should understand each of the following.

form	Standard American English
function	types of grammar
immediate constituent (IC) analysis	descriptive grammar
phrase structure tree diagram	pedagogical grammar
phrase marker	prescriptive grammar
prototype theory	transformational generative
prototypical cases	grammar
peripheral cases	types of grammatical rules
Reed-Kellogg diagram	descriptive rules
syntax	prescriptive rules

ENDNOTES

1. When we are discussing items that occur in both spoken and written English, we will use the word *speaker* as a shortcut to refer simultaneously to speakers and writers of English. In the same way, we will use *hearer* to refer both to hearers and readers of language.
2. Joseph P. Pickett et al., ed., *The American Heritage Dictionary of the English Language,* 4th ed. (Boston: Houghton Mifflin, 2000).
3. In this book, an asterisk (*) will be placed before phrases and sentences that a native speaker (someone who has learned to speak English as a child) would never use.

Varieties of English 2

Chapter 2 establishes a context for the discussions of English structure in later chapters by viewing English as a continuum of dialects and styles that contrast with each other in pronunciation, vocabulary, and grammar. Regional, social, and international dialects reflect who speakers are and where they come from geographically and socially.

CHAPTER GOALS

At the end of this chapter, you should be able to

- Notice *language differences* in everyday usage.

- Understand the difference between *regional* and *social* dialects.

- Recognize that *Standard American English* provides a relatively uniform speech variety.

Prior study of English grammar has usually left students with the impression that English is or ought to be uniform. Teachers and textbooks have often given students the idea that, in an ideal world, everyone would speak and write a uniform "proper" English, with little or no variation from an agreed-upon standard of correctness.

We do not want to give you that impression, for in fact it is the normal condition of English and of every other language to vary along a number of dimensions. Efforts to put the language (or its speakers) in a linguistic straightjacket by insisting on conformity at all times to a uniform standard are doomed to fail, for they go against the very nature of language: to be flexible and responsive to a variety of conditions related to its users and their purposes.

There are, in fact, as many varieties of English as there are groups of speakers, and the word used for such varieties is **dialect:** a variant of a language spoken by a group of people sharing the same time (historical period) or space (geographical or social environment). All native speakers of English speak a dialect that identifies them as

- living in the twenty-first century (compare your way of speaking with Shakespeare's: "Thou shouldst not have been old till thou hadst been wise," from *King Lear*);
- residing in a specific country (in the United States, the luggage carrier in a car is the *trunk;* in England it is the *boot*); and
- belonging to a specific socioeconomic group—people sharing similar cultural backgrounds, income levels, and amounts of education (some speakers usually pronounce the initial sound of words like *this*, *these*, and *those* as if they began with *d* rather than *th,* while other speakers seldom use this pronunciation).

In addition, their speech varies depending on their psychological state at the moment and whether they are speaking to people of the same sex, age, interests, religion, or profession. There is, in fact, hardly any aspect of our social existence that is not reflected to some extent in the way we speak—in our choice of words, our selection of grammatical structures, our pronunciation.

Because each of us belongs to different social groups, we each speak a language variety made up of a combination of features slightly different from those characteristic of any other speaker of the language. The language variety unique to a single speaker of a language is called an *idiolect*. Your idiolect includes the vocabulary appropriate to your various interests and activities, pronunciations reflective of the region in which you live or have lived, and variable styles of speaking that shift subtly depending on whom you are addressing.

As a speaker of English, you react—sometimes consciously, sometimes unconsciously—to variations in the language used around you, and you vary your own language in response to your environment. As a person educated about language, you will want to be aware of how you and others respond to variation in language and to ensure that your own responses are based on reason and not on stereotype.

Consider an example of how you make judgments based on the varieties of language you observe. You make guesses about where speakers are from based on their **regional dialects.** For instance, for Southerners, words like *park* and *pork* may sound alike, whereas for Northerners, they have different vowels. What's more, Southerners may use the term *roasting ears* to refer to what Americans from other regions call *corn-on-the-cob.* You also make judgments about speakers' socioeconomic levels on the basis of their **social dialects** (for example, attributing a lower economic or educational level to a speaker who regularly says *I seen it* rather than *I saw it*). Language also signals the speaker's sex and age. Men and women differ in their language patterns; for example, research suggests that men interrupt women more than women do men (a finding that surprises most men but not most women). And different age groups—children, teenagers, middle-aged adults, and very old persons— each have distinctive ways of using the language (such as calling parents *Mommy* and *Daddy*, in contrast to *Mom* and *Dad* or *Mother* and *Father*). The word *dialect* refers to any language variety spoken by people who form a subgroup of society (whether their affinity is based upon age or gender or shared interests, for example) who develop a way of speaking when they are together that identifies them as members of that group.

REGIONAL DIALECTS

The first English-speaking immigrants to what would become the United States brought with them from England their own seventeenth-century local British dialects. Local dialect diversity in England then, as now, was far greater than the regional diversity that came to characterize American English. In fact, historians of the English language in America agree that, during the seventeenth and eighteenth centuries, the dialects that the colonists brought with them underwent a process of *leveling*—that is, dialect differences in the colonies became less marked as the early Americans moved about and accommodated their speech to that of speakers of other dialects. At the same time, diminished communication with England and a growing interest in having an American language different from that of England encouraged the development of pronunciation and vocabulary distinct to the New World.

Another influence on American English came from the language of West African slaves, who, according to current research, spoke a version of English (sometimes called Plantation Creole) that had evolved from the pidgin English (a simplified form of English) used to conduct African trade, including the slave trade. In contact with the English spoken by whites, Plantation Creole gradually evolved into the dialect today called *Black English Vernacular (BEV)* or *African-American Vernacular English (AAVE)*. The centuries of contact also influenced the language of whites and had an especially great impact on the southern dialect.

During the nineteenth century, regional dialect differences in American English grew for several reasons. The eastern seaboard was in closer contact with England than the rest of the country and adopted some of the changes happening there; it was probably during this time, for instance, that the *r*-less pronunciation of coastal New England (*pahk the cah*) developed, following the British fashion. Settlement patterns as the nation spread westward tended to follow major geographical boundaries such as rivers and mountain ranges; these divide the chief regional dialects still today. And both geographical and cultural differences between the South and the North, such as the influence of Black English on Southern White English, fostered growing differences between the speech of the two regions.

Today, most linguists describe three major regional varieties of American English: the Northern, Midland, and Southern dialects (see Figure 2.1), with boundaries based on contrasting patterns in pronunciation, vocabulary, and grammar in the eastern half of the United States. In the western half of the country, settlers from all three regions mixed to a great degree. As a result of that mingling and of continuing mobility, the major dialects have blended in the west, with Midland features predominating.

In most ways, the three varieties of American English are alike—that is, regardless of region, Americans tend to use the same words most of the time, to pronounce them alike, and to follow similar patterns of grammar. The distinctions are noticeable to native speakers of American English, but in most cases, they are relatively minor when compared with how much of the language all Americans have in common.

However minor they are, we do notice and respond to regionalisms in the speech of others. Thus, though most speakers of American English are probably unaware that they speak a regional dialect, they are aware of regionalisms in the speech of people from other areas. Judging by humorous dictionaries of regionalisms available around the United States, we not only notice differences,

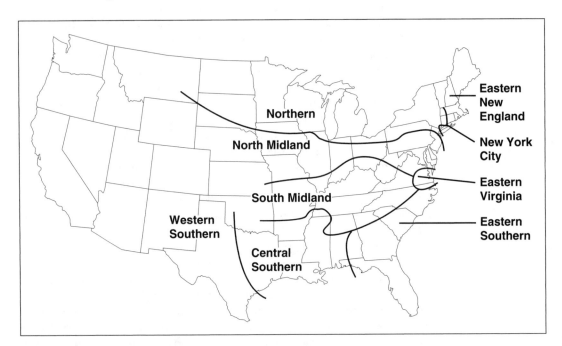

Figure 2.1   Major Regional Dialects of American English[1]

but we also think that people from other regions "talk funny." Consider these examples:

Southern Speech[2]

watt	a color	*Cotton is watt.*
raid	a primary color	*The American flag is raid, watt, and blue.*
par	electric current	*Turn off the par.*
poke	bacon meat from a pig	*We had poke and eggs for breakfast.*

Boston Speech (Northern)[3]

Cuber	the Caribbean island ruled by Fidel Castro
draw	a compartment in a chest for storing clothes; a *drawer*
drawering	a sketch made with a pencil, pen, or crayon
cod	a small, flat piece of stiff paperboard for playing bridge and poker

SOCIAL DIALECTS

Despite their amusement, Americans are quite tolerant of speakers of regional varieties and have elected presidents from every region of the country. This openness to regional variation in dialect doesn't always carry over into attitudes toward social dialects, however, where departures from the most prestigious patterns, particularly in grammar, are often stigmatized as mistakes caused by ignorance. Understanding, as linguists do, that each dialect is, in fact, a self-contained, rule-governed system, offers a more constructive and accurate alternative to such negative judgments. When we look at dialects as systematic, equally valid forms of the language, which children acquire naturally and completely as part of growing up, we see the variations among them as patterned differences rather than failures to speak English "correctly."

Large cities like New York, Washington, D.C., Detroit, Chicago, and Los Angeles exhibit complex *sociolinguistic stratification*—that is, their residents are divided along social class lines that can be identified by regular patterns of linguistic variation. The social dialect of educated, middle-class professionals, people who enjoy the benefits of wealth and power, is at one end of a continuum of prestige and is usually considered standard in the community; the social dialects of those without education, wealth, and power are at the other end, where they are labelled **nonstandard.**

Within these urban speech communities, speakers are very sensitive to the social meanings of dialect differences. For example, middle-class speakers in New York City seldom omit the *r* in words like *guard* and *horse* and hardly ever say *ting* for *thing* or *dese* for *these*, as the speakers of nonstandard dialect do.

Yet speakers of all social classes immediately respond to these kinds of linguistic markers of social class. While social dialects differ observably in vocabulary and pronunciation, the grammatical features that distinguish them (such as the occurrence of nonstandard subject-verb patterns like *they was* and *he done it*) are more stigmatized than other kinds of differences.

Sometimes the migration of large groups of people results in a regional dialect becoming a social dialect. This sort of shift occurred with Appalachian English when large numbers of speakers from the Appalachian region moved to northern cities in search of jobs. New dialect patterns were added to an already complex urban language environment. Children came to school with speech that showed systematic and predictable differences from local dialects and from the language found in textbooks. For example, according to the rules of Appalachian dialect, verbs that are considered singular in textbook English agree with plural subjects. Speakers might say *they was, the cars is, those people makes,* and *her children has.* Are these errors? According to traditional schoolroom definitions of correctness, such examples would be considered mistakes. In fact, however, Appalachian speakers who combine the subject *they* with the verb *was* are following the agreement patterns of Appalachian English. Such a construction is consistent with the rules that govern their speech.

A similar situation exists throughout the Southwest with speakers of Hispanic background, who may systematically substitute *ch* for *sh* so that *shin* and *chin* sound the same. The extensive use of unmarked tense, which is found among Vietnamese speakers, for example, saying *Sam walk to school yesterday* instead of *Sam walked to school yesterday,* is also governed by regular rules. In a like manner, African-American Vernacular English is a rule-governed system that differs from other dialects of American English in patterned ways. One distinction involves the African-American Vernacular English use of the verb *be.* Although a complete exploration of these patterns is beyond the scope of this chapter, several examples will illustrate the systematic nature of the African-American Vernacular English rules for using *be*—and how different they are from the standard English patterns described in later chapters of *Analyzing English Grammar.*

1. *Be* without inflection, or sometimes as *bees* or *be's,* is mainly used to indicate something that occurs habitually.

   Our bus be late every day.

   I see her when I bees on my way to school.

   They be slow all the time.

   That kid always be messing up.

2. If the event or situation is one that doesn't occur habitually or repeatedly, then the *be* is omitted.

   Our bus late today.

   I see her when I on my way to school.

   They slow last night.

   That kid messing up right now.

3. *Be* can also indicate future time, depending on the context.

Our teacher be in class tomorrow.	(future *be*)
Our teacher be in class every day.	(habitual *be*)
I be studying math tonight.	(future *be*)
I be studying math all the time.	(habitual *be*)[4]

Because standard written English does not have these uses of uninflected *be* (nor does it include the pattern of omitting *be* for nonrecurring actions or conditions), Americans not familiar with African-American Vernacular English may be at a loss to interpret its highly structured grammatical patterns. Children who come to school speaking African-American Vernacular English have in the past been treated as deficient in some way because their native dialect includes patterns not found in schoolroom grammars of English. Fortunately, today teachers are more knowledgeable about variations in American dialects and are more likely to understand differences like these between African-American Vernacular English and standard written English.

People who migrate to urban centers, as many African Americans and Appalachians have, often feel lonely and isolated in their new communities. Not only may they look different; they also speak differently and often dress, eat, and live differently from the local population. Those differences, which may become an excuse for ridicule by the locals, are an essential part of the identity of the migrants, who associate them with home, love, and the values they have been raised with and are therefore reluctant to give up. Appalachian migrants to eastern cities in the United States frequently go home to the hills on weekends to assuage their feelings of loss. The economic advantages of embracing the mainstream urban dialect and culture is counterbalanced for many migrants by a severe sense of human loss.

This dilemma is often played out in the classroom, where children are expected to conform to a new and often hostile culture and abandon a familiar, comfortable one. Teachers who understand and appreciate the nature of dialect variation can take delight in helping all of their students to enjoy learning about differences among dialects. Doing so may help migrant children make more rapid progress in adding a mastery of standard written English to their repertoire of skills.

STANDARD AMERICAN ENGLISH

Giving students a mastery of **Standard American English (SAE)** is usually accepted without much discussion as one of the primary goals of American education. But what is Standard American English? In many other countries, asking a similar question about the national language would have a simpler answer than it does in the United States. In France, for example, a national academy has the duty of determining what shall be included in standard French. Although proposals for similar academies to legislate correct English have repeatedly been defeated, Americans have traditionally had plenty of respect for language authorities, especially in the classroom. Dictionaries, spelling books, and school grammars have been given the status of absolute authorities, even more powerful than the often feared English teacher. Although we continue to look to these sources to tell us what is standard, the term *Standard American English* is used with several meanings.

Although the United States has no official standard, many features of pronunciation, vocabulary, and grammar are widely shared by middle-class, urban, educated speakers of the language. These common features have led to the perception of a General American dialect that many people refer to as Standard American English. Interestingly, people who use the term in this way often consider their own dialect to be a pretty good example of standard English, even though they will readily acknowledge that they "make a few errors now and then" and could probably improve their usage. Sometimes, these same people will deny that they speak a dialect, saving that term for varieties of the language different from their own.

The artificially created dialect of radio and television probably comes closest to what most people consider standard spoken American English. We might call it *Broadcast Standard English* or *Network Standard*. It is a mixture of widely used pronunciations and vocabulary with grammar drawn pretty much from the prescriptive handbooks familiar to anyone who has taken a freshman writing class. The Northern and Midlands flavor of the vocabulary and pronunciations of this dialect probably represents the bias of the media centers, New York City and Los Angeles.

Language professionals often try to compensate for the ambiguity of the term *Standard American English* by using it to refer to the variety of the language that actually is relatively uniform throughout the country: written American English. The standard form of the written language that is taught in schools and encoded in writers' handbooks is called **standard written English,** or sometimes *standard edited English,* emphasizing the careful revisions and corrections that are usually necessary in formal writing. As a linguist looks at American English, the only really accurate use of the term *Standard English* is to refer to this edited form of written English, as there is no single standard among spoken dialects.

Because the written language changes more slowly than any spoken dialect, standard written English tends to be less subject to change and tolerant of variety than is current American speech. An advantage of its resistance to change is that the written form of English has remained relatively uniform throughout the world, assuring that documents written in one area can easily be read anywhere else. A disadvantage is that the spoken form continues to change and, as a consequence, constantly moves away from the written version. This helps to explain why the task of teaching it occupies so much school time and why all children, whatever their background, may have to struggle to master some of its arbitrary rules. Yet standard written English carries with it great benefits for those who develop competence in using it, for it is the language of public life. The ability to handle easily the language of books, newspapers, magazines, and public institutions brings with it access to power through educational and professional advancement and through increased skill in manipulating the bureaucracies that impinge on all of our lives.

College students have had many years of experience to verify the powerful influence of standard written English in our society. Schools demand that you be able to read and write it. The standardized tests that control educational gateways crucial to later economic success expect you to be able to respond to difficult questions about it. And people who have power and authority in business, industry, and the professions often have strong negative reactions to writing that does not conform to the norms of standard written English. The power of standard written English and its prestigious place among the various American social dialects mean that most of us use more than a single dialect and all of us use a range of styles as we adjust to various communicative situations. A job interview, an appearance in court, an oral exam, a public speech—situations like these motivate speakers to shift their language closer to the patterns of the standard, whatever their social class dialect. This **style shifting,** in which the speaker tries to produce speech closer to standard English, sometimes causes **hypercorrection,** in which speakers "go one better," and it has been found to be a characteristic of second-ranking groups in many communities.

A simple example of hypercorrection is saying *between you and I* instead of *between you and me.* When children use the form *me and you* (as in *Me and you bought candy*), parents and teachers often correct them, pointing out that it should be *you and I.* Possibly, *you and I* begins to sound more correct and cultured than *you and me* in all contexts, and as a consequence, some speakers overgeneralize, using *you and I* even when the phrase occurs as the object of a preposition. Evidently, **linguistic insecurity** and the desire to be correct leads some speakers to overcorrect. One American linguist suggests that, because American schoolteachers have traditionally come from the lower middle class, they may have the sort of excess linguistic insecurity that leads to hypercorrection and intolerance of other dialects.

To understand the relation between the Standard American English that the schools strive to teach and the dialects that each of us brought to school as children, you may find it helpful to consider language acquisition and development in terms of exposure to the linguistic environment as represented in Figure 2.2.

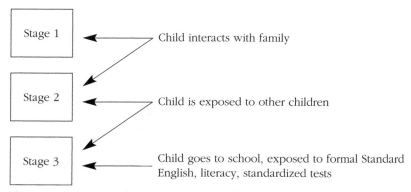

Figure 2.2 Stages of Language Acquisition

In stage 1, infants begin to acquire language through interaction with family members; whatever dialect (or language) is spoken in the home will be the one that very young children first acquire. In stage 2, children are exposed to other children outside the home, and language development continues under the dual influence of family and peers. Only in stage 3, when children first go to school, do they receive their initial exposure to standard English as part of formal instruction in literacy, followed quickly by the beginning of a long string of standardized tests to assess their mastery of the language. However, formal schooling typically begins *after* children have mastered a native spoken dialect. School language is, therefore, at best something that is added on outside the natural setting in which children learn their first language. Standard written English is a second language for all children, but it is obviously closer to the dialect spoken by some speakers than to that spoken by others. As children spend years in the process of mastering the complex reading, writing, and thinking skills that we associate with standard English, their learning will be enhanced by respect from teachers for the dialects most closely associated with who they are and from where they come.

▪ *EXERCISE 2.1*

Hypercorrection is the tendency of speakers to overcorrect their speech in formal situations. One linguist explains overcorrection by relating it to the speaker's great anxiety about speaking properly, rather than naturally. Might this also offer a means of understanding the occurrence of sentences like *Whom did you say is calling?* and *We will accept whomever applies,* in which *who*, rather than *whom*, is the correct form? What explanation for this common "error" would you propose?

STYLES

In contrast to these *user-related* varieties of English—that is, varieties that reflect something about the identity of the speaker, as regional and social dialects do—*use-related* varieties of the language reflect not so much who we are but the occasions and purposes for our use of language. We make choices in **style** of speech or writing based on our assessment of the relative formality or informality of the situation (for instance, by using a greeting like *Hi! How's it goin'?* in contrast to *Good afternoon. How are you?*).

Simply by sharpening your observation of your own and others' speech, you can become acutely aware of how widely language varies along the stylistic dimension. At one end of the continuum of verbal style lies the private, almost wordless language of lovers; at the other is the highly elaborate, fancy formality of some public speakers. In this text, we are concerned with language use between those two extremes: the public language of everyday life. That kind of language falls on the same continuum, approaching the style of intimacy at one end and that of elegant rhetoric at the other. Gradations of formality are reflected in subtle changes in the kind of language speakers choose to use, stylistic changes that account for the variety in everyone's speech.

Toward the intimate end of the continuum is *casual speech,* characterized by conversation that treats the listener as an insider who shares much knowledge with the speaker. In casual style, *ellipsis* is frequent—that is, parts of sentences can be omitted, as the article is in *Coffee's good* and as the subject and verb are in *Nice day today.* Participants in casual conversation are on a first-name basis. They may use slang and informal vocabulary, employing a variety of set formulas like *What's up?* and *See ya later!* Of course, speakers who initiate casual conversation with people they do not know well may do so for a variety of purposes. The used-car salesman who says *Call me Cal,* puts his arm around your shoulder, and offers you, his new buddy, a special low price, may have objectives other than expressing sincere friendship.

When adults are exchanging information with superiors or people they do not know well, they usually switch from casual to *consultative style.* For example, walking up to the manager's desk in a bank, you might say: *Excuse me, my name is Fred Brown, and I'd like to speak to someone about opening a new account.* The manager, in turn, might reply: *Good afternoon, Mr. Brown. I'll be happy to help you. What type of account do you wish to open?* Both speakers provide all of the information needed to understand the business being conducted; they do not assume that they will be understood without it. The listener plays an active role, responding as the bank manager does in the example or, when listening for a longer period, inserting attention signals such as *yes, uh-huh, right, I see,* and so on. When conducting business in consultative style, Americans generally use the grammar, pronunciation, and meanings of standard English or shift their speech in that direction.

An even more *formal style* occurs in speech intended for public occasions. It is used by a speaker addressing a large group. Participation by the listeners is controlled by convention: They may not interrupt until called on to do so. The formal speaker typically employs careful pronunciation and intonation, reflecting the goal of informing the audience. Formal language may be planned in advance, even written down, thereby replacing the spontaneity of less formal styles with the communicative advantages of coherence and careful organization. The speaker is often detached and impersonal in formal style, using expressions such as *one may suppose that* rather than the less formal *I think that.*

The language used varies with each style. When we are feeling at ease and are speaking casually, we tend to relax our control of the finer rules of the language. Conversely, when we believe we must monitor our language carefully because we are addressing someone who is more powerful, belongs to a higher social class, or has more education, we find it hard to relax. Most of us feel required to attempt to match the manner of speaking of the person with higher status. Compare, for example, the speech style you might use in offering a ride to a friend at work or at school (*Wanna lift?*) with that used to address a superior (*Would you like a ride?*). In some contexts, you might answer the phone with *This is she,* and in others, *This is her* or *This is me.* In talking with friends, you may not worry about whether to use *lie* or *lay,* but in conversation with your English teacher, you may pause to think about the distinction.

Writing, too, falls along this kind of continuum. At one end are the private notes written to oneself and at the other, writing intended for publication. The less the writer knows the reader personally, the more necessary it is that all essential information be supplied and that the conventions of standard written English be observed. When we speak of *formal writing,* we mean writing that will be read by people unknown to the author. Business correspondence, research papers, and official documents, to name a few, are representatives of formal writing. They are usually edited carefully to be certain that they conform to the standards described in dictionaries and usage handbooks.

Most of the writing and speech you produce or encounter will fall along the continuum between casual and formal, and it is the language used along this continuum that is the subject of our book. As we discuss usage in the chapters that follow, we occasionally point out items that occur in **formal** usage but may not occur in **informal** styles. When we do so, we are referring to the stylistic continuum apparent in everyone's use of the language, including speakers of standard English, a continuum ranging from informal, casual speech with friends on the one end to formal public address and formal writing on the other.[5]

■ *EXERCISE 2.2* _____

Although the full range of speech styles can be observed in college classrooms, the language tends to shift between consultative and formal styles. College and university classes are often referred to as *lectures,* and some instructors have the title, *lecturer.* Think about the speech style of the instructors in the classes that you are currently taking. Consider the degree to which the presentation approaches the formality of written English and how often students interrupt with contributions and questions. How would you place the lectures on the continuum from casual to consultative to formal? Do you find that you monitor your own speech more in a formal classroom situation than in a casual one?

■■■■■ *SECOND LANGUAGE ACQUISITION* ■■■■■

When young children are exposed to more than one language, they seem to acquire the languages they are exposed to equally well and in definite stages. Adult second language learners acquire a new or "target" language in stages similar to those that children go through when acquiring their native tongue, but the first stage of adult learning of a second language exhibits features of both the new language and the native language of the speaker. This **interlanguage** phase includes two types of errors in using the new language. Errors of the first type involve the same kind of mistakes that children make in acquiring their first language. For example, in learning English, children acquiring English as a native language and nonnative speakers learning English as a second language may try to regularize the past tense of irregular verbs, saying *bringed* instead of *brought,* or *drived* instead of *drove.* Because most verbs in English form the past tense by adding *-ed,* both first- and second-language learners master this general pattern early on, and extend it to all verbs. Later they learn the individual exceptions to this general pattern. Because mistakes like these represent an apparently universal stage in the development of English language proficiency, they are called **developmental errors.**

Errors of the second type occur only in second language learning, when learners transfer to the new language a feature from their first language. For example, a native Spanish speaker may say *espeak* instead of *speak* because in Spanish the sound of *s* followed by *p* cannot begin a word without a vowel coming first. The Spanish speaker transfers to English this particular Spanish sound pattern. Such substitutions are called **transfer errors.**

Researchers in the area of second language acquisition who investigate how people gain proficiency in the actual use of a language other than their mother tongue suggest that becoming a skilled user of a second language requires not only the development of proficiency in the new grammar (**linguistic competence**) but also the ability to use the new language in a variety of circumstances (**communicative competence**). Drawing from psychological theories of learning, from linguistic theories of language structure, and from studies within many disciplines of how people interact in social settings, scholars have concluded that to communicate successfully, a second language learner must be proficient in several other dimensions of the language in addition to its grammar.

For example, skilled speakers of a second language must have **textual competence**—that is, knowledge about units of language larger than single sentences in speech or in writing, units such as stories, conversations, lectures, letters, poems, sermons, jokes, exchanges of greetings, expressions of apology and sympathy, and so on. In acquiring textual competence, the second language speaker learns the rules that govern how speakers organize information and link sentences in the new language. Mastering American English, for example, involves learning that, when engaging in informal conversation, native speakers use such colloquial linking expressions as *Well, y'know,* and *Not to change the topic, but…* to tie together separate units of speech, providing an element of cohesion and at the same time marking boundaries such as changes of topic or point of view. In very formal discourse, on the other hand, they may use connectives such as *If I may interject* and *With all due respect for my opponent* instead.

In addition to knowing ways of organizing information into coherent structured wholes (textual competence), successful communication requires **pragmatic competence,** which refers to knowledge of the use of language in social settings. Pragmatic competence includes understanding conventions such as the appropriate use of forms of address and titles in English—for instance, when to say *Excuse me, sir* instead of *Hey, man!* and when to refer to your father-in-law as *Bill* rather than as *Mr. Smith.* The socially appropriate use of a language requires knowledge of rules for turn-taking behavior in conversation and how properly to signal your desire to have your turn—for example, by inserting *Pardon me, but…* or *I don't wish to interrupt, but….* Pragmatic competence also includes knowing when to use or to switch between more formal and less formal styles of speech (in speaking to a group, starting out with the formality of *My dear colleagues and guests* in contrast to the colloquial *Listen up, guys!*). They include knowing what vocabulary and delivery are appropriate in specific situations—knowing, for example, that one might say of the death of a relative *My uncle passed away*, in contrast to how one might refer to the death of a pet fish, *Goldie croaked.*

Second language learners, in making the same shifts, may, in addition, switch between the second language and their native language. If they have learned the second language informally, outside the classroom, they may know only a casual "street" variety and rely on their native language, rather than on the second language, for more formal expressions and situations. If, on the other hand, they learned the second language primarily or solely through classroom instruction and reading, they may know only a formal variety and, because they are unable to move easily into an informal, "friendlier" style, they may seem aloof or "stiff" to native speakers of the language. Children of immigrants may learn to speak the native language of their parents at home, and in a conversation with their siblings, they may easily switch languages, even in the middle of the sentence. However, without any formal training in the parents' native language, they may be unable to use its standard variety, or to read and write it efficiently. In either case, switching styles may force them to change languages as well. Becoming proficient in a second language thus depends on a variety of factors, including the range of styles to which a learner is exposed, the degree of interaction the learner has with native speakers, and the personal and psychological circumstances in which speech and writing take place.

ENGLISH IN AN INTERNATIONAL CONTEXT

Today, a greater variety of languages may be spoken in the United States than ever before. The impact, particularly in cities where immigrants settle in large numbers, is evident. The University of California at Los Angeles reports that students in Los Angeles County schools speak more than 100 different languages!

Predictably, some Americans oppose the costs of providing multilingual services, and many more feel threatened by such linguistic and cultural diversity. Some have even organized attempts, which have been successful in some states, to pass laws making English the official language. According to the organization U.S. English, which lobbies to have English made the official language of government in the United States, by 2003 24 states had adopted laws or constitutional amendments making English their official language. Thus far, these laws are mostly symbolic, expressing citizens' fears for the primacy of English but having little or no effect on the day-to-day operations of state governments and not impinging on previously enacted measures like those mandating multilingual ballots or court interpreters for non–English-speaking defendants in criminal trials. But a federal judge nonetheless nullified an Arizona constitutional amendment making English the language "of all government functions and actions," ruling that it violated federally protected free speech rights.

Does the United States need laws to protect and promote English? We don't think so. For one thing, cultural uniformity can't be achieved by force of law and threat of penalty. But equally important, the English language is under no threat. Today, English is a world language, a native language to more than 377 million people and a second language to more than 98 million. In addition, English serves as a lingua franca, an agreed-upon vehicle of communication for specific purposes among speakers who may not share any other language, and for countless others ranging from airline pilots to computer scientists.

Recently, the BBC quoted statistics showing that there were a billion English learners on the planet in 2000; language researchers estimated that two billion (a third of the people on earth) will be learning English in the next decade. Globally, American English is only one of a number of major national dialects with their own unique features. Some of the larger communities of speakers of distinctive dialects of English as a first language include those who speak British English (56 million speakers); South Asian English, including the people of India, Bangladesh, Pakistan, Sri Lanka, Nepal, and Bhutan (number uncertain); Canadian English (16 million); Australian English (15 million); Irish English (3.3 million); New Zealand English (3.4 million); South African English (3 million); and Jamaican English (2.4 million). But there are many other "world Englishes," as Figure 2.3 indicates.[6]

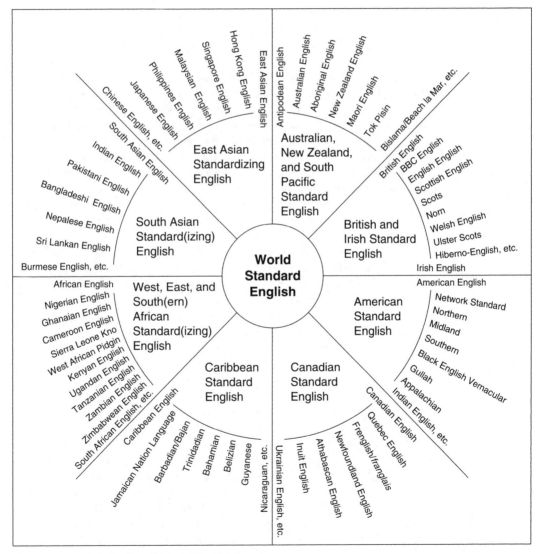

Figure 2.3   The Circle of World English[7]

Worldwide, British and American English have been most influential on learners of English as a foreign language through the major involvement by speakers of those dialects in teaching English as a foreign language (EFL). But none of the varieties, including British and American, can claim preeminence on linguistic grounds as the standard for the others. Each is a legitimate version of English. Just as that abstract entity *American English* is in the broadest sense the sum of its regional and social dialects, so *Global English* must be defined as the sum of various national and local varieties.

Within the United States, English also exists in an international context as one language amid many. This nation founded by immigrants welcomes those arriving at New York Harbor with that symbol of liberty on which is inscribed the invitation:

> *Give me your tired, your poor,*
> *Your huddled masses yearning to breathe free . . .*

Yet in reality, Americans have sometimes had mixed feelings about new arrivals and their languages. As early as the mid-eighteenth century, Benjamin Franklin was concerned about the language situation in Pennsylvania. He wrote, in 1751, "Why should Pennsylvania, founded by the English, become a colony of aliens, who will shortly be so numerous as to Germanize us instead of our Anglifying them, and will never adopt our language or customs any more than they can acquire our complexion?" However great the contributions of German immigrants to American culture have been, the German language has not replaced English nor ever really challenged its dominance. Yet fears like Franklin's, sometimes focused on German but also on a variety of other languages, have recurred periodically in the 250 years since then. As new immigrants settled in the United States, the first generation often continued to speak the native language they brought with them, but the second generation usually became fluent in English. Later generations have tended to lose the family language altogether. Even in those areas where Spanish is most prominent, Latino immigrants are switching to English at about the same rate as the German, Italian, and Polish immigrants who came before them. By the third generation, almost all Latino immigrants are predominantly English speakers, even though they learn Spanish at home. In those parts of the country where Spanish is flourishing, immigration of Latinos is continuing, but the pattern of language shift from Spanish to English is continuing as well. A study done in 1992 found that a great majority of those whose background is Hispanic believe strongly that English should be the first language of Latinos in the United States. In short, the use of English is so pervasive in the United States and increasing so rapidly in the rest of the world that laws and constitutional amendments cannot possibly increase its prominence or raise the motivation among immigrants to learn it. Students of English need to shift their focus beyond the artificial monotony of the school grammars and handbooks that still tend to dominate the formal study of the language. Exploring the rich diversity of styles and regional, social, and international dialects and accents that constitute the real language—as living human beings speak it—can provide a lifetime of fascinating discovery.

▥ *EXERCISE 2.3*

Noah Webster (1758–1843)—who is famous for, among other things, his early American dictionaries, spelling books, and grammars—warned repeatedly in the late eighteenth century against the dangers of borrowing foreign words and incorporating them in American English, whether directly from abroad or through the influence of foreign immigrants. In spite of his (and others') alarms, many words have indeed entered our language through such borrowing. Just a few examples of words borrowed into English during the eighteenth and nineteenth centuries include:

Italian	*casino, mafia, malaria, studio*
Spanish	*cigar, rodeo, patio, frijoles, macho*
German	*waltz, iceberg, semester, hamburger*
Arabic	*genie, candy, safari*
Indian	*cashmere, pajamas, dinghy*
Dravidian	*tea, ketchup*
Native North American	*raccoon, moccasin, skunk*

There are hundreds of other examples. As our language seems not to have been harmed but, if anything, enriched by such borrowing, how can we account for the dire predictions?

SUMMARY

Regional and social dialects reflect the diversity within American society. Superimposed on the variations in speech that evolve naturally in any complex community are value judgments about which varieties are standard and non-standard. No naturally occurring spoken dialect of American English is *the* standard variety, but the standard written English taught in schools and encoded in writers' handbooks is used by educated Americans throughout the country as a shared medium of public written communication. Worldwide, American English is but one of many Englishes spoken as a first language by hundreds of millions of people and as a second language by many more. Within the United States, language diversity is evident in the rich array of Native American and immigrant languages that supplement English. The language and dialect you use identifies who you are: by national origin, region, and social class. In contrast to this user-related variation, language also shows meaningful variation according to the purposes that it serves. Prominent among such use-related variations are stylistic levels that vary according to situation and speaker-hearer relationship along a continuum from informal, even intimate, through the businesslike consultative style, to the most selfconsciously formal varieties used primarily for prepared speeches, ceremonies, and rituals. For young children whose first language is not English, learning English as a second language involves stages and developmental errors similar to those that characterize native language acquisition. Adult learners of English as a second language may also make developmental errors, but, in addition, they move through an interlanguage phase, in which features and patterns from their native language are transferred to the new language. Mastering a second language is not simply a matter of learning the rules of grammar but also of mastering the complex ways in which communities use language for a wide array of purposes.

KEY TERMS

American English
  nonstandard
  standard
  standard written
communicative competence
  linguistic competence
  textual competence
  pragmatic competence
dialects
  regional
  social

hypercorrection
interlanguage
  developmental errors
  transfer errors
linguistic insecurity
style
  informal style
  formal style
  style shifting

ENDNOTES

1. From Roger W. Shuy, *Discovering American Dialects* (Urbana, IL: NCTE, 1967), p. 47. Copyright 1967 by the National Council of Teachers of English. Reprinted with permission.
2. From Jim Murray, "Olympic Guide to Diction," *Los Angeles Times,* 28 October 1990, pp. C1, C13.
3. From Dana L. Wilson, *Boston English Illustrated* (Lincoln, NE: Centennial Press, 1976), pp. 28, 37, 43, 28.
4. Based on Geneva Smitherman, *Talkin and Testifyin: The Language of Black America* (Boston: Houghton Mifflin, 1977), pp. 19–23.
5. Martin Joos, in *The Five Clocks* (New York: Harcourt, Brace & World, 1967), named five styles of speech. Because they generally do not occur in everyday public speech, we have omitted from our discussion the styles at the ends of the continuum: intimate (spoken between two people who are communicating with few words) and frozen (used in speeches and addresses to large groups of people).
6. All statistics taken from David Crystal, *The Cambridge Encyclopedia of the English Language* (Cambridge: Cambridge University Press, 1995), pp. 108–109.
7. From "The English Languages?" *English Today*, 11 (July 1987), p. 11, published by Cambridge University Press. Used with permission.

The Morphology of English

3

CHAPTER PREVIEW

Chapter 3 discusses some basic ways in which speakers construct meaning out of the resources provided by the English language. The units of meaning considered fundamental in a language are its morphemes, the components of words.

CHAPTER GOALS

At the end of this chapter, you should be able to

- Differentiate *morphemes* from *words* and *syllables*.
- Differentiate between *bases* and *affixes*.
- Identify *bound* and *free bases*.
- Distinguish *prefixes* from *suffixes*.
- Identify *allomorphs* of a *morpheme*.
- Recognize and produce examples of all eight *inflectional morphemes*.
- State whether or not a *derivational morpheme* has changed the part of speech of the base to which it is attached.

Although we tend to think of words as the meaningful units used in creating sentences, the shortest sequence of sounds that is capable of conveying meaning is often less than a word. The word *smallest*, for instance, contains not only information about size, *small*, but also information about size in relationship to similar things, *-est*. (The superlative ending on the word states a relationship to other small things.) Sometimes, as is true in *smallest*, each syllable of a word is a meaningful unit, but even a one-syllable word may contain more than one unit of meaning. For example, a one-syllable word like *walked* signifies the meaning of the verb *walk* and indicates that the verb is in the past tense. Meaning may extend across more than one syllable as well. We have many multisyllable words, like *able* or *museum*, that cannot be broken down into more than one meaningful chunk.

MORPHEMES

The word **morpheme** is used by linguists to name the smallest unit of meaning in a language. In order to differentiate morphemes from words and syllables, braces are used to surround sequences of sounds identified as morphemes {-est}. If a word cannot be divided into any smaller meaningful components, then it, too, is a morpheme. For example, the word *readable* consists of two morphemes, {read} and {-able}, the first of which is also an independent word, *read*.

Although the term *morpheme* may be unfamiliar to you, the morphological system is not; you use it constantly in creating and in understanding sentences of English. If it had been necessary for you to master a unique word for each new concept encountered while learning English, you would have had to memorize an enormous word stock. Instead, you have learned patterns for creating words and rules for fitting new words into the system. For example, when you learned that the adjective *bold* is the basis of an adverb *boldly*, the pattern helped you recognize other adjective/adverb pairs, like *sweet/sweetly*, *generous/generously*, *happy/happily*, and *rough/roughly*. You were also able to create these regardless of whether you had ever heard them spoken. At some point, you learned to create yet another set of words from the same material by prefixing {un-}. In fact, an important part of your knowledge of English is an awareness of which words accept a negative prefix (*unkindly, ungenerously, unhappily*) and which do not (**unsweetly, *unroughly*).

The use of morphology as a resource for forming and comprehending new words remains important even after you have acquired language because you are continuously encountering new words. Soon after the appearance of the noun *funk* ("pop art created from bizarre objects") in the 1960s, an adjective (*funky*) followed and from that a second noun, *funkiness*. Anyone acquainted with the meaning to the art world of *funk* could immediately understand the other two coinages. Also consider *Watergate*, the name of the apartment complex in Washington, D.C., in which the Democratic National Committee had their offices. After the infamous break-in of the 1970s, American English gained a new morpheme, {-gate}, meaning "scandal involving government figures." Several immediately understandable words have subsequently been coined by the news media, like *Koreagate* (1976), *Oilgate* (1978), *Irangate* (1986), *Whitewatergate* (1994), *Monicagate* (1998), *Iraqgate* (2004), *Memogate* (2005), and *FEMAgate* (2005).

■ EXERCISE 3.1

As a speaker of English, you already know how to create new words and how to guess at the meaning of words you have never heard before. Suppose that you hear someone use the newly coined noun, *glub,* and are told that it means "a silly remark"; next, you encounter an adjective formed from the noun, *glubby.* You may be able to guess that it characterizes an act or person as being silly. Using these two words as the basis, see how many of the following words you can create or understand.

1. From the noun *glub,* create a verb that means "to say something silly." (*They always* _glubbing_ *during discussions.*)
2. From the noun *glub,* create another noun meaning "someone who makes a silly remark." (*Sometimes she can be such a* _glubber_ .)
3. From the noun *glub,* create an adjective other than *glubby.* (*That was certainly a* _glubberous_ *thing to say.*)
4. From the *adjective* created in #3, create an adverb. (*Jack always speaks so* _glubberously_ *about his brother.*)
5. From the noun *glub,* create another noun meaning "one who hates silly remarks."

In addition to serving as resources in the creation of vocabulary, morphemes supply grammatical tags to words, helping us to identify on the basis of form the parts of speech of words in sentences we hear or read. For example, in the sentence *Morphemes supply grammatical tags to words,* the plural morpheme ending {-s} helps identify *morphemes, tags,* and *words* as nouns; the {-ical} ending underscores the adjectival relationship between *grammatical* and the following noun, *tags,* which it modifies. Most speakers of English can tell a great deal about the following nonsense sentence by using morphological clues:

(1) Why is that groony stronker wigrifying his klummitzes so briggily?

Because *groony* ends in {-y} and comes between *that* and a nounlike word ending in {-er}, most students will guess that it is an adjective. *Stronker* appears to end in the morpheme often used to create nouns meaning "one who does": *biker, streaker, teacher. Wigrifying* ends in two verbal morphemes: {-fy}, used to create verbs like *falsify, magnify,* and the verb ending {-ing}, found on participles like *biking, streaking, teaching. Klummitzes* looks like a plural noun because of its ending; and *briggily* seems to have the adverbial ending we have seen above on *unkindly* and *unhappily.*

Our purpose in discussing morphemes is to provide enough information so that you can use your knowledge of morphology to help identify parts of speech and to understand the inflectional system of English (that is, the morphemes used to convey grammatical information, like the noun plural on *cats* or the verb past tense on *walked*). If you are a native speaker of the language, you already know and use the morphological system of English every time you speak. What we want to do is bring to a conscious level what you already know intuitively.

RULES OF THUMB

Characteristics of a Morpheme

---

1. Has a meaning that can be at least vaguely stated.
2. Contains only one unit of meaning.
3. Can be used with the same meaning within other words or as a word itself.

Figure 3.1

Before doing Exercise 3.2, review the characteristics of a morpheme in Figure 3.1.

▪ *EXERCISE 3.2*

Decide how many units of meaning each of the following words contains. First, draw a line between each unit; see if you can state the meaning of each unit or describe how it changes the word to which it attaches. Second, try to show that each unit can stand alone as an independent word or else be used with the same meaning in another word. An example has been done for you. (You may find a dictionary helpful in doing this exercise; however, the important point is to try dividing the words into meaningful bits.)

EXAMPLE

Unequal

Un | equal

*{un-} means "not, or contrary to" and negates the meaning of "equal." It is also used in **unfair**.*

{equal} is a word meaning "having the same capability, quantity, or effect as something else."

1. underscore	4. cowardly	7. nonbeliever	10. unfashionable
2. reform	5. childish	8. clueless	11. reignited
3. darken	6. doughnuts	9. disapproval	12. declassify

▪ *EXERCISE 3.3*

Follow the steps of morphological analysis outlined in Figure 3.2 in order to identify each morpheme in the following sentence.

Yesterday, the baker's oldest daughter ran away with the banker's younger son.

In Figure 3.2, we suggest that you begin by drawing a line between each word because every word of English contains at least one morpheme. Many words, like *the* and *with*, contain only one unit of meaning; others contain two or more. How did you divide *yesterday?* You probably drew a line between *yester* and *day* because there is a word *day* that has the same meaning (a 24-hour period) both in *yesterday* and by itself. The remaining part, *yester*, is less than a word, but it has a recognizable meaning ("previous one before this"), which also occurs in *yesteryear*. Can it be divided into two or more morphemes? It can only if you are able to show that the units divided off can be reused with the same meaning in other word combinations. The *yes* of *yester* does not have the meaning of assent found in the initial word of *Yes, you may go,* and you will probably be unable to think of a meaning for or a way to reuse *ter*. Therefore, {yester} is considered a single morpheme, not capable of further reduction.

Baker's and *banker's* are alike. Each contains a full word (*bake, bank*), followed by a suffix {-er} that means "one who bakes (or banks)," and both words end in a possessive suffix {-'s}. Thus, each contains three morphemes. *Oldest* contains the superlative morpheme {-est} we discussed above, when it appeared on *smallest*. *Daughter* ends in *-er*, but this ending is not the morpheme appearing in *baker* and *banker;* the meaning of the whole word is not "one who *daughts." (Remember that the asterisk is used in linguistics to mark forms that do not occur in the language.) You might suspect that the *-er* ending—which also appears on *mother, father, sister,* and *brother*—relates to the fact that all are kinship terms. But cutting off the suffix would leave parts that are not reused in other words in modern English: *{moth-}, *{fath-}, *{sist-}, and *{broth-}. Because these bits are not used to create other words with meanings related to *mother, father, sister,* and *brother*, the words cannot be cut into morphemes. {Daughter}, therefore, constitutes a single morpheme. The *-er* ending on *younger* is not the same as that on *baker* and *banker*. It does

---

RULES OF THUMB

Steps of Morphological Analysis

1. Draw a vertical line between words and between whatever parts of words seem to you to be meaningful units in the sentence.
2. Go back and check each division you made.
   a. Be sure that each contains only one unit of meaning.
   b. Try to state what the meaning or function of each unit is.
   c. Try to think of a way that you can use the unit with a similar meaning in another word or as a word itself.

Figure 3.2

not mean "one who does." It is the comparative morpheme used to show the varying degrees of adjectives: *old* (normal), *older* (comparative), and *oldest* (superlative). *Away* is made up of two morphemes: the word *way* and a prefix {a-}, which turns words into adverbs (*bed/abed, board/aboard*).

Ran is a more complex case: It is a single-syllable word containing two kinds of information, the word *run* ("to move rapidly") and a vowel change that signals that the verb is in the past tense. If you compare *run/ran* with similar pairs of verbs (*want/wanted, treat/treated*), where two different syllables signal the two meanings, you may see more clearly why *ran* is interpreted as having two morphemes: {run} + a signal of the past tense.

A prototypical morpheme consists of a bit of sound that can be isolated in the way {-ed} can be separated from {want}. Not only does such a segment pass each of the tests we have used in identifying morphemes, but in addition, it has clear boundaries that allow us to draw a line between it and the other morphemes to which it is attached. The past-tense morpheme in *ran* is not a prototypical case. Although it meets our basic test of signaling a single meaning, it is not easily isolatable as a unit. The change from present to past tense in the verb *run* is clearly signaled by the change of the vowel in *run* to the one in *ran*. A change in vowels signals the change from present tense to past tense in quite a few other verbs: *write/wrote, bind/bound, shake/shook, blow/blew*. Some other verbs signal past tense with even more unpredictable contrasts (for example, *go/went; am, is, are/was, were*), and a few have past-tense forms identical to their present-tense forms (like *spread/spread, burst/burst, cost/cost*).

Rather than grow frustrated in trying to make all morphemes fit exactly the mold of the prototype, we can recognize that the past-tense morpheme {-ed} in verbs like *wanted* is an example of a prototypical morpheme, one that is easy to recognize because of its clear boundaries. Other contrasts that signal past tense (such as the vowel change in *run/ran*) are more *peripheral* cases of the same morpheme: They meet some of our criteria but lack the clear boundaries that characterize the prototype. Thus, although we can't draw a line between the separate morphemes of *ran*, we can think of it as having the morphological structure {run} + {-ed}.

■ *EXERCISE 3.4* _____

> Try dividing the words in the sentences below into morphemes. At first, divide on the basis of your intuition, and then test each morpheme to be sure (1) that it contains a single meaning that you can state, and (2) that you can reuse the morpheme with the same meaning in another word or as an independent word.

1. Fred finds the old elevator unbearable.
2. The manager listened impatiently as the clerk's claims became increasingly incredible.

Allomorphs

Exercise 3.4 raises some questions we have not yet encountered. One has to do with the spelling of morphemes. Is there a difference in meaning between the {-able} of *unbearable* and the {-ible} of *incredible?* Probably not. Both have similar pronunciations and both mean "capable of the action" suggested by the base. In discussing morphemes, pronunciation and meaning are more important than spelling. What would you say of the final syllables on *shopper* and *operator?* Are they the same morpheme? Do both create nouns meaning "one who performs the action"? Then despite the difference in spelling, both are considered variants of a single morpheme.

What if the pronunciation of a morpheme changes? Consider the contrast between *incredible*, in which the second syllable of {-able} sounds like *bull*, and *incredibility*, in which the same syllable sounds like *bill*. The morpheme {-able} is pronounced differently in each. Does this mean that we are dealing with two different morphemes? No. Although the meaning must be identical for two items to be considered a single morpheme, the pronunciation can vary. Both are considered variants, or **allomorphs,** of the morpheme {-able}, as no difference in meaning coincides with the difference in pronunciation. As a matter of fact, this morphological pattern occurs each time {-ity} is added to {-able}, thus producing a variety of pairs, such as *usable/usability; readable/ readability; marketable/marketability; credible/credibility.*

INFLECTIONAL MORPHEMES

We have seen two kinds of morphemes in the analysis above: **derivational morphemes,** used to create new words ({-er} in *baker*), and **inflectional morphemes,** used to show grammatical relationships ({-s} in *baker's*). English has a small set of inflectional morphemes, used every time we speak, to show grammatical relationships between the words in a sentence.

If you have studied any European language other than English, you have encountered a far more complex inflectional system than is found in English today, where only eight **inflections** still exist, all of them suffixes: two for nouns, four for verbs, and two for adjectives and adverbs. This is an astonishingly small number of inflections compared with the number of inflections on nouns and verbs in other inflected Western European languages, such as Spanish, French, and Italian.

An important distinction between derivational and inflectional morphemes is the nature of the base before and after affixing occurs. When derivational morphemes are attached to a base, they create words with new meanings: *Walk* names an activity, but *walker* refers to a person who performs the activity. When inflectional morphemes are added, the essential meaning and the part of speech of the word remain unchanged; the appended morpheme simply contributes additional information about the concept. Both *walk* and *walked* are verbs naming an activity; the latter differs from the former only in tense, the designation of the time at which the activity took place.

Figure 3.3 summarizes the kind of information supplied by the eight inflectional morphemes. You are already familiar with *homophones* in English: two words that sound alike but have different meanings (*won* and *one*, for instance). As you can see in Figure 3.3, it is also possible to have two or more morphemes that sound alike but have different meanings. Three different meanings are signalled by the suffix pronounced *s:* noun plural (*three cats*), noun possessive (*Janet's hat*), and verb third-person singular present tense (*Leslie walks*). We can differentiate among them by calling them {-s$_1$} for the plural, {-s$_2$} for the possessive, and {-s$_3$} for the third-person singular present tense of the verb. For most English verbs, the past-tense and the past-participle forms are also identical (*I **owned** that book once; I have **owned** it for some time*). However, because a number of verbs have past participles ending in {-en} (*ridden, eaten, frozen*), linguists have named the past-participle morpheme {-en} in order to contrast it with the past-tense morpheme {-ed}.

SUMMARY			
English Inflectional Morphemes			
Morpheme Function	Form	Combined Form	Resulting Word
Nouns			
Plural	-s	book + -s	books
Possessive	-s	Barbara + -s	Barbara's
Verbs			
Present tense (3rd-person singular)	-s	walk + -s	walks
Past tense	-ed	walk + -ed eat + vowel change	walked ate
Past participle	-en	walk + -ed eat + -en	walked eaten
Present participle	-ing	walk + ing	walking
Adjectives			
Comparative	-er	big + -er	bigger
Superlative	-est	big + -est	biggest

Figure 3.3

Only a few grammatical items are worth memorizing, and the inflectional suffixes are among them. First of all, there are only eight. Second, you already know them and use them without any problem; only the terminology may be new to you. Third, identification of inflectional morphemes becomes especially important when you are trying to classify parts of speech and sentence types. In Figure 3.4, we provide some sentence frames that may help you fix these eight inflections in memory.

Noun Inflections

The elaborate system of inflections added to nouns to indicate distinctions of gender, number, and case, historically known as the *declension* of nouns, is much simpler in English than it is in many other European languages. Today in English only two noun inflections survive, one identifying number (the plural) and one identifying case (the possessive).

In writing, the regular versions of the plural are usually signaled by adding an -*s* or an -*es* to the base form of the noun (*book/books, box/boxes*). In speech, there are three pronunciations of the **noun plural inflection.** It occurs as the [s] sound in some words (*pots*), as the [z] sound in others (*pans*), and as a syllable ending in the [z] sound in still others (*glasses*). The choice of which ending to use is determined by the nature of the preceding sounds, producing a pattern discussed in the Appendix, "The Sounds of American English." Other allomorphs occur as well. For some words, the plural is signaled by changing -*um* to -*a* (*datum* becoming *data* and *medium* becoming *media*); for some,

SUMMARY	
Examples of Inflectional Suffixes	
Inflection	Frame
{-s₁} noun plural	He has three *desserts*.
{-s₂} noun possessive	This is *Betty's* dessert.
{-s₃} verb present tense	Bill usually *eats* dessert.
{-ed} verb past tense	He *ate* the dessert yesterday.
{-en} verb past participle	He has always *eaten* dessert.
{-ing} verb present participle	He is *eating* the dessert now.
{-er} adjective comparative	His dessert is *larger* than mine.
{-est} adjective superlative	Her dessert is the *largest*.

Figure 3.4

an *-en* is added (*oxen*); and for some, the plural is not expressed at all (*one sheep/three sheep*). Linguists sometimes refer to this as the **zero allomorph,** representing it with the null sign Ø, as in {sheep} + {Ø}. Not all speakers of English agree on where the zero allomorph occurs. Compare *two fish* and *two fishes*, for example. Do you use both? If so, do they have different meanings?

Another sort of variation in the pronunciation of inflectional morphemes occurs as a result of regional and social dialects and styles of speech, as we discussed in Chapter 2. For example, children growing up in inner-city communities may not pronounce consonant sounds in some contexts, such as at the ends of words when several consonants occur together in a series or cluster. *John watches TV* may be pronounced the same as *John watched TV*, with *watches* and *watched* both pronounced as *watch*. Does this mean the speaker does not understand the difference between present and past tense? Not at all. In other circumstances the present tense and past tense morphemes will be pronounced. What we are observing is simply a particular pattern of pronunciation, not a difference in meaning. In fact, few, if any, speakers pronounce the {-ed} inflection in sentences like *Mary loved Don*, unless they are speaking very slowly and deliberately.

The **noun possessive inflection** is a remnant of the earlier genitive case in English. It has the same pronunciations as the plural, depending on the final sound of the word to which it attaches. No matter which way it is pronounced, it is usually written as *'s*. When a singular noun ends in *-s* or *-z*, the possessive is pronounced as a syllable ending in the [z] sound and written *'s* (*the boss's desk, the cruise's end*). The possessive of a plural noun is indicated by a simple apostrophe after the final *s* (*five days' work*). Writers are generally guided by pronunciation. If they add the sound of an [s] in speech to signal the possessive, they write the possessive *'s;* if they don't add an [s] in speech, they write only an apostrophe.

Some speakers of American English have a zero allomorph of the possessive morpheme. They may indicate possession either by using the {-s$_2$} versions we have noted or simply by juxtaposing the two nouns involved, as in *Have you seen **Mary book?*** As in the case of the zero allomorph of the present and past tense morphemes (in which *John watches TV* and *John watched TV* may be pronounced the same as *John watch TV*), the zero allomorph of the possessive tends to occur where two or more consonants come together. In *Mary's book*, the [z] sound of the possessive suffix and initial consonant of *book* create the environment in which the possessive morpheme may not be pronounced. Such a pronunciation pattern is one of the many minor ways in which one dialect of English may differ from another without affecting meaning. Teachers of children who routinely use the zero allomorph of the possessive (*Mary book*) in speech can help them to become conscious of the correct *spelling* of the possessive, for they are likely, at least initially, to write possessive nouns as they pronounce them.

Because in many instances there is an equivalence of meaning between the possessive formed by adding the inflectional morpheme {-s$_2$} to a noun and using that same noun as the object of the preposition *of*, it has become traditional to think of the possessive as having two forms: the -'s possessive morpheme and the *of* possessive phrase. We can say either *the country's president* or *the president of the country* without a significant change of meaning. The *of* possessive is used somewhat more often for inanimate things and the -'s possessive more often for humans. (In the examples that follow, a question mark is placed before items that not all speakers of the language will find acceptable.)

(2) ?the house's door   Patricia's knee

the door of the house   ?the knee of Patricia

Verb Inflections

Many languages have complicated verb *conjugations*, inflections identifying person, number, tense, mood, voice, and aspect for every verb. As we shall see below, only four verb inflections survive in Modern English: one for number (third person singular), one for tense (past), and two for aspect (perfect and progressive). Language resources other than conjugation are used to identify some of the distinctions once expressed by inflections. For example, for future time we combine helping verbs and adverbs (*I **will** write my paper **later***); we use helping verbs to indicate the conditional mood (*I **might** not answer his letter*); and we express the subjunctive mood by changing the expected verb form (*If he **were** here, he would answer for himself*).

The uninflected form of the verb is the **infinitive** form, named this because it is the form used to create an infinitive (*to sit, to see, to be*). When the subject is a third-person singular noun or pronoun (*he, she, it,* or nouns to which these pronouns can refer), the **present-tense inflection** has exactly the same allomorphs as the noun plural: [s] (*sits*), [z] (*grows*), and a syllable ending in [z] (*loses*). The verb in the sentence *I usually sit here* is in the present tense, even though there is no visible morpheme marking it as such. The same is true in *We grow tomatoes, You always object*, and *They see the point now.* These verbs are identified as present tense by default (they are *not* past tenses) and by analogy: If the pronoun is changed to *she*, the present-tense inflection occurs on the verb.

The present-tense inflection is marked only when the subject is a third-person singular noun or pronoun, with one important exception. Notice the irregularity of the present tense forms in (3). All of these are present-tense forms of the verb *be:*

(3) I *am*

he, she, or it *is*

we *are*

The **past-tense inflection,** although usually written *-ed*, has three common allomorphs in speech: [t] (*sipped*), [d] (*strolled*), or a syllable ending in [d] (*waded*). (The reason for this alternation is discussed in the Appendix.) Other allomorphs, including a change of the vowel in the base (*run/ran,* *eat/ate, ride/rode*) and the **zero allomorph** (*cut/cut, hit/hit, put/put*), signal past tense for a large set of irregular verbs in English. No matter what combinations of allomorphs are used to form the past tense, all are seen as belonging to a single morpheme, {-ed}. Thus, morphologically, we could write *went* as {go} + {-ed}.

The **past-participle inflection** is often identical to the past tense (*I walked yesterday/I have always walked, he cut/he has cut*), but for many irregular verbs, it is the syllable *-en* (*I have eaten; I have ridden*). For this reason—and to differentiate it from the past-tense morpheme—linguists label the past-participle morpheme {-en}, even though more verbs in English form their past participles by adding *-ed* than by adding *-en*.

The past-participle inflection has two important uses in English. It attaches to verbs following the helping verb *have* to form the present perfect (*We have received his answer*) and past perfect (*We had received his answer*) aspects of the verb. (The perfect is discussed in more detail in Chapter 6.) It also attaches to verbs following the helping verb *be* (*His answer is/was received*) to form the passive voice. (The passive is discussed in more detail in Chapter 8.)

The past participle form of the verb often occurs as a noun modifier (*an **admitted** freshman*) and is related to a larger phrase such as *a freshman who was admitted*. After long usage, some noun modifiers that began as past participles cross over and become true adjectives (*the **excited** crowd, the **troubled** nation*), capable of being qualified (*very excited/troubled*) or compared (*more excited/troubled*). Others do not. Because we cannot say **a very/more admitted freshman*, it is clear that *admitted* is simply a verb past participle used to modify the noun. We discuss the differences between past participles and adjectives in Chapter 12.

Figure 3.5 summarizes the major allomorphs of the past-tense and the past-participle morphemes in English.

SUMMARY		
Major Verb Past-Tense and Past-Participle Allomorphs		
Regular Verbs	*Past Tense {-ed}*	*Past Participle {-en}*
Past-tense and past-participle forms are identical.	She *walked/tapped.* It *stayed/opened.* He *waited/waded.* They *stopped.*	She has *walked/tapped.* It had *stayed/opened.* He has *waited/waded.* They were *stopped.*
Irregular Verbs	{-ed}	{-en}
Vowel change No change in form	She *ate/rode.* He *sang/wept.* They *found.* They *hit.* They *cut.*	She *has eaten/ridden.* He *has sung/wept.* They were *found.* They have *hit.* They were *cut.*

Figure 3.5

▣ *EXERCISE 3.5*

The present tense is used in English not only to signify that an action is occurring in the present, but also for any of the following:

A. A regular activity or state assumed to occur in the past, present, and future

B. Something in a narrative that occurred in the past but is told as though it were happening in the present

C. Something that is continuously ongoing in the past, present, and future

D. Something that will occur in the future

E. Something that occurs at an indefinite time

Consider the following sentences and try to match the highlighted present-tense verb in each with the time in which the action occurs. An example has been done for you.

EXAMPLE

*Some children **floss** their teeth after every meal.*

TIME = A: A regular activity

1. Mia usually *rides* a horse named "Velvet."
2. Our semester *ends* soon.
3. The early bird *gets* the worm.
4. So the salesman *says,* "I'll have to ask my manager about that."
5. Mary Lou *orders* a vegetarian meal when she *flies.*
6. Everyone *thinks* that Melanie *looks* just like her poodle.
7. Marnie *hopes* our final *is* easier than the midterm.
8. Macbeth *kills* Duncan because he *believes* in the witches' prophecy.

▣ *EXERCISE 3.6*

Identify the past-tense and past-participle morpheme of each of the following verbs, using Figure 3.5 as a guide. Compare your answers with those of others in your class. Speakers of different dialects have different forms for the past-tense and past-participle versions of some of these verbs.

EXAMPLE

sing

Present	*I **sing** for the school choir every afternoon at five o'clock.*
Past	*Yesterday, I **sang** from five to nine o'clock. (Change of vowel)*
Past Participle	*I have **sung** for the school choir many times. (Change of vowel)*
[In the passive voice]	*The National Anthem was **sung** at the beginning of the concert.*

1. think	4. sweep	7. turn	10. hit
2. sink	5. bleep	8. swim	11. grit
3. blink	6. burn	9. trim	12. sit

The fourth inflection, the **present-participle inflection** {-ing}, has a single form, always occurring as *-ing: walking, singing, calling.* The present-participle form also often occurs as a noun modifier (*the **sleeping** baby, a **rolling** stone*) and is related to a larger phrase such as *a baby that is sleeping* or *a stone that is rolling.* Some present participles used as noun modifiers become adjectives over a period of time (*a **pleasing** personality, a **deserving** student*), capable of being qualified or compared (*very/more pleasing, very/more deserving*). The majority, however, remain verb present participles used to modify nouns. They cannot be qualified or compared (**the very/more sleeping baby, **the rather rolling stone*). We discuss more fully the differences between present participles and adjectives in Chapter 12.

Adjective and Adverb Inflections

In some languages, adjectives share the declensions of nouns, inflecting to show gender, number, and case. In English, however, there are only two possible inflections for adjectives, the comparative and the superlative. The **adjective comparative** and **superlative inflections** {-er} and {-est} are quite regular, but they can be added only to one- or two-syllable words in English. We have *tall, taller, tallest* and *heavy, heavier, heaviest* but not *visionary, *visionarier, *visionariest.* Adjectives of more than two syllables do not accept inflectional morphemes; for them, entire words, rather than morphological suffixes, are used to indicate the comparative (*more visionary*) and superlative (*most reluctant*).

Note that the comparative and superlative inflections also appear on a small number of adverbs: *He drove longer and faster than anyone else.* Many adverbs, too, can be compared or made superlative by using *more* and *most* (*more securely, most effectively*).

FUNCTIONAL SHIFT

It is not unusual in English to find that a word can accept more than one kind of inflection. A word like *meet*, for instance, can be a verb (*The committee must **meet** this week*) and accept all verb inflections (present tense, *meets;* past tense, *met;* past participle, *met;* and present participle, *meeting*). As a noun, *meet* can also accept the plural inflection in contexts like *three swap meets.* Many English words that started out as nouns have become verbs as well simply by our using them as verbs with verb inflections: *network* (as in *We have **networked** all of our computers*), *interface, position, contrast, race,* and *lunch* are examples. The process of converting one part of speech into another without changing its basic form in any way is called **functional shift** (or *conversion*) and has given us numerous new nouns from words that were originally verbs: for instance, *worry, laugh, mistake, nap,* and *run.* As they learn new words in English, people also learn what kinds of inflections they can take.

WHAT'S THE USAGE? *Noun and Verb Inflections in AAVE*

Standard American English differentiates between singular and plural nouns (*book : books*) and marks grammatical agreement between a subject and its predicate, as in *she walks : they walk.* African-American Vernacular English often does not mark the plural of nouns (*those girl*), nor the agreement between subjects and verbs (*They was very happy*). When regular verbs occur with the third person singular subject, the {-s} present tense morpheme is omitted (*Jan walk to school*). Such features are also encountered in the dialects of other speakers of English, such as Vietnamese, Chinese, and Japanese, whose native languages do not inflect. These speakers routinely omit the {-s} for the plural nouns, and the {-s} which marks the third singular of the present tense.

One reason these omissions can occur without disrupting communication is that information dictating the choice between singular and plural noun and verb inflections may be available elsewhere in the context, and often, the plural is marked redundantly: twice in *they were,* where both the pronoun and verb indicate the plural, and three times in *those two pretty girls,* where *those, two,* and *girls* all indicate the plural, with only the adjective being neutral. At an early period in our history, all four words, including the number and adjective, would have had plural morpheme suffixes. However, numbers and adjectives no longer inflect to show the number in English, nor does the article (*the girl/the three girls*). The plural inflection in Standard American English has gradually simplified over its history, as has the present tense verb inflection. No present tense marker is required for the verb in *I/we sing, you sing,* or *they sing.* The tense marker survives only for the third person singular in SAE: *she sings.* The AAVE rules, which have done away with some of those redundancies for the plural and present tense inflections, have simply taken that regularization one step further.

EXERCISE 3.7

Which types of inflection can each of the words below accept? Identify and give examples. Some can accept only one kind of inflection; some can accept more than one. An example has been done for you.

EXAMPLE

record

Noun   *Court **records** show that attorneys prefer to plea bargain.*

Verb   *The cryptographer **recorded** the statements of the defendant.*

1. concrete	3. star	5. drink	7. free
2. reconcile	4. table	6. far	8. long

DERIVATIONAL MORPHEMES

Not all morphemes show grammatical relationships. Many are used to create (or derive) new words by recycling parts of existing words into new combinations. Derivational morphemes provide an efficient, transparent method of forming new words, one that simplifies the mastery of vocabulary in a language. If you know the words *asteroid*, *android*, and *humanoid*, you can quickly derive the meaning of *inhumanoid*, a monsterlike creature that happens to have glow-in-the-dark teeth and movable appendages, which a local toy store advertised for $22.99 each. Even without a context, you can probably guess at the meaning (if you do not already know it) of *agribusiness* or *deselect* or *whiffability*. Derivation is also a useful way of making one word fit many contexts. For example, by attaching a variety of **affixes** (morphemes added to the beginnings or ends of words) to the basic noun *friend*, you can create other nouns (*friendship, friendliness, unfriendliness, friendlessness*), adjectives (*friendly, unfriendly, friendless*), and a verb (*befriend*).

■ *EXERCISE 3.8* _____

Before reading on, do this experiment. Following the example of derivations from the word *friend*, begin with the word *act*. See how many words you can build by attaching affixes to it and to any new word created in the process.

In creating words based on *act*, you probably used both **prefixes** (morphemes attached to the beginnings of words) and **suffixes** (morphemes attached to the ends of words). Prefixes and suffixes are considered **bound morphemes** because they are incapable of standing alone as words; they must be connected (bound) to other morphemes. Such morphemes are written with a hyphen indicating where they attach to other words. Morphemes that can stand alone as words are said to be **free morphemes.** We have summarized some of the combinations possible with *act* in Figure 3.6, showing where affixes attach to other morphemes. Using Figure 3.6, you can get *active, actively, inactive, inactively, activity, inactivity, activate, inactivate, react, reactive, reactivate, enact, reenact, enactment,* and *reenactment.* You may see other possibilities as well. There are many more.

Our purpose in studying morphology is to learn to analyze the structure of words and to use that analysis to help identify the parts of speech to which words belong. Notice that some derivational morphemes change the part of speech; for instance, the noun or verb *act* becomes the adjective *active.* Others do not change the part of speech; *enact* and *reenact* are both verbs. Some morphemes identify the part of speech; because {-ive} creates adjectives from other words, its presence helps you locate adjectives. Again, others do not help.

SUMMARY		
An Example of Derivational Morphology: {act}		
Derivational Bound Prefixes	*Free Base*	*Derivational Bound Suffixes*
{in-}	{act}	{-ive} + {-ly}
{in-}	{act}	{-ive} + {-ity}
{in-}	{act}	{-ive} + {-ate}
{re-}	{act}	{-ive} + {-ate}
{en-}	{act}	
{re-} + {en-}	{act}	{-ment}

Figure 3.6

The prefix {in-} simply negates the meaning of words to which it attaches, leaving them the same part of speech. It can occur as a prefix on both adjectives (*inactive*) and nouns (*inaction*).

An important point to remember is that derivational morphemes change the *meaning* of the words to which they attach. *Act, enact, reenact,* and *reenactment,* for instance, all have different meanings. In each case, the attachment of the derivational morpheme ({en-}, {re-}, or {-ment}) accounts for the change in meaning of the new word.

Not all morphemes are affixes. Each word contains a meaningful core, or **base,** to which prefixes and suffixes are attached (*act* in the examples above). Not all bases are free morphemes, able to stand alone as words. Bound bases also occur. Figure 3.7 shows a bound base {-ject}, which has come into English from Latin with the meaning of "throw" or "force," together with a variety of derivational prefixes and suffixes. See how many words you can compose using these bound morphemes. (Some of the derivational suffixes can be used with bases other than those with which they appear.)

■ *EXERCISE 3.9*

Divide the words below into morphemes. Note whether each is bound or free and whether it is a base or a derivational prefix or suffix. For those that are used to create specific parts of speech, identify the part of

SUMMARY		
An Example of Derivational Morphology: {-ject}		
Derivational Bound Prefixes	*Bound Base*	*Derivational Bound Suffixes*
{e-}	{-ject}	{-able} + {-ity}
{de-}	{-ject}	{-ion}
{e-}	{-ject}	{-or}
{in-}	{-ject}	
{inter-}	{-ject}	{-ion} + {-al} + {-ly}
{inter-}	{-ject}	{-or} + {-y}
{pro-}	{-ject}	{-ion} + {-ist}
{re-}	{-ject}	{-ee}
{sub-}	{-ject}	{-ive} + {-ness}
{sub-}	{-ject}	{-ive} + {-ity}
{sub-}	{-ject}	{-ive} + {-ism}
{sub-}	{-ject}	{-ive} + {-ist} + {-ic}
{sub-}	{-ject}	{-ive} + {-ize} + {-ation}

Figure 3.7

speech created. Reuse each affix and bound base in another word. Remember that each morpheme must be usable with the same meaning in another word or as an independent word. An example has been done for you.

EXAMPLE

rearrangement

{arrange}   *free base*

{re-}   *bound derivational prefix; means "to do again"; can be used in* **reapply**

{-ment}	bound derivational suffix; creates nouns meaning "result of an action"; can be used in **displacement**

1. foreshadow   3. hyphenate   5. bestir   7. marvelous

2. disapproval   4. technocrat   6. enthronement   8. enclosure

■ EXERCISE 3.10 _____

An advantage of derivational word creation is that we often can guess the meaning of a word on the basis of the morphemes combined to create it. Can you match the phobias below with the fear they name?

acrophobia	fear of bees
claustrophobia	fear of being looked at
hydrophobia	fear of being shut in an enclosed space
agoraphobia	fear of being alone
gamophobia	fear of birds
ornithophobia	fear of crowds
ponophobia	fear of dampness
melissophobia	fear of death
demophobia	fear of eating
thanatophobia	fear of fish
phagophobia	fear of frogs
ichthyphobia	fear of heights
genophobia	fear of marriage
arachnophobia	fear of open spaces
ophidiophobia	fear of poverty
xenophobia	fear of seeing, handling, or playing a flute
gynophobia	fear of sex
triskaidekaphobia	fear of snakes
autophobia	fear of spiders
scopophobia	fear of strangers
hygrophobia	fear of thirteen
batrachnophobia	fear of water
peniaphobia	fear of women
alophobia	fear of work

New words enter the language because users of the language create them in order to express concepts or name things for which no existing word will do. Try making up the name of a new phobia.

Figure 3.8 summarizes the main differences between derivational and inflectional suffixes.

SUMMARY	
Differences Between Derivational and Inflectional Suffixes	
Derivational	Inflectional
1. Always precede any inflectional suffixes. Example: {-ize} in *authorizing* {author} + {-ize} + {-ing}	1. Always follow any derivational suffixes. Example: {-s} in *statements* {state} + {-ment} + {-s}
2. Often change part of speech of base. Example: *boy* (noun) *boyish* (adjective)	2. Never change part of speech of base. Example: *boy* (noun singular) *boys* (noun plural)
3. Usually can combine with only a few subgroups of bases belonging to one or two parts of speech. Example: *human > humanize* **humanify* **humanate*	3. Combine with almost all members of single part of speech. Example: *human > humans* *pencil > pencils* *car > cars*
4. Have some lexical (or dictionary) meaning. Example: {-ize} > *humanize* Creates verbs meaning "to cause to become."	4. Have grammatical meaning. Example: {-s} > *humans* Creates plural of a word that retains its original meaning.

Figure 3.8

FORM CLASSES AND STRUCTURE CLASSES

Not all words can change form through the addition or subtraction of morphemes. You have probably been taught to consider the following words as verbs, but notice that they cannot accept any of the verb inflections discussed above nor can you add any derivational morphemes to them:

can, may, will, shall, must, might, could, would, should

In the process of acquiring language and of learning which inflections a word can undergo, children and adults learning English as a second language sometimes attempt to make these words conform to the verb pattern, saying, *"She mights" or *"He coulds," but these forms do not occur in English. Eventually, children and ESL students discover that the nine "verbs" above form a special class (called *modals*), each of which occurs in a single, uninflected form.

Words that can change form through the addition of derivational or inflectional morphemes belong to a category called **form-class words:** nouns, verbs, adjectives, and adverbs, the categories of words traditionally referred to as the four *parts of speech*. Membership is determined by the ability of the word itself to inflect or by its ability to substitute for another word that inflects. Other words are incapable of changing form through inflection or derivation; they belong to a separate category called **structure-class words.** Both form and structure classes are discussed in the following chapters.

■ *EXERCISE 3.11*

Many kinds of words are like the modals listed in the preceding paragraph in that they accept neither inflectional nor derivational morphemes. From the following list, identify those that are capable of changing form through the addition of morphemes as well as those that are not.

1. fast	4. might	6. cook	8. among
2. quite	5. backwards	7. attractive	9. imagine
3. river			

■ *A WORD ABOUT WORDS* ■

In our discussion of morphology, we have demonstrated how words are created through **derivation,** the adding of prefixes and suffixes to existing words of English. Although derivation is by far our richest source of new words, it is not the only source. Another way we have of extending the vocabulary is through **compounding,** combining two words into one. This method is a common practice of English. Some words (*chalkboard*) are obvious compounds; others have been around long enough that we no longer think of them as combining two words (*slipshod*); and still others have been around so long that we can no longer perceive that they originated as compounds (*daisy* from *day's eye*).

Compounds are not always written as one word. They may be hyphenated (*real-life*) or even written as two words (*real estate*). Compounds are identified by pronunciation, not by spelling. Contrast the pronunciation of the following pairs, and see if you can hear the difference between the compound (the first pair of words) and the phrase (the second pair): *real estate/real tragedy, tie in/tie together; blackball/black diamond.*

The study of the origin and historical development of compounds, or of any word, for that matter, is the field of **Etymology.** If you wish to know the etymology of a word, look it up in a desk dictionary or an unabridged dictionary. At the beginning or end of the word's entry, you will find the historical source of the word, usually in brackets. For example, *The American Heritage*

Dictionary entry for *compound* will tell you that the word entered Middle English from Old French. It originated in a Latin derivation that combined the prefix *com-* ("together") with the word *ponere* ("to put").

Centuries after it entered the English language, *compound* still means "to put together," but the meanings of words are not always so stable. Our vocabulary is in a constant state of change, as we adapt old words to cover new meanings, or acquire new words that supplant or dislodge the old. Thus, even a word that keeps the same form through centuries can undergo a change of meaning over a period of time.

Changes in meaning or vocabulary intrigue people. Linguists who have studied this area of grammar have isolated two major kinds of semantic change, **extension** and **narrowing.**

Extension (also called *generalization*) refers to the process by which the meaning of a word changes through time, referring to more categories than it did originally. For example, *bench* entered the language meaning "a seat." That meaning still exists, but the word has been extended to mean "the office of someone in authority, such a judge or bishop," as in *The bench is the judicial arm of the government. Bench* can also refer to a carpenter's worktable. In sports, it refers to the place where nonparticipants sit, but also to the nonparticipants (or reserves) themselves. It can refer to a level area of land along a shore and, in surveying, some elevated point of reference (a *bench mark*). You may be able to think of additional meanings, as well.

Narrowing (or *specialization*) occurs when the opposite happens: The reference of a word may become more exclusive over time. For example, the word *starve* originally meant "to perish" from any cause. *Starve* has been supplanted by the word *die,* and its own meaning has narrowed to refer only to dying from a lack of food.

Changes in meaning occur through our usage of words in different contexts which expand the inventory of items to which a word refers. Changes in the **connotation** (or *suggestiveness*) of words also occur. Neutral words may gradually pejorate, or acquire negative connotations, as has happened with *notorious*. Originally, it referred simply to someone or something that was widely known. Today, it has been supplanted by *famous,* and its own reference has narrowed to a smaller set: those known widely, but regarded unfavorably.

Words with negative connotations often revive, reclaiming their neutrality. In the nineteenth century, *breast* and *leg* or *thigh* were taboo in mixed company; as a consequence, one expressed a preference for *light meat* and *dark meat* of chicken or turkey. Today *breast, leg,* and *thigh* have ameliorated, reclaiming all or most of their neutrality, while *light meat* and *dark meat* have pejorated, acquiring sexual and, hence, socially negative connotations.

Semantics is the study of meaning, and there are many more kinds of semantic change than we have room to discuss here. If you do a Web search of "word formation," "semantics," or "semantic change," you will be led to fuller discussions of etymology and semantics, and you will find cross references to relevant books and articles.

■ *EXERCISE 3.12*

Practical Applications—Semantics

1. See if you can find words in current slang illustrating the following methods of word formation.

   a. **Compounding**—Discussed above.

   b. **Blends**—The combining of parts of two words into one: *smog* from *smoke* and *fog*.

   c. **Acronyms**—The combining of the initial letters of words into a new word: *radar* from *radio detecting and ranging*.

   d. **Proper names**—The use of a proper name as a general term: *xerox*.

   e. **Abbreviations**—The shortening of an existing word: *gas* from *gasoline*.

   f. **Back formation**—The assumption that a word is derived from a base that doesn't really exist: *laze* is derived by removing a supposed adjective-forming morpheme from *lazy* by analogy with *craze* and *crazy*.

2. *Gay* originally meant "mirthful." Did it pejorate when it began to refer to human sexuality? Has it ameliorated in recent years?

3. Look at the names of musical groups, and at the lyrics and titles of their songs. How have new words been created? What kinds of semantic change can you observe as a result of the language of current music?

SUMMARY

Morphemes, the smallest units of meaning in a language, consist of bases and affixes. Bases may be bound or free. Affixes are, by definition, bound; they may precede the base (prefixes) or follow it (suffixes). To analyze morphemes, we divide a word into its meaningful parts (the morphemes), state the meaning or function of each, and show that each occurs with a similar meaning or function as part of other words in the language. English has eight inflectional morphemes (morphemes that show grammatical relationships): two for nouns (plural, possessive), four for verbs (present tense, past tense, present participle, and past participle), and two for adjectives and adverbs (comparative, superlative). All the remaining morphemes are derivational (morphemes used to create words in the language).

REVIEW EXERCISES

Morphological Analysis

This exercise tests your ability to recognize and interpret all of the aspects of a morpheme listed in the chapter goals: to differentiate between bases (bound or free) and affixes (prefixes or suffixes) and to recognize such allomorphs as, for example, bound versions of a free morpheme. Separate the words below into morphemes and list them (using your dictionary if necessary). Identify the base morpheme as bound or free and give its meaning. Then state whether the remaining morphemes are prefixes or suffixes, and give the meaning or function of each affix. (Its function may be to change the part of speech of a word.) Finally, use it with the same meaning or function in another word (or as an independent word). An example has been done for you.

EXAMPLE

statements

{state}	*free base; "to say";* **state**
{-ment}	*derivational suffix; creates nouns;* **government**
{-s}	*inflectional suffix; plural;* **days**

1. baggage	4. semiconductor	7. painterly	10. redeployment
2. stylistic	5. outside	8. marginalize	11. undecipherable
3. indigestion	6. grumpiest	9. incapability	12. householders

Inflectional Morphemes

In the following passage, a number of words are in bold type. Each includes an inflectional morpheme. Write the word and the inflectional morpheme it contains:

noun plural	verb present tense
noun possessive	verb past tense
adjective (adverb) comparative	verb past participle
adjective (adverb) superlative	verb present participle

The first one has been done for you as an example.

EXAMPLE

Alaska's   noun possessive

Alaska's agricultural industry **is** the **smallest** in the nation, but the **state's** short **growing** season **is** not **keeping** people who live in Alaska from **becoming** vegetable **gardeners. It's** possible to produce outstanding **crops** within the Arctic Circle, despite the adverse climate. What **vegetables have lacked** because of the brief growing season, they can make up for by growing **faster.** During the long summer **days,** vegetables and **fruits** grow at a pace unknown to the ordinary American gardener. One man **reported** that his **cabbages** often **grew** an inch a day under a summer sun that hardly set. Even though the nights **were** short, the difference in temperature before and after sunrise could be so great that one day his cabbages, which **had been chilled** during the short night, **exploded** as the sun **rose.** Afterwards, he **said,** "There **was** coleslaw everywhere." The result of such rapid growth is **bigger** vegetables, so much bigger that they often set world **records** for size. One gardener, who **holds** seven annual world records for his giant vegetables, **has produced** a 39-pound turnip, a 45-pound cabbage, and a 19-pound carrot. His carrot set a world record, but his cabbage **was** a wimp. The **largest** cabbage ever grown **weighed** more than 105 pounds. It, too, was **grown** in Alaska.

Practical Applications—New Coinages

The word "wiki," which comes from the Hawaiian *wiki wiki,* meaning "quick" or "informal," is being used to refer to Internet sites that allow users to add to or modify the content of the Web pages. Some new coinages using the morpheme {wiki} are listed below. See if you can guess the meaning (if you don't already know it) of the words and identify the morphemes involved in the new creation.

1. wikipedia
2. wiktionary
3. wikiblog
4. wikitorial

Using {wiki} as your base morpheme, see if you can create words with the following meanings:

5. A verb meaning "the act of adding content to someone else's interactive Web page"
6. A noun meaning "someone who sits all day modifying wiki pages"
7. A noun meaning "the world of wiki pages"
8. Another word for a blog that allows others to add content
9. A link added to a wiki page

Practical Applications—Changing Language

Investigate the following questions and write up a report of your findings. You can find data for your answer by listening to others, by asking others what they have noticed, and by Googling both topics on the Internet.

1. We have seen two ways of showing the comparative and superlative in English: the morphemes {-er} and {-est}, and the qualifiers *more* and *most.* Generally, one or the other is used to form the comparative, but *more* and *most* may be encroaching on the territory of the morphemes. Can you find more examples like the following, which are equally acceptable to some speakers of English?

   She is even prettier than she used to be.

   She is even more pretty than she used to be.

Are both of the following equally acceptable?

She looks the prettiest in that green hat.

?She looks the most pretty in that green hat.

2. Irregular verb forms have been disappearing for centuries, but we still have about 200 irregular verbs. As evidence of change underway, you will often find verbs regularized by some writers, but not by others. Compare the following:

wake, woke, has woken   *wake, waked, has waked*
burn, burnt, has burnt   *burn, burned, has burned*
knit, knit, has knit   *knit, knitted, has knitted*

Can you find printed examples of these two versions of irregular verbs? Can you think of other irregular verbs that appear with more than one past participle form?

KEY TERMS

affix
  suffix
  prefix
ameliorate
base
compounding
connotation
derivation
etymology
extension
form-class words
inflections
  adjective/adverb comparative
  adjective/adverb superlative
  noun plural
  noun possessive
  verb present tense (third-person
    singular)
  verb past tense
  verb past participle
  verb present participle

morpheme
  allomorph
  zero allomorph
  bound morpheme
  free morpheme
  derivational morpheme
  inflectional morpheme
narrowing
pejoration
semantics
structure-class words

Form-Class Words

4

CHAPTER PREVIEW

Chapter 4 discusses nouns, verbs, adjectives, and adverbs, the four major form classes of English words, the core of what traditional grammarians call the parts of speech.

CHAPTER GOALS

At the end of this chapter, you should be able to

- Identify examples of the four form classes: *nouns, verbs, adjectives,* and *adverbs.*

- Differentiate between *subclasses* of nouns.

- Differentiate between *attributive* and *predicative* adjectives.

- Differentiate between *subclasses* of adverbs.

- Give supporting criteria of *form* (morphology) and *function* (sentence position) to justify the assignment of a word to a given form class.

An unabridged dictionary of the English language has close to a half million words defined in it. If the probability existed that you might hear any one of those words at any time, you would have to pay very close attention to the speech around you. All dictionaries contain a substantial number of words that are not used in everyday speaking and writing, and any speech situation limits the probable topics to be discussed. Thus, in a given situation, some words are more likely to be uttered than others. In addition, the words used form predictable sequences and patterns. For example, you predict that the subject will occur at the beginning of a sentence you are hearing, and so you immediately start listening for clues to help you to identify it. Because not all possible word combinations can serve as subjects, you expect to find nouns and nounlike phrases near the beginning. The English language uses words like articles (*a, an, the*) to signal that a noun is coming, so you are alert for those as you listen to someone else's utterances.

All these restrictions on word selection constitute a kind of redundancy in language; you do not have to hear everything that is said in order to understand what someone is trying to communicate. You guess enough of the message from those portions of it that you are able to hear to participate in a conversation despite considerable interference from outside noise, listen to two conversations at once, or even hear another conversation while you are speaking yourself. The reduction of chance increases the efficiency with which people communicate because both speaker and hearer share a set of assumptions about the order in which information will be presented.

Remember the two versions of the same "sentence" presented in Chapter 1?

(1)   *Stands corner little the on house old of and 12th that Vine the* belongs to me.

       The little old house that stands on the corner of 12th and Vine belongs to me.

The second version is easier to say, easier to understand, and easier to remember because the words occur in patterns specified by the rules of English. To describe the patterns that we use to communicate, it is necessary to have labels for the categories of words that belong to those patterns. The most important of these are the four parts of speech: nouns, verbs, adjectives, and adverbs.

FORM AND FUNCTION

The four **parts of speech**—nouns, verbs, adjectives, and adverbs—are labeled **form classes** because members of each class share the ability to change their **form** by accepting derivational and/or inflectional morphemes. The term *form* refers literally to the shape of the word (or phrase, or clause)—its pronunciation and its spelling. For example, you know just by looking at it that *scarcity* is a noun: It ends in -*ity*, a morpheme used to create nouns (*capacity, velocity*). On the other hand, nothing about the form of the word *desk* signals that it is a noun, but you can identify it as one because it can also occur in the plural form *desks* with the meaning of "more than one desk." The isolated form of a word like *scarcity*, with its derivational suffix, and the variable form of a word like *desk*, which can combine with inflectional suffixes, provide clues that young children apparently use as a guide to what kinds of words fit into what positions in an English sentence.

We also recognize parts of speech because of the way they behave—that is, by their **function.** Most nouns can follow articles (***a** scarcity,* **the** *desk*) or can fit into the blank in a sentence like the following: *The _____ seemed surprising/ugly/atrocious.* When you define nouns in terms of where they can occur or what words they can appear with, you are giving an *operational,* or *functional,* definition: "A *noun* is a word that can do *x, y,* or *z.*" It is necessary to have two ways of identifying parts of speech because forms can overlap. Consider the word *runs,* for example. You know that it occurs in at least two forms: *run* and *runs*. Is *runs* a plural noun or a third-person singular verb? It could be either, as the sentences below demonstrate:

(2) He made two *runs* yesterday.

This car *runs* well.

It is impossible to distinguish the part of speech of *runs* on the basis of form alone because, as our discussion of morphemes showed, the same suffix may have two or more different meanings: {-s} may be a noun plural (*books*), a noun possessive (*snake's*), or a verb present-tense marker (*reads*). This identity of form sometimes leads to amusing ambiguity, as these headlines demonstrate:

(3) PRINCIPAL TRANSFERS UPSET PARENTS
(*Des Moines Register*, 12 May 2001)

JUDGE FACING SEX CHARGES AHEAD IN EARLY RETURNS
(*Los Angeles Times*, 6 March 2002)

ER DELAYS KILLING HEART PATIENTS
(*Globe and Mail*, 26 November 2004)

In order to decide whether a word is functioning as a noun or a verb, English speakers use a variety of clues, to be discussed below.

■ *EXERCISE 4.1*

This exercise demonstrates how much you rely on form and function to recognize parts of speech. Identify the italicized words in the nonsense sentence below as nouns, verbs, adjectives, or adverbs. Are you using formal features (the word's appearance) or functional ones (its position in the sentence, its occurrence with another word, or both) as clues in your identification? For instance, consider this sentence:

After the *widgeluggers plinkered* one of the *groodies*, the *blunksy frigoldkins morfelled grobously* with their *prithereens*.

Forms with Overlapping Functions

Things and *actions* appear to be the basic categories into which speakers divide their experience of the world. They categorize their universe into the things that they perceive, on the one hand, and into the actions that those things perform or undergo, on the other. In English, we use nouns to name things and verbs to express actions, and we assume that these are two quite separate categories and that there is no overlap. The traditional definitions of a *noun* as "the name of a person, place, or thing" and a *verb* as "an action" help reinforce the notion that we are dealing with two entirely separate categories. But, in fact, things and events exist on a continuum, with unequivocal things at one end (*cat*) and actions at the other (*sing*). A little thought will demonstrate that some nouns name events (*lightning*) and that some words name both things and actions (*flame*). Defining a *noun* as "the name of a person, place, or thing" does not help differentiate between words that can occur both as nouns or as verbs. Compare the following:

(4)   a. He may *study* in Europe next summer.   (verb)

        b. My *study* is in the front of the house.   (noun)

        c. The wind usually *blows* from the west.   (verb)

        d. He suffered three *blows* to the head.   (noun)

Because the italicized words in each pair are both identical in form and related in meaning, how do you decide which ones name an action and which do not? Although you may be unaware of it, you differentiate between (4a) and (4b) by observing the position of *study* in the two sentences. In fact, it is only after you have recognized that *study* is functioning as the main verb in (4a) that you decide it is naming an action. Because it is functioning as the subject of (4b), you identify it there as a noun and say that it is the name of a thing. In (4c) and (4d), however, the distinction is not so clear. In both sentences, *blows* names an action.

Because of the division English makes between nouns and verbs, we restructure our perception of an event based on the way the language describes it. After the fact, when a noun names an action, as in (4d), we are usually quite comfortable with insisting that we perceive the event as a thing. However, this means that the traditional definitions of nouns as things and verbs as actions can be used to identify only those nouns that occur uniquely as people, places, or things (*girl, Paris, magazine*) and those verbs that occur uniquely as actions (*ratify, revolve*). For less typical nouns and verbs, the traditional definitions don't help us very much.

To verify this for yourself, answer this: Is *out* a noun? It can be, either as a component of the game of baseball (*The Tigers have two* **outs**) or as a label for someone who is not in office or lacks power and prestige (*The* **outs** *versus the* **ins**). But it can also be a verb meaning "to become publicly known" (*The truth will* **out**) or an adjective describing what is not fashionable (*Wide lapels are really* **out** *this year*). In addition, *out* can be an adverb (*The sun came* **out**) or a preposition indicating direction (*The cat ran* **out** *the door*).

NOUNS

Because in English a single word can serve so many functions, you usually need clues other than meaning to decide what part of speech a word can belong to. One of the clues we depend on is the word's form. In identifying **nouns,** for instance, we are helped by knowing that some nouns have been created from other words by adding as an affix a noun-making derivational morpheme (*consist****ency***, *commun****ism***); we know by looking at them that they are nouns. Most nouns, as we have seen, also inflect; they can become plural (*girl/girls*) or possessive (*girl's*). This ability to inflect helps us to differentiate between nouns and adjectives that have identical base forms. In (5a), *green* functions as an adjective; it does not become plural in (5b), but it does accept an adjective inflection in (5c):

(5)   a. That *green* hat is not becoming to her.

    b. Those *green* hats are not becoming to her.

    c. The *greenest* hat is the most becoming to her.

Green can also function as a noun, accepting the plural morpheme in contexts like (6b):

(6)   a. That *green* is darker than this one.

    b. Those *greens* are darker than this one.

Not all adjectives can both follow a determiner and be pluralized, as *green* does in (6). We cannot say **that happy* or **those happies;* but adjectives that can accept noun inflections have become nouns in English. Deciding whether such words refer to a quality or a thing does not help us differentiate reliably between adjectives and nouns. When a word like *green* functions as an adjective, as in examples (5a) and (5b), then we say that it names a *quality;* when it is functioning as a noun, as in examples (6a) and (6b), we arbitrarily say that it names a *thing,* even though the reference in each case is to a quality of color.

We also identify nouns by using functional clues—that is, by noticing what words precede them or where they occur in sentences. Many nouns can appear after articles (***the*** *girl,* ***a*** *girl*), possessives (***her*** *girls*), numbers (***three*** *girls*), or demonstratives (***that*** *girl*). In fact, articles occur only in combination with nouns or nounlike words; because they never occur alone, they are reliable signs that nouns follow.

The functional behavior of nouns enabled structural linguists to construct a **frame sentence** to help identify nouns. The frame is a sentence with an empty slot (indicated by a blank line) in the subject position. Most of the words that can be used in the subject position are nouns.

(The) _____ seem(s) all right (inevitable/necessary).

Noun Frame Sentence

Three points are important to notice and remember about the frame sentence:

1. The article *the* appears in parentheses because not all nouns can follow *a, an,* or *the.* An article may or may not appear in the test sentence (*The boy seems all right, Edna seems all right*).

2. The adjective phrase *all right* can be varied (*unacceptable, short, slow*), depending on the meaning of the noun.

3. Only a single word at a time can be tested in the noun slot of the frame sentence.

Because most of the words that can fit into the empty slot will be nouns, children learning the language need only hear a sentence like *The glonk seems all right* in order to enable them to sort *glonk* as a noun and to infer other possible forms and combinations in which it can occur: *glonks, glonk's, a glonk, of the glonk, with the glonk*. Conversely, of course, if they just hear someone mention *three glonks*, they guess, without ever hearing the combination, that it will fit into a sentence like *The glonk seems all right*. To determine whether something is or can be a noun, you can test against each of the characteristics we have given in Figure 4.1 as Rules of Thumb for identifying nouns. A noun *must* fit the frame sentence and have at least one of the characteristics listed.

■ *EXERCISE 4.2*

Test each of the words below against the five characteristics of nouns summarized in Figure 4.1. Which words are nouns? How many of the criteria are valid for each? An example has been done for you.

EXAMPLE

tree

Noun   *(4)*

Applicable   *(2) pluralizes; (3) can become possessive; (4) can directly follow an article; (5) can fit in the frame sentence*

Not Applicable   (1) no noun-making morpheme

The, a   1. virus   3. e-mail   5. Web site   7. chatting ← functional noun

2. viciousness   4. provider   6. online   8. mailing

RULES OF THUMB	
Tests for Nouns	
Formal Proof	
1. Has noun-making morpheme.	govern*ment*
2. Can occur with the plural morpheme.	government*s*
3. Can occur with the possessive morpheme.	government*'s* decision
Functional Proof	
4. Without modifiers, can directly follow an article and create a grammatical unit.	*the* government, *a* government
5. Can fit in the frame sentence.	(The) _____ seem(s) all right.

Figure 4.1

Prototypes and Peripheral Cases

After doing Exercise 4.2, you may wonder where we place the limits for words belonging to the noun category. Look again at the differences between *diligence* and *refusing*. *Diligence* fulfills two of the characteristics of nouns: It contains a noun-making morpheme (used to create nouns like *competence* and *intelligence* from adjectives like *competent* and *intelligent*), and it can fit in the frame sentence (*Diligence seems necessary*). It ordinarily does not pluralize or become possessive, and, when it stands alone without any modifiers, it cannot follow an article (*a/the diligence*). With just two noun characteristics, *diligence* is not a good example of a prototypical noun, but it is nonetheless a noun, one created by derivation from an adjective and, in fact, one that never occurs as anything but a noun. Theoretically, a word could meet only a single noun criterion and still be categorized as a noun by default if it was created by means of a noun-derivational morpheme and if it never occurred as any other part of speech.

But look at *refusing*. It fulfills one noun criterion: It can fit in the frame sentence (*Refusing seems all right*). However, in every other way it is a verb. It ends with an *-ing* verb inflection and in various forms occurs as a fairly prototypical verb. Words such as *refusing* can be used in noun positions—they fit the frame sentence—but they stand outside the periphery of the noun category and are called **gerunds,** verbs that occupy noun positions in sentences; the label indicates that they are not true nouns.

If you think of the category of nouns as a continuum, it looks something like Figure 4.2. Notice that prototypical nouns occur in the center (A), and nouns derived from other parts of speech occur closer to the periphery (B, C, D, and E). Adjectives and verbs that can appear in noun positions but that do not have any

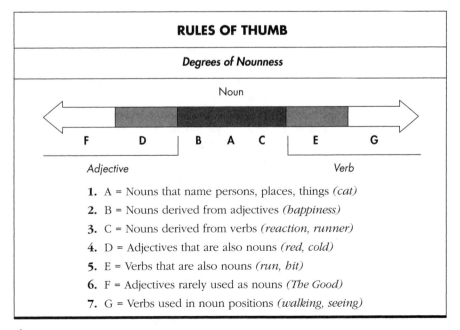

RULES OF THUMB

Degrees of Nounness

Noun

F   D   B   A   C   E   G

Adjective   Verb

1. A = Nouns that name persons, places, things *(cat)*
2. B = Nouns derived from adjectives *(happiness)*
3. C = Nouns derived from verbs *(reaction, runner)*
4. D = Adjectives that are also nouns *(red, cold)*
5. E = Verbs that are also nouns *(run, hit)*
6. F = Adjectives rarely used as nouns *(The Good)*
7. G = Verbs used in noun positions *(walking, seeing)*

Figure 4.2

other attributes associated with nouns occur outside the periphery (F, G), indicating that they are simply words from another class that are able to function as though they were nouns. Even when used in noun positions, they retain their identity as adjectives and verbs. Prototypical nouns tend to display more of the features summarized in Figure 4.1 than do peripheral examples of the noun class, and they best fit the traditional definition of "naming a concrete person, place, or thing."

▇ EXERCISE 4.3

Return to Exercise 4.2. Decide which of the seven degrees of nounness summarized in Figure 4.2 best describes each of the words listed in that exercise.

▬▬▬▬▬ SUBCLASSES AND FEATURES ▬▬▬▬▬

We recommend that you memorize the criteria for membership in the four form classes (contained in the charts throughout this chapter headed Rules of Thumb). Using them will enable you to classify words reliably as nouns, verbs, adjectives, and adverbs, a critically important step for understanding how the English language works and for learning to analyze English grammar. Once you are familiar with the prototypical grammatical characteristics of each of the four broad classes of words, you can better comprehend how these open-ended groups can be further described according to a variety of grammatical and semantic traits that both reflect and affect how we use them.

How would you respond to the following sentence?

(7)   *Merle's wristwatch is plotting to kill him.

You might wonder about the mental soundness of the person who spoke it, or you might admire it as a strangely creative way of trying to express something. However, any speaker of English would recognize that this sentence is unusual. Why? Because we normally require a human subject for *plotting*, whereas *wristwatch* is distinctly nonhuman. Elements of meaning like *human* and *nonhuman* are called **semantic features.** From a very early age, as they rapidly add words to their **lexicons** (their mental dictionaries), children simultaneously learn semantic features like these as part of the meanings of words. Such features play an important role in how they organize and use their vocabularies, which eventually grow to include thousands of items.

Compare the following two sentences:

(8)   *That plate craves liver.

My cat craves liver.

What is wrong with the first sentence, in contrast with the second, can once again be described in terms of semantic features, but this time the features are not human and nonhuman, for neither *plate* nor *cat* is human. The verb *crave* requires a subject like *cat* that has the semantic feature *animate* ("alive and capable of movement and feeling"), whereas *plate* is *inanimate*. The presence of some features implies that others will also be present. For example, any noun that has the feature human will also have the feature animate, as humans are by definition animate beings; thus, the sentence *My sister craves liver* is also completely acceptable.

Linguists consider the meaning of each form-class member as being made up of a cluster of semantic features. We can see, for example, that some words having the features animate or human also incorporate the features male or female because of contrasting pairs such as *doe* and *buck, mare* and *stallion, girl* and *boy, uncle* and *aunt, niece* and *nephew*. Some words with the feature inanimate must also include the features solid or liquid to explain the contrast between sentences like these two:

(9)   *I poured a cup of furniture.

I poured a cup of coffee.

All speakers of the language recognize the semantic subclasses into which nouns, verbs, adjectives, and adverbs fall on the basis of features like these, and most of the time they "follow the rules" in combining words that are semantically compatible. But knowing the language includes being able to use it creatively and metaphorically by consciously violating the normal rules:

(10)   My car devours gas when the air conditioner is on.

Shirley must have been poured into those jeans she wore last night.

Devour usually requires an animate subject, and *pour* normally involves a liquid, yet these two sentences communicate their meanings quite clearly.

As you can see, words are not simple things. Important subclasses exist on the basis not only of features of meaning, like animate and inanimate, but also on the basis of **grammatical features,** traits that are important to us because they influence grammatical choices and create subclasses of nouns, verbs, and adjectives.

Noun Subclasses

Nouns are classified as being either **common** (*pebble, table, idea, boy*) or **proper** (*New York, Hungary, James Joyce, General Motors, Thanksgiving*). Proper nouns, capitalized in writing, are the names of specific places, persons, or events. It is not difficult to discover that the distinction between common and proper nouns has grammatical consequences. For example, common nouns can appear following articles (*a, an, the*), but proper nouns usually cannot:

(11) | **Common Nouns** | **Proper Nouns** |
|---|---|
| on the holiday, on a holiday | on Thanksgiving (*on the Thanksgiving) |
| in the city, in a city | in New York (*in the New York) |
| the author, an author | James Joyce (*the James Joyce) |

One of the functions of the definite article (*the*) is to distinguish one thing from another. Because there is only one holiday called *Thanksgiving,* one city called *New York,* and one famous author named *James Joyce,* no article is necessary. If for some reason we want to refer to such a unique entity as if there were, at least in imagination, more than one of them, then we use an article:

(12)   Do you remember *the Thanksgiving* of 1987?

         They know only *the New York* of the very rich.

         He spoke of *the young James Joyce.*

Sometimes an article has become part of a proper name or is used with it by convention. Names of newspapers like *the Los Angeles Times*, institutions like *the Getty Museum*, geographical references such as *the Atlantic Ocean*, and plurals like *the United States* all occur with an article.

Common nouns are subcategorized as **count nouns** or **noncount (mass) nouns.** Count nouns—like *pencil, telephone, cousin*—refer to things that are considered separate entities. They occur with *many* and other determiners (words that function like articles and precede nouns) that make distinctions in number:

(13)   a. many pencils, a pencil, every telephone, these cousins

         b. one pencil, two pencils, three telephones, four cousins

Noncount nouns, on the other hand, refer to entities that we think of as not countable but occurring in a mass, such as *money, water, electricity, sunshine,* and *bread*. These nouns occur only in the singular with *much* and other indefinite determiners that do not include the notion of number:

(14)   a. much money, some electricity, less water, a lot of bread

         b. *one money, *two monies, *three electricities, *four sunshines

Expressions like *a lot of* occur frequently with noncount nouns, allowing us to refer to various amounts of what we can't easily count. Similarly, we can preface noncount nouns with countable ones to form phrases like the following:

(15)   three pints of blood

         four bushels of wheat

         three pages of information

In some contexts, we can convert mass nouns into count nouns by using them to refer to particular types or varieties of the material they name or the source from which they come:

(16)   Our favorite French bakery makes 14 breads.

         The wines of California are being exported to Europe.

■ **EXERCISE 4.4**

Describe each of the following nouns by listing the features that characterize it. Select from this list:

count, noncount (mass)   human, nonhuman
common, proper   male, female
animate, inanimate

Use only those features that seem appropriate to the particular word.

1. calculus   3. graph   5. paper   7. student
2. analysis   4. mathematician 6. arithmetic 8. Euclid

VERBS

Verbs have been defined traditionally as words that "express action," a characteristic that seems to be true of the most prototypical of verbs—for example, *sit, speak, see, sing, read, write*. Yet, as we have seen, this meaning-based criterion doesn't help us to distinguish between verbs and words that are or can be nouns naming actions, like *attack, storm, delivery, departure*, or *lightning*. Young children appear initially to classify words as verbs if there is an *agent* (someone who does something) performing an *action* (the thing done), as in *The baby ate*. Later, they recognize that verbs name *states* (*The cat lay before the fire*) and *conditions* (*The house remained unlocked over the weekend*) as well. When a noun is used as a verb, the verb means that someone or something behaves in some way like the thing named by the noun (*You must dog their footsteps*) or uses the thing named in an activity (*He will head home at five o'clock*).

Because it is impossible to identify all verbs as actions or all actions as verbs, speakers use other clues of form and function as well. Some verbs are recognizable by form because they have been created from other parts of speech with derivational verb-making morphemes (*falsify, enrage*). Verbs are also recognizable because of their ability to change form through inflection, by taking endings that indicate third-person singular (*eats*), past tense (*ate*), past participle (*eaten*), and present participle (*eating*). But in isolation, without a context, it is impossible to tell whether words like *dog/dogs* and *head/heads* are nouns or verbs. They contain no derivational morphemes, and the inflectional suffix {-s} could be either the noun plural or the verb present-tense marker. In such cases, the function of the word is helpful, for verbs behave in ways that other words cannot. They can be negated (*The baby didn't eat*); many can be made into commands (*Eat!*); and all can follow a modal auxiliary (*You must eat*). The latter ability gives us a frame sentence for testing verbs.

> **They must _____ (it).**

Verb Frame Sentence

The parentheses around *it* indicate that a noun or noun substitute may or may not be required following the verb; some verbs have them, and some do not. Try out the test frame with these verbs: *sell, listen, advise, call, sleep*. Placed in the slot, each makes a grammatical sentence. Compare what happens if you try to use a noun, like *construction*, or an adjective, like *happy: *They must construction, *They must construction it, *They must happy, *They must happy them*.

Because some verbs can be followed by an adjective, a second frame provides an alternative test to the first.

> **They must _____ good.**

Verb Frame Sentence: Alternative Version

Try placing the verbs *be, remain, seem, look,* and *smell* in the slot. Each can be used with an adjective following, but no other part of speech will function grammatically there: *They must construction good, *They must happy good*. The Rules of Thumb in Figure 4.3 can help you in identifying verbs. To be a verb, a word *must* have one or more of the qualities listed there.

EXERCISE 4.5

Test each of the verbs below against the eight possible characteristics of verbs summarized in Figure 4.3. Which words are verbs? How many of the criteria are valid for each? An example has been done for you.

EXAMPLE

speak

Verb	*(7)*
Applicable	*(2) can take present-tense morpheme; (3) can be made past tense; (4) can become a present participle; (5) can become a past participle; (6) can be made a command; (7) can be made negative; (8) can fit the frame sentence.*
Not Applicable	*(1) contains no verb-making morpheme.*

1. engulf	3. sink	5. fortify	7. recede
2. warn	4. hit	6. flee	8. quake

RULES OF THUMB	
Tests for Verbs	
Formal Proof	
1. Has verb-making morpheme.	critic*ize*
2. Can occur with present-tense morpheme.	criticiz*es*
3. Can occur with past-tense morpheme.	criticiz*ed*
4. Can occur with present-participle morpheme.	criticiz*ing*
5. Can occur with past-participle morpheme.	had fall*en*, was criticiz*ed*
Functional Proof	
6. Can be made into a command.	*Criticize* this novel!
7. Can be made negative.	They did *not criticize* the novel.
8. Can fit in one of the frame sentences.	They must _____ (it). They must _____ good.

Figure 4.3

■ *EXERCISE 4.6* _____

Decide whether each of the following words is a noun, a verb, neither, or both, using the tests for membership in those classes summarized in Figures 4.1 and 4.3.

EXAMPLE

globe

*Noun only. (2) Occurs with plural (**globes**); (3) occurs with possessive (**the globe's axis**); (4) can follow an article (**a globe**); (5) fits in frame sentence (**The globe seems all right**). Cannot be a verb: ***They globed it.***

1. frighten	3. treat	5. tot	7. candy
2. costume	4. princess	6. fantasize	8. bewitch

Verb Subclasses

Like nouns, verbs have a number of grammatical features that determine their membership in subcategories. In Chapter 3, we contrasted regular and irregular verbs on the basis of their inflectional patterns. Another important distinction among the members of this form class is the contrast between *transitive, intransitive,* and *linking verbs.* Grammarians classify a verb into one or more of these subclasses based on its ability to enter into relationships with other major elements of a sentence. Because we devote a major portion of Chapter 7 to discussing verb subclasses in connection with the basic structure of sentences, we will postpone further discussion of verbs until then.

ADJECTIVES

Nouns and verbs are the basic building blocks of language; all other words are subsidiary to them in some way, acting either as relational links or as modifiers. Most students learn that **adjectives,** for example, are words that stand for a quality and modify or describe nouns, and most adjectives do. We might think first of prototypical examples like *a **red** balloon, a **tall** woman, an **affectionate** dog, a **heavy** weight.* But not all words that modify nouns are adjectives, and not all adjectives modify nouns.

Let's begin by clarifying the notion of **modification.** Suppose you have a series of figures that are alike:

If we modify one of these boxes, it stands out from the others in the series:

That is the purpose of modification: The **modifier** differentiates one member from all other members of the same class. In English, we can modify nouns with adjectives: *The **tall** man* differentiates one man from others who are not as tall as he. We can also use nouns for the same purpose: *The **kitchen** sink* differentiates one kind of sink from others in a house. We can use participles and participle phrases to modify nouns: *The cat **sleeping in the sun*** identifies a specific cat. We can even use prepositional phrases: *A bottle **of milk*** names a bottle that differs from *a bottle **of wine*** and *a bottle **of soda.*** In each case, we have done with words (*tall, kitchen, sleeping in the sun, of milk*) what we did with asterisks in the box above: We have modified one member of a class so that it stands apart from all others.

Because so many kinds of grammatical structures can modify a noun, how can we identify adjectives? Adjectives have several characteristics not shared by the other kinds of noun modifiers. One is their form. Some adjectives are derived morphologically from other parts of speech—for example, *funny, barnlike, porous, livable, weekly*. We can guess by looking at them that they are or can be adjectives. In addition, adjectives can be made comparative or superlative, either through inflection (*the sadder man, the saddest man*) or by using *more* and *most* (*a more profitable contract, the most profitable contract*). As we have seen, nouns and participles may function like adjectives in modifying nouns, but they cannot be made comparative or superlative (**the kitchener cabinet, *the sleepingest cat*).

Adjectives also differ from nouns and participles in their ability to be modified in degree by the addition of words, often called **qualifiers** or **intensifiers,** that are similar to *more* and *most* and that specify the degree or quantity of the quality for which the adjective stands. Examples include *very, rather, somewhat, quite, really, fairly, too, awfully,* and *pretty,* some of which have other functions, as well.

The ability to follow the intensifier *very* is used to create a frame sentence for adjectives.

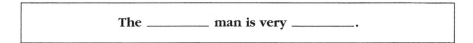

The _____ man is very _____.

Adjective Frame Sentence

To use the frame as a test, it is necessary to place the base form of the same adjective (one without any comparative or superlative inflection) in both slots: *The **sad** man is very **sad***. The repetition may seem a bit silly, but the sentence is grammatical, and the feature that distinguishes adjectives from other words that can modify nouns is their ability to function in *both* positions. (Compare our test frame sentence using *sad* with the ungrammatical results of placing the modifiers *repair* and *sleeping* in the test positions: **The **repair** man is very **repair**; *The **sleeping** man is very **sleeping***. Neither *repair* nor *sleeping* is an adjective, and neither fits in the second adjective position of the frame sentence.)

The first slot in the frame sentence contains what is called an **attributive adjective** (one that modifies a following noun), and the second slot contains a **predicative adjective** (one that follows a verb and identifies a quality of the subject of the sentence). In using the frame sentence, remember that not all adjectives can modify all nouns, so it may be necessary to change the noun in the frame. *The **grapey** man is very **grapey*** is a strange sentence, but *The **grapey** wine is very **grapey*** is not.

RULES OF THUMB	
Tests for Adjectives	

Formal Proof
   1. Has adjective-making morpheme.
  2a. Takes comparative or superlative morpheme.
	happ*y*, lov*able*, fool*ish*
	soft*er*, soft*est*

Functional Proof
  2b. Can be made comparative or superlative by using *more* or *most*.
   3. Can be qualified.
   4. Can fit both slots in the frame sentence.
	more sensitive, *most* sensitive
	
	rather soft
	The _____ man seems very _____.

Figure 4.4

The Rules of Thumb in Figure 4.4 summarize the criteria that characterize adjectives. Any word that has an adjective-making morpheme (Test 1) or can fit in both slots in the frame sentence (Test 4) must be an adjective.

■ EXERCISE 4.7 _____

Test each of the words below with the tests for adjectives summarized in Figure 4.4. Which words are adjectives? How many of the criteria are valid for each adjective? An example has been done for you.

EXAMPLE

selfish

Adjective   *(4)*

Applicable   *(1) has adjective-making morpheme {-ish}, as in **girlish, greenish**;*
                *(2) can be made comparative or superlative with **more, most;***
                *(3) can be qualified—**very selfish;** (4) fits the frame sentence.*

    1. alluring   3. skinny   5. diet   7. controlled

    2. eating   4. pale   6. tall   8. hungry

Adjective Subclasses

One way in which adjectives are subclassified is according to how they can be used in sentences. Adjectives are called *attributive* when they occur before a noun, usually attributing (ascribing) a quality to that noun:

(17)   our **sleepy** *child*

the **hot** *sun*

Adjectives are called *predicative* when they occur in the predicate of a sentence and without a following noun:

(18)   Our *child* is **sleepy.**

The *sun* became **hot.**

The adjective frame sentence illustrates both kinds of adjectives:

(19)   The _____ man was very _____.

         attributive   *predicative*

Most adjectives can be used as both attributives and predicatives, but some function exclusively one way or the other. For example, *entire, outright,* and *utter* always occur as adjectives, but can be used only in the attributive slot of the frame sentence, as the following examples illustrate:

(20)   The *entire* pizza disappeared.   (attributive)

*The pizza was *entire*.   (predicative)

Geraldine told an *outright* lie.   (attributive)

*The lie was *outright*.   (predicative)

He spoke *utter* nonsense.   (attributive)

*The nonsense was *utter*.   (predicative)

The adjectives *aghast, alive,* and *afraid,* in contrast, normally function only as predicatives.

(21)   Our teacher was *aghast*.   (predicative)

*Our *aghast* teacher continued to lecture.   (attributive)

That spider looked *alive*.   (predicative)

*I saw an *alive* spider.   (attributive)

Some predicative adjectives accept or even require complements—that is, phrases that complete them:

(22)   Our cat seems to be *afraid of that dog.*

Our cat seems to be *afraid.*

My brother is *fond of frozen yogurt.*

*My brother is *fond.*

In contrast to *afraid,* which can occur with or without the complement *of that dog, fond* requires a complement like *of frozen yogurt.* Adjectives that are only attributive or only predicative will not fit in both slots of the adjective test frame, as the first position is attributive and the second is predicative. Nevertheless, we identify them as adjectives because they meet other adjective tests, and they don't fit into any other form class.

WHAT'S THE USAGE?   *Adjectives*

For the past two centuries, prescriptive grammarians have argued about another subclassification of adjectives, one based on their ability to occur with qualifiers like *more, most, very, rather, less,* and so on. Most adjectives are **gradable**—that is, we can arrange them on a scale of intensity that we indicate with qualifiers: *somewhat late, rather late, very late, extremely late.* However, some adjectives don't seem to be gradable. For example, *double, triangular, nuclear,* and *vertical* don't normally occur with a qualifier: *The **nuclear** reactor was very **nuclear,** *The **vertical** pole was rather **vertical.** And other **nongradable adjectives** seem by their meaning to defy comparison or qualification: *dead, mortal, eternal,* and *endless,* for example, and adjectives with technical meanings, such as *hydrochloric* and *paleozoic.*

The problem occurs with the use of adjectives such as *unique, perfect,* and *correct.* Some authorities frown on their use in sentences like *He bought a really unique T-shirt* or *Mary's entry in the soufflé contest was more perfect than Harry's,* arguing that something is either *unique* or *perfect* or it isn't; logically, these qualities can't be compared. However, the one thing certain about language is that it changes. In 1964, *The American Heritage Dictionary* argued that nongradable adjectives like *unique* could be qualified by words that did not indicate degree, such as *nearly* (suggesting that something just misses the mark) or *truly* (meaning "Believe it or not"). In the intervening years, they find, advertisers and travel writers have used *unique* so loosely that it has acquired a second meaning, "extraordinary," and is used in this sense by excellent speakers and writers, citing sentences like *Chicago is no less unique an American city than New York or San Francisco.*

Other adjectives that have traditionally been nongradable are also undergoing change in their meanings. Can you use *sincere, honest, round, single,* and *empty* with qualifiers like *rather, very, more,* and *most?*

■ *USAGE EXERCISE 4.8* _____

Are the following adjectives attributive, predicative, or both? Create sentences showing how each can be used.

EXAMPLE

hypnotic

Streisand gave a **hypnotic** *performance.*   (attributive)

or

Her performance was/seemed **hypnotic.**   (predicative)

1. magical   3. ghostly   5. mysterious   7. surprising
2. demonic   4. asleep   6. ultimate   8. unusual

━━━━━━━━━ **ADVERBS** ━━━━━━━━━

In talking about the world around us, we use nouns as a major category, naming what we perceive. Verbs, which describe what those things are doing, also form a major category. Adjectives act in a secondary way, telling what nouns are like. **Adverbs** are even further removed from tangible experience; they modify verbs (*Sue swims* **quickly**), adjectives (*Bill's car is* **mechanically** *sound*), other adverbs (*Andrew drove* **incredibly** *fast*), and even whole sentences (**Obviously,** *someone ate the rest of the pizza*). Perhaps this is why they are the most difficult of the four form classes to identify and understand.

Other factors contribute to the complexity of adverbs, however. One problem is that there is some overlapping of form between adjectives and adverbs. Words like *fast* and *slow* once had different adjectival and adverbial forms, but in the course of the development of English, the differences between them disappeared, and the two forms became identical:

(23)   That horse likes a *fast* track.   (adjective)
         Don't drive so *fast*.   (adverb)
         They are *slow* learners.   (adjective)
         Go *slow*.   (adverb)

Slow has developed a new adverb form, *slowly*, one which alternates with *slow*. Both of the following are correct:

(24)   He drives too *slowly*.   (adverb)
         He drives too *slow*.   (adverb)

Inflectional and derivational morphemes overlap, as well. Adverbs share with adjectives the ability to be compared, either by using inflectional morphemes (*she ran faster, she ran fastest of all*) or by using *more* and *most* (***more** slowly, **most** slowly*). Although the suffixes {-wise} and {-ways} are reliable markers of adverbs derived from nouns (*lengthwise, clockwise, sideways*), as is the derivational suffix {-ward(s)} (*afterward[s], backward[s]*), they are relatively rare. The most common adverb-making morpheme {-ly} is also used to create adjectives (*friendly, lovely, leisurely*); hence, this derivational suffix does not by itself provide a reliable means of distinguishing between adverbs and adjectives. We attempt to clarify the distinction between these two {-ly} morphemes at the end of our discussion of adverbs.

One characteristic of adverbs not shared by other parts of speech is their mobility. Although their normal position is immediately following the verb or at the end of the sentence, it is often possible, for emphasis and stylistic effect, to move adverbs about within a sentence. In fact, the mobility of adverbs is one of their most distinctive characteristics.

(25)   He drove through the town *slowly*.

He drove *slowly* through the town.

Slowly he drove through the town.

Because adverbs can almost always occur last and because they are usually not essential to the sentence, the frame sentence for identifying adverbs is a complete sentence, to which a single word—if added—must be an adverb.

The man told his story _____.

The woman walked her dog _____.

Adverb Frame Sentences

The specific nouns and verbs in the frame sentences can be changed. What is important is the pattern: a complete sentence, with the final slot available for an optional adverb.

Because of the complexity of adverbs as a class, no single criterion listed in Figure 4.5 among our Rules of Thumb for testing adverbs works for every adverb.

■ *EXERCISE 4.9* _____

There are two {-ly} morphemes: one {-ly$_1$} used to create adjectives and one {-ly$_2$} used to create adverbs. To understand the difference, begin by sorting the following words into two groups: adjectives and adverbs. Use the criteria given in Figure 4.5 to verify your classification. Can you see a pattern in the part of speech to which the adjective-making {-ly} morpheme is added? How about the adverb-making {-ly}?

1. lovely   3. absolutely   5. timely   7. worldly
2. foolishly   4. maniacally   6. paternally   8. ghostly

EXERCISE 4.10

After you have done Exercise 4.9, think about the words below. Each raises a different problem related to the classification you worked out above.

1. hourly   This derives from a noun. Is it an adjective only, or can it occur as an adverb as well?

2. leisurely   This derives from a noun. Is it an adjective only, or can it occur as an adverb as well?

RULES OF THUMB	
Tests for Adverbs	
Formal Proof	
1. Has adverb-making morpheme.	sudden*ly*, cross*wise*, home*ward*
2a. Takes comparative or superlative morpheme.	She ran *faster.* She ran *fastest.*
Functional Proof	
2b. Can be made comparative or superlative with *more* or *most.*	*more* suddenly, *most* suddenly
3. Can be qualified.	*rather* suddenly
4. Can be moved within a sentence.	The door opened *suddenly.* The door *suddenly* opened. *Suddenly* the door opened.
5. Can fit in the frame sentence.	The man told his story _____.

Figure 4.5

■ *EXERCISE 4.11* _____

Test each of the words below against the five criteria for adverbs summarized in Figure 4.5. Which words are adverbs? How many of the criteria are valid in each case? For each word, create a sentence illustrating its use as an adverb and/or other parts of speech as appropriate. An example has been done for you.

EXAMPLE

straight	*(3)*
Applicable	*(2) can be made comparative or superlative; (3) can be qualified; (5) can fit the frame sentence.*
Not applicable	*(1) has no adverb-making morpheme; (4) cannot move in its sentence.*
Part of speech	*Adverb—Our pitcher can't throw **straight.***
	*Adjective—Helen planted a tree with a **straight** trunk.*

1. quietly	3. fatherly	5. Sunday	7. seriously
2. reverently	4. upward	6. early	8. edgewise

Adverb Subclasses

Adverbs are often categorized on the basis of the kind of information they provide. For our discussion of sentence structure in later chapters, the most important kinds of adverbs tell **manner** (how), **time** (when), or **place** (where).

(26) The horses ran *quickly/steadily/slowly/well/reluctantly.*   (manner)
Our guest arrived *yesterday/then/immediately.*   (time)
Your boss called *here/somewhere/around/outside.*   (place)

Other common semantic groupings of adverbs include those of **degree, frequency and number,** and **duration:**

(27) She is *strikingly/incredibly/amazingly* beautiful.   (degree)
They met *often/twice/seldom/frequently.*   (frequency and number)
He *always/still/briefly* bragged about it.   (duration)

■ *EXERCISE 4.12* _____

Awareness of the kinds of information they supply can help you identify adverbs in a sentence. Decide whether each of the examples below is an adverb of time, place, manner, degree, frequency and number, or duration. Can any be used more than one way?

1. soon   *time*
2. anxiously   *manner*
3. somewhere   *place*
4. utterly   *degree*
5. often   *frequency*
6. carelessly
7. once   *frequency*   *duration*
8. eternally

ANALYZING FORM AND FUNCTION

When members of a form class occur in prototypical functions, we often have little trouble in identifying them, even when some signals of class membership are ambiguous. For example, consider the following two sentences:

(28)   He had two *runs* yesterday.

This car *runs* well.

Because the noun plural suffix {-s} and the third-person singular present-tense suffix {-s} are identical, the word *runs* can be either a noun or a verb. By looking at it in isolation from the sentences in which it is used, we cannot tell to which form class it belongs. (When we say that its signals of class membership are ambiguous, we mean that the suffix {-s} could be either a verb inflection or a noun inflection.)

However, when we analyze the word *runs* in the context of each sentence in which it occurs, we can quickly resolve the ambiguity by replacing the ambiguous form *runs* with other words, prototypical nouns or verbs that belong to only one category. If you take a prototypical noun like *desk* and try substituting it in both of the examples, you find that it fits in the first (*He had two **desks** yesterday*) but not in the second (**This car **desks** well*). Continuing with the same process, try substituting a prototypical verb, such as *operates*, for each instance of *runs*, and you find that it fits the second (*This car **operates** well*) but not the first (**He had two **operates** yesterday*).

Sometimes, however, classification is made difficult by the ability of one form (noun or verb, for example) to function as though it were another. *Noun, verb, adjective*, and *adverb* are terms reserved for single words in English belonging to specific form classes. The functions such words most often perform are called *nominal, verbal, adjectival*, and *adverbial*. Many of the "exceptions" that are the despair of grammar students arise because form and function do not always match in English.

We have seen, for example, that a small group of nouns can function as though they were adverbs:

(29)   Charlie Brown had to take Snoopy *home*.

Home is not an adverb; it is a noun performing an adverbial function. Similarly, verb participles often function as though they were nouns:

(30)   *Walking* is Maddy's favorite form of exercise.

In form, *walking* is a verb participle. In function, it is nominal. It passes none of the tests for nouns, other than its position in the sentence; nevertheless, it is perfectly acceptable in the noun slot of the frame sentence (*Walking seems all right*). Grammarians have a label (*gerund*) for verb forms functioning as though they were nouns, a label that reminds us of the difference between the form (verb) and its function (nominal).

The adjectival function is even more complex. Three forms can modify nouns: adjectives, other nouns, and verb participles. Compare the following:

(31)   a. Homer needs some *new* shoes.

b. Homer needs some *baseball* shoes.

c. Homer needs some *walking* shoes.

If we apply the adjective tests (Figure 4.4) to the italicized words in these examples, we find *new* in (31a) to be a prototypical adjective. It accepts adjective inflections (*newer shoes, newest shoes*), and it fits both slots of the adjective test frame sentence (*His new shoes seem very new*). However, neither *baseball* nor *walking* pass any of the tests. Neither can fit in the second slot of the adjective frame sentence (**His baseball shoes seem very baseball. *His walking shoes seem very walking.*), and neither can be made comparative or superlative (**walkinger, *walkingest shoes; *My shoes are more baseball than yours. *Those shoes are the most baseball of all.*). In fact, the only inflections *baseball* accepts are those associated with nouns (*three baseballs, baseball's Hall of Fame*), and *walking* contains an inflectional verb morpheme, the participial ending {-ing}.

Like a chemist applying a series of chemical tests to identify an unknown substance, linguists classify words on the basis of shared characteristics, not by guessing or doing a partial analysis only.

In (31b) and (31c), *baseball* and *walking* function adjectivally—that is, they appear in a position usually occupied by an adjective. They function like adjectives, yet by default they remain a noun and verb respectively, as we clearly showed by applying the tests for nouns, verbs, and adjectives. In the three columns below, notice how the modifier position we associate prototypically with adjectives is filled first with an adjective, then with a noun, and finally with a verb (in either the present-participle or past-participle form).

Adjective	Noun	Verb
a *sharp* knife	a *steel* knife	a *sharpened* knife
the *young* teacher	the *philosophy* teacher	the *snoozing* teacher
that *rusty* truck	that *delivery* truck	that *loaded* truck
some *white* papers	some *mathematics* papers	some *stacked* papers
an *old* lantern	a *kerosene* lantern	a *shining* lantern
two *fresh* flowers	two *spring* flowers	two *wilting* flowers
your *soft* blanket	your *cotton* blanket	your *woven* blanket

SUMMARY		
Adjectivals (Words That Modify Nouns)		
Words That Have Adjective Characteristics	*Words That Do Not Have Adjective Characteristics*	
1. Can be made comparative or superlative. 2. Can be qualified.	Words that usually function as nouns.	Words that usually function as verbs.

Figure 4.6

As these examples illustrate, the same function (in this case, the adjectival function) can be performed by members of several form classes. Why not just go
ahead and call them all adjectives? First of all, the purpose of grammatical analysis is to discover the natural classes into which words fall. The pattern seems
to be something like that summarized in Figure 4.6.

Sooner or later, any description of English must take into account that so-
called adjectives fall into these three groups. Traditional grammarians have generally classified all noun modifiers as *adjectives,* blinking away the fact that those
derived from nouns and verbs do not behave as other adjectives do.
Contemporary linguists call any word that can modify a noun an *adjectival* (like
nominal, a word describing function rather than form) and classify adjectivals
into three major groups: adjectives, nouns, and verb participles. In addition, a
variety of phrases and clauses can function adjectivally (that is, modify nouns),
as we demonstrate in later chapters. In fact, we repeatedly stress that becoming skilled in grammatical analysis requires that you clearly distinguish form and
function. What a word *is* (its form: noun, verb, adjective, adverb) is not always
the same as what it *does* (its function: nominal, verbal, adjectival, adverbial).

■ *EXERCISE 4.13*

The 14 italicized words in the following passage occur in positions normally occupied by nouns, adjectives, or adverbs. However, not all of these
words belong to the form class you might expect, if you consider only the
word's function. Carefully apply the tests for nouns, verbs, adjectives, and
adverbs to classify the words correctly. In your answer, state the form
class to which each italicized word belongs, and then identify how that
word is functioning, whether *adjectivally* (functioning as though it were
an adjective), *adverbially* (functioning as though it were an adverb), or
nominally (functioning as though it were a noun). Be prepared to explain
what tests justify your classifying of the form and function of the word as
you did.

EXAMPLE

Wei loves The *Learning* Channel.

Learning *is a verb functioning adjectivally as the modifier of the noun* ***Channel.***

The concert ***Saturday*** started ***late.*** The soloist wore a ***green*** dress with a ***beaded*** jacket and a ***fur*** collar. The audience expected to hear ***country*** music, but the soloist chose from the ***classical*** repertoire. She began with a ***short*** song about ***loss*** and ***sadness.*** Her ***singing*** was beautiful, but when we went ***outside*** at intermission, many people were ***already*** going ***home.***

Comments and Suggestions

A Note on Terminology

At about this point, some of you are thinking: Attributive? Predicative? Transitive? Gradable? What is the use of all of these technical terms? Maybe you won't believe us when we say that we're sympathetic with those of you who feel this way. It's certainly not easy learning so much abstract terminology in the space of a few weeks, especially when you're probably facing the same kind of challenge in other classes, from psychology to physics to music to literary criticism. In part, the terminology of linguistics *is* like the technical language of other disciplines, and this text, like other introductions to a discipline, has a healthy dose (or unhealthy overdose?) of terminology. Without such special terms, we would have no way of talking (or even thinking) about the concepts that each discipline has evolved in exploring its special corner of the universe. However, linguistic terminology is unique in that it reflects the attempt of linguists to use language to talk about language itself. In contrast to physicists, for example, who use language to talk about the physical universe, linguists must invent language to describe language. (They even have a term for their "language about language": *metalanguage.*) As you strive to internalize the key terms used in this book, please be patient with us, knowing that we aren't trying to overwhelm you with jargon but only to introduce you to the language necessary for thinking and talking in an educated way about language. At the end of each chapter we list what we consider to be just the essential terms associated with the concepts covered in the chapter. In the Glossary at the end of the book, we define those terms, as well as other, less central linguistic terms that have occurred in the course of our discussion.

A Word About Pragmatics

The linguistic field of *pragmatics* deals with the influence of social context on how language is interpreted. For example, *It's midnight* can be described linguistically as a sentence stating the time. However, to interpret what meaning such a sentence conveys, we need to know who said it and to whom it was addressed, as well as where they were and what they were doing when it was uttered. Said to someone setting a watch, it would be a simple statement of fact. Said by the supervisor of a midnight-to-eight workshift, it might mean "It's time to go to work." On a four-to-midnight workshift, it might mean "It's time to go home." Said by one spouse to another at a party, it might mean the same thing. If they had agreed to stay until one or two, however, it might mean "It's not yet time to go home." Said by anxious parents, it might mean "Why hasn't Flora come home from the party yet?" And so it goes.

An important aspect of pragmatics, for our purposes, is the fact that people often distort syntax or strain the literal meanings of language for effect. Just about any word can be used as a verb (*She is always computering* or *He pianoed a tune*), and although we may be struck by its strangeness, we won't have trouble interpreting it. Idioms, metaphors, and poetic license enrich our language, but of course, they complicate its description. We have had to decide, in the interests of brevity, to restrict ourselves to describing fairly literal, mainstream usage. Bear in mind always that the exceptions you think of may simply be instances of wonderfully imaginative language use. On the other hand, they may invalidate our generalizations. Test them. You will be operating as linguists do.

A Suggestion

The four form classes constitute natural sets of words that behave in similar ways in English. We suggest that you stop reading for a while and review what you have learned about them. Digest what you have read before going on. When you come back, preferably at another sitting, try the review of form class differences in Exercise 4.14.

■ EXERCISE 4.14

Read the following passage, and then answer the questions that follow it.

> The way people talk about the **color spectrum,** and **even perceive it,** varies from one **speech community** to another, although all **human eyes** see the same colors because colors have their own reality in the **physical world.** Color consists of **visible wavelengths** which **blend imperceptibly** into one another. No sharp breaks in the spectrum separate one color from another, such as orange from red. But when speakers in most **European communities** look at a rainbow, they imagine they see six sharp bands of color: red, orange, yellow, green, blue, and purple.[1]

1. In *color spectrum*, what part of speech is *color?* What formal or functional evidence supports your identification?

SUMMARY	
Major Tests for Parts of Speech	

Nouns
 Formal Criteria
    1. Can occur with the plural or possessive morpheme.
 	
    2. May have a noun-making morpheme.
 Functional Criteria
    3. Can fit in the frame sentence.
	government*s*
	 government*'s* decision
	
	 govern*ment*
	
	 (The) _____ seem(s) all right.

Verbs
 Formal Criteria
    1. Can occur with verb inflectional morphemes.
 	
    2. May have a verb-making morpheme.
 Functional Criteria
    3. Can fit in one of the frame sentences.
	criticiz*es*, criticiz*ed*,
	 had fall*en*; was criticiz*ed*,
	 is criticiz*ing*
	
	 critic*ize*
	
	 They must _____ (it).
	 They must _____ good.

Adjectives
 Formal Criteria
    1. May have an adjective-making morpheme.
 	
  2a. Can be made comparative or superlative by using inflectional morphemes.
 Functional Criteria
  2b. Can be compared by using *more* or *most*.
 	
    3. Can fit both slots in the frame sentence.
	lov*able*
	
	 soft*er*, soft*est*
	
	 more soft, *most* soft
	
	 The _____ man seems very _____.

Adverbs
 Formal Criteria
    1. May have an adverb-making morpheme.
  2a. Can be made comparative or superlative by using inflectional morphemes.
 Functional Criteria
  2b. Can be made comparative or superlative by using *more* or most.
    3. Can move in its sentence.
 	
    4. Can fit in the frame sentence.
	cross*wise*
	
	 She ran fast*er*.
	 She ran fast*est*.
	
	 more suddenly, *most* suddenly
	
	 The door opened *suddenly*.
	 The door *suddenly* opened.
	 Suddenly the door opened.
	 The man told his story _____.

Figure 4.7

2. In *even perceive it*, what part of speech is *perceive?* What formal or functional evidence supports your identification?

3. In *speech community*, what part of speech is *speech?* What formal or functional evidence supports your identification?

4. In *human eyes*, what part of speech is *human?* What formal or functional evidence supports your identification?

5. In *physical world*, what part of speech is *physical?* What formal or functional evidence supports your identification?

6. In *visible wavelengths*, what part of speech is *visible?* What formal or functional evidence supports your identification?

7. In *blend imperceptibly*, what part of speech is *imperceptibly?* What formal or functional evidence supports your identification?

8. In *European communities*, what part of speech is *European?* What formal or functional evidence supports your identification?

Figure 4.7 summarizes the major characteristics of each of the four form classes.

SUMMARY

The vast majority of words in the English language belong to one of the four major form classes: nouns, verbs, adjectives, and adverbs. Not only are there far too many members of each of the groups for you to memorize, but every day, new form-class words are being created, thereby expanding these open-ended categories still further. By examining prototypical and peripheral members of each group, linguists have identified specific features of form (derivational and inflectional morphemes) and function (typical positions and frequently co-occurring words) that mark nouns, verbs, adjectives, and adverbs and enable us to recognize them. Young children learning the language acquire an unconscious understanding of these same cues, which are essential for decoding the structure and meaning of sentences. Within each of the four form classes, important semantic and grammatical features separate the members into subcategories that reflect as well as affect how we use them.

REVIEW EXERCISES

Form Classes in Context

Here you are tested on your ability to identify examples of the four form classes and to give criteria of form and function to support your assignment of a word to a given form class. Referring as necessary to the Summary in Figure 4.7, identify the form class to which each of the following boldfaced words belongs. State the characteristics of form and function that allow you to make the classification.

Crop circles are designs **embedded** in fields of grain. They appear **overnight** in fields that show no **physical** evidence of having been entered by machines or people. In the early 1970s they were simply circles, but more **complicated** designs have begun to appear since then. A few people have **admitted** making some of the circles. **British** reporters **estimate** that there are 7 to 10 teams of pranksters operating in England in the summer, indulging in a behavior called "crop circle **hoaxing.**" Everything is done in **complete** secrecy, and no one has ever been **caught** in the act. Most of the circles have been found in Wessex, in **southern** England, but **recently** the **phenomenon** of crop circles has become **international.**

Form Classes in Isolation

Referring as necessary to the Rules of Thumb in Figures 4.1, 4.3, 4.4, and 4.5, and summarized in Figure 4.7, for isolating nouns, verbs, adjectives, and adverbs, identify the form classes to which the following words can belong. Some fit into more than one category. Create a sentence to illustrate each word functioning as a member of the form class or classes to which it can belong.

1. slippery   3. sudden   5. soggy   7. steadily

2. mist   4. skid   6. shelter   8. shower

Subclasses

Provide a noun, verb, adjective, or adverb to exemplify each of the following sets of grammatical and semantic features. Use each word in the context of a sentence.

1. adverb, frequency, comparative
2. noun, proper, inanimate, noncount
3. adjective, gradable, both attributive and predicative
4. adverb, manner, superlative
5. noun, common, animate, human, female
6. noun, proper, animate, nonhuman, male
7. adjective, attributive but not predicative
8. adjective, predicative but not attributive

Practical Applications: Language Creativity and Shifting Parts of Speech

1. An article in the *Los Angeles Times* suggested that people might put some bling onto boring white iPods by adding jewels or covering them

with python skin. A few days later, after it was reported that Serena Williams wore $40,000 earrings in a match at the New York Open, a columnist speculated that if she played Mary Pierce, that there might be a bling-bling women's final. Is it your sense that *bling-bling* is a true adjective? How many ways can *bling* and *bling-bling* be used?

2. Online, there have been long discussions of the *Wussification of America*. What is the source of the word *Wussification?* What is its meaning? If it isn't in your dictionary, do you know where to look? What other words have you encountered that are formed on the same base as *Wussification?*

3. To what form classes do *pretty* and *how* belong? In the title of the poem "anyone lived in a pretty how town" by e. e. cummings, how do *pretty* and *how* function?

4. A comic strip character ordered a dozen doughnuts for a comparison study he was doing and said to the clerk, "You will *comp* these for me, won't you?" Did the cartoonist create the verb *comp,* or was it already in current use? Check its status in a dictionary copyrighted before 2002.

KEY TERMS

adjective
  attributive versus predicative
  gradable versus nongradable
adverb
  of manner, time, place, degree,
    frequency and number, and
    duration
form
form classes, parts of speech
frame sentence
function
gender
  feminine

masculine
neuter
gerund
grammatical features
lexicon
modification, modifier
noun
  common versus proper
  count versus noncount (mass)
number (singular, plural)
qualifier (intensifier)
semantic features
verb

ENDNOTE

1. From Peter Farb, *Word Play: What Happens When People Talk* (New York: Knopf, 1973), p. 172.

Structure-
 Class Words 5

Structure-class words form the basic structure of English sentences. In addition, they modify and signal the grammatical relationships between form-class words and phrases within the sentence.

CHAPTER GOALS

At the end of this chapter, you should be able to

- Identify *structure-class words.*

- Recognize *determiners, auxiliaries,* and *qualifiers.*

- Distinguish among *prepositions, adverbs,* and *verb particles.*

- Recognize the types of pronouns: *personal, indefinite, interrogative, possessive, reciprocal, reflexive,* and *relative.*

- Know the purposes and punctuation of the types of *conjunctions.*

STRUCTURE-CLASS VERSUS FORM-CLASS WORDS

As we saw in Chapter 4, English has a core vocabulary made up of nouns, verbs, adjectives, and adverbs, words used to label and describe the things and activities we perceive in the world around us. These words have been called **content words** because they are considered to *contain* meaning independent of one another. We assume that it is possible to say what *cat, happiness,* or *pretty* refers to, even when it stands alone. We think of each as having **lexical meaning,** the kind of meaning that is given in a dictionary definition for a word like *cat:* "a carnivorous mammal (*Felis catus* or *F. domesticus*), domesticated since early times as a catcher of rats and mice and as a pet and existing in several distinctive breeds and varieties" (*The American Heritage Dictionary of the English Language,* 4th ed., 2000).

However, some content words are better examples of lexical meaning than others. If we think of a continuum from the center to the periphery, the prototypes of nouns, verbs, adjectives, and adverbs are the best examples of content words, as all have visible, verifiable qualities as part of their lexical meaning. Toward the periphery are abstract nouns, verbs, and adjectives and many adverbs. You can imagine writing dictionary entries, like the one for *cat,* for form-class members with a lot of lexical meaning—*finger, tree, swim, humid*—but trying to compose such an entry for those that lack relatively clear and independent meanings—such as *thing, do, nice,* and *then*—would be more difficult.

There is even less lexical meaning in **structure-class words,** or **structure words;** rather, they contribute **grammatical meaning** to a sentence. They signal the structural relationships that words have to one another and are the glue that holds sentences together. Consider the following "sentence":

(1) The *winfy prunkilmoger* from the *glidgement mominkled* and *brangified* all his *levensers vederously.*

What clues here enable you to recognize the members of the form classes?

Even though we converted all of the content words into nonsense syllables and consequently deprived them of lexical meaning, (1) sounds like a sentence because all of the important signals of structure are in place. These include derivational morphemes like the *-y* on *winfy* and *-er* on *prunkilmoger,* inflectional morphemes like the *-ed* on *mominkled* and *brangified,* and structure-class words like *the, from, and, all,* and *his.* Such clues help you to identify *prunkilmoger, glidgement,* and *levensers* as nouns; *mominkled* and *brangified* as verbs; *winfy* as an adjective; and *vederously* as an adverb. In addition, these clues help to signal the grammatical relationships of those words. Even without lexical meaning, we can say a great deal about what this sentence "means." For example, we know that:

- A *prunkilmoger* did something.
- What the *prunkilmoger* did was the actions of *mominkling* and *brangifying.*
- The *brangifying* and possibly the *mominkling* were done to his *levensers.*
- The *brangifying* and possibly the *mominkling* were done in a *vederous* manner.
- The *prunkilmoger* had the quality of *winfiness.*
- The *prunkilmoger* that did the *mominkling* and *brangifying* was from the *glidgement.*

What happens when we reverse the process, replacing the form-class words and turning the structure words into nonsense syllables?

(2) *Glop* angry investigator *larm blonk* government harassed *gerfritz* infuriated *sutbor pumrog* listeners thoroughly.

The result does not sound like an English sentence. Although the words containing lexical meaning are in place, it is hard to find them in (2). Moreover, the sentence is incomprehensible because the *grammatical meaning*—that which is signaled by the structure words—is obscured.

Structure-class words like *the, from, a, and, all,* and *his* help you to identify the form-class words and provide essential signals of the syntactic structure associated with English sentences. But in doing so, they contribute some lexical information of their own as well. Notice how a change in structure words changes the meanings of the following sentences:

(3)   I am waiting for a train *to* Chicago.

I am waiting for a train *from* Chicago.

Who has *a* key to this door?

Who has *the* key to this door?

Mary was upset when John couldn't find the key to *her* car.

Mary was upset when John couldn't find the key to *his* car.

Structure-class words do not lack content, as you see. More importantly, however, they provide essential information about the form-class words with which they occur and signal their grammatical relationships. Because the primary significance of structure words lies in the grammatical operations they perform rather than in their lexical meaning, they are called **function words** by some linguists, and their grammatical meaning is sometimes referred to as **functional meaning.**

Two other differences between the structure classes and the form classes are significant. First, as we observed in Chapters 3 and 4, nouns, verbs, adjectives, and adverbs can undergo important morphological form changes by the processes of derivation and inflection. In contrast, the members of the structure classes for the most part show no such changes in form, as is evident in recalling some examples of prepositions (*to, from, of, on*), conjunctions (*and, or, nor, but*), and modal auxiliaries (*must, may, will, can*). Each member of these important structure classes occurs in a single form.

Second, the form classes include extremely large numbers of members, and through the various processes of word creation and derivation, their size is constantly growing. In contrast, the structure classes typically have a limited, usually quite small number of members, and that membership is essentially fixed. For example, English has only three articles, nine prototypical modal auxiliaries, a few dozen pronouns, and a few dozen frequently occurring prepositions, and no new ones are being created. This is clearly in contrast to the open-ended nature of the lists of nouns, verbs, adjectives, and adverbs.

Figure 5.1 summarizes the main differences between the form and structure classes. Structure words do not usually stand alone. Their association with specific form classes provides a signal that a member of that class is coming. For example, *determiners* (like *the*) and *prepositions* (like *between*) never occur without an accompanying noun; *modal auxiliaries* (like *should*) require a verb to complete their meaning; and *qualifiers* (like *very*) are always

SUMMARY	
Contrasts Between Form and Structure Classes	
Form Classes	Structure Classes
1. They are open-ended, not limited in the number of their members.	1. They are mostly closed, relatively small groups.
2. Their members usually undergo changes in form.	2. Their members generally do not change form.
3. Their members usually have lexical meaning.	3. Their members have mostly grammatical meaning.

Figure 5.1

followed by an adjective or an adverb. Once we encounter any one of these structure words, the possible kinds of words that can follow are reduced: We listen for the anticipated noun, or verb, or other form-class word.

English has a considerable number of structure word groups, some quite small and specialized in their functions. In this chapter, we discuss the most important classes, beginning with the ones just mentioned and including *relatives* (such as *who* in *the friend who called me*), *interrogatives* (words like *who, what, when,* and *where* when they are used to ask questions), *pronouns,* and *conjunctions* (like *and* and *or,* which function to join words, phrases, or groups of related words). Some of the other structure words appear in the context of later chapters, where we will see clearly what they contribute to the structure of sentences. Figure 5.2 will help you to remember the major form and structure classes.

SUMMARY	
Form Classes (Content Words)	Structure Classes (Function Words)
Nouns	Determiners
Verbs	Auxiliaries
Adjectives	Qualifiers
Adverbs	Prepositions
	Conjunctions
	Pronouns
	Relatives
	Interrogatives

Figure 5.2

DETERMINERS

A **determiner** is a structure word that precedes and modifies a noun, the prototypical members of the set being the articles *a/an* and *the*. We could define a *determiner*, in fact, as "a structure word that can substitute for *a/an* or *the*." The main subgroups of determiners are listed in Figure 5.3.

To say that determiners precede and modify nouns does not, of course, distinguish them from most adjectives. But determiners differ from adjectives in several important ways:

- Determiners don't occur with any of the adjective-forming derivational suffixes, like *-able* and *-ly*.
- Determiners don't have comparative or superlative forms: *tall, taller, tallest; this, *thiser, *thisest*.
- Determiners do not fit in both slots of the adjective test frame sentence: The _____ man seems very _____.
- Determiners always *precede* any adjective or noun modifiers of a noun, as does *the* in *the expensive car stereo*.

The is called the **definite article** and *a/an* the **indefinite article.** The contrast between the two is related to knowledge about the noun that the speaker (or writer) shares with the hearer (or reader). When *the* is used with a noun, the hearer presumably knows specifically what is being talked about. When *a* or *an* is used, such knowledge is not assumed. Consider these contrasting examples:

(4)   a. Please wash *the car*.

b. Please wash *a car*.

c. Did you see *the dog?*

d. Did you see *a dog?*

SUMMARY	
Main Groups of Determiners	
Articles	a/an, the
Demonstratives	this, these, that, those
Possessives	my, our, your, his, her, its, their
Indefinites	some, any, no, every, other, another, many, more, most, enough, few, less, much, either, neither, several, all, both, each, . . .
Cardinal Numbers	one, two, three, four, . . .
Ordinal Numbers	first, second, third, . . . last

Figure 5.3

In (4a) and (4c) the speaker assumes that the hearer knows which specific car and dog are being referred to. In such a context, we can use either the definite article or one of the demonstratives, which also identify definite persons or things: *Please wash **that car,** Please wash **this car.*** However, in (4b) and (4d), the speaker has no specific car or dog in mind. The indefinite article in these sentences could be replaced with one of the other indefinite determiners without changing that aspect of the meaning: *Please wash **some car,** Please wash **any car.*** Common count nouns are considered to be indefinite when they occur in the plural without any determiner:

(5) *Cars* are becoming more expensive every year.

Dogs are good pets.

Without determiners, *cars* and *dogs* refer to any or all cars and dogs but no specific ones.

Native speakers of English seldom think about the complex grammatical meanings signaled by determiners or about the intricate patterns governing their use, for these individuals have acquired an unconscious understanding of how to use and interpret determiners as part of the natural process of learning the language as children. People who learn English as a second language are not so fortunate, however, and many struggle with the English determiner system long after having mastered most of the other important elements of the language. In order to use determiners idiomatically, one must, for example, properly correlate determiners with the count/noncount distinction we discussed in Chapter 4. As you can see in the following examples, noncount nouns can occur with the definite article (*the*) or without any article, but they never occur with the indefinite article (*a/an*):

(6) *The sand* got in my shoe.

Sand got in my shoe.

*A sand got in my shoe.

The air is essential for our survival.

Air is essential for our survival.

*An air is essential for our survival.

Singular, proper count nouns usually occur without a determiner:

(7) *Peter* went to *Seattle.*

*The Peter went to *the Seattle.*

But a singular common count noun cannot stand alone; it must be preceded by an article or some other type of determiner:

(8) *A train* passes this way regularly.

*Train passes this way regularly.

My bicycle is broken.

*Bicycle is broken.

The indefinites *many* and *few* occur with count nouns, whereas *much* and *little* accompany noncount nouns:

(9)   Count: The children gathered *many stones.*

*The children gathered *much stones.*

Few trains pass this way anymore.

*Little trains pass this way anymore.

Noncount: These solar panels generate *much electricity.*

*These solar panels generate *many electricity.*

*Few milk was left in the carton.

Little milk was left in the carton.

If English is your native language, you already know when to use indefinite and definite articles (*a/an* and *the*). If you are a nonnative speaker or have to explain to such a person how to use the article system in English, then the information provided about count and noncount or mass nouns will be helpful. Even advanced speakers of English as a second language may use the wrong article, leave out an article when one is called for, or use one when none is necessary or appropriate. However, such persistent, minor variations are probably best thought of as being similar to a slight "foreign accent," something that doesn't cause serious problems and goes away, if at all, only gradually.

Usually, only one determiner precedes a noun. However, this restriction doesn't apply to all determiners. Some appear in combination with others, as these examples illustrate:

(10)   *half **the*** Belgian chocolate   ***the*** *first two* successful tries

*all **those*** dirty windows   ***those*** *last* bars of music

*both **my*** English classes   ***their*** *only* daughter

Demonstratives, indefinites, and cardinal numbers (see Figure 5.3) can function either as determiners modifying nouns or as nominal substitutes for nouns (pronouns). In the following pairs, which example illustrates the determiner function and which the pronoun function?

(11)   Have you seen *these* new shoe styles?

Have you seen *these?*

This house will be yours someday.

This will all be yours someday.

Some people like it hot, and *other* people like it cold.

Some like it hot, and *others* like it cold.

In each pair, the first example illustrates the determiner function, and the second indicates the nominal use. In *Have you see these,* for example, *these* can stand either for something previously mentioned (such as *these new shoe styles*) or for something to which the speaker is pointing. Possessives, too, can serve either as determiners or pronouns. Some have two forms (see Figure 5.4), depending on their function:

(12) Is that *her* convertible?   (determiner)

Is that *hers?*   (pronoun)

Possessive nouns have the same distribution. When a possessive noun occurs before another noun, we consider it a determiner, even though it may have its own determiner and modifiers, as in (13c).

SUMMARY		
Possessives		
	Determiner Function	*Nominal Function*
First-Person		
singular	*my*	*mine*
plural	*our*	*ours*
Second-Person		
singular	*your*	*yours*
plural		
Third-Person		
singular — masculine	*his*	
singular — feminine	*her*	*hers*
singular — neuter	*its*	
plural	*their*	*theirs*

Figure 5.4

(13) a. Is that *Kate's* convertible?   (determiner)

  b. Is that *Kate's?*   (noun)

  c. Is that *the blonde girl's* convertible?   (determiner)

  d. Is that *the blonde girl's?*   (noun)

Because Asian languages do not have such complex rules for determiner use, native speakers of these languages face a difficult task in learning the English determiner system. Their English may be accompanied by a grammatical "accent" that results in singular common count nouns being used without determiners:

(14) *I bought *automobile* from *car dealer.*

  *Is *library* open today?

  *We watched *movie* last night.

  *He wrote *perfect computer program.*

Speakers of English as a second language whose native language is French or Italian might have difficulties with other aspects of the determiner system that conflict with the patterns they learned as children. Instead of *People use these trails for jogging,* they may insert a definite article called for by the grammatical rules of their own languages and say, *People use these trails for the jogging.*

Not surprisingly, native speakers of English encounter equally difficult problems in attempting to master new languages. In fact, even within the English-speaking world, differences in the use of determiners exist:

(15) American English   My friends enrolled in the university.

  British English   My friends enrolled in university.

  American English   She is in the hospital.

  British English   She is in hospital.

We need not go outside of American English to find unpredictable inconsistencies, for although we say *in the university,* we also say *in high school* and *in college.* And although we say *at the theater* and *at the museum,* we say *at church* and *at temple.* The rules governing determiners are complex indeed, and we have not exhausted those complexities here.

■ EXERCISE 5.1

List the determiners used in the following sentences, remembering that adjectives are not determiners. Then, go back to your list and classify each determiner as one of the following:

definite or indefinite article

demonstrative

possessive

indefinite

cardinal number

ordinal number

1. Two small moons orbit Sylvia, a large main belt asteroid.

2. It was the first asteroid found to have multiple moons.

3. Of the two small moons that orbit Sylvia, Remus was the second moon to be discovered.

4. These moons were probably broken off the asteroid by an impact at some point in the past.

5. Because its density is small, Sylvia is quite porous.

6. Scientists believe that other, smaller moons may yet be found.

Diagrams and Trees

For visual learners, sentence diagrams and phrase structure trees help to clarify visually the relationship between determiners and the nouns they modify. In a Reed-Kellogg diagram, modifiers appear on lines slanted away from the headword they modify. As headwords are placed on horizontal lines, noun phrases (groups of words that can substitute for nouns) look like this:

(16)

■ *EXERCISE 5.2*

Draw Reed-Kellogg diagrams of the following noun phrases. Remember that the noun headword goes on the horizontal line and modifiers go on lines slanting downward away from it, as is shown in (16) in the text.

1. other moons

2. its density

3. the second moon

4. the only other asteroid

Before showing how tree diagrams represent the same information, let's look at the way trees are drawn. They are called either *phrase structure trees* or *phrase markers* because they attempt to represent visually the way words are grouped into phrases (groups of words that can substitute for nouns, verbs, adjectives, or adverbs) to create sentences. A noun and its determiners, for example, are considered to constitute a *noun phrase* (abbreviated NP), and there is a phrase structure rule like the following:

(17) NP = (Determiner) + Noun

Phrase structure rules (abbreviated PS rules) say that the item on the left-hand side of the equals sign consists of the items on the right, and the rules give the order in which items occur. The structures on the right thus are the *constituents* of whatever structure is named to the left of the equals sign. In this case, the rule states that a noun phrase (NP) consists of (=) an optional determiner (the parentheses indicate that the determiner is optional) and a noun. The lack of parentheses around *noun* means that a noun or a noun substitute must be present in order for the structure to qualify as a noun phrase. Constituents that appear in parentheses in phrase structure rules are optional: They need not be present. Because the determiner is parenthesized above, the rule specifies that a noun phrase may consist simply of a noun or a determiner followed by a noun. According to the rule in (17), therefore, both of the following are noun phrases:

(18) books (Noun)
a book (Determiner + Noun)

You can confirm that both *books* and *a book* have the same grammatical structure by showing that one can substitute for the other in a sentence:

(19) *Books* fell to the floor.
A book fell to the floor.

Actually, noun phrases can be far more complicated than this suggests, but for the moment, we will consider just noun phrases like those analyzed in (16). To draw a phrase marker, begin by writing down the item that appears to the left of the equals sign in the PS rule (in this case, NP). This constitutes the *node,* or the place from which constituents branch off. Below the node, draw branching lines to whatever occurs on the right of the equals sign. Your phrase markers for *a car* and *all the cars* should look like this:

(20)

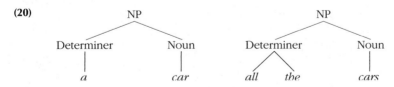

EXERCISE 5.3

Draw properly labeled phrase markers of the noun phrases for which you drew Reed-Kellogg diagrams in Exercise 5.2.

━━ AUXILIARIES ━━

Auxiliary verbs either signal that a main verb is coming or serve as a substitute for the verb phrase. By affecting the form of the main verb and altering its meaning in systematic ways, auxiliary verbs also play an important role in the intricate grammatical patterning of the main verb phrase, which we discuss in Chapter 6. Figure 5.5 lists the **modal auxiliaries,** none of which inflect, and gives the main forms of **have, be,** and **do,** which have a number of inflections: number (present and plural), tense (past and present), and participle {-en} and {-ing} forms.

Modal Auxiliaries

The modal auxiliaries always precede the main verb as well as any other auxiliaries that are present.

(21)   a. The fireworks display **will** *start* in five minutes.

b. The fireworks display **may** *have started* five minutes ago.

c. The fireworks display **should** *have been starting* by now.

In the first example, the modal is followed immediately by the main verb. In (21b), the modal is followed by another auxiliary verb, *have,* and then by the main verb, *started,* and in (21c) the modal is followed by two other auxiliaries, *have* and *been,* as well as the main verb, *starting.*

To understand why linguists do not consider the nine modal auxiliaries—*can, could, will, would, shall, should, may, might,* and *must*—to be true verbs, look again at the characteristics used in Chapter 4 to identify a verb. None of them consistently applies to modals. For example, modals usually cannot

SUMMARY			
Auxiliary Verb Forms			
Modal Auxiliaries	**Have**	**Be**	**Do**
can	have	be	do
could	has	am	does
will	had	is	did
would	having	are	done
shall		was	doing
should		were	
may		been	
might		being	
must			

Figure 5.5

1. Have a verb-making morpheme.

2. Occur with a present-tense morpheme.

3. Occur with a past-tense morpheme.

And they cannot

4. Occur with a past-participle morpheme.

5. Occur with a present-participle morpheme.

6. Be made into a command.

7. Be made negative.

8. Fit in one of the frame sentences:

They must _____ *[it].*

They must _____ *good.*

Although it may seem to you that modals can be made negative, in fact, this is not the case. A sentence like *She must not* or *She cannot* is incomplete because you don't know what the person must not or cannot do. It is the deleted main verb (the headword) and not the modal that is being negated: *She must not (repeat that mistake)* or *She cannot (find the scissors).* In fact, the modal auxiliaries do not ordinarily fulfill any of the criteria for true verbs.

Some linguists consider *could, would, should,* and *might* the past tense of *can, will, shall,* and *may.* However, this is not reliably the case. They are not used without adverbs to express past time:

(22)   I could swim *when I was younger,* and I still can.

We would often light a fire on cold evenings *when I was young.*

All the modals are used most often to signal specific meanings (such as condition, probability, obligation, and possibility) listed for them in Chapter 6, Figure 6.8.

Modals are prototypical structure words in that they never function alone; they have been called *helping verbs* because they must always occur with a true verb following them—either explicit, as in the first half of (23), or implied, as in second half:

(23)   Janice *can meet* us here tomorrow, but Joe *can't* [*meet* us here tomorrow].

Have

As an auxiliary, *have* always occurs before the past participle {-en} form of another verb to express the perfect (completed) aspect of the verb. When *have* is in the present tense, it creates the present-perfect form of the verb:

(24)   A bright green bird *has nested* there.

The critics *have written* their reviews.

When in the past tense, the auxiliary *have* creates the past-perfect form:

(25)   A bright green bird *had nested* there.

The critics *had written* their reviews.

Have as a True Verb

In addition to being an auxiliary, *have* also functions as a true verb having many meanings, including:

(26)   Kelly *has* the dictionary.   (to possess)

Marge *has* red hair.   (to be characterized by)

Fred *has* chicken pox.   (to be ill with)

I *had* the shrimp in white wine   (to eat)
with marinated asparagus tips.

Martina *had* a baby.   (to give birth to)

You *had* the courage to refuse.   (to display a quality or trait)

Be

As an auxiliary, *be* has two main functions. One is to express the progressive (ongoing) aspect of the verb. It occurs before the present participle {-ing} form of the main verb to create either the present-progressive form when *be* is in the present tense,

(27)   Harvey *is cooking* squash again.

The football players *are lifting* weights.

or the past-progressive form when *be* is in the past tense,

(28)   Harvey *was cooking* squash again.

The football players *were lifting* weights.

Its other auxiliary function is to create passive verbs. A form of *be* followed by the past participle of another verb marks the passive voice in English. The examples in (29) show common examples of the passive:

(29)   a. At each game, the National Anthem *is sung* by the whole crowd.

b. The letter *was written* by the school principal.

c. Joey likes to hear the National Anthem *sung* by a football crowd.

d. The letter *written* by the school principal looked ominous.

(29a) and (29b) show the full passive: a form of the verb *be* followed by the past participle of the main verb (*is sung, was written*). (29c) and (29d) show the reduced passive: *be* has been removed, and the past participle remains as a modifier of the preceding noun (*the National Anthem sung by a football crowd, the letter written by the school principal*). We discuss the passive in greater detail in Chapter 8.

Be as a True Verb

Like *have, be* can function as a true verb as well as an auxiliary. In its nonauxiliary function, *be* links its subject to a phrase in the predicate that describes or identifies the subject:

(30) That gas station *is* open.

The club members *were* mostly business people.

Do

As an auxiliary verb, we employ *do* in a number of grammatical processes, which we study in later chapters. For example, we use *do* when we create certain kinds of questions:

(31) He *leaves* tomorrow.

Does he *leave* tomorrow?

She *wants* some of these delicious chocolates.

Does she *want* some of these delicious chocolates?

Do is also used to form negatives:

(32) They *want* that wall-sized television after all.

They ***don't*** *want* that wall-sized television after all.

and emphatic statements:

(33) The moon *looks* like a big pizza pie tonight!

The moon ***does*** *look* like a big pizza pie tonight!

Do as a Pro-Verb

In its other auxiliary use, the relation of *do* to verbs is similar to that of pronouns to nouns: You could call *do* in this function a "pro-verb."

(34) We want that trophy more than they *do*.

I'll taste your raw-beet casserole if Fred *does*.

In the first example, *do* stands for *want that trophy,* and in the second, *does* substitutes for *tastes your raw-beet casserole.*

Do as a True Verb

As a true verb, *do* has a variety of meanings, including:

(35)	Jack will *do* the work without complaining.	(to perform)
	A full night's sleep *did* you a lot of good.	(to cause)
	I wonder what Mary *did* after college.	(to work at, especially as a vocation)
	In Cosmetics 101, we learned to *do* eyes and cheeks.	(to apply cosmetics to)
	Shirley *did* her living room in Neo-Baroque.	(to decorate)
	We all helped to *do* the dishes.	(to wash)

▪ EXERCISE 5.4

Identify the auxiliary verbs in the following sentences.

1. The windmill farm near Livermore, California, is one of the largest providers of wind energy in the world.
2. Environmentalists have reported that large numbers of birds fly into turbine blades and die.
3. They have a monitoring system that tracks the number of birds that are killed every day.
4. Those that have been killed include raptors, meadowlarks, flycatchers, and warblers.
5. The government will shut down some of the windmills this winter and may replace the turbines with taller ones that could reduce the bird kill.
6. These measures do not entirely satisfy environmentalists, who have argued that they do not do enough to reduce the carnage.
7. The farms must strike a balance between protecting the birds and producing renewable energy for California.

Diagrams and Trees

Diagrams show auxiliary verbs as part of the main verb, placing them on the horizontal line along with the verbs they modify:

(36)	Jane	has been jogging	Edgar	should apologize

Phrase structure trees show the relationship between auxiliaries and main verbs much more clearly; they are discussed in detail in Chapter 6.

QUALIFIERS

Qualifiers usually precede adjectives or adverbs, increasing or decreasing the quality signified by the words they modify (*more colorful, less frequently*). The test frame for adjectives in Chapter 4, which includes the prototypical qualifier *very,* provides a slot that can help you identify most qualifiers.

(37)   The *handsome* man seems _____ *handsome.*

<u>very</u>

<u>quite</u>

<u>rather</u>

Figure 5.6 lists the most common qualifiers. As we have already seen, some of them serve other functions as well. Notice that although most are single words, some phrasal qualifiers (qualifiers made up of more than one word) also occur.

Traditional grammarians usually classified qualifiers as adverbs of degree, and at first glance, judging on the basis of meaning and function, this seems reasonable. Degree adverbs—like *completely, absolutely, extremely,* and

SUMMARY		
Examples of Qualifiers		
very	so	pretty
quite	just	even
rather	enough	a bit
somewhat	still	a little
more	almost	a (whole) lot
most	fairly	a good deal
less	really	a great deal
least		kind of
too		sort of

Figure 5.6

excessively —can fit into the same position as the prototype, and they have similar meanings:

(38)   The man seems <u>very</u>_____ good.

<u>completely</u>

<u>absolutely</u>

<u>extremely</u>

<u>excessively</u>

However, are qualifiers true adverbs? Exercise 5.5 will help you to contrast adverbs and qualifiers.

▌ *EXERCISE 5.5* _____

Below are the main tests for determining if a word fits the adverb class. Try these tests on qualifiers from the list in Figure 5.6.

1. Adverbs modify verbs—that is, they fit in the adverb frame sentence:

    The man told his story *slowly.*

    What happens when you substitute the prototypical qualifiers *very, quite,* and *rather* in the frame sentence in place of the prototypical adverb *slowly?*

2. Adverbs can be made comparative and superlative:

    fast*er,* fast*est*

    more suddenly, *most* suddenly

    Can you make comparative and superlative forms for *very, quite,* and *rather?*

3. Adverbs can be qualified:

    somewhat sadly

    What happens when you try to qualify *very, quite,* and *rather?*

4. Adverbs frequently have adverb-making suffixes:

    sudden*ly,* cross*wise,* home*ward*

    Do the prototypical qualifiers you are testing occur with such morphemes?

5. Adverbs can be moved within a sentence:

    The door opened *slowly.*

    The door *slowly* opened.

    Slowly, the door opened.

    Test the qualifiers in a sentence like the following. Can they be moved?

    Although Paula became very tired quite early in the marathon, she finished it.

Based on your application of the adverb tests to qualifiers, should qualifiers be considered adverbs?

Not all qualifiers function in the same way. For example, *more* and *most* are qualifiers used to form the comparative and superlative with multisyllable adverbs and adjectives—that is, those formed from other parts of speech by means of derivational morphemes (*more extensive, more extensively*), as most of the others form the comparative and superlative with *-er* and *-est* (*quicker, later*).

Some qualifiers—including *even, rather, no, lots, a (whole) lot, a (good) bit, a great deal, a little*, and quite a few rather informal words and phrases, ranging from *heaps* and *tons* to off-color forms that we'll leave to your imagination—can modify comparative forms:

(39)   The midday temperature became <u>somewhat</u> hotter.

<u>much</u>

<u>still</u>

A few qualifiers—including *just, somewhat, a bit*, and *a little*—can modify prepositional phrases:

(40)   We left *just after dawn.*

Diagrams and Trees

In sentence diagrams, qualifiers, like other modifiers, appear on slanted lines leading to the word they modify.

(41)

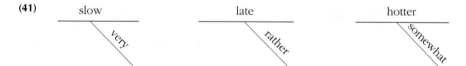

If the headword is already on a diagonal line, then the qualifier is placed under it:

(42)

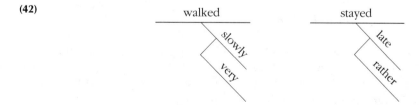

Qualifiers and the words they modify create phrases in which the headword is an adverb or an adjective. To give an example, a modified adverb constitutes an adverb phrase (abbreviated ADVP), described by the phrase structure rule below:

(43)   ADVP = (Qualifier) Adverb

Using this rule as a guide, you would draw a tree of *very slowly* by beginning with ADVP, the element to the left of the equals sign. It would branch to the elements on the right (qualifier and adverb). (Notice that the qualifier appears in parentheses in the rule above, a way of noting that it may be part of, but is not essential to, an adverb phrase.)

(44)

The same kind of rule generates an adjective phrase (ADJP) and provides a guide for creating a phrase marker representing qualified adjectives.

(45)   ADJP = (Qualifier) Adjective

WHAT'S THE USAGE?   *Qualifiers*

Not all qualifiers occur in formal writing. Some tend to be used only in speech, in informal writing, or in specific regions of the country, and some are omitted from Figure 5.6 because they are considered unprintable. If you were to consult a usage guide, you might find distinctions such as the following:

Formal   The weather was *rather* hot.
              The weather was *very* hot.
Informal   It's *pretty* hot today.
              It's *real* hot today.
Regional   It's *powerful* hot today.

We should, perhaps, remind you that schoolroom grammars and usage guides lag behind actual norms of usage. *Pretty hot* is quite likely to occur in the writing of many educated Americans and *real hot* in their speech, even though traditional guidebooks disapprove.

As a student of linguistics, how would you describe *totally* and *all* in the following sentences we overheard on our campus?

(46)   Christine is *totally* angry at her boyfriend.

        After Bill called, my sister is *all* "I told you so."

Should these words be considered qualifiers?

A Review and a Reminder

We have given detailed descriptions of the characteristics of determiners, auxiliaries, and qualifiers to help you focus on which words belong to which categories. Don't become overwhelmed by trying to memorize those differences. If you are a native speaker, you already know them at a tacit level. You know, for instance, that determiners always come first in a noun phrase and that some of them precede or follow others. You already know most or perhaps all of the characteristics we have provided. Because it is incomplete, don't try to memorize the list of determiners in Figure 5.3. Try to get a feel for the category so that you understand that determiners are structure words that precede nouns and provide specific kinds of information about the nouns they modify.

    The most useful test for identifying determiners is to try substituting them for articles *a, an,* or *the* in a sentence. Because articles occur only before nouns, you will have constructed your own frame containing a noun that the determiner will modify. For example, make up a pair of phrases beginning with an article, one singular and one plural, and then try substituting words for the articles. Words that fit, if they are not nouns or adjectives, will be determiners:

(47)   Prototypical Determiners

    a. *a* new house

    b. *the* new houses

    Look back at Figure 5.3, and you will see that all the determiners can replace either *a* or *the* in 47.

    At a subconscious level, you also know that modals always come first in a verb phrase. You probably never accidentally say **He have must gone out* instead of *He must have gone out.* We mention the word order characteristics of modals and their failure to inflect to help you to see them as a class and to acquaint you with the criteria that have led linguists to classify them as a separate group of words. Because there are only nine modals, we generally urge students to memorize them. They form pairs and a triplet, a pattern that helps to simplify the memorization of this group of words:

(48)   Modals

can	will	shall	may
could	would	should	might
			must

In discussing qualifiers, we have stressed their differences from adverbs because many students will have been taught that they *are* adverbs. Why separate them into a class by themselves? Why not continue to call them adverbs? Because they behave differently: They do not modify verbs, they do not change form through the addition of morphemes, and they often cannot stand alone, without either an adjective or an adverb following.

To fix the category in your mind and to help identify members of the set, try using the following phrases. In the qualifier slot, the first contains *very* and the second, *much*. Most qualifiers will fit in one slot or the other.

(49)   Prototypical Qualifiers
       a. *very* polite

       b. *much* more polite

At this point, we suggest that you stop and review what you have learned about determiners, auxiliaries, and qualifiers. Then, when you come back to the text (preferably at another time), try doing Exercise 5.6, a review of what you have just read.

■ *EXERCISE 5.6*

In the following sentences, identify all of the determiners, auxiliary verbs, and qualifiers.

1. Jack FM radio plays very catchy '80s music for members of Generation X: classic rock, a few oldies, and some rap.

2. Jack radio has remained mostly a music station, without any weather, traffic, or chatter, and its commercials are shorter than the usual.

3. The originators of the first Jack radio station thought they would sell their concept to AM stations.

4. However, its format has spread to 17 Jack radio FM stations; it is so popular that it is spawning copycats like Bob FM and Dave FM.

Once you develop a sense of which words will substitute for various classes, you can begin to test fuzzy instances yourself. For example, in the following, do you think *many* is more like a determiner or like a qualifier? In other words, does *many* modify *songs* or *more?*

5. Listeners like knowing they will hear many more songs and fewer commercials on Jack FM.

In the following sentence, is *ought to* more like a main verb or a modal? Why?

6. Perhaps as their cool music repeats itself over and over on Jack radio, Generation Xers ought to begin to think about moving on to something new.

PREPOSITIONS

Prepositions are reliable signals that a noun is coming. They occur before (in "*pre*-position" to) a noun phrase (a noun and its modifiers, if any). Together, the preposition and noun phrase constitute a **prepositional phrase:**

(50) *in* the attic   *after* lunch   *below* that street sign

      up the path   *since* Easter   *for* a very good reason

The noun or noun phrase following the preposition (such as *the attic* in *in the attic*) functions as the **object of the preposition.** Prepositions connect their noun phrase objects to some other word or phrase in a sentence, thereby modifying that other word or phrase by adding information of the sort provided by adverbs (place, time, manner, and such) or by adding the kind of descriptive information usually supplied by adjectives.

(51) the voice *of the people*   (adjectival: modifies the noun *voice*)

      hurried *to the store*   (adverbial: modifies the verb *hurried*)

      sorry *for the interruption*   (adverbial: modifies the adjective *sorry*)

When prepositional phrases function as though they were adverbs, they are called *adverbial modifiers,* and when their role is similar to that of adjectives, they are called *adjectival modifiers.* In each of the following examples, the preposition serves as a link to the verb that the prepositional phrase modifies:

(52) **Prepositional Phrases Functioning Adverbially**

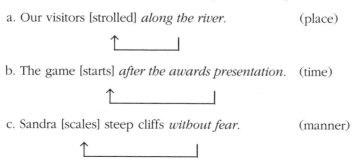

      a. Our visitors [strolled] *along the river.*   (place)

      b. The game [starts] *after the awards presentation.*   (time)

      c. Sandra [scales] steep cliffs *without fear.*   (manner)

When they function adjectivally, prepositional phrases modify a noun or noun phrase:

(53)   **Prepositional Phrases Functioning Adjectivally**

1. Mrs. Carter owns [the house] *with the tile roof.*

2. [The class] *after lunch* is the most difficult.

With the tile roof tells which house is being referred to, and *after lunch* specifies which class is the most difficult.

Is there a prototypical preposition? One student told us that she had been taught that a preposition was anything a mouse could do to a clock. Such a creative characterization of prototypical prepositions seems intuitively almost right: The prepositions that express relationships of time, place, and direction (such as *after, since, in, on, under, over, up, toward*) seem to provide the clearest examples of what a preposition is. But one of the most frequently occurring prepositions is *of,* which usually expresses nothing about location or direction.

Without trying to specify a precise group of prototypes, Figure 5.7 lists some of the most common prepositions. For convenience, we have divided the prepositions in our chart into two groups: *simple,* those that consist of a single word, and *phrasal,* those that consist of more than one word (*along with, in case of, on top of*).

Diagrams and Trees

Prepositional phrases are diagrammed so that the preposition appears on a line slanting downward from the word the phrase modifies; the object of the preposition appears on a horizontal line following it; and modifiers of the object appear on slanted lines below, in the position we have already observed with determiners:

(54)

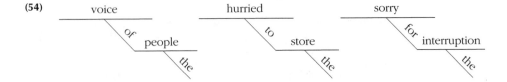

SUMMARY			
Common Prepositions			
Simple Prepositions			
about	besides	into	since
above	between	like	through
across	beyond	near	throughout
after	but (= except)	of	to
against	by	off	toward(s)
along	concerning	on	under
among	despite	onto	underneath
around	down	opposite	until (till)
as	during	out	unto
at	except	outside	up
before	for	over	upon
behind	from	past	via
below	in	pending	with
beneath	including	regarding	within
beside	inside	round	without
Phrasal Prepositions			
according to	due to	in view of
across from	except for	inside of
alongside of	for the sake of	instead of
along with	in accordance with	off of
apart from	in addition to	on account of
aside from	in back of	on behalf of
away from	in case of	on top of
because of	in connection with	out of
by means of	in front of	outside of
by reason of	in place of	regardless of
by virtue of	in reference to	short of
by way of	in regard to	together with
down from	in spite of	up to

Figure 5.7

A phrase structure rule describes the structure of a prepositional phrase (abbreviated PrepP):

(55)   PrepP = Preposition + NP

This rule specifies that a prepositional phrase consists of a preposition followed by a noun phrase. To draw a phrase marker of *of the people,* we would branch from the element on the left of the equals sign to those on the right:

(56)

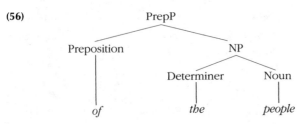

Differences Between Prepositions and Adverbs

Sometimes a word can be a preposition in one context and an adverb in another. In the following examples, you can differentiate the preposition from the adverb by searching for an object. Diagrams may help clarify this distinction for you. In (57a) and (57c), recognizing *the dorm* as the object of *inside* and *the stairs* as the object of *down* allows you to say with confidence that in those sentences, *inside* and *down* are prepositions. The two words are interpreted as adverbs of place in (57b) and (57d), as no noun follows them.

(57)   a. They were not supposed to be playing with   (preposition)
           Frisbies **inside** the dorm.

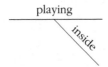

        b. House rules did not allow playing with Frisbies **inside.**   (adverb)

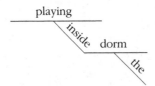

        c. The little boy fell **down** the stairs.   (preposition)

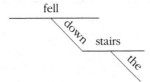

d. The little boy fell ***down.*** (adverb)

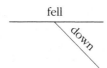

Differences Between Prepositions and Verb Particles

To complicate matters a bit more, many of the forms that serve both as adverbs and as prepositions also function as **verb particles.** Some very common verbs are created by combining a verb with a verb particle, resulting in a **phrasal verb.** Two examples are the particles *up* in *look up* and *in* in *turn in*.

(58) Oscar *looked up* the word.

At midnight we *turned in.*

As you can see, the particle is essential to the meaning of the verb in these two examples. *Look up* means "search for in a dictionary," and *turned in* means "went to bed."

How can we distinguish the particles *up* and *in* from their homophonous prepositions? In (59a), *looked up* is a unit meaning "find in a dictionary." *The word* is the object of the phrasal verb *looked up*. However, in (59b), *looked up* is not a unit. Rather, *up the road* is a prepositional phrase (consisting of the preposition *up* followed by its object, *the road*), telling where Oscar *looked:*

(59) a. Oscar looked up the word.

b. Oscar looked up the road.

Another test can distinguish a verb particle from a preposition: If the phrasal verb is transitive—that is, followed by an object—the particle can usually be moved to a position following the object, as example (60) illustrates. Remember that the arrow (↓) means "is equivalent to" whatever follows.

(60) Oscar *looked up* the word.
↓
Oscar *looked* the word *up.*

In contrast, a preposition can never be moved to a position after its object. In (61), it is impossible to create an equivalent version with the preposition following *the road:*

(61) Oscar looked *up the road.*
↓
*Oscar looked *the road up.*

Differences Between Verb Particles and Adverbs

Verb particles are often identical to adverbs. How do you differentiate between a particle and an adverb? First, because adverbs are often optional, they can usually be omitted without changing the meaning of the verb. Particles are not optional and thus cannot be omitted. In the following, notice that the meaning of the verb remains unchanged regardless of whether or not the adverb is included. In both the (a) and (b) versions of (62), the verb retains the sense of "turning an automobile":

(62)   a. At the entrance to the parking lot, we should *turn in*.   (adverb)

   b. At the entrance to the parking lot, we should *turn*.

In (63), on the other hand, the meaning changes if *in* is removed. In fact, the (b) version is strange, because we do not know how to interpret the meaning of *turn:*

(63)   a. At midnight, we should *turn in*.   (particle)

   b. ?At midnight, we should *turn*.

Second, as modifiers, adverbs usually add information regarding time, place, or manner. Particles do not. Thus, in (64), the adverb *in* can be replaced by other adverbial modifiers of direction (*left,* for instance), whereas the particle cannot.

(64)   a. At the entrance to the parking lot, we should *turn in*.   (adverb)

   b. At the entrance to the parking lot, we should *turn left*.

   a. At midnight we should *turn in*.   (particle)

   b. ?At midnight we should *turn left*.

Finally, the sentence containing *in* as an adverbial modifier of direction or place can answer a question beginning with *where*. The sentence containing a particle cannot.

(65)   a. At the entrance to the parking lot, where should we turn?
   We should *turn in*.

   b. At midnight, where should we turn?
   ?We should *turn in*.

In is a particle in *At midnight, we should turn in,* not an adverb. It cannot be replaced by an adverb, nor can it be questioned using *where* without completely changing the meaning of the verb.

■ *EXERCISE 5.7*

> The italicized words in the sentences that follow are either prepositions, adverbs, or verb particles. Decide how to classify each. Remember that prepositions have noun or noun phrase objects; verb particles are essential to the meaning of the verb; and adverbs often can be moved within the sentence, or even be deleted.

1. *Since* the cloning *of* Dolly the sheep *in* 1996, scientists have gone *on* to clone mice, rabbits, horses, and cats.
2. The founder *of* Genetic Savings & Clone doled *out* $19 million *to* no purpose, hoping to have a dog cloned.
3. A Texas A&M team that cloned a cat *on* its second try, gave *up* its dog-cloning program several years ago.
4. Part *of* the problem has been the difficulty *of* finding *out* when a dog is *in* heat so that eggs can be harvested.
5. *Recently,* Korean scientists finally seem to have worked *out how* to clone a dog.
6. To clone Snuppy the puppy, the Koreans often put *in* 18- *to* 20-hour days monitoring their laboratory dogs, waiting *patiently for* the right moment.
7. Genetic Savings & Clone is hoping to cut *back on* the inefficiencies related *to* dog cloning, but even if it succeeds, cloning Fido won't be cheap.
8. GS&C is charging $32,000 *for* a cloned cat; pet-lovers will have to dig even *deeper into* their pockets *for* a copy *of* their dog.

■ PRONOUNS ■

One of the most striking distinctions between form classes and structure classes is that form-class words (nouns, verbs, adjectives, and adverbs) are subject to change in form through the addition of derivational and inflectional morphemes. Structure-class words, on the other hand, occur in a single form. Pronouns, however, are an exception to that generalization. Although they are structure words—they depend on other words for their function and meaning—many of them are capable of inflection. We discussed *demonstrative* and *possessive pronouns* in the section on determiners at the beginning of this chapter. We end the chapter on structure words with a discussion of *interrogative* and *relative pronouns*. In this section, we discuss other pronouns: *personal, reflexive, reciprocal,* and *indefinite pronouns.*

Pronouns as Noun-Phrase Substitutes

A **pronoun** is traditionally defined as a "noun substitute," but that is not exactly accurate. Consider what happens if we replace the noun in the sentence *That* *old torn **hat** is lying there* with a pronoun: **That old torn **it** is lying there.* In fact, a pronoun can substitute not only for a noun but also for a whole noun phrase—that is, a noun and whatever modifiers and determiners occur with it. Replacing the noun phrase *that old torn hat* with the pronoun *it* results in a grammatical sentence: *It is lying there.*

However, *It is lying there* is a peculiar sentence. Without any context, we would have no idea what *it* refers to. In our actual use of pronouns, we depend very strongly on either verbal or nonverbal context to determine meaning. If someone spoke that sentence to you while gesturing toward an old torn hat, a hammer someone had lost, or some other object, you would know from that nonverbal gesture what the referent of *it* was. Or the referent might be identified verbally by a preceding sentence, as in the following:

(66)   a. You know *that hammer we lost? It* is lying there.

b. Are you looking for *that old torn hat? It* is lying there.

In such cases, we call the words that identify a pronoun's referent its **antecedent.** *That hammer we lost* is the antecedent for *it* in (66a); *that old torn hat* is the antecedent for *it* in (66b).

Personal Pronouns

Personal pronouns refer to people or things that are physically present or that have been mentioned in the preceding text. In English, pronoun inflections are remnants of an earlier, more elaborate declension of nouns, adjectives, and pronouns; they enable pronouns to be differentiated on the basis of person, number, gender, and case. The **first-** and **second-person personal pronouns** (*I*, *we*, and *you*) are used to refer to the speaker and other participants in a conversation. The **third-person personal pronouns** (*he*, *she*, *it*, and *they*) refer to other persons and things. Unlike the four form classes, whose members number in the thousands and to which new members are constantly being added, the pronouns constitute a small set that is closed—that is, no new members can be added to the set by the derivational processes we have studied. However, like the form classes, some pronouns do show inflectional changes in their forms.

All of the personal pronouns except *you* have distinct forms signaling **number,** either **singular** or **plural.** Only the third-person singular pronouns have distinct forms signaling **gender: masculine** (*he/him*), **feminine** (*she/her*), and **neuter** (*it*). Masculine and feminine personal pronouns are also sometimes used for a few other kinds of referents. Ships and airplanes are frequently considered feminine (*The* Queen Mary *lost some of **her** dignity when **she** was turned into a hotel and tourist attraction*), and sometimes, in rather literary language, abstract ideas like nature and love, countries, geographical features, and cosmic bodies are treated as if they had gender (*Kingly death keeps **his** pale court; France readied **her** forces for war*). The neuter gender form *it* is used to refer to practically all other nonhuman referents.

Pronouns inflect for **case** to show whether they are functioning as subjects of sentences, as objects of verbs or prepositions, or as possessives. Figure 5.8 shows the forms of the personal pronouns in the subject and object case. We have already seen the possessive case in Figure 5.4. The **subject case** (traditionally called the *nominative case*) is considered the base form. As its name implies, the subject case is the form of the personal pronoun used when the pronoun functions as a subject:

SUMMARY			
Personal Pronouns			
		Subject Case	*Object Case*
First-Person			
singular		*I*	*me*
plural		*we*	*us*
Second-Person			
singular		*you*	
plural			
Third-Person			
singular	masculine	*he*	*him*
	feminine	*she*	*her*
	neuter	*it*	
plural		*they*	*them*

Figure 5.8

(67)   *They* rented an apartment.

         Bob revealed that *he* had enrolled in law school.

         In formal usage, the subject case is also used when the pronoun follows *be* or certain other verbs that take subject complements (a topic discussed in Chapter 7). But in informal usage, the object case is frequent:

(68)   Formal   It is *I*.

                       That is *she*.

         Informal   It's *me*.

                       That's *her*.

         The **object case** is used when the pronoun serves in any object function:

(69)   Rodney saw *them*.   (direct object of a verb)
         Rodney showed *her* the apartment.   (indirect object of a verb)
         Rodney showed an apartment to *him*. (object of a preposition)

         Only the second-person *you* and the third-person neuter *it* do not have separate forms for the subject and object cases.

         ### WHAT'S THE USAGE?   *Personal Pronouns*
         The conventions of standard written English require that subject and object case forms be used appropriately, even when informal usage may be somewhat less consistent, as the examples in (68) above illustrate. Another structure that sometimes causes confusion about proper pronoun case is a prepositional phrase with two pronouns as objects, especially when the prepositional phrase comes at the beginning of a sentence, where we expect subjects to be. In this situation, the subject case can sound deceptively correct. However, you should be aware that the substitution of subject for object pronouns in sentences like the following is often stigmatized (considered nonstandard or unacceptable) by grammar handbooks.

(70)   Nonstandard   Just between *you* and *I*, Fred really shouldn't wear those yellow plaid pants.

         Standard   Just between *you* and *me* . . . (*You* and *me* are objects of the preposition *between*.)

         Nonstandard   For *Carla* and *he*, life seems to offer nothing but interesting challenges.

         Standard   For *Carla* and *him*, . . . (*Carla* and *him* are objects of the preposition *for*.)

Nonstandard   He bought *Ed* and *I* a new car.

Standard   He bought *Ed* and *me* a new car. (*Ed* and *me* are objects of the verb *bought*.)

A change seems to be underway in the use of object pronouns in American English. The forms in (70) labeled as nonstandard are often used by speakers of standard English. Will the distinctions between the nonstandard and standard forms cease entirely to function as social status markers in American English? While we await the outcome of this linguistic change, the following analytic tests may help you to check your pronoun usage when you are in doubt:

1. Try the pronouns one at a time, alone. For example, when deciding between *For Carla and I* and *For Carla and me*, omit *Carla and*. Usually, you'll be able to tell at once that *For me* is correct and **For I* is not.

2. Substitute other pronouns for the entire phrase. For example, when deciding between *Just between you and I* and *Just between you and me*, substitute *we* and *us* for *you and I* or *you and me*. You may have a clearer intuition that *Just between **us*** (the equivalent of *you and me*) is correct, but **Just between **we*** (the equivalent of *you and I*) is not.

■ *USAGE EXERCISE 5.8*

In the sentences below, select the pronouns that are most appropriate in formal, standard usage. Be ready to explain why you made the choices you did.

EXAMPLE

Like you and *I/me*, President Smith enjoys billiards and pizza.

Me** is the appropriate choice, because both **you** and **me** are objects of the preposition **like.

1. When you and *he/him* start planning the end-of-the-semester party, drop a note to Eddie and *she/her*.
2. If *he/him* and *she/her* find out in time, they can help plan the refreshments.
3. Our group will provide live music if you let Jason and *I/me* know the date.
4. Unless both *he/him* and *I/me* study this weekend, we may have nothing to celebrate.
5. Professor Snorf is going to ask you and *she/her* whether he will be welcome at the party.

Reflexive Pronouns

When a sentence contains two references to the same noun or noun phrase, one in the subject and one in the predicate, the second becomes a **reflexive pronoun** (one ending in *-self* or *-selves*). The reflexive endings serve as a reminder that the antecedent is to be found within the immediate sentence and not, as is true with other pronouns, in a preceding sentence or in the nonverbal context. In the following examples, subscripts ($_1$) mark words that have the same referent.

(71)   Phil$_1$ criticized Phil$_1$.

   ↓

   Phil$_1$ criticized *himself*$_1$.

   Somehow, our horses$_1$ freed our horses$_1$.

   ↓

   Somehow, our horses$_1$ freed *themselves*$_1$.

   Katherine$_1$ vowed to Katherine$_1$ never again to marry a bookie.

   ↓

   Katherine$_1$ vowed to *herself*$_1$ never again to marry a bookie.

   Another function of the reflexives is to give special emphasis to a noun phrase, either by following that noun phrase immediately or by coming at the end of the sentence. For example:

(72)   Senator Gillis *himself* showed up at our party.

   Joanne prepared the entire report *herself*.

   The forms of the reflexive pronouns are summarized in Figure 5.9.

WHAT'S THE USAGE?   *Reflexive Pronouns*

Usage handbooks advise not using a reflexive pronoun unless its antecedent appears within the same sentence.

(73)   Nonstandard   *Fred* and *myself* produced a fabulous term paper.
   Standard   *Fred* and *I* . . .

   Nonstandard   Their comments about *Betty* and *myself* were vicious.
   Standard   Their comments about *Betty* and *me* . . .

Nevertheless, nonstandard sentences like those in (73) occur frequently in the speech and writing of respected, successful people. Compare your own reactions to the *me/myself* alternatives above with those of your classmates.

SUMMARY		
Reflexive Pronouns		
First-Person		
singular		*myself*
plural		*ourselves*
Second-Person		
singular		*yourself*
plural		*yourselves*
Third-Person		
singular	masculine	*himself*
	feminine	*herself*
	neuter	*itself*
plural		*themselves*

Figure 5.9

Social norms no doubt establish a usage as acceptable before handbooks record the fact. Is that what is happening here?

Reciprocal Pronouns

When two sentences might be needed to describe a two-way action, as in (74), a single sentence, using the **reciprocal pronouns** *each other* and *one another*, may substitute for them.

(74) Cecile loves Ernest, and Ernest loves Cecile.
↓
Cecile and Ernest love *each other*.

Reciprocal pronouns are like reflexives in that they may substitute for the second instance of a repeated noun phrase, but reciprocals are used when two-way actions are involved—that is, when actor and recipient are identical or act mutually. Compare the following:

(75) a. Reflexive   Can you imagine 23 faculty members₁ shouting at *themselves₁*?

b. Reciprocal   Can you imagine 23 faculty members₁ shouting at *one another₁*?

In (75a), each faculty member is presumed to be shouting at himself or herself. In (75b), the members are shouting at other members. (*Each other* tends to be used with reference to two participants and *one another* with reference to more than two, as the examples in (74) and (75) illustrate.)

Indefinite Pronouns

Indefinite pronouns include pronouns made with *one, some, any, no, every,* and *other,* as well as a miscellaneous group of others. They usually have no specific referent and therefore no antecedent, as in these examples:

(76) *Nobody* came to our party.

The personnel office is advertising for *somebody* to do secretarial work.

Some indefinites can be used either as pronouns or as nouns. When they occur alone, without modifiers, they lack specific reference and are interpreted as indefinite pronouns; when they follow articles, they name definite things and are thought to be nouns.

(77) Pronoun   *One* should always be on time.

Noun   That book is *the one* that I ordered.

The majority of the indefinite pronouns are presented in a summary chart, Figure 5.10.

SUMMARY					
Indefinite Pronouns					
one	some	any	none	everyone	another
oneself	someone	anyone	no one	everybody	any other
	somebody	anybody	nobody	everything	no other
	something	anything	nothing		others
many, more, most, enough, few, less, much, either, neither, several, all, both, each					

Figure 5.10

WHAT'S THE USAGE?   *Indefinite Pronouns*

Two personal pronouns—*they* and *you*—also occur as indefinites:

(78)   *They* say an honest man will never get rich.

   You never know what the future will bring.

   You should always treat others as *they* would like to be treated.

The indefinites *they* and *you* can be paraphrased as "people," "someone," or "no one," depending on the context. However, because *they* and *you* normally refer to specific persons or antecedents, their use as indefinites tends to be contradictory. Used as indefinites, the pronouns appear to refer to someone specific when in fact they do not. Careful writers try to avoid such possibly misleading vagueness, choosing the versions in (79b) and (79d):

(79)   a. They are going to raise taxes again.

   b. The state legislature is going to raise taxes again.

   c. You can't find a house for less than $250,000 in our town.

   d. No houses are available for less than $250,000 in our town.

Some of the indefinite pronouns continue to stimulate arguments about proper usage. Which option would you choose in the following examples?

(80)   Somebody always forgets to do *his/her/their* homework.

   Nobody could remember where *he/she/they was/were* supposed to sit.

   Everyone took *his/her/their* shoes off.

In each example, the antecedent for the italicized personal pronouns is an indefinite pronoun. Grammatically, *somebody*, *nobody*, and *everyone* are singular, and it would therefore seem to be grammatically correct to choose a singular pronoun, either *his* or *her*, to refer back to them. Sometimes context makes that decision easy, as in the third example, if we revise it just a bit:

(81)   Everyone in the Girl Scout troop took off *her* shoes.

However, most of the time, we either don't know the sex of the persons that indefinite pronouns like *everyone* are referring to or the indefinite words are referring to a mixed group of males and females. In these situations, conflict arises. On the one hand, older conventional rules of usage recommend using the masculine form as a generic pronoun—that is, to refer to anyone, male or female, in a group of mixed or unknown sex. On the other hand, many writers and speakers wish to avoid the possibly sexist practice of using a masculine pronoun to refer to girls and women, thereby appearing to deny their presence and diminish their importance. A glance back at the summary chart of personal pronouns (Figure 5.8) shows the bind into which English places us, for we have no third-person singular personal pronoun that can refer to a human without specifying gender. One rather awkward solution to this dilemma is to use expressions like *he or she* and *his or her*:

(82)   Somebody forgot *his or her* hat.

An alternative that is currently chosen frequently in American English is the gender-neutral plural:

(83)   Somebody forgot *their* hat.

The attractiveness of this usage is clear: The third-person plural pronoun refers to males and females equally. Using the plural pronoun *they* with the indefinites *everyone* and *everybody* may seem even more natural than with *somebody,* as these words, in spite of being grammatically singular, seem to refer to groups of people.

(84)   Everyone forgot *their* books.

One way to avoid this number-agreement problem while uncomfortable language change is occurring is to use plural alternatives to singular indefinite pronouns or singular nouns in your writing:

(85)   Instead of this: Everyone forgot their books.
             Use this: All the students forgot their books.

             Instead of this: Everyone came in their own cars.
             Use this: The guests all came in their own cars.

This same strategy works when the antecedent is a noun rather than an indefinite pronoun:

(86)   Instead of this: Every citizen should exercise his or her right to vote.
             Use this: All citizens should exercise their right to vote.

             Instead of this: A doctor must do what is best for his patients.
             Use this: Doctors should do what is best for their patients.

By revising sentences in this way, you can be grammatically correct and semantically accurate without violating traditional conventions of good usage or using sexist forms of expression.

■ *USAGE EXERCISE 5.9*_____

> Revise the following sentences so that they are semantically accurate, grammatically correct, and stylistically graceful. For class discussion, note which sentences you feel are satisfactory as written.
>
> 1. If anyone wants to enter the watermelon-eating-contest, he or she should sign up today.
> 2. Each contestant should give his completed application to Maureen.
> 3. Both Perry and myself are reluctant to fill out an application.
> 4. Last year, no one could finish his fourth watermelon.
> 5. Someone couldn't even eat his third watermelon.
> 6. Everyone who takes part in the contest will receive a watermelon T-shirt with their name printed on it.

▬▬▬▬ *CONJUNCTIONS* ▬▬▬▬

The structure class of **conjunctions** includes two types—*coordinating* and *subordinating conjunctions*—together with a related category traditionally considered with conjunctions, *conjunctive adverbs*. All of the conjunctions have the function of *joining* grammatical structures; however, each group does so in quite distinctive ways. It is probably worthwhile to memorize the set of coordinating conjunctions. There are not many, and nothing about their form or behavior will help you identify them. If you know which conjunctions are coordinators, you can use tests to differentiate between the much larger sets of remaining ones: conjunctive adverbs and subordinators.

Coordinating Conjunctions

The prototypical **coordinating conjunction** (and no doubt the most frequently used) is *and*. The other common members of the group are *but, or, yet, nor, for,* and *so*. **Coordinators** join grammatical structures of similar form, transforming them into a single grammatical unit. They join words;

(87)   John *and* Mary

phrases (sequences of words that can substitute for a noun, verb, adjective, or adverb);

(88)   very tasty *but* rather fattening

under the stairway *or* in the closet

washed by the rain *and* dried by the sun

or entire clauses (sequences of words containing both a subject and a predicate);

(89)   after he graduated from college *yet* before he got a job

if she won the lottery *and* if her junk bonds tripled in value

When single words or phrases are joined, the result is a *phrase*. When two sentences are joined by coordinating conjunctions, the result is a **compound sentence.**

(90)   Pedro threw a temper tantrum, *but* his sister ignored him.

Kabira stayed home, *for* she had work to do.

Either someone is going to have to start cooking, *or* we will have to go out for dinner.

Correlative Conjunctions

Correlative conjunctions are coordinating conjunctions (*and, or, but*) paired with other words that extend the meaning of the first: *both…and, either…or, neither…nor,* and *not only…but also.* Like the other coordinators, the correlative conjunctions connect syntactic units that, according to convention, have the same grammatical form: a single word can be joined to a word, a phrase to a phrase, or a clause to a clause.

(91)   *both* students *and* faculty   (two nouns)

not only composes the music   (two verb phrases)
but also writes the lyrics

Either you know the answer *or* you don't.   (two clauses)

Most of the coordinating and correlative conjunctions can join any kind of grammatical unit—words, phrases, clauses, or sentences—but some have a more limited distribution. The coordinators *for, yet,* and *nor* (unless accompanied by *neither*) join only sentences.

(92)   She hasn't telephoned us, *nor* has she written.

She has *neither* telephoned *nor* written.

But not: *She hasn't telephoned *nor* written.

The correlative pair *both . . . and* does not join complete sentences but can join any of the other structures that occur within sentences:

(93)   He offended both *his friends* and *his enemies.*   (two noun phrases)

Both *because he was tired* and *because he*   (two dependent clauses)
had no money, Charlie decided to spend the
evening with a good book.

WHAT'S THE USAGE? *Punctuating Sentences with Coordinating Conjunctions*
As our examples of sentences joined by coordinating conjunctions illustrate,
a comma precedes the coordinator in a compound sentence:

(94) The committee didn't want to be disturbed, *so* they closed the door.

Either she must have this report by tomorrow, *or* she will have to cancel the
board meeting.

If the sentences are very short, the comma may be omitted:

(95) She sang and he hummed.

However, no comma occurs when the two units joined are less than full
sentences:

(96) peanut butter and jelly

in a cup or in a glass

If three or more words are joined, the result is a list (or series), and commas follow each item in the list except the last:

(97) We gobbled *peanuts, popcorn, **and** potato chips* at the circus.

The marines serve with dedication *in the sky, on the sea, **or** on the land.*

Some usage authorities advise that a comma is not needed before the coordinator in cases like these. However, placing a comma before the conjunction
in a series of three or more items can often prevent confusion and ambiguity.
For example,

(98) Wilbur has always respected his parents, Albert Einstein and Mother Theresa.

Are the parents Albert Einstein and Mother Theresa, or has Wilbur respected
four people? A comma clarifies the meaning.

(99) Wilbur has always respected his parents, Albert Einstein, and Mother Theresa.

Conjunctive Adverbs

Conjunctive adverbs are on the periphery of both conjunctions and adverbs. They are like conjunctions in that they connect and signal relationships between two sentences; they are like adverbs in the kinds of meaning they express:

(100)   Contrast

however, instead, nevertheless, on the contrary, on the other hand, still, having said that

Margot's friends made reservations at an expensive restaurant; *however,* they couldn't really afford to eat there.

Addition

also, besides, furthermore, in addition, moreover

My driver's license has expired; *furthermore,* my bus pass has lapsed.

Cause and effect

accordingly, as a result, consequently, hence, so, therefore, thus

The electricity is off; *as a result,* everything in the freezer has melted.

Example or restatement

for example, that is

Robert is a serious collector of jazz recordings; *for example,* he owns practically everything Miles Davis ever recorded.

Time

afterward(s), earlier, finally, in the meantime, later, meanwhile, then

On the way here, I received a speeding ticket; *afterwards,* I had a flat tire.

The clauses joined by conjunctive adverbs retain their status as independent sentences. They are punctuated with either semicolons or periods, as though they contained no conjunction at all:

(101)   a. We are going to go to the movies; afterwards, we will have dinner.

b. We are going to go to the movies. Afterwards, we will have dinner.

Like other adverbs, conjunctive adverbs can be moved about in the sentence. They are usually set off from the rest of the sentence by commas, as

<table>
<tr><td colspan="2" align="center">**SUMMARY**</td></tr>
<tr><td colspan="2" align="center">*Coordinators and Conjunctive Adverbs*</td></tr>
<tr><td colspan="2">**Coordinating Conjunctions**
and, but, or, nor, yet, for, so
Correlative Conjunctions
both . . . and, either . . . or, neither . . . nor, not only . . . but also</td></tr>
<tr><td colspan="2">**Conjunctive Adverbs**</td></tr>
<tr><td>Contrast, opposition</td><td>however, instead, nevertheless, on the contrary, on the other hand, still, anyway</td></tr>
<tr><td>Addition</td><td>also, besides, furthermore, in addition, in fact, moreover</td></tr>
<tr><td>Cause and effect, conclusion</td><td>accordingly, as a result, consequently, hence, therefore, thus</td></tr>
<tr><td>Example, restatement</td><td>for example, for instance, namely, that is</td></tr>
<tr><td>Time</td><td>afterward(s), earlier, finally, in the meantime, later, meanwhile, then, subsequently</td></tr>
<tr><td>Choice</td><td>otherwise</td></tr>
<tr><td>Emphasis</td><td>indeed, that is to say, to be sure</td></tr>
</table>

Figure 5.11

in (102a) and (102b), although some writers omit the comma when the conjunctive adverb comes at the beginning of the sentence, as in (102c):

(102)   a. For years, she had listened to his complaints; she decided, *finally,* to divorce him.

b. For years, she had listened to his complaints; *finally,* she decided to divorce him.

c. For years she had listened to his complaints; *finally* she decided to divorce him.

Figure 5.11 lists the most common coordinating conjunctions and conjunctive adverbs.

Subordinating Conjunctions

As we have seen, coordinators, correlatives, and conjunctive adverbs all join sentences or parts of sentences that are grammatically *equivalent.* In contrast, **subordinating conjunctions** (or **subordinators**) create **complex sentences** by joining grammatically *unequal* elements: a subordinate (or dependent) clause to a main (independent) clause.

We present a detailed discussion of the differences between independent and dependent clauses in Chapter 9. For the present, we point out merely that a subordinate clause is one that cannot stand alone as a sentence; it begins with a word that makes it dependent on some other clause. The main clause of a sentence is the clause that can stand alone; it is complete on its own. (The reverse arrow in the examples that follow means "is derived from" or "comes from" whatever follows it.)

(103)   Harold sang old sea ditties *while* he prepared dinner.

↑

Harold sang old sea ditties.   (main clause)

while he prepared dinner   (subordinate clause)

Subordinating conjunctions cannot move about in their sentences; they always come first in the subordinate clause. However, the entire clause containing the subordinator can often be moved to the front of the sentence, as in (104b). When a subordinate clause appears in the initial position of a sentence, a comma follows it:

(104)   a. He couldn't order a steak dinner   (No comma needed)
        because *he had forgotten his wallet.*

        b. ***Because*** *he had forgotten his wallet,*   (Comma needed)
        he couldn't order a steak dinner.

The subordinate clause performs an adverbial function in the complex sentence—that is, it modifies a verb, an adjective, an adverb, or the entire sentence, providing information about time, place, manner, and so forth. In Chapter 9, we analyze adverbial clauses in more detail; here we simply introduce the structure-word group that makes such clauses possible. Subordinators fall into subgroups according to the kinds of meaning they convey, as summarized in Figure 5.12.

Sometimes students feel unsure of their ability to distinguish between subordinating conjunctions and conjunctive adverbs. It may help to remember that the conjunctive adverb can be moved about within its clause, but its clause cannot move. In contrast, the subordinating conjunction cannot move; it must always come at the beginning of its clause. Because the subordinator creates an adverbial modifier, the entire clause that contains it can usually be moved about in the sentence of which it is a part. Notice the difference in the behavior of subordinators and conjunctive adverbs.

(105)   **Subordinator**
        a. He shortened his talk ***so that*** *they could ask questions.*

SUMMARY	
Subordinating Conjunctions	
Time	after, as, as soon as, before, once, since, until, when, while
Manner	as, as if, as though, like
Contrast, opposition	although, though, whereas, while, except (that)
Cause and effect	because, in that, now that, since, so that
Condition	if, in case, provided (that), unless
Purpose	so that, in order that
Comparison	as . . . as, more than, less than, than

Figure 5.12

b. ***So that*** *they could ask questions,* he shortened his talk.

The entire subordinate clause in (105), *so that they could ask questions,* is adverbial, and like other adverbials, it can be moved to different positions in the main clause. In (106), the clause introduced by the conjunctive adverb is independent. *Consequently, they could ask questions* cannot be moved to precede *He shortened his talk.* However, because the conjunction itself is adverbial, it is movable, as is illustrated in (106c).

(106) **Conjunctive Adverb**

a. He shortened his talk; ***consequently,*** *they could ask questions.*

b. *****Consequently,** they could ask questions; he shortened his talk.

c. He shortened his talk; they could, **consequently,** ask questions.

Differences Between Subordinators and Prepositions

Some of the words listed as subordinators also occur as prepositions. Remember that you can recognize a preposition by the fact that it is followed by a noun phrase object. A subordinator, in contrast, is followed by an entire clause that, without the subordinator and with appropriate punctuation, could be an independent sentence.

(107)   He insulted me ***before*** *he left the room.*   (*Before* is a subordinator.)
He left the room. = clause

He insulted me ***before*** *our dinner.*   (*Before* is a preposition.)
our dinner = noun phrase

■ *EXERCISE 5.10*

> Decide whether the italicized words in the following sentences are preposi-
> tions or subordinating conjunctions. Remember that a preposition precedes
> a noun phrase (a noun and its modifiers); a subordinating conjunctions joins
> two clauses (structures containing both subject and verb).

1. *While* the British military were stationed in Bermuda, their summer uniform included shorts and knee socks *during* the hot months.
2. *After* the military departed, Bermuda businessmen continued to wear just-above-
   the-knee shorts and knee socks with shirts, ties, and jackets.
3. *Since* the 1920s, Bermuda shorts have been accepted as formal attire only *if* they
   were worn with cuffed knee socks and leather slip-on loafers.
4. They were even considered appropriate business attire for members of Parliament
   until ten years ago.
5. *Since* that time, Bermuda has begun to rid itself of its British colonial identity and
   its formality.
6. *After* dress-down Friday became a daily fashion, Bermuda shorts spread to the
   younger generation.
7. *Since* the shorts are suited to Bermuda summer weather, they have remained popular with young businessmen, who wear them without ties and jackets, and without
   the knee socks.

■ *EXERCISE 5.11*

> List all of the conjunctions in the sentences below; then, identify whether
> each is a coordinating conjunction, subordinating conjunction, or con-
> junctive adverb.

1. After the Baseball Hall of Fame opened in Cooperstown, N.Y., in 1939, fans came
   from all over the U.S. to honor both the players and the sport.
2. Subsequently, other sports followed suit. A Pro Football Hall of Fame opened in
   1963, and a Pro Basketball Hall of Fame followed in 1968.
3. Today there are museums devoted to Motorsports, Stock Car Racing, and Auto
   Racing; nevertheless, five major cities are seeking the right to open a NASCAR Hall
   of Fame.
4. Because a hall of fame can create tourism dollars for a community, the notion has
   spread from honoring celebrated athletes to honoring nearly anyone or any hobby.
5. It has already been receiving school groups for over a year, but the Trucking
   Hall of Fame near Des Moines is not scheduled to open until next year. It will
   honor not only trucks, but also drivers who have had long careers and excellent
   safety records.

6. A Beer Hall of Fame is set to have a rooftop beach, several beer gardens, and a karaoke bar when it opens in Cincinnati in 2007. However, no one knows what criteria will have to be satisfied before someone can be inducted into the Beer Hall of Fame.

WHAT'S THE USAGE? *Comma Splices and Run-On Sentences*

Among the various conventions of standard written English that writers are expected to follow, few assume greater importance than appropriately marking the boundaries of a sentence by placing a capital letter at one end and a period or other end punctuation (such as an exclamation point or question mark) at the other. Inseparable from the written conventions of marking sentence boundaries is the proper use of coordinating conjunctions, conjunctive adverbs, and subordinating conjunctions to join sentences and clauses. When an appropriate conjunction is not used, the result can be a comma splice or a run-on sentence.

A **comma splice** results when two independent sentences are joined solely by a comma:

(108)   *He is always boasting, no one seems to mind.

A **run-on sentence,** really two sentences without any punctuation or conjunction between them, is identical to the comma splice but without the comma:

(109)   *He is always boasting no one seems to mind.

A period or semicolon after *boasting* correctly marks the sentence boundary:

(110)   He is always boasting. No one seems to mind.
         He is always boasting; no one seems to mind.

However, conjunctions offer other alternatives for linking these two sentences. They not only join two clauses but also express relationships between the two.

(111)   He is always boasting, *but* no one seems to mind.   (coordinator)
         He is always boasting; *however,* no one seems   (conjunctive adverb)
         to mind.
         Although he is always boasting, no one seems   (subordinator)
         to mind.

Attending an American high school or college virtually guarantees that you have experienced personally or at least observed the stigma attached to violating the convention that forbids comma splices and run-ons in formal, edited writing. Somehow, many people in the United States have come to equate even minor failures to observe this convention with near illiteracy. While it may seem irrational to place so much weight on what is, after all, only one redundant detail in the complex code of the English writing system, you, as an individual, have little power to modify what has become so well established. Until the slow but inevitable processes of linguistic change alter or at least relax these conventions, it will be of great value for you to observe them scrupulously when writing for an audience that expects carefully edited work. Figure 5.13 will help you to keep in mind the main alternatives for handling potential sentence boundaries in written English.

RULES OF THUMB	
Words Used to Connect Clauses	
Coordinators and Correlatives	
and, but, or, nor, yet, for, so either . . . or, neither . . . nor, not only . . . but also	**Punctuate with a comma**: The wind blew softly, and the crickets chirped. Either the teacher is late, or we are early.
Subordinators	
Examples *after, since, when, although, whereas, because, so that,* etc.	**Punctuate with a comma if subordinate clause comes first:** The mosquitoes became active after the sun set. After the sun set, the mosquitoes became active.
Conjunctive Adverbs	
Examples *afterward(s), later, however, nevertheless, as a result, besides, for example,* etc.	**Punctuate with a semicolon or period. Set off the conjunctive adverb with a comma, or with a pair of commas if it is inside its clause:** Ted spoke; however, no one listened. Ted spoke. However, no one listened. Ted spoke. No one, however, listened.

Figure 5.13

■ *USAGE EXERCISE 5.12*_____

Correct each of the following run-ons and comma splices in at least two ways, using a coordinating conjunction, a conjunctive adverb, or a subordinating conjunction. For any one sentence write corrections drawing on connectors from different categories. (You may want to rearrange elements of the sentence.) Pay close attention to the logical relationship between the two clauses you are joining, and choose a connector that clarifies that relationship. An example has been done for you.

EXAMPLE

A run-on sentence: *You can't be a good example, then you'll have to be a horrible warning.*

a. Punctuation: *You can't be a good example. Then you'll have to be a horrible warning.*

b. Coordinator: *You can't be a good example, so then you'll have to be a horrible warning.*

c. Subordinator: *If you can't be a good example, then you'll have to be a horrible warning.*

d. Conjunctive adverb: *You can't be a good example; as a result then, you'll have to be a horrible warning.*

1. Everything seems to be going well, you have obviously forgotten something.
2. The early bird gets the worm the second mouse gets the cheese.
3. Be nice to your kids, they will choose your nursing home.
4. There can't be a crisis today, my schedule is already full.
5. You can smile when things go wrong, you have someone else to blame.
6. Hard work pays off in the future laziness pays off now.
7. He who asks is a fool for five minutes he who does not ask is a fool forever.
8. God could not be everywhere he made mothers.

■ *EXERCISE 5.13*_____

Practical Applications

Consider the sentences you created for Exercise 5.12 and choose the version(s) you think are most effective. Be prepared to discuss why you have chosen some and rejected others.

RELATIVES

We might well have included the short list of *relatives* (*who, whom, whose, which, that*) with the pronouns we discussed earlier, but because they share an important feature with subordinating conjunctions, we have included them here. Both subordinating conjunctions and relatives connect a dependent clause to the rest of a sentence. The clauses connected by subordinators usually function adverbially in the sentence—that is, modifying verbs, adjectives, adverbs, or the sentence as a whole. The clauses connected by the relatives (called **relative clauses**) function adjectivally within a sentence, modifying nouns as part of a noun phrase. In the next two examples, the relative clauses are italicized. Notice that *who* is used when the relative functions as the subject of its clause and *whom* when it is the object of the verb.

(112)   a. [The woman] ***who** married Rusty* is an aerospace engineer.

        b. [The woman] ***whom** Rusty married* is an aerospace engineer.

Like other pronouns, the **relative pronoun** has an *antecedent* (a preceding noun to which it refers). Here and in the following examples in this section, the antecedents of relatives are set off in brackets. *The woman* is the antecedent for *who* in (112a) and for *whom* in (112b); the relative clauses specify which woman is the topic of the sentences. In addition to referring to an antecedent outside of the relative clause, a relative has a grammatical function within its own clause. In (112a), *who* is the subject of *married,* and in (112b), *whom* is the direct object of *married.* If we replace the relative pronouns with their antecedents, the difference is clearer:

(113)   a. ***who*** married Rusty
          ↑
          The woman married Rusty.

        b. ***whom*** Rusty married
          ↑
          Rusty married *the woman.*

In (113a), *who* occupies the same position as *The woman:* the subject slot. In (113b), *whom* and *the woman* are both objects of the verb *married.* We have more to say about how to choose between *who* and *whom* when we discuss relative clauses in Chapter 9.

Whose is the possessive form of the relative. Within a relative clause, *whose* functions as a determiner, just as a possessive pronoun or noun would do in its place:

(114)   [The bicyclist] ***whose*** *helmet fell off* kept riding.
↑

The bicyclist kept riding.
The bicyclist's helmet fell off.

The bicyclist is the antecedent of *whose.*

Who, whom, and *whose* refer to human antecedents and, varying with the speaker, to some animals. *That* has a single form, which functions as either subject or object in relative clauses. It can refer to both human and nonhuman antecedents.

(115)   [The train trip] ***that*** *intrigues me most*   (*That* functions as subject and
        visits the Copper Canyon in Mexico.   refers to inanimate noun, *trip.*)

        [The child] ***that*** *they adopted*   (*That* functions as direct object of
        spoke his first words at six months.   *adopted* and refers to human
                                                  noun, *child.*)

Which also has a single form, which serves in both subject and object function. Its antecedents are things, animals, and sometimes a general idea expressed by the rest of the sentence:

(116)   a. [Those apple trees], ***which*** *belong to our neighbor,* bear beautiful fruit.

        b. [Carlo read all of *War and Peace* over the weekend], ***which*** *astounded his friends.*

In (116b), no specific word or phrase is the antecedent of the relative; instead, *which* refers to the idea expressed in the entire preceding portion of the sentence. Some authorities and usage handbooks consider it an error to use a pronoun like *which* without a specific noun or noun phrase as an antecedent.

Because *which* and *that* have no possessive form, *whose* often refers to inanimate antecedents as well:

(117)   He tossed aside [the lock] ***whose*** *key was missing.*

        The company manufactured [a device] ***whose*** *circuits were made of a secret, superconducting ceramic material.*

SUMMARY	
Relatives	
Pronominal relatives	who, whom, whose, which, that
Adverbial relatives	where, when, why

Figure 5.14

Perhaps *whose* is used because the alternatives seem overly complex. The alternative to the relatives in (117) would be *the lock to which the key was missing* and *a device for which the circuits were made of a secret, superconducting ceramic material.*

In addition to the relative pronouns already mentioned, *where, when,* and *why* can function as **relative adverbs.** For example:

(118)   We visited [the place] ***where*** *the Vikings landed.*

Our great-grandparents lived at [a time] ***when*** *the environment was less polluted.*

Please explain [the reason] ***why*** *you can't turn in the assignment.*

These relative clauses function adjectivally: They modify the nouns bracketed in the sentences above. However, the relatives *where, when,* and *why* function adverbially *within their own clauses,* as you can see if we rephrase the relative clauses as independent sentences:

(119)   The Vikings landed *there* (or *at that place*).

The environment was less polluted *then* (or *at some time*).

You can't turn in the assignment *for some reason.*

Many of the words listed in the summary of relatives (Figure 5.14) also function in other ways, including as interrogatives, the subject of the next section. When they are relatives, these words have antecedents (a preceding noun to which they refer); if you find no antecedent, the word may be functioning as something other than a relative.

■ *EXERCISE 5.14*

Underline the relatives in the following sentences. Circle their antecedents.

1. Abraham Lincoln is the only ex-President who has his own national association of impressionists.

2. The Association of Lincoln Presenters has attracted 160 Lincoln impersonators since 1990, the year when it was founded.

3. There are many reasons why Lincoln attracts so many impersonators.

4. His honesty and integrity are the basis on which most build their characterizations.

5. One man got the idea of becoming an impersonator at a mall, where he learned that the man that he was watching was making money by pretending to be Lincoln.

6. The pretend Lincolns, most of whom are white and over 60, do not all have Lincoln's build.

7. The impersonators trade secrets online, such as places where you can buy a beaver top hat like Lincoln's.

8. The pretend Lincolns are especially popular with children, whose favorite question is "Aren't you dead?"

INTERROGATIVES

The **interrogative** and **relative** structure classes have almost identical members. Often called *question words* because of their function or *wh-words* because of their most common initial letters, this short list includes *who, whom, whose, which, what, where, why, when,* and *how.*

Interrogatives begin direct questions. In addition to signaling that a question will follow, each plays some grammatical role in the sentence that it begins. Sometimes the grammatical function of the interrogative word is clearer if you answer the question, substituting an appropriate word for the interrogative. In (120a), *who* is the subject of the sentence, having the same role as *someone* in the answer. In (120b), *which* is a determiner preceding the noun *cheesecake,* functioning like *this* in the answer. And in (120c), *when* plays an adverbial role, standing for a time expression in that sentence.

(120) a. *Who* left this envelope on my desk?   (question)
          Someone left this envelope on my desk.   (answer)

       b. *Which* cheesecake did they like best?   (question)
          They liked *this* cheesecake best.   (answer)

       c. *When* are you leaving?   (question)
          You are leaving *then/at some time.*   (answer)

Interrogatives also function to introduce indirect questions:

(121) I wonder **who** *left the envelope on my desk.*

       Tony asked them **which** *cheesecake they liked best.*

The indirect questions—*who left the envelope on my desk* and *which cheesecake they liked best*—are dependent clauses functioning as the objects of

SUMMARY	
Interrogatives	
Pronominal interrogatives	who, whom, whose, which, what *whatever*
Adverbial interrogatives	where, why, when, how

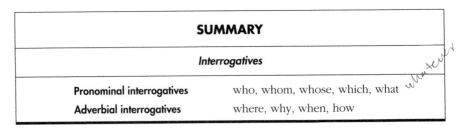

Figure 5.15

wonder and *asked* in our examples. Chapter 10 deals more extensively with the function of such clauses. A summary of interrogatives is provided in Figure 5.15.

■ *EXERCISE 5.15*_____

Underline the interrogatives and double underline the relatives in the following sentences. Remember that relatives have antecedents, whereas interrogatives do not. Circle the antecedent of each relative.

1. When they are asked what the most feared fault in the U.S. is, most people name the San Andreas, which is 750 miles long.
2. After seeing years of no major activity along the fault line, many scientists believe the pressure on it is reaching a point where something will have to give.
3. No one can guess where the next quake will be centered.
4. Researchers have set out "trap lines" that are designed to catch even the slightest movement along the San Andreas.
5. They are also building the San Andreas Fault Observatory at Depth (SAFOD), an underground observatory at a point where a quiet section of the fault subject only to microquakes meets a violent section of the fault.
6. What scientist hope to find are precursors signaling that a quake is coming.
7. Recently a magnitude-6 earthquake, whose rumbles were felt far away, surprised researchers, who found nothing unusual in advance of the quake except for very small signs that showed stress may have increased the day before it took place.
8. Whatever happens along the fault in the future, scientists hope SAFOD will eventually help them predict when and where an earthquake will strike.

SUMMARY

For the most part, the structure classes are small, closed sets with little lexical meaning, whose members tend to occur in a single form. Their primary function is to signal grammatical structure and relationships. Determiners are cues to and supply aspects of meaning for a following noun. Articles (*a/an* and *the*) are prototypical for the entire determiner group. Auxiliaries accompany or substitute for main verbs and signal important elements of grammatical meaning within the intricate verbal system. The modals and *have, be,* and *do* constitute the main English auxiliaries. Qualifiers accompany adjectives and adverbs, either increasing or reducing the intensity of the quality denoted by the form-class word. *Very* provides a useful prototype of this class of structure words. Prepositions function to connect their object noun phrases to other parts of the sentence. A preposition with its noun phrase object constitutes a prepositional phrase, which may function as either an adjectival or adverbial modifier. The personal, reflexive, reciprocal, and indefinite pronouns have a close grammatical relationship with nouns and noun phrases, and many of them, unlike prototypical structure-class words, undergo changes in form similar to those that characterize nouns. Coordinating conjunctions join grammatically equivalent units—whole sentences and their parts. Conjunctive adverbs connect complete sentences, signalling the logical relationships between them. Subordinating conjunctions link subordinate clauses as adverbial modifiers to verbs, adjectives, adverbs, and whole sentences. Relatives link relative clauses to the nouns or noun phrases they modify. Interrogatives introduce direct and indirect questions. All of these structure classes, as well as other function words and groups yet to be described, play significant roles in the grammatical structures introduced in later chapters.

REVIEW EXERCISES

Structure Identification

Identify the structure class/subclass to which the italicized words in the following sentences belong.

1. *When* we first arrived at Camp Runamok, *did* you notice the *two* nervous-looking campers *whose* jackets bulged *as if* they *might* each *be* carrying *rather* large quantities of food *under their* arms?

2. *Some of* the campers grumbled *fairly* loudly about the sun reflecting *off* the shimmering waters of Lake Potawatawichi, *which had* temporarily interfered with *our fourth* attempt to signal the girls at Camp Rogununda.

3. Harold gathered *up all his* pet snails quickly *enough* to keep them hidden *from one* tent counselor, *but neither he nor his* buddies *could* understand *why the* camp cook was eyeing them *with* so much interest.

4. *Our* camp counselor, *whose* nickname was "The Dome," was *rather* sensitive *about* being bald. It was, *therefore, quite* natural that we, *his most* devoted campers, presented *him with a* different wig *at* the end of our stay.

Pronouns

Indicate whether the italicized pronouns in the following sentences are personal, possessive, reflexive, reciprocal, indefinite, relative, or interrogative.

1. Judy and *I* batted tennis balls back and forth while *we* waited for *our* partners to arrive.

2. Geoff tried to repair by *himself* the dripping faucet *that* was driving *him* crazy.

3. The difference between *you* and *him* is that *everyone* knows *you* and no one knows *him*.

4. Does *anyone* know *whose* book is lying on the desk?

5. *One* can only hope that *everyone who* is seated in the back of the auditorium can hear *us*.

6. Motivated by *their* hatred for *each other, which* started two seasons ago, the two football teams worked *themselves* into a frenzy.

7. Because *your* cactus preserves were the best of the jellies *that* were entered in the competition, *you* should have won first prize.

8. *Someone* ought to ask *who* is scheduled to give a report next week.

Practical Applications: Using Structure Words Effectively

Try to combine the sentences below into a coherent, correctly punctuated paragraph. Use pronouns, conjunctions, and other structure words to provide transition and avoid repetition.

1. In November 2000, Merv Grazinski bought a new 32-foot Winnebago motor home.

2. Merv Grazinski was on his way home from the Winnebago agency.

3. Merv Grazinski entered a freeway.

4. Merv Grazinski set the cruise control at 70 mph.

5. Merv Grazinski left the driver's seat.

6. Merv Grazinski went to the back of the Winnebago.

7. Merv Grazinski started to make himself a cup of coffee.

8. The Winnebago left the freeway.

9. The Winnebago crashed.

10. The Winnebago overturned.

11. Merv Grazinski sued the manufacturer.

12. The Winnebago handbook had not advised Merv Grazinski that Merv Grazinski should not leave the steering wheel unattended.

13. Merv Grazinski won his lawsuit.

14. Merv Grazinski was awarded $1,750,000.

15. Merv Grazinski was awarded a new Winnebago.[1]

Practical Applications: Missing Structure Words

Each of the following headlines has two possible meanings. Write two versions of each headline by adding missing structure words where needed.

1. BODY FOUND IN VAN DONATED TO SALVATION ARMY
   (*The Kansas City Star*, 16 August 2002)

2. AMERICAN ACCUSED OF DESERTING HOSPITALIZED
   ([Springfield, Illinois] *The State Journal-Register*, 19 July 2004)

3. CELLPHONE MESSAGE LEADS BELGIAN POLICE TO MURDER SUSPECTS
   (*The Vancouver Sun*, 18 August 2004)

4. REPORTS ON BIN LADEN DRYING UP
   ([Minneapolis-St. Paul] *The Star Tribune*, 18 December 2001)

5. DEER AND TURKEY HUNT FOR DISABLED PEOPLE
   ([Newark, Ohio] *The Advocate*, 19 October 2002)

6. SOFTWARE HELPS BLIND COMPUTER USERS
   (*Detroit Free Press*, 12 September 2002)

KEY TERMS

antecedent
article
  definite
  indefinite
auxiliary verb
  be auxiliary
  do auxiliary
  have auxiliary
  modal auxiliary
case
  subject case
  object case
comma splice
complex sentence
compound sentence
conjunction
  conjunctive adverb
  coordinating conjunction,
    coordinator
  correlative conjunction
  subordinating conjunction,
    subordinator
content word
demonstrative
determiner
function word

interrogative clause
  interrogative pronoun
  interrogative adverb
meaning
  functional meaning
  grammatical meaning
  lexical meaning
phrasal verb
prepositional phrase
  object of a preposition
  preposition (simple, phrasal)
pronoun
  indefinite pronoun
  personal pronoun
    first, second, third person
  possessive pronoun
  reciprocal pronoun
  reflexive pronoun
qualifier
relative clause
  relative adverb
  relative pronoun
run-on sentence
structure word
structure-class word
verb particle

ENDNOTE

1. This is one of the most famous of the many "urban legends" that appears regularly in print and is used as proof that our legal system is insane. Like many of the "legends," this Winnebago story is completely false.

Phrases 6

CHAPTER PREVIEW

Chapter 6 introduces the kinds of phrases that are combined to create sentences, including noun phrases, verb phrases, adjective phrases, and adverb phrases. We conclude with the main verb phrase, the verb combined with whatever helping verbs are used with it to form complex verb forms.

CHAPTER GOALS

At the end of this chapter, you should be able to

- Identify and diagram the most important *constituents* of sentences: *noun phrases, verb phrases, adjective phrases,* and *adverb phrases.*
- Understand and use the *Main Verb Formula.*
- Understand the differences among *time, tense,* and *aspect.*
- Recognize the difference between *main verbs* and *auxiliary verbs.*
- Recognize the meaning of *modal auxiliaries.*

SUBJECTS AND PREDICATES

Sentences are spoken one word at a time, and they are heard that way as well. Listeners do not, however, understand the meaning of sentences by interpreting one word after another. In fact, processing language word by word would put such a strain on short-term memory that we would be unable to comprehend long, complex sentences. We would lose our place, as we do when we hear a long string of unrelated numbers. We simplify the understanding process as we listen or read by dividing information into meaningful chunks.

At the sentence level, the largest segments into which we divide the material are **subject** and **predicate.** The linguistic division of information into subjects and predicates reflects what may be a universal trait of human perception. We tend to see two aspects of events—things and actions—and in describing them, we usually name first the thing most prominently involved (the *topic* or *subject* of the sentence) and then the event that involved it or what is said about it (the *comment* about the topic, or the *predicate* of the sentence).

Users of any language share expectations about the way information will be organized in discourse, and the speaker who wishes to be understood will arrange information according to those expectations. For a conversation to take place, the speaker must have something to say, and the listener must be able to understand it. Language structure provides a pattern that helps the speaker to present information in predictable patterns and the listener to process that information efficiently.

To begin with, the listener assumes (1) that there is a topic the speaker wants to talk about and (2) that the speaker has something to say about it. An English speaker usually names the thing to be talked about first, before making a comment about it. If the topic is something the listener knows nothing about, then the speaker must introduce it, often by using a question such as "Do you know that store down the street?" to focus the listener's attention on what is to be the topic of a conversation. Unless there is special preparation, listeners expect that the topic will be identified at the beginning of a sentence and that it will be old information, something they have already heard of (information they share with the speaker); they expect that the second part of the communication will provide *new* information—a comment—about the topic.

To see how much we assume that this will be the pattern, suppose the speaker violates it by commenting on a topic that has never been mentioned to the listener; the result is likely to be something like the following:

(1) *Eleanor:*   My new officemate is rather unpleasant.
    Darrell: What new officemate? What happened to William?

In this example, Eleanor assumes that Darrell already knows that she has a new officemate. Darrell's response shows that Eleanor was mistaken.

Identifying the subject is crucial to our understanding of what is said or written because only when we have oriented ourselves to that aspect of the discourse is our attention free to turn to the understanding of the new information presented about it: the *predication* (the expression of what something *does* or *is like*) of the sentence. The conventional placement of subject and predicate in conversation helps with the identification. We expect to find the subject (the *who* or *what* a sentence is about) at the beginning of the sentence, and once that is identified, we expect the rest of the sentence to tell what the subject *does* or *is like.*

Our experience as speakers of the English language has taught us to assume that, once the verb appears in a sentence, we have heard the entire subject. Because of our intuitive awareness of the structure of English, we can even divide nonsense sentences into subjects and predicates. Given the following nonsense sentence—

(2)   The glaggety woodgies climmed brudgingly to the weegster.

and told to divide it into two parts, most speakers of English will interpret *The glaggety woodgies* as the subject (even identifying it as a plural subject) and *climmed brudgingly to the weegster* as the predicate containing a past-tense verb (*climmed*).

As a speaker of English, you have a tacit knowledge of the two-part division of sentences into subjects and predicates. Before reading on, do the following exercise, in which you are asked first to divide sentences into two parts intuitively and then to test your intuition by substituting a single pronoun for the segment you have identified as the subject.

■ *EXERCISE 6.1*

1. How would you divide the following sentences into two parts, subjects and predicates? Underline the subjects. (Note that some words that appear at the beginning of the sentence may not be part of the subject.)

   a. Edward grows tomatoes as large as grapefruit.

   b. The students in Math 101 have always disliked taking exams.

   c. Usually, people find Bill Cosby funny.

   d. The house that we own sits on a small lot.

2. Test your intuition by trying to substitute a single pronoun (*he, she,* or *it*) for the subject you have underlined.

Most speakers of English would agree intuitively that the division between the subject and predicate of the first sentence should be as follows:

(3)   Edward   grows tomatoes as large as grapefruit.

Edward names a topic (the *who* of the sentence, presumably known by both speaker and hearer). *Grows tomatoes as large as grapefruit* gives new information about Edward, telling something that he *does*. Other possible divisions of the sentence won't work. For example, *as large as grapefruit* belongs with *tomatoes,* so no division is possible after *tomatoes:*

(4)   ?Edward grows tomatoes   as large as grapefruit.

Because no single noun or verb will substitute for either part that has been divided here, we have not cut the sentence into subject and predicate. The entire phrase *tomatoes as large as grapefruit* belongs with *grows,* so you can't make the main division of the sentence after *grows,* either. A noun cannot be substituted for *Edward grows* nor a verb for *tomatoes as large as grapefruit.*

(5)   ?Edward grows   tomatoes as large as grapefruit.

  The second sentence in Exercise 6.1 is just a bit more difficult to process. Understanding what others say or write is, in part, a guessing game. As we listen, we make rapid calculations about relationships and categories. Once we have heard *The students,* we may guess that it is the entire subject, thus being led momentarily into dividing the sentence into a subject and a predicate as follows:

(6)   ?The students   in Math 101 have always disliked taking exams.

  Although the first part, *the students,* is like a subject (it names *who* or *what* performs the action in this sentence), the second part, *in Math 101 have always disliked taking exams,* is not a logical unit acting as a predicate: It does not tell what the students *are* or *do.* In fact, the appearance of the preposition *in* rather than the expected verb warns us that more of the subject is being presented. Thus, we quickly reanalyze the sentence into the following two parts, the first identifying the subject and the second providing new information about it.

(7)   The students in Math 101   have always disliked taking exams.

  Although we expect the subject to constitute the first segment of an English sentence, for variety or emphasis a speaker may move some part of the predicate into that position. As long as the fragment from the predicate is not too long or too complex, we do not become confused about what belongs to the subject and what belongs to the predicate. Look again at the third sentence. Adverbs may appear between the subject and the verb (*People **usually** find Bill Cosby funny*) or even before the subject (***Usually,** people find Bill Cosby funny*). We have little trouble in recognizing derived adverbs like *usually* as belonging to the predicate, no matter where they appear in the sentence:

(8)

Usually, | people   find Bill Cosby funny | usually.

  The fourth sentence (*The house that we own sits on a small lot*) contains two verbs: *own* and *sits.* We can differentiate the main verb of the sentence (*sits*) from others by signals like the relative pronoun *that,* which warns us to interpret the following verb as part of a relative clause *that we own* and not as the main verb in the sentence.

(9)   The house that we own   sits on a small lot.

That we own is a relative clause identifying which house is being discussed; as such, it is part of the subject, not part of the predicate.
  One way to represent the two-part, subject/predicate pattern of sentences graphically is by means of a phrase structure tree, or phrase marker, one of numer-

ous methods available for displaying the constituent structure of sentences (the parts that make up the sentence). As you may recall, the tree is drawn by following phrase structure rules that specify the constituents of the sentence or phrase. The rule that gives the structure of English sentences is as follows:

(10)   S = NP + VP

This rule says that a sentence of English is made up of a noun phrase (NP) followed by a verb phrase (VP). To draw the tree, whatever occurs to the left of the equals sign becomes the top point, and the structures on the right branch from it. Thus, if we begin with the rule in (10) and then fill in the two parts of the sentence, we get:

(11)

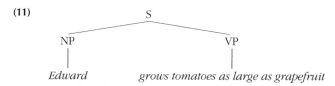

The phrase structure tree shows that the noun phrase, *Edward,* is functioning as what has traditionally been called the subject of the sentence, and the verb phrase, *grows tomatoes as large as grapefruit,* is functioning as its predicate.

This simple phrase marker describes equally well the underlying structure of all four of our example sentences. It shows how they are alike in structure. Notice in each case that the subject noun phrase tells *who* or *what* the sentence is about, and the verb phrase tells what the noun phrase *does* or *is like*. All that needs to be changed in the tree is the specific noun phrase functioning as subject or the verb phrase functioning as predicate.

(12)

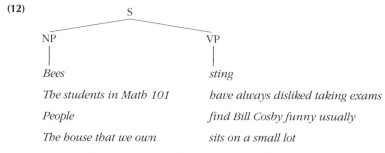

An alternative way of representing the same information visually is available with the Reed-Kellogg diagram, in which the subject and predicate appear on a horizontal line, divided by an intersecting vertical line:

(13)   Bees | sting

In such a diagram, all of the words that are part of the subject appear to the left of the vertical, and all of the predicate appears on the right. We go into more detail about drawing trees and diagrams at places in the text where we think they help clarify grammatical concepts.

■ *EXERCISE 6.2* _____

We have been using simple examples to illustrate the two-part nature of English sentences. If you have ever had difficulty in recognizing the subject of a complicated sentence, the kind of personal pronoun substitution we have used above can help you. We suggest here two other tools that can help verify your intuition of what constitutes the subject of a sentence.

a. ***Tag question test.*** The tag question comes at the end of a statement and seeks the listener's agreement with the statement. (*Arnold is Rollerblading./Arnold is Rollerblading, **isn't be?***) As Exercise 1.1 showed, speakers of English have a tacit knowledge of how to form tag questions. Because forming the tag requires that the entire subject be replaced by a pronoun, speakers also have a tacit knowledge of subjects. Therefore, creating a tag question with a suspect sentence can verify your identification of the subject.

b. ***Yes/no question test.*** Speakers of English also have a tacit knowledge of how to turn a statement into a question (*Arnold is Rollerblading./Is Arnold Rollerblading?*) In creating the question, the speaker moves a modal, an inflected auxiliary verb, or *be* around the subject. A comparison of the two versions shows what constitutes the subject.

EXAMPLE

Leaving before the lecture ended yesterday was a big mistake.

1. Tag question: ...*wasn't **it?***
2. Yes/no question: *Wasn't **leaving before the lecture ended yesterday** a big mistake?*

After studying the examples, identify the subjects in the sentences below.

1. The next car that I buy must be fuel efficient.
2. The best car for me would be one with an EPA estimate of at least 45 miles to the gallon.
3. The EPA's combined fuel economy formula is based on 55 percent of city driving miles per gallon and 45 percent of highway miles per gallon.
4. Buying a car that is listed as fuel efficient does not guarantee that the car will deliver the mpg listed on the sticker.
5. Failing to pay attention to recommended careful driving habits can decrease the fuel efficiency of a car by 20 percent.
6. Accelerating a little more slowly can improve fuel efficiency.
7. Removing the foot from the accelerator a little sooner before a stop sign will also help.
8. Running the air conditioning increases the work that the engine has to do and lowers the fuel efficiency of a car.

▬ *FORM AND FUNCTION* ▬▬▬▬▬▬▬▬▬▬▬▬▬▬▬▬▬▬

In our discussion thus far, we have been careful to distinguish **form** from **function.** Let's review the distinction we've been making.

One of the first form/function contrasts we made in this chapter was in describing the basic structure of sentences. We said that a noun phrase (*form*) served as the subject (*function*), and that a verb phrase (*form*) served as the predicate (*function*) of a sentence. A sentence is thus made up of a noun phrase subject and a verb phrase predicate. These two phrases, we said, determine the *form* of a sentence. But what exactly do we mean by *form*?

Earlier, in Chapter 4, we used *form* as one of the ways of recognizing different parts of speech, or word classes. When we used the term *form* in connection with classes of words, we meant the specific prefixes and suffixes that attach to and change the form of each kind of word. For example, the past-tense suffix {-ed} occurs with verbs, and its presence enables us to recognize a member of the verb class, even when the specific "word" is a sequence of nonsense syllables, like *fibbled.* Similarly, the derivational suffix {-tion} enables us to recognize nouns like *addition* and *concentration,* and the suffix {-al} helps us to identify members of the adjective class like *additional* and *functional.*

Not all words can be identified on the basis of form. Some words are not capable of accepting affixes (*after, that*), and others can take the inflections of more than one word class (*She is **cutting** out a dress; He has three **cuts** on his arm*). In such cases, its position in a phrase or sentence is what helps us in identifying the class to which a word belongs. That is why we used sentence frames to help us identify nouns, verbs, adjectives, and adverbs in Chapter 4. If a word can occupy a slot in a frame sentence, we can demonstrate its ability to *function* as the part of speech identified by that slot. In testing for adjectives, for instance, we substitute one word after another in the adjective slots; if a word fits, we have demonstrated that English treats it as an adjective.

In discussing phrases, we continue to use *form* with the same meaning: It refers to the physical shape or the internal structure that enables us to classify a phrase. In this chapter, for instance, we show how a noun phrase may consist of (1) a single noun:

(14) honey *Honey* tastes sweet.
Jesse *Jesse* is outside.

(2) a determiner plus a noun:

(15) the milk *The milk* tastes sweet.
my car *My car* is outside.

Or (3) a determiner plus one or more adjectives plus a noun:

(16) that cold drink *That cold drink* tastes sweet.
a sleek, old black cat *A sleek, old black cat* is outside.

The pattern of a noun preceded by a possible determiner and one or more possible adjective modifiers provides us with a prototypical *form* for all noun phrases. The noun is the **headword** of the noun phrase, the word that other words modify.

The principle of *substitution* is essential in grammatical analysis. We cannot possibly hope to characterize all of the possible noun phrases of English on the basis of form. Just thinking about the possible structures that can serve as subjects of sentences should convince you that an exhaustive catalog of noun phrases would be, if at all possible, incredibly long and complex. Consider, as a single example, the subject of the preceding sentence: *Just thinking about the possible structures that can serve as subjects of sentences*. In form, this string of words is nothing like the prototypical noun phrases described above, yet a pronoun can substitute for it (*It should convince you*), and it functions quite naturally in a noun phrase slot. In fact, remembering that parentheses indicate optional items, you will find that the entire sequence fits in the noun slot of the frame sentence (*The*) _____ *seem(s) all right/silly:*

(17)   *Just thinking about the possible structures that can serve as subjects of sentences* seems all right/silly.

It is reasonable to argue, then, that a noun phrase in English is any of the prototypical forms identified above *or* any sequence of words that can be substituted for those forms. If we define a phrase on the basis of its structure, we are using its *form* as our basis. If we define a phrase on the basis of its ability to substitute for an equivalent phrase (or to occupy a sentence slot), we are using its *function* as our basis. Analyzing the structure of sentences requires us to use both form and function to define noun, verb, adjective, and adverb phrases.

RECOGNIZING PHRASE TYPES

Subjects and predicates can become quite long and complex in writing and, indeed, in the most ordinary conversation. To facilitate understanding as we read or listen to someone speak, we divide what can be large chunks of meaning into the phrases that are the chief **constituents** of sentences—that is, the parts or components from which sentences are constructed. Because those phrases have predictable patterns, we are able to understand rapid conversation, even though, at any given time, we are probably hearing one sentence after another that we have never heard before. As we listen, we divide the material into familiar patterns—structures that make the information easier to store and remember than it would be if every word had a novel relationship to every other word.

We have seen two phrases combine to create sentences: noun and verb phrases. In the rest of this chapter, we look at the four kinds of phrases that combine to create predicates in English: noun phrases (NP), main verb phrases (MVP), adjective phrases (ADJP), and adverb phrases (ADVP). As sentence and predicate constituents, they can be defined as follows:

- *A **noun phrase** is a noun or any group of words that can substitute for a noun.* The simplest prototypical noun phrase consists of a single noun, like *Edward* or *people*. Equally basic is a phrase consisting of a noun headword preceded by a determiner: *the lamp, a cup, her boyfriend.* However, the headword of a noun phrase can also be modified by other words

---

(*the **blue** car*), phrases (*the students **in Math 101***), or clauses (*the house **that we own***). In Chapters 10, 11, and 12, we discuss other forms (phrases and clauses) that can function as noun phrases.

- A ***main verb phrase*** *is the main verb of the sentence plus its auxiliary or helping verbs.* The main verb phrase may consist of a single **main verb,** such as *fell* in *That tree fell.* When there are auxiliary (or helping) verbs, like *might* and *have* in *That tree might have fallen,* they are also part of the main verb phrase. The main verb is the headword of the phrase.

- An ***adjective phrase*** *is an adjective or any group of words that can substitute for an adjective.* The prototypical adjective phrase consists of a single adjective, *tall* in *Sally is **tall,*** or an adjective headword and a qualifier, *very tall. Even taller than the woman who coaches her volleyball team* is more elaborate, but because it can substitute for the single adjective *tall* (*Sally is **even taller than the woman who coaches her volleyball team***), you can recognize it as an adjective phrase.

- An ***adverb phrase*** *is an adverb or any group of words that can substitute for an adverb.* The prototype of an adverb phrase consists of a single adverb (*strongly* in *The wind blew **strongly***), or an adverb headword accompanied by a qualifier (*very strongly*). Because you can substitute the subordinate clause *as if we were in the midst of a hurricane* for the adverb *strongly,* you can recognize the larger constituent as an adverb phrase (*The wind blew **as if we were in the midst of a hurricane***).

Figure 6.1 sums up substitution tests that are useful in identifying phrase types. You cannot hope to memorize all of the combinations that can function as noun, adjective, or adverb phrases. Learn the tests for identifying them, instead. The main verb phrase is different. Because it contains a small and fixed number of words, its constituents can be memorized.

Let's return to the sentences above and see if we can analyze their *constituent structure,* the arrangement of their parts. Remember that the constituents

RULES OF THUMB	
Substitution Tests Useful in Identifying Phrase Types	
Noun Phrase	Try to substitute a single noun or pronoun (like *someone* or *something*) for it.
Main Verb Phrase	We will discuss these in detail below.
Adjective Phrase	Try to substitute a related single adjective for it.
Adverb Phrase	Try to substitute a related single adverb (like *there, then,* or *somehow*) for it. Then move it to a position following the verb.

Figure 6.1

of the sentence are a noun phrase functioning as the subject and a verb phrase functioning as the predicate. Predicates must include a main verb phrase, but they may also include noun phrases, adjective phrases, and adverb phrases as constituents. *If you find a phrase for which there is no single word substitute, it is not a constituent of the sentence or of the predicate. It must be part of another, larger phrase.*

(18)   Edward grows tomatoes as large as grapefruit.

- *Edward,* the subject, is a single noun and is, according to our definition, a noun phrase as well.

- The main verb *grows* stands alone without any auxiliaries and is the entire main verb phrase.

- Although *tomatoes,* by itself, could be a noun phrase, in identifying constituents of the sentence, we are looking for the largest sequences of words that can be replaced by a single part of speech: a noun, a verb, an adjective, or an adverb. Two facts suggest that *tomatoes as large as grapefruit* be considered as a single unit. First, in this sentence, the entire phrase can be replaced either by the single word *tomatoes* (or by a pronoun like *something*), yielding a complete sentence: *Edward grows tomatoes* or *Edward grows something.* Second, if you divide this structure, no single word can replace *as large as grapefruit* in this structure, while supplying similar information about the tomatoes. If, for example, you try to substitute a simple adjective like *big* for the phrase, you get **Edward grows tomatoes big.* Thus, the complete sequence *tomatoes as large as grapefruit* is a noun phrase constituting part of the predicate, and we identify the sentence constituents as follows:

(19)   A noun phrase subject: *Edward*

A verb phrase predicate: *grows tomatoes as large as grapefruit*

The predicate has two constituents consisting of

(20)   A main verb phrase: *grows*

A second noun phrase: *tomatoes as large as grapefruit*

A phrase structure tree of the sentence looks like this:

(21)

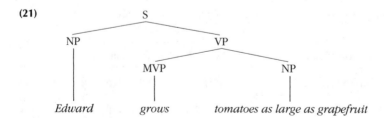

The constituents in the next sentence are a bit more difficult to identify.

(22)   The students in Math 101 have always disliked taking exams.

- *The students* is a noun phrase; it can be replaced by a single word (such as *they* or *students*). However, we can demonstrate that it is part of another, larger noun phrase, *The students in Math 101*. In the first place, the same pronoun (*they*) or single noun (*students*) can be substituted for the larger phrase to which it belongs. In the second place, *in Math 101* is not a constituent of the sentence. No single word can substitute for it. In fact, as a modifier telling *which* students are being referred to, it is part of the subject noun phrase it helps to identify.

- Although *always* comes in the middle of the main verb phrase (*have disliked*), it is an adverb that could appear either at the beginning or end of the predicate; therefore, it is an adverb phrase.

- The main verb phrase contains the present-tense form of the helping verb *have* followed by the past-participle form of the main verb *dislike*.

- We are left with the words *taking exams*. Because the phrase forms a unit for which we can substitute a single noun (*exams*) or a pronoun (*something*), it is a noun phrase telling *what* students dislike.

Thus, we can identify the following constituents:

(23) **Sentence Constituents**

A noun phrase subject:	*The students in Math 101*
A verb phrase predicate:	*have always disliked taking exams.*

Predicate Constituents

A main verb phrase:	*have disliked*
A second noun phrase:	*taking exams*
An adverb phrase:	*always*

Example (24) is a phrase structure tree of (22).

(24)

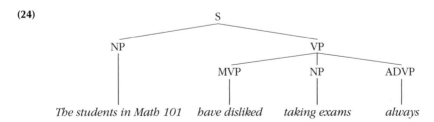

The third sentence is fairly straightforward.

(25) Usually, people find Bill Cosby funny.

The only question arising in this sentence is what to do with the sequence *Bill Cosby funny*. Your intuition will probably suggest to you that this is not a single unit. You can replace it with *him* or *Cosby,* but some of the sense is lost because two kinds of information are supplied in the predicate of (25): the person (*Bill Cosby*) and a word that describes him (*funny*). The first phrase, because it is the name of a person, is easily identified as a noun phrase, and the second, a simple adjective, is an adjective phrase. Thus, the constituents of the sentence can be identified as follows:

(26) **Sentence Constituents**

A noun phrase subject:	*people*
A verb phrase predicate:	*find Bill Cosby funny usually*

Predicate Constituents

A main verb phrase:	*find*
A second noun phrase:	*Bill Cosby*
An adjective phrase:	*funny*
An adverb phrase:	*usually*

The constituent structure of (25) can be analyzed with the following phrase structure tree:

(27)

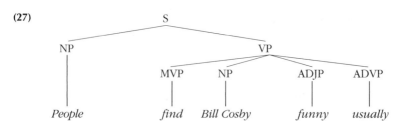

The last sentence in our examples presents an additional difficulty: It contains a relative clause, *that we own:*

(28)   The house that we own sits on a small lot.

- *The house that we own,* even though it contains a noun and a clause, must be a noun phrase because we can replace the entire phrase with a pronoun like *it* or *something* (***It** sits on a small lot*). *That we own* is not a sentence constituent; no single word can substitute for it.
- *Sits* is the entire main verb phrase.
- *On a small lot* is a prepositional phrase. Because it tells *where* and can be replaced by a simple adverb *there*, it is functioning as an adverb phrase in this sentence. Remember that *on a small lot* is a prepositional phrase in **form,** but it is an adverb phrase in **function.** Prepositional phrases can function as adjectivals (*a house **of our own,*** in which *of our own* modifies *house*), and as adverbials (*sits **on a small lot,*** in which *on a small lot* modifies *sits*). We cannot tell the function of a prepositional phrase until we see its place in a sentence. Notice that although the adverbial prepositional phrase contains a noun phrase (*a small lot*), we do not, at this stage

of our analysis, divide the prepositional phrase into smaller constituents. If we did, we would be left with the preposition *on,* for which we could not substitute any single noun, verb, adjective, or adverb. Because we cannot, *on* is not a constituent of the predicate.

The constituents of this sentence are as follows:

(29) **Sentence Constituents**

A noun phrase subject:	*The house that we own*
A verb phrase predicate:	*sits on a small lot*

Predicate Constituents

A main verb phrase:	*sits*
An adverb phrase:	*on a small lot*

The phrase structure tree for (28) is

(30)

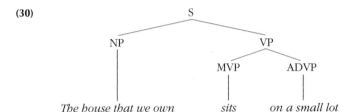

EXERCISE 6.3

Divide each of the following sentences into its subject and predicate. Label its sentence constituents: NP, MVP, ADJP, ADVP. Remember that an adverb phrase may have been moved away from its normal position at the end of the sentence. If it has, move it to the end before trying to analyze the phrase structure of the sentence. An example has been done for you.

EXAMPLE

Our youngest son probably hit that ball into the neighbor's yard.

Our youngest son	*hit*	*that ball*	*into the neighbor's yard*	*probably*
NP	MVP	NP	ADVP	ADVP

1. Gilroy, California, calls itself "The Garlic Capital of the World."
2. Every July Gilroy holds a three-day Garlic Festival.
3. Organizers expect more than 250,000 people for the festival this year.
4. A newly crowned Miss Gilroy Garlic will reign at this year's festival.
5. The festival committee has ordered two tons of garlic from local farms.
6. Not all people are delighted with the garlic ice cream.

7. In earlier years, festival sponsor Listerine provided free Cool Mint Pocket Packs to attendees.

8. This year, it is BYOBM (Bring Your Own Breath Mints).

THE MAIN VERB PHRASE

The most important constituent of the predicate is the main verb phrase. Its headword is the main verb, which tells what the subject *does* or *is like*. English requires that the main verb of a sentence be a **finite verb**—that is, that it be inflected for tense, either in itself (*eat/ate*) or else by way of helping verbs (*is eating/had eaten*). Helping verbs include:

Modals	*can, could, will, would, shall, should, may, might, must*
Have	*have, has, had*
Be	*am, is, are, was, were, be, been, being*

These forms combine in a systematic inflectional pattern that we describe with the **main verb phrase formula,** sometimes also referred to as the **verb expansion rule.**

Before analyzing that formula, recall the five principal forms in which English verbs occur. They are each listed in Figure 6.2, along with frame sentences for which each form of the finite (or inflected) verb is appropriate. Following the slot in each test frame sentence are the optional words (in parentheses), *something* and *good,* for verbs that require a following noun or adjective, respectively.

The **base form** is uninflected and is the version of the verb that is listed in a dictionary and that occurs with the infinitive marker *to.* The **simple present-tense form** ends in allomorphs of {-s} if the subject is a third-person singular noun phrase (one for which *he, she,* or *it* can be substituted).

SUMMARY	
Principal Parts of English Verbs	
Base Form	It might _____ (something/good). She wants to _____ (something/good).
Simple Present-Tense Form {-s}	He _____ {-s} (something/good) sometimes.
Simple Past-Tense Form {-d}	You _____ {-d} (something/good) then.
Past-Participle Form {-en}	We have _____ {-en} (something/good) always.
Present-Participle Form {-ing}	They are _____ {-ing} (something/good) now.

Figure 6.2

The **simple past-tense form** of regular verbs is formed by adding allomorphs of {-d} to the base form, with a number of irregular verbs, as we have seen, indicating past tense by a change of vowel (for example, *ride/ rode*). The **past-participle form** is usually created with an inflection identical with that of the past tense (*walked/have walked*), but many irregular verbs have *-en* as the past-participle marker (for example, *ridden*). The **present-participle form** is always formed with *-ing* (see Figure 3.3).

■ *EXERCISE 6.4*

Look at the sentences below, paying particular attention to the order in which verbs and helping verbs occur and the forms they take. Then answer the following questions about them:

a. Which verb (or helping verb) shows tense?

b. What happens to tense when there is a modal?

c. What form of the verb follows a modal?

d. What form of the verb follows HAVE?

e. What form of the verb follows BE?

1. Charlie had been driving for hours.
2. Charlie may have driven the car for them.
3. Charlie will be driving us tomorrow.
4. Charlie should always drive the car.
5. Charlie was driving the car yesterday.
6. Charlie has driven for a long time.
7. Charlie must have been driving the car today.
8. Charlie drove the car last.

You will have noticed in doing Exercise 6.4 that the three kinds of auxiliaries illustrated in the eight sentences always precede the main verb. They may be absent entirely (as in #8), or they may appear in any combination. However, they always occur in the same order:

- First comes the modal, if there is one.
- Next comes a form of *have,* if it occurs.
- Then comes a form of *be,* if there is any.
- Finally, following any or all of the above, comes the headword, the main verb.

If we categorize all the auxiliary verbs as members of a single component of the main verb phrase, the **auxiliary (AUX),** it is possible to represent this information about English verbs by extending the tree diagram as follows:

(31)

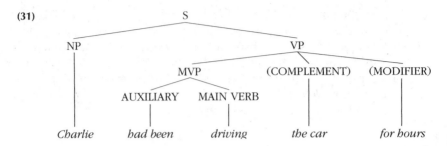

As you will recall, this tree diagram begins with a sentence (S) and says that it consists of a noun phrase subject (NP) followed by a verb phrase predicate (VP). To this is added a new branching, based on the following rule:

(32)   VP = MVP + (COMPLEMENTS)

According to (32), the verb phrase consists of a main verb phrase (MVP), which may be followed by one or more **complements:** the noun phrases, adjective phrases, or adverb phrases that complete the meaning of the main verb and that are part of the predicate. In Chapter 7, we analyze the phrases that can occur as complements of the verb. For the remainder of this chapter, we discuss just the main verb phrase.

The main verb phrase formula is as follows:

(33)   MVP = AUX + MV

This says that a main verb phrase in English is created by combining the helping verbs that constitute the auxiliary with the main verb itself.

We have already seen some of the elements that occur as auxiliaries (the modals, *have*, and *be*). Using parentheses to indicate items that are optionally present (that is, that may or may not occur in a sentence) and capital letters to indicate that *have* and *be* are functioning as auxiliaries (HAVE auxiliary and BE auxiliary), we may create a formula that captures the order in which the helping verbs must occur and indicates that each is optional:

(34)   AUX = (MODAL) + (HAVE) + (BE)

Such a formula puts the helping verbs into the proper order, but notice that parts of the main verb phrase are not accounted for. Inflectional affixes—either verb tense or participle endings—occur on some of the verbs in the sentences we examined above.

Look again at the verb sequences in the sentences of Exercise 6.4, as they are summarized in Figure 6.3, noticing especially what inflections are added to HAVE, BE, or the main verb and what immediately precedes those inflected forms.

The pattern you can see in Figure 6.3 is the following:

1. The unmarked base form of a verb appears after modals:

may *have*   should *drive*
will *be*   must *have*

Main Verb Phrases of Exercise 6.4			
may	had	been	driving
will	have		driven
should		be	driving
			drive
		was	driving
	has		driven
must	have	been	driving
			drove

Figure 6.3

2. The past-participle morpheme occurs on the verb immediately following the helping verb HAVE:

had *been*   has *driven*
have *driven*   have *been*

3. The present-participle morpheme occurs on the verb immediately following the helping verb BE:

been *driving*   was *driving*
be *driving*   been *driving*

Another way of expressing this would be to say that the first element of the main verb phrase is a modal, if it is present, and that it causes no change in the verb form that follows; the second is HAVE, which must be followed by the *past-participle* form of a verb; and the third is BE, which must be followed by the *present-participle* form of a verb. Notice, too, that, except for modals (which do not inflect), whatever comes first in the main verb phrase will be inflected for past or present tense.

had been driving   has *driven*
was driving   *drove*

We must include a provision for verb **tense** in our formula as well.

A formula showing the constituents of the auxiliary and representing all of these inflectional morphemes would look like the following:

(35)   AUX = TENSE + (MODAL) + (HAVE + {-en}) + (BE + {-ing})

According to this formula, the only required constituent of the AUX is tense—TENSE is not enclosed in parentheses. This is a way of representing the fact that, in English, we must always decide whether the verb is in the present or past tense. MODAL stands for any of the nine modal auxiliary verbs; HAVE stands for a form of the auxiliary verb *have;* {-en} symbolizes the past-participle inflection that occurs on verbs following the auxiliary *have;* BE represents the auxiliary verb *be;* and {-ing} stands for the present-participle inflection required on the verb following the auxiliary *be.*

This formula underscores the relationship between the auxiliaries *have* and *be* and the participle forms that must follow them. If the auxiliary verb *have* is present in a sentence, then the verb phrase will also contain a past-participle morpheme; both parts, *have* + {-en}, will be present (for example, **have written**). If the auxiliary verb *be* is present in a sentence, then the verb phrase will contain a present-participle morpheme; both parts, *be* + {-ing}, will be present (for example, **is writing**). If the auxiliaries *have* and *be* are both present, then the verb phrase will include both a past participle following the *have* and a present participle following the *be* (for example, **has been writing,** in which *has* is followed by *been,* the past-participle form of *be,* and *been* is followed by *writing,* the present-participle form of *write*).

English has two tense inflections: present {-s}, marked when the subject is a third-person singular noun phrase, and past {-d}, which, as you learned in Chapter 3, occurs in a variety of allomorphs. Thus, an additional step is needed in our formulaic description of English main verb phrases:

(36) TENSE = $\begin{bmatrix} \text{present} \\ \text{or past} \end{bmatrix}$

Finally, we have used MODAL to represent any of the nine modal auxiliaries, and that information can also be summarized in a formula:

(37) MODAL = *can, could, shall, should, will, would, may, might, must*

Figure 6.4 contains a tree diagram representing all of this information about the main verb phrase.

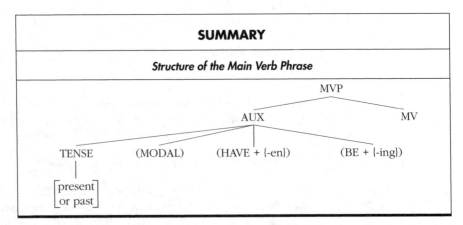

Figure 6.4

Creating Verb Phrases

The information contained in the tree diagram in Figure 6.4 can be expressed as the main verb phrase formula, given in Figure 6.5.

Both the tree diagram in Figure 6.4 and the main verb phrase formula in Figure 6.5 suggest how it is possible for you to create a vast number of English main verb phrases simply by selecting combinations of constituents to include in the auxiliary with a particular main verb and subject. Having selected those constituents, you must make sure that the elements that are affixes get attached to or incorporated into the appropriate word in the verb phrase you are creating.

Suppose, for example, you select three constituents: past tense (tense must always be included), HAVE + {-en}, and the verb *write*. Those basic constituents can be represented as:

(38)

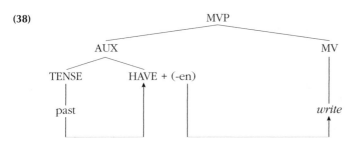

This abstract representation of the underlying structure becomes an actual main verb phrase by incorporating inflections into the verb forms that follow them. The horizontal arrow, like the vertical one, means "becomes" or "is transformed into" whatever follows. We use the horizontal arrow here so that the two items can appear side by side:

(39)   past + HAVE + {-en} + *write*   ⟶   *had written*

past + HAVE   ⟶   *had*

{-en} + *write*   ⟶   *written*

SUMMARY
Main Verb Phrase Formula
1. MVP = AUX + MV **2.** AUX = TENSE + (MODAL) + (HAVE + {-en}) + (BE + {-ing}) **3.** TENSE = $\begin{bmatrix} \text{present} \\ \text{or past} \end{bmatrix}$ **4.** MODAL = *can, could, shall, should, will, would, may, might, must*

Figure 6.5

The past tense attaches to and inflects HAVE, creating the form *had*. The past-participle marker {-en} becomes part of the verb *write*, converting it to *written*. If, on the other hand, the underlying structure had included only two elements, past + *write*, then the inflection would combine with the MV itself:

(40)

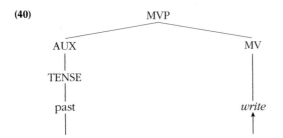

The result would be the simple past-tense main verb phrase *wrote:*

(41)   past + *write* ⟶   *wrote*

Consider another example. First, you might select the following constituents for the underlying main verb phrase structure:

(42)

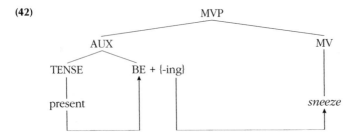

In order to know what form of a verb will result with present tense, you need to know the grammatical **person** and **number** of the subject. Suppose, for this example, that the subject is a third-person singular subject (*he, she, it,* or an equivalent noun). In this case, the following will result:

(43)   present + BE + {-ing} + *sneeze* ⟶   *is sneezing*

present + BE   ⟶   *is*

{-ing} + *sneeze*   ⟶   *sneezing*

Present tense will convert BE to *is*. Then {-ing}, the present-participle marker, will become part of *sneeze,* producing the verb phrase *is sneezing,* as in the sentence *He is sneezing.* If the subject is first-person singular (*I*), then BE will become *am* when present tense is incorporated into it, resulting in *I am sneezing.* A second-person subject (*you*) or a plural subject (*we, they*) will mean that present tense followed by BE will result in *are,* as in the sentences *You/We/They are sneezing.*

Notice how arrows in Figure 6.6 show the pattern of incorporating into the following verb form the grammatical information normally signaled by affixes (tense, past participle, present participle). To use this chart, you supply a subject in the first column and a main verb in the last column. In the examples provided, *Carol* is the subject, *speak* is the main verb, and in the last four examples, *should, will, could,* and *must* are the modal auxiliaries. Become familiar with the regularity of this pattern as you complete the next exercise.

When students initially study the structure of the English main verb phrase, they often respond first to its apparent complexity. It certainly is not simple to describe. Yet as students become familiar with the regularity of its patterning and more comfortable with the attempt by linguists to represent that regularity in the main verb phrase formula, they recall with amazement that small children acquire great skill in using English verb phrases at an early age, long before anyone even considers requiring them to take a formal course in English grammar.

■ EXERCISE 6.5 _____

Referring as necessary to Figure 6.6, convert each of the following into a sentence by converting the abstract representation of its verb phrase into an actual verb phrase. An example has been done for you.

EXAMPLE

No one + **present** + **HAVE** + {**-en**} + *telephone*   →   ***No one has telephoned***

Present + HAVE   →   ***has***

{*-en*} + *telephone*   →   ***telephoned***

1. Our plane + **present** + **be** + at the gate. *[is]*
2. The crew + **past** + **arrive** + some time ago. *[arrived]*
3. They + **present** + **should** + **HAVE** + {**-en**} + **load** + the luggage by now. *[should have loaded]*
4. They + **present** + **HAVE** + {**-en**} + **have** + time enough to be ready to go. *[have had they]*
5. Nothing + **present** + **BE** + {**-ing**} + **happen** + right now. *[is happening]*
6. The passengers + **present** + **HAVE** + {**-en**} + **BE** + {**-ing**} **wait** + for a long time. *[have been waiting]*
7. Something unusual + **present** + **must** + **HAVE** + {**-en**} + **BE** + {**-ing**} + **keep** + the plane here. *[must have been keeping]*
8. Perhaps we + **present** + **will** + **be** + {**-ing**} + **leave** + soon. *[will be leaving]*

Without associating the tree diagram in Figure 6.4 with actual main verb phrases, it can be difficult to remember what each part represents. The following paragraphs present and explain each possibility represented by the diagram.

Remember that TENSE is not optional in either the formula or the tree. All main verb phrases in English sentences are presumed to signal past or present tense. The unmarked base form signals present tense (*I usually walk*), unless the subject is the third-person singular (*He usually walks*).

SUMMARY

Creating Verb Phrases from Underlying Structures

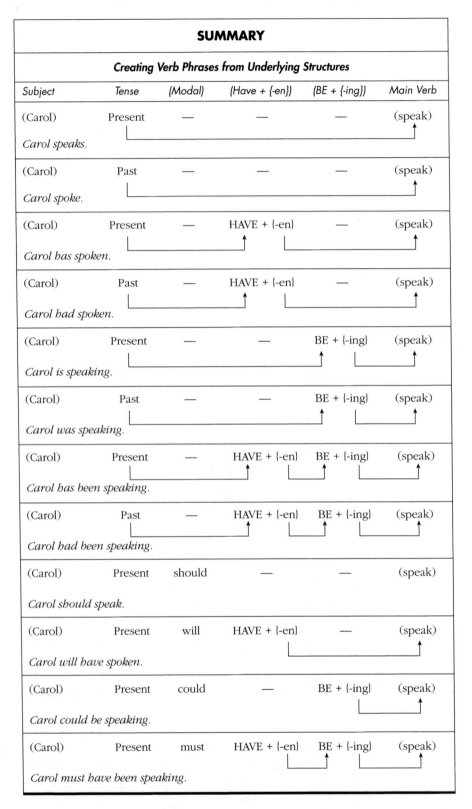

Subject	Tense	(Modal)	(Have + {-en})	(BE + {-ing})	Main Verb
(Carol)	Present	—	—	—	(speak)
Carol speaks.					
(Carol)	Past	—	—	—	(speak)
Carol spoke.					
(Carol)	Present	—	HAVE + {-en}	—	(speak)
Carol has spoken.					
(Carol)	Past	—	HAVE + {-en}	—	(speak)
Carol had spoken.					
(Carol)	Present	—	—	BE + {-ing}	(speak)
Carol is speaking.					
(Carol)	Past	—	—	BE + {-ing}	(speak)
Carol was speaking.					
(Carol)	Present	—	HAVE + {-en}	BE + {-ing}	(speak)
Carol has been speaking.					
(Carol)	Past	—	HAVE + {-en}	BE + {-ing}	(speak)
Carol had been speaking.					
(Carol)	Present	should	—	—	(speak)
Carol should speak.					
(Carol)	Present	will	HAVE + {-en}	—	(speak)
Carol will have spoken.					
(Carol)	Present	could	—	BE + {-ing}	(speak)
Carol could be speaking.					
(Carol)	Present	must	HAVE + {-en}	BE + {-ing}	(speak)
Carol must have been speaking.					

Figure 6.6

Consider what happens when the auxiliary includes only TENSE and no auxiliary verbs:

(44)

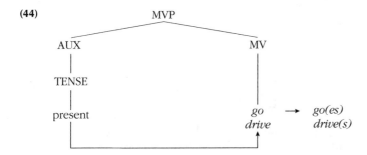

TENSE can be either present or past. If it is present, the verb will occur either in the base form or with an allomorph of the {-s} verb inflection—for example, *I go, you go, we go, they go,* but *Sue goes.* We indicate this following our trees by including the arrow (→), which means "is transformed into" whatever follows. In this tree, the main verb takes on appropriate allomorphs of the present tense.

If TENSE is past, the main verb will acquire an allomorph of {-ed}:

(45)

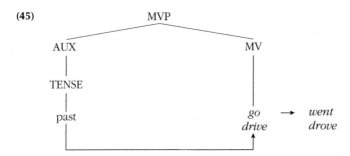

Let's consider main verb phrases with the helping verb HAVE as a constituent of the auxiliary. Because HAVE comes immediately after TENSE, it will inflect for past or present, becoming *has* or *have* if the tense is present. The {-en} attaches to the verb that follows, turning it into a past-participle form—*gone* and *driven* in examples (46) and (47).

(46)

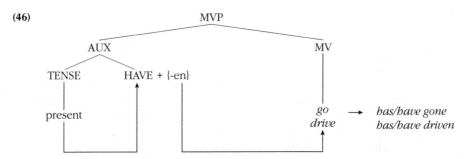

If TENSE is past, the inflection will create *had:*

(47)

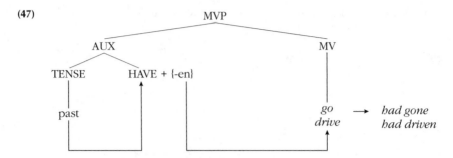

Another option included among the possible main verb phrase structures represented in Figure 6.4 is one that includes TENSE and the auxiliary verb BE. When BE immediately follows TENSE, it inflects to show the present or past tense, becoming *am, is,* or *are* if the tense is present. The {-ing} morpheme attaches to the main verb, which follows, as in examples (48) and (49):

(48)

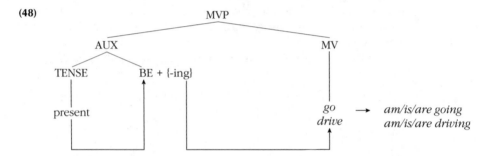

If TENSE is past, BE will become *was* or *were,* depending on whether the subject was singular or plural, and again the {-ing} in the tree diagram converts the following verb into a present participle form (*going* and *driving*) in these examples.

(49)

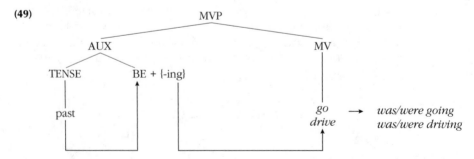

The auxiliary can include both HAVE and BE as helping verbs, as in examples (50a) and (50b). If both are present, HAVE, which comes first, signals tense, either present (*has been going, have been driving*) or past (*had been going, had been driving*). The presence of {-en} following HAVE tells us that the verb following HAVE will be in the past-participle form, as *been* is in these examples. The {-ing} after BE in the tree diagram represents the fact that the verb that follows BE in a verb phrase will be in the present-participle form (*going* and *driving*):

(50) a.

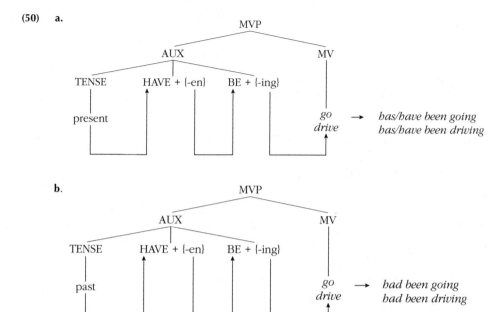

b.

If the AUX includes a modal as a helping verb, TENSE is not signaled by an inflection, as modals constitute a set of verbs that do not take any inflections. We will assume that all modals are present tense. Verbs that follow modals are always in the base form: *will go, might drive*. Example (51) illustrates a main verb phrase with *will* as a modal auxiliary:

(51)

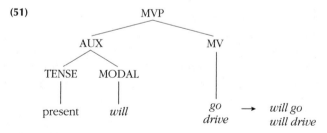

(The exact meaning of modals in combination with other verbs is complex, as we discuss a bit later.)

■ *EXERCISE 6.6*

Analyze the main verb phrases in the sentences below, and write out the words and morphemes you have identified. If there is a modal, consider it to be in the present tense. An example sentence has been done for you by following the steps:

EXAMPLE

| *TENSE* | *MODAL* | *HAVE + {-en}* | *BE + {-ing}* | *MAIN VERB* |

Several students have forgotten their lunches today.

| *present* | — | *HAVE + {-en}* | — | forget |

1. *Main verb phrase is **bave forgotten**.*
2. *TENSE is present (as can be seen from **bave**).*
3. *MODAL does not occur.*
4. *HAVE + {-en} occurs (**bave forgotten** is made up of HAVE followed by a verb ending in a past-participle morpheme).*
5. *BE + {-ing} does not occur.*
6. *The main verb is **forget**.*

1. Everyone is enjoying the performance of *Aida* tonight.
2. Several fans were standing outside the stage door in order to catch a glimpse of the tenor before the opera.
3. However, he had arrived at the theater before them.
4. The fans should have taken their seats.   *Present + modal + have + {en} + take*
5. Most of the audience had been sitting in the auditorium for some time already.
6. The soprano should be singing especially well.   *Present + modal + Be {ing} + sing*
7. She has sung the role of *Aida* many times.   *Present + have + {en} + sing*
8. We may want to see the opera again next week.

■ *EXERCISE 6.7* _____

After you feel you understand the examples in Exercise 6.6, try reversing the process. Below, you are given a chart indicating which elements of the auxiliary are to be part of the main verb phrase. Write the appropriate form of the verb *sleep* in the space that follows. An example has been done for you.

EXAMPLE

	TENSE	MODAL	HAVE + {-en}	BE + {-ing}	*sleep*
John	present	—	HAVE + {-en}	BE + {-ing}	= has been *sleeping*
1. John	past	—	—	—	= _____
2. John	present	must	—	—	= _____
3. John	past	—	HAVE + {-en}	—	= _had slept_

4. John	present	may	—	BE + {-ing}	=	_____
5. John	present	will	HAVE + {-en}	—	=	*have slept*
6. John	present	—	—	BE + {-ing}	=	*is sleeping*
7. John	present	might	HAVE + {-en}	BE + {ing}	=	*might have been sleeping*
8. John	past	—	HAVE + {-en}	BE + {ing}	=	*had been sleeping*

Time, Tense, and Aspect

It may be helpful to keep in mind the distinction between form and function to explain how English verbs signal *time, tense,* and *aspect*. Remember that the term *form* refers to the physical shape or configuration of a grammatical unit, and the term *function* indicates the role it plays in a larger grammatical structure.

Main verb phrases contain tense morphemes that help to signal the time when an action took place. Unfortunately for students of English, time and tense do not always match. To begin with, we have only two tense markers—past and present—but we think of time as being divided at least three ways—into past, present, and future. The inflection of the verb identifies its tense, but the time referred to is often determined by other elements in the sentence, especially by adverbs. The identification of the meaning of tense is complicated by our need to specify special aspects of the verb, depending upon whether an action represents a single occurrence or a repeated one, whether it is or was an action that went on for some time (*progressive*), and whether it has been completed (*perfect*).

Simple Tenses

When neither HAVE + {-en} nor BE + {-ing} occurs in the AUX, we have *simple tenses,* and only two inflections are possible: past or present.

The Simple Present Tense Form (present + MV)

The simple present tense can express a variety of actual times:

(52) I *feel* good today.   (present time)

Ed *swims* every afternoon.   (repeated action: past, present, future implied)

She *leaves* for Chicago tomorrow.   (future time)

Notice how important the adverb phrases *today, every afternoon,* and *tomorrow* are for signaling the meaning of the present tense.

The Simple Past Tense Form (past + MV)

The simple past tense expresses past time:

(53)   We *saw* a good movie last night.

I *devoured* six pieces of pizza for dinner.

There is no future-tense morpheme in English, no affix that can be attached to a verb to indicate that the action will take place in the future. Simple **future time** must be expressed by other words in the sentence:

(54)   **Modals**

I *shall* be out of town all week.

Larry definitely *will* be at the party.

Present Tense + Adverbial Modifiers

This class *ends* **at 11:00.**

Leave a message **when you call.**

Susan *is leaving* for New York **on Thursday.**

Finite and Nonfinite Verb Forms

The main verb phrase must include a verb inflected for tense. That inflected verb is said to be a **finite verb:**

(55)   a. He *eats*.   Finite verb *eat*, present tense

b. He *ate*.   Finite verb *eat*, past tense

c. He *is* eating.   Finite auxiliary verb *be*, present tense

d. He *was* eating.   Finite auxiliary verb *be*, past tense

e. He *has* eaten.   Finite auxiliary verb *have*, present tense

f. He *had* eaten.   Finite auxiliary verb *have*, past tense

Our description of grammatical sentences of English, based upon these examples using third-person singular subjects, assumes that tense is a required part of the main verb phrase, even when there is no visible marker present.

(56)   a. I *eat*.   Finite verb *eat*, present tense

b. He *might* eat less.   Finite modal verb *might*, present tense

There is no visible morpheme to justify our calling the verb *eat* or the modal *might* in (56) examples of the past or present. As you may recall, we used the concept of the zero allomorph of a morpheme to account for instances where we intuitively believe something to be indicative of a plural:

(57)   one sheep   Singular noun (unmarked)

three sheep   Plural noun (unmarked)

or of a past or present tense:

(58)   Watch while I *hit* the ball.   Present tense (unmarked)

I just *hit* three home runs in a row.   Past tense (unmarked)

Linguists have assumed, on the basis of analogy, that if the noun in *one dog* is singular and in *three dogs* is plural, then in *one sheep* the noun is singular and in *three sheep* it is plural. Still using analogy as their basis, they infer the present and past tense forms of the verb *hit* in (58) after comparing them with the sentences in (59):

(59)   Watch while he *bats* the ball.   Present tense (marked)

He just *batted* three home runs in a row.   Past tense (marked)

Alternative explanations for sentences (55) through (59) exist. One can explain (56b), for instance, by arguing that main verb phrases of English can contain *either* TENSE or MODAL. We prefer an explanation that assumes that TENSE is the defining element of the finite verb in the predicate of a sentence.

However these sentences are explained, speakers of English generally agree that all of the sentences in (55) through (59) contain finite main verb phrases. Nonfinite verbs also play an important role in English sentences. Notice the present and past participles *eating* and *eaten* in the sentences of (55c) through (55f). The participles are inflected verbs, but they are not finite: they do not indicate tense. Rather, they indicate whether an action is thought of as in progress (present participle) or as completed (past participle). Consequently, for most speakers of English, participles cannot serve as the predicate of a sentence:

(60)   *They *eating*.

*They *eaten*.

As we have seen above, present and past participles occur following inflected auxiliaries in finite main verb phrases. They also serve as headwords in nonfinite verb phrases like the following:

(61)   While *eating* dinner, he sometimes read.   Present participle

Having *eaten* dinner, he watched TV.   Past participle

and as noun modifiers:

(62)   Do you see that dog *eating* from the table?   Present participle

What happened to the *half-eaten* pie?   Past participle

Nonfinite verbs function in a variety of ways in English sentences. They are so important, in fact, that we devote four chapters (Chapters 9 through 12) to contrasting the differences between finite and nonfinite verbs and verb phrases. Meanwhile, you will encounter them in our exercises and examples because they are so common in English that it is difficult to write sentences without them. Remember that the finite verb is the one inflected for tense.

WHAT'S THE USAGE? *Verb Tense and Aspect in AAVE*

African American Vernacular English (AAVE) has its own syntactical structure, one that differs from that of Standard American English (SAE). AAVE speakers may use the inflectional past tense morpheme {-ed} in many contexts, but in others they may convey the past tense through the present tense plus adverbial expressions of past time, such as *last night, yesterday,* or *on Sunday.* Because AAVE pronunciation rules call for the simplification of clusters of two or more consonants in succession, words like *fact* may be pronounced *fac.* In a sentence like *He pass the exam,* for example, it is hard to decide whether the speaker intended to use the past tense but dropped the *t* between the consonant at the end of *pass* and the consonant at the beginning of *the,* or whether the past tense has been omitted altogether. Some speakers of English as a second language also omit the {-ed} marker of the past tense if their native language is uninflected for tense.

AAVE has a complex tense-aspect system that differs markedly from SAE. In *He be readin' all day,* the use of *be* marks habitual, continuative aspect. The addition of *all day* intensifies the continuative aspect. SAE would require something like *He spends all of his days reading.* In *He bin readin' to her,* the form *been* has perfect progressive meaning, similar to SAE *has been reading.* Finally, *He done did it* emphasizes the perfect aspect of an action, as expressed in SAE by *He already did it.*

Compound Verb Forms—Perfect and Progressive

Compound verb forms are those containing participles. Traditionally, these forms have been said to express **aspects** of the action: whether ongoing (progressive aspect) or completed (perfect aspect). Remember that the terms *present* and *past* name the tense of the finite verb (its form), and they also refer to time. The terms *perfect* and *progressive* indicate whether a particular state or action has been completed or is in progress. When tense and perfect are combined, the function of tense changes. Instead of signaling simple time, it indicates whether an action has been completed before the present time (present perfect) or before some past time (past perfect). As we have seen above, participles occur in the following patterns:

(63)   The presence of HAVE + {-en} always means that the following verb will be in a *perfect* form.

The presence of BE + {-ing} always means that the following verb will be in a *progressive* form.

This reliable correlation allows us to simplify our symbolic representation of the auxiliary portion of the main verb phrase. Instead of:

(64)   AUX = TENSE + (MODAL) + (HAVE + {-en}) + (BE + {-ing}) we can abbreviate the formula to:

(65)   AUX = TENSE + (MODAL) + (PERFECT) + (PROGRESSIVE)

We can also revise the tree diagram in Figure 6.4 to incorporate these terms:

(66)

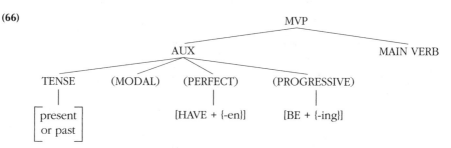

If you recall that HAVE + {-en} equals the *perfect* and BE + {-ing} equals the *progressive,* you need not memorize the names of compound verb forms. You can "read" them by decomposing the main verb phrase. Their labels are derived from their tense (past or present) or else from the presence of the modals *will* or *shall* (future) in combination with HAVE + {-en} (perfect) and BE + {-ing} (progressive).

Perfect verb forms, created by using the auxiliary verb HAVE followed by a past-participle form of a verb (written as HAVE + {-en}) in the main verb phrase, emphasize the beginning or the completion of an action. Because of the inclusion of the past participle, students tend to think of all of these as past tenses, but often they are not; in addition to the past perfect, it is possible to have both a present perfect and a future perfect, all formed by combining the helping verb HAVE with a past participle form of the verb that follows.

The Present Perfect (present + Perfect + MV)

The present perfect (present + HAVE + {-en} + MV) refers to an action that was completed in the immediate past or one that began in the past and contin-ues in the present:

(67)   I *have finished* the book you lent me.   (immediate past)

He *has taught* at Harvard for 20 years.   (past, into the present)

Students sometimes find the present perfect confusing because it exhibits a mismatch between time (past) and tense (present). Remember, however, that tense is marked by the form of the first verb in the main verb phrase. The perfect aspect always involves past *time:* Some action has been complet-ed in the past. Its *tense* gives a point of reference relative to the present time. If the completion occurred at an indeterminate time before now, the tense used is present, and it means "before the present moment." If the completion occurred before some definite time in the past, the tense used is past, forming a past perfect, and it means "before a specific time or action in the past."

The Past Perfect (past + Perfect + MV)

The past perfect (past + HAVE + {-en} + MV), which always expresses past time, expresses an action that took place before another one:

(68)   After he *had shoveled* the walk, it began to snow again.

Past action	*it began to snow again*
Previous past action	*he had shoveled the walk*

He believed that the play *had* already *ended.*

Past action	*He believed*
Previous past action	*the play had already ended*

The Future Perfect (present + will/shall + Perfect + MV)

The future perfect (present + *will/shall* + HAVE + {-en} + MV) signals an action that will occur before some time or event in the future:

(69)   On August 30, Jan *will have owned* the same car for 20 years.

Future time	*On August 30*
Future action complete	*Jan will have owned the same car for 20 years*

The airplane *will have left* before we reach the airport.

First future action	*The airplane will have left*
Second future action	*we reach the airport*

Progressive verb forms, formed by using the auxiliary BE followed by the present participle (BE + {-ing}) in the main verb phrase, are used to stress that an action or state is or was ongoing; the time referred to may be past, present, or future.

The Present Progressive (present + Progressive + MV)

The present progressive (present + BE + {-ing} + MV) is used to express an ongoing action or state in the present time or, as is true of the simple present tense, either a habitual or a future action:

(70)   A dog *is barking* in the yard next door.   (present time)
Edward *is leaving* for South America tonight.   (future time)
John *is* always *snarling* at someone.   (habitual action)

The Past Progressive (past + Progressive + MV)

The past progressive (past + BE + {-ing} + MV) signifies an action that was ongoing in the past. Although the past progressive can occur in a simple sentence,

(71) A hearty soup *was simmering* on the back of the stove. (past time)

this verb form is most often paired with another verb to express an action that was occurring at some time in the past when something else was going on, as well:

(72) The telephone *was ringing* when I opened the front door.

Ongoing past action	*The telephone was ringing*
Other past action	*I opened the front door*

The Future Progressive (present + will/shall + Progressive + MV)

The future progressive (present + *will/shall* BE + {-ing} + MV) signals that an action will take place in the future:

(73) I *shall be seeing* him tomorrow afternoon. (future time)

or that an action will occur in the future while something else is going on:

(74) It *will be snowing* by the time we get to the mountains.

Ongoing future action	*It will be snowing*
Other future action	*we get to the mountains*

Perfect progressive verb forms result when both the auxiliary HAVE followed by a past participle (HAVE + {-en}) and the auxiliary BE followed by a present participle (BE + {-ing}) occur in the same main verb phrase. These forms combine the emphasis of the perfect on the beginning or ending of an event with the expression by the progressive of its ongoing nature.

The Present-Perfect Progressive (present + Perfect + Progressive + MV)

The present-perfect progressive (present + HAVE + {-en} + BE + {-ing} + MV) signifies an action that began in the past and is still ongoing in the present:

(75) They *have been testing* our phone for the last hour.

The Past-Perfect Progressive (past + Perfect + Progressive + MV)

The past-perfect progressive (past + HAVE + {-en} + BE + {-ing} + MV) identifies an action that began before a time or another action in the past:

(76) By 11:00, she *had been singing* for three hours.

Past time	*11:00*
Past action	*she had been singing for three hours*

They *had been waiting* for 25 minutes when we arrived.

Past action   *we arrived*

Previous past action   *They had been waiting for 25 minutes*

The Future-Perfect Progressive
(present + will/shall + Perfect + Progressive + MV)

The future-perfect progressive (present + *will/shall* + HAVE + {-en} + BE + {-ing}) expresses an action that began at some unspecified time before another time or event in the future and that continues into the future:

(77)   By Friday, that cup *will have been sitting* there for ten days.

Future time   *Friday*

Future action   *that cup will have been sitting there for*
                                                    ten days

When you get this card, I *will have been traveling* for three weeks.

Future action   *you get this card*

Previous future action   *I will have been traveling for three weeks*

Figure 6.7 recapitulates the information on time, tense, and verb form given above.

■ EXERCISE 6.8

Identify by name the form of each of the italicized main verb phrases in the following sentences. Break each into its underlying structure. An example has been done for you.

EXAMPLE

Woody Allen *will be appearing* at the film festival next spring.

will be appearing: *future progressive form; present + will + BE + {-ing} + **appear***

1. A huge rabbit from Austria recently *invaded* Italy.
2. A Viennese art group *has erected* a giant pink bunny on an Italian mountainside.
3. The 200-foot-long rabbit *has been lying* on Mt. Colletto Fava in Northern Italy for several months.
4. Dozens of women *must have contributed* to the knitting of the giant rabbit.
5. It *will be lying* on its back there for the next 20 years.
6. The art group *is allowing* people to clamber up the rabbit's 20-foot sides.
7. People *can* also *lie* on its big pink stomach when they *are feeling* tired of climbing.
8. It *is* pretty in pink today, but it *will* not *be* very attractive by 2025.

SUMMARY	
Traditional Names of English Verb Forms	
Form Name *[structure]*	**Example**
Simple Present [present]	*Our dog barks.*
Simple Past [past]	*Our dog barked.*
Future Time [present + MODAL]	*Our dog will bark.*
Present Progressive [present + BE + {-ing}]	*Our dog is barking.*
Past Progressive [past + BE + {-ing}]	*Our dog was barking.*
Future Progressive [present + MODAL + BE + {-ing}]	*Our dog will be barking.*
Present Perfect [present + HAVE + {-en}]	*Our dog has barked.*
Past Perfect [past + HAVE + {-en}]	*Our dog had barked.*
Future Perfect [present + MODAL + HAVE + {-en}]	*Our dog will have barked.*
Present-Perfect Progressive [present + HAVE + {-en} + BE + {-ing}]	*Our dog has been barking.*
Past-Perfect Progressive [past + HAVE + {-en} + BE + {-ing}]	*Our dog had been barking.*
Future-Perfect Progressive [present + MODAL + HAVE + {-en} + BE + {-ing}]	*Our dog will have been barking.*

Figure 6.7

The Meaning of Modals

Modals, as we saw earlier, do not inflect to show tense like ordinary verbs. Although they were more like other verbs at an earlier stage in the history of English, through centuries of linguistic change, they have become a unique group of auxiliary verbs that affect the meaning of other verbs in special ways.

Sometimes, the multiple meanings of the same modal seem to be related to one another. For example, *can* often refers to "the ability to do something," as in the sentence, *Sharon can pilot jet aircraft.* A somewhat related meaning of *can* indicates a potentiality to do something: *Winds near the eye of a hurricane can reach speeds close to 200 miles per hour.* A third common meaning of *can*, "having the permission to do something," also seems related to the other two: *Professor Brown says we can turn in our papers late.*

However, other meanings of modals seem only distantly related, if at all. *Might*, for instance, sometimes refers to "a rather weak potentiality," as in *It might rain.* But at other times, it seems to indicate (through sarcasm) "an unfulfilled obligation to do something": *You might show some gratitude.*

Without pretending to exhaust all of the more subtle meanings of modals, in Figure 6.8 we list some of the more important ways in which modals contribute to the meanings of verb phrases.

WHAT'S THE USAGE?   *Can and May*

In Figure 6.8 we list "permission" as one of the meanings of both *can* and *may*. At one time, *can* referred to the ability to do something (*We can swim across the lake*) and *may* expressed permission (*You may swim here if you wish*). Because speakers of English have failed to maintain the distinction between the two, most handbooks and dictionaries no longer prescribe that the difference between them be preserved. For most speakers of American English, *can* is now used interchangeably with *may* in sentences like *You can/may swim here if you wish.* Observe your own usage and that of your friends, teachers, and others. What patterns, if any, do you find in the use of *can* and *may*?

Other Auxiliaries

The modal auxiliaries form a special class because of their function in the sentence and because of their inability to inflect for tense. Other verbs and verb phrases perform similar functions as helping verbs in the main verb phrase, but are excluded from the MVP formula because of idiosyncrasies in their behavior. In the following examples, the word(s) functioning as helping verbs are shown in contrast with modal auxiliaries:

(78)

Modal	**Other**
They *must* leave.	They *have to* leave.
	They *have got to* leave.
It *will* rain soon.	It *is going to* rain soon.
They *should* be on the table.	They *ought to* be on the table.
Sometimes, we *would* disagree.	Sometimes, we *used to* disagree.

SUMMARY		
Meanings of Modal Auxiliaries		
Modal	Meaning	Example
can	ability permission potentiality	*Mike can play tennis.* *Yes, you can go to the movies.* *A redwood can grow to be extremely tall.*
could	ability permission potentiality	*I could ride a bike when I was seven.* *He said I could go with you.* *It could rain.*
may	potentiality permission	*It may rain.* *Yes, you may go to the movies.*
might	potentiality obligation	*It might rain.* *You might show some gratitude.*
will	promise certainty command future time	*I will be there.* *The sun will rise tomorrow.* *Sophomores will report at 10 a.m.* *They will probably be late.*
would	past habit obstinacy	*Sometimes he would sing for us.* *You would do that, wouldn't you?*
shall	promise legal command future	*I shall be there.* *The Vice President shall preside.* *We shall have to redo this report.*
should	weak obligation possibility	*You should study for the test.* *If he should come, tell him I called.*
must	strong obligation deduction	*You must pay your taxes.* *The streets are wet. It must have rained.*

Figure 6.8

All of the auxiliary verbs in (78) are followed by the unmarked infinitive form of the verb. A few others, however, are followed by verbs in the *-ing* or *-ed* form, as in *keep talking, start working, get finished.*

Some dialects of American English have helping verbs not included in our discussion. Some African American dialects, for instance, have available to their speakers an invariant form of *be* that can be used to indicate future time. Speakers of standard English, lacking that form, express the equivalent meaning by using a modal:

(79)   Our teacher be in class tomorrow. (some African American dialects)[1]
           Our teacher will be in class tomorrow. (Standard English dialect)

   Some dialects of Chicano English express the progressive simply by using the helping verb BE without the morpheme {-ing}.

(80)   They're play. (some Chicano English dialects)[2]
           They're playing. (Standard English dialect)

   Speakers of both dialects may omit BE in creating the progressive form:

(81)   He sleeping with a bear. (some Chicano English dialects)
           That kid messing up right now. (some African American dialects)

   Many speakers of Appalachian English have an auxiliary verb not included in our discussion: *done* + {-en}, used as an emphatic present perfect. Speakers of standard English would express the same information using *completely* or—more informally—*totally*:

(82)   He done wiped them out. (some Appalachian English dialects)
           He completely wiped them out. (Standard English dialect)

   We discuss two other constituents of the auxiliary when we discuss transformational rules in Chapter 8. One is BE + {-en} as a component used in forming passive sentences, such as *The book was written by a young author.* The other is *do,* which we use to form interrogative and negative sentences in English.

Have and *Be* as Main Verbs

In all of the examples in this chapter, *have* and *be* have appeared only as auxiliary verbs. However, unlike modals, which occur only as auxiliaries, *have* and *be* can be used as main verbs, auxiliaries, or both:

   1. The dinner is already on the table.
   [TENSE (present) + *be*]
   Be is a main verb.

   2. Those children are being noisy.
   [TENSE (present) + BE + {-ing} + *be*]
   The first *be* is an auxiliary verb, and the second one is the main verb.

   3. They have three automobiles in their garage.
   [TENSE (present) + *have*]
   Have is the main verb.

   4. He has had three colds this winter.
   [TENSE (present) + HAVE + {-en} + *have*]
   The first *have* is an auxiliary, and the second is the main verb.

   As a main verb, *be* has little or no meaning; it simply links the subject with some noun, adjective, or adverb phrase in the predicate. It seems to be used in standard English because our rules for forming sentences require that we have a verb inflected for tense. Some languages (Russian, for example) express the same information without a verb, simply by placing the subject and its complement side by side. In informal speech, perhaps many speakers occasionally omit the linking verb in sentences where it has contracted (*You're doing well* alternating with *You doing well*). In some dialects of American English, the omission of the relatively meaningless contracted form of *be* is a regular feature:

(83)   This a school. (some dialects of Chicano English)
        Our bus late today. (some African American dialects)

■ *EXERCISE 6.9*

In each of the following sentences, draw a line under the subject and circle the main verb phrase. Then break each main verb phrase into its underlying structure and indicate whether *have* and/or *be* are auxiliary verbs or main verbs. Ignore the rest of the predicate. An example has been done for you.

EXAMPLE

Don (will be having) surgery next Monday if his doctor (is) available.

[*will be having*] = TENSE *(Present)* + MODAL + BE {-ing} + **have**

BE is an auxiliary and **have** is the main verb.

[*is*] = TENSE *(Present)* + **be**

Be is the main verb.

1. The National Zoo is hoping to reopen its Panda House soon; it will be ready for huge crowds.
2. Zoo keepers had closed the house to the public just before their mother panda gave birth in July.
3. The public has been able to see just the father panda, who has been spending time outside in his yard.
4. The mother has only occasionally appeared in her yard, and visitors have not yet seen the baby. (Remember that *only occasionally* and *not yet* are modifiers; they are not part of the main verb phrase.)
5. When the Panda House reopens, zoo officials will be giving out timed admission tickets.
6. Officials are expecting that the male baby cub will have a name by then.
7. Visitors to the zoo's Web site have been submitting names for the panda since his birth.
8. So far, they have sent in close to 150,000 names, but the zoo is being quiet about its choice.

WHAT'S THE USAGE? *Shall and Will*

Many grammar handbooks suggest a rule for the use of *shall* and *will*. Shall, according to this rule, should be used with first-person subjects (*I* and *we*) and *will* with second- and third-person subjects (*you* and all others) to express statements about the future:

(84)   *I **shall** probably graduate in June.*
*They **will** repair your car this afternoon.*

For emphasis, as in expressing a demand, a threat, or a promise, the pattern should be reversed, according to these handbooks:

(85)   *I **will** sue him no matter what he does.*
*You **shall** turn in every assignment or fail this class.*

▪ USAGE EXERCISE 6.10_____

The "rule" for distinguishing between *shall* and *will* illustrates how usage changes. Fifty years ago, students were routinely drilled on observing the distinction described here between *shall* and *will*. Drill was necessary because the difference was disappearing, even though grammar handbooks and dictionaries continued to prescribe that the two should be kept separate. You will probably find in your classroom that some students know the rule and try to follow it, some know there is a rule but are uncertain about how apply it, and some do not know that such a rule has ever existed. To which group do you belong?

SUMMARY

In this chapter, we have discussed the phrases that function as the most important constituents of sentences: noun phrases, verb phrases, adjective phrases, adverb phrases. Understanding how the main verb phrase functions is useful in identifying and (as you will find in later chapters) classifying the main verbs of sentences and understanding a variety of sentence structures, including passives, questions, commands, exclamations, negatives, and others. In the grammar of English, the systematic patterning of the main verb phrase auxil-

SUMMARY
Main Verb Phrase Formula (Revised)
1. MVP = AUX + MV
2. AUX = TENSE + (MODAL) + (PERFECT) + (PROGRESSIVE)
3. TENSE = past or present
4. MODAL = *can, could, will, would, shall, should, may, might, must*
5. PERFECT = [HAVE + {-en}]
6. PROGRESSIVE = [BE + {-ing}]

Figure 6.9

iary is unique. The main verb phrase formula represents the regularity of its underlying structure (see Figure 6.9).

We have seen that the subject of a sentence is always a noun phrase, and the predicate is always a verb phrase. The verb phrase functioning as predicate must include at least a main verb phrase, but it may also include other phrases—noun phrases, adjective phrases, and adverb phrases—that function as complements (completers) of the verb. Chapter 7 includes discussion of the complements that can be important constituents of the verb phrase.

Figure 6.10 summarizes graphically this chapter's discussion of the phrase structure of sentences, with special emphasis on the importance of the main verb phrase.

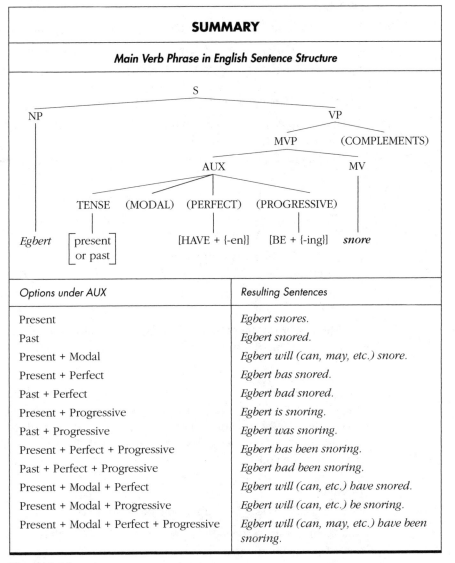

SUMMARY

Main Verb Phrase in English Sentence Structure

Options under AUX	Resulting Sentences
Present	*Egbert snores.*
Past	*Egbert snored.*
Present + Modal	*Egbert will (can, may, etc.) snore.*
Present + Perfect	*Egbert has snored.*
Past + Perfect	*Egbert had snored.*
Present + Progressive	*Egbert is snoring.*
Past + Progressive	*Egbert was snoring.*
Present + Perfect + Progressive	*Egbert has been snoring.*
Past + Perfect + Progressive	*Egbert had been snoring.*
Present + Modal + Perfect	*Egbert will (can, etc.) have snored.*
Present + Modal + Progressive	*Egbert will (can, etc.) be snoring.*
Present + Modal + Perfect + Progressive	*Egbert will (can, may, etc.) have been snoring.*

Figure 6.10

REVIEW EXERCISES

Sentence Constituents

The ability to identify sentence constituents remains important throughout the remainder of the text, as we analyze ever more complex sentences and attempt to see how these can be reduced to simple patterns based on the four phrase types studied in Chapter 6. Divide each of the following sentences into its subject and predicate. Then label its sentence constituents: NP, MVP, ADJP, ADVP. The first one has been done for you.

EXAMPLE

The radio announcer   will probably give the composer's name.

The radio announcer	*will give*	*the composer's name*	*probably*
NP	*MVP*	*NP*	*ADVP*

1. Americans have taken chicken wings to their hearts.
2. Wing Nights at chain restaurants like KFC and Domino's have sent chicken wing prices sky-high.
3. Wingnuts is the first California restaurant to specialize in chicken wings.
4. Wing Ding fundraisers are popular throughout the United States.
5. The Jacksonville, Florida, Chamber of Commerce is sponsoring a Wing Ding Chicken Wing Cook-Off this year.
6. At a Wing Ding in Miami, one man ate 124 buffalo chicken wings in 12 minutes.
7. He was 10 chicken wings shy of the chicken-wing-eating world record.
8. The Placer County, California, Wing Ding features a world famous chicken-bone-throwing contest.

Main Verb Phrase

Break each of the italicized main verb phrases in the following sentences into its underlying structure. Then give the name of the verb form. Notice that the main verb is always last in the Main Verb Phrase. An example has been done for you.

EXAMPLE

Arnaud *has been telling* us about his new motorcycle.

has been telling: *present + HAVE + {-en} + BE + {-ing} + tell;* present perfect progressive form

1. Several students have been studying together for the math final.

2. They may be feeling fairly confident that they will pass easily.

3. In fact, Lauren is probably already waiting outside the classroom.

4. Ted might have been studying alone for the exam.

5. He had not had time to study until yesterday.

6. No one has seen him since yesterday morning.

7. Bob should have been mastering addition and subtraction while he was dreaming of becoming a high school math teacher.

8. He thought he had understood everything until he began to study.

Practical Applications: Modal Auxiliaries

In this exercise, you are asked to draw on of the meaning of modal auxiliaries and use other auxiliaries to relate an action to a specific time (past, present, or indefinite) and aspect (perfect or progressive). Use the bolded words in your response to the following suggestions.

1. Using the simple present tense, write a sentence describing something a friend **always** does.

2. Write a sentence describing something you **can** do very well. Identify the time of the action and the tenses of each main verb phrase.

3. Write a sentence describing something you **could** do once but that you no longer **can.** Identify the time of the action and the tenses of each main verb phrase.

4. Write a sentence describing what a university **could** do to make registration simpler. Identify the time of the action and the tenses of each main verb phrase.

5. Write a sentence describing something you **are** doing right now. Identify the time of the action and the tenses and aspects of each main verb phrase.

6. Write a sentence about something that you are pleased to **have** finally finished. Identify the time of the action and the tenses and aspects of each main verb phrase.

7. Write a sentence describing something you **will** do next week. Identify the time of the action and the tenses of each main verb phrase.

8. Write a sentence describing something you once believed **had** happened but later discovered had not. Identify the time of the action and the tenses and aspects of each main verb phrase.

KEY TERMS

adjective phrase, ADJP
adverb phrase, ADVP
aspect
auxiliary verb, helping verb, AUX
BE auxiliary
complement
constituent
finite verb
form
function
future time
HAVE auxiliary
headword
main verb phrase, MVP
main verb phrase formula (verb
  expansion rule)
modal, modal auxiliary

noun phrase, NP
number
perfect progressive verb forms
perfect verb forms
person
predicate
principal parts of English verbs
  base form
  past-participle form
  present-participle form
  simple present-tense form
  simple past-tense form
progressive verb forms
subject
tense
verb phrase, VP

ENDNOTES

1. Examples are based on Geneva Smitherman, *Talkin and Testifyin: The Language of Black America* (Boston: Houghton Mifflin, 1977), pp. 19–23.
2. Chicano examples are based on Gustavo Gonzalez, "Chicano English," in *Chicano Speech in the Bilingual Classroom,* eds. Dennis J. Bixler-Marquez and Jacob Ornstein-Galicia (New York: Peter Lang Publishing, 1988), pp. 77–78. All rights reserved.

Five Basic Sentence Types

7

CHAPTER PREVIEW

In this chapter, we will analyze the entire predicate, focusing upon the main verb itself and any noun phrases, adjective phrases, or adverb phrases that are required to complement (complete) it. While analyzing complements, we will ignore the auxiliary (AUX), to which we gave so much attention earlier, not including it in the phrase structure trees or formulas presented. You already understand how it is structured, and no variations that occur in it affect the analysis of predicates that we are undertaking to clarify here.

CHAPTER GOALS

At the end of this chapter, you should be able to

- Distinguish among *be, intransitive, linking,* and *transitive* verbs.
- Recognize the *five basic sentence types* on the basis of the verb and its complements.
- Differentiate between *adverbial* and *adjectival verb complements.*
- Recognize both *adjectival* and *nominal subject complements.*
- Distinguish among *direct objects, indirect objects,* and *object complements.*
- Draw phrase structure trees and Reed-Kellogg diagrams for each of the five sentence types.

Like all other languages, English consists of a potentially infinite set of sentences. If, in order to analyze English grammar, we first had to collect and study all of the possible English sentences, our task would be impossible. Fortunately, we can begin to understand how to analyze the grammatical structure of sentences without worrying about each individual one of the billions that have already been (or that are still waiting to be) spoken and written. Learning to recognize just five simple patterns that underlie almost all of the sentences of English is a crucial first step.

BINARY STRUCTURE

The five basic sentence types of English are alike in that each reflects the binary (two-part) structure that characterizes the simplest sentences of the language. Underlying such prototype sentences, we can, as we saw in Chapter 6, discover a **noun phrase** (NP) functioning as **subject** and a **verb phrase** (VP) functioning as **predicate.** Look at these examples:

(1) Jenny   purred.
      Our neighbor's pet   is outdoors constantly.
      The tomcat curled up on the cushion   seemed very friendly.
      The smallest kitten   became a family member.
      A furry female   eyed a bowl of tuna.

In each of these simple sentences, the left-hand constituent is a noun phrase functioning as the subject. Remember that a noun phrase is either a noun or a group of words that can substitute for a noun, and as the example sentences demonstrate, any noun phrase can be the subject of a sentence. Thus, the first subject is a single noun; the others are noun phrases that could be interchanged with it.

The right-hand constituent of the sentence is a verb phrase functioning as its predicate. Like the noun phrase subjects, the verb phrases in the sentences above are interchangeable. Any of the predicates may occur with any of the subjects to form complete sentences.

In some sentences of English, the verb phrase consists solely of a main verb phrase with its single verb constituting the entire predicate; in others, the main verb phrase may be accompanied by other words, phrases, and clauses that are called either **complements** (because they *complete* the predicate) or **modifiers** (because they *add to* or *modify* the meaning of the verb). Complements are required to complete the verb; modifiers are optional. Notice, again, that the verb phrases in the sentences above are interchangeable: Any of the right-hand constituents may occur with any of the subjects to form complete sentences.

As we saw in Chapter 6, one of the ways linguists represent the structure of sentences is by drawing phrase structure trees. To do so, they begin with the largest category, the sentence (S), and hypothesize that all sentences in English are made up of subject noun phrases (NP) and predicate verb phrases (VP). They represent this information in the *phrase structure rule,* using a single arrow that means "can be written as" or "consists of":

(2)   S $\longrightarrow$ NP + VP

This general rule describes the basic form of all sentences of English and suggests that, to convey information in English, we create sentences that contain subjects (either explicit or implied) and predicates. If the order of the constituents is reversed (**Is outdoors all the time our neighbor's pet*), the structure is not a grammatical English sentence; if one of the constituents is missing (*Is outdoors all the time*), the structure is a sentence *fragment*.

To draw a phrase structure tree diagram, put the item to the left of the arrow at the top and branch from it to the items on the right. The branching point (*S* in this tree) is called a *node;* any terminal point in a branch can become a node for another branching, as we shall see below. In a phrase structure tree (or phrase marker), each node and each terminal point is labeled with the name of the syntactic category to which it belongs.

A phrase structure tree diagram representing the subject-predicate structure of each of these prototypical sentences would look like this:

(3)

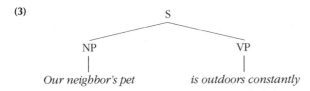

S

| NP | VP |
| *Our neighbor's pet* | *is outdoors constantly* |

This simple phrase marker describes equally well the underlying structure of all five of our example sentences. It shows how they are alike in structure. All that needs to be changed is the specific noun phrase or verb phrase that occurs as subject or predicate.

(4)

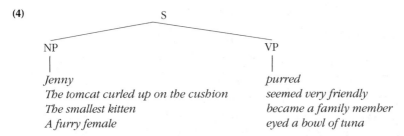

S

NP	VP
Jenny	*purred*
The tomcat curled up on the cushion	*seemed very friendly*
The smallest kitten	*became a family member*
A furry female	*eyed a bowl of tuna*

It is, in fact, the structural differences in the verb phrase that distinguish the five basic sentence types. In the remainder of this chapter, we discuss these distinct kinds of sentences, numbering them with roman numerals: Types I, II, III, IV, and V. However, there is nothing sacred or even traditional about our numbering scheme. Assigning each type a number simply provides us with an easy way of referring to them.

To review what you learned in Chapter 6 about identifying sentence constituents, including the constituents of the verb phrase, complete the following exercise.

■ *EXERCISE 7.1*

Each of the strings of words below contains a subject and a main verb phrase. Some of them are complete sentences as they stand. Others need additional words (complements) in order to become sentences. Add only NPs, ADJPs, or ADVPs that are necessary to complete each sentence and then identify what kind of phrase you have supplied. If two or more phrases are required, note what kinds they are. If the string is already complete, leave it alone.

EXAMPLE

The post office employees quickly sorted _____.

The post office employees quickly sorted **the mail.**   *(NP)*

1. Before the storm the sun was _____.
2. Then the clouds looked quite _____.
3. The weatherman predicted _____.
4. The National Hurricane Center named _____.
5. I felt _____.
6. Automobiles clogged _____.
7. Rescue workers patrolled _____.
8. Trees fell _____.

TYPE I—THE INTRANSITIVE TYPE

Consider the following examples:

(5)	Fish	swim.
	A telephone	is ringing.
	Jan	snores loudly.
	The customer	complained persistently.
	Carla	must have enrolled rather early.

If you divide each of these sentences to show its constituent structure, you will find that each contains a noun phrase subject and a main verb followed either by nothing at all or else by an adverb phrase. Notice that the adverb phrases are optional, and there are no noun phrases or adjective phrases functioning as constituents in the predicates of these sentences. The verbs are complete by themselves.

The simplest Type I sentences consist of a subject followed by a predicate in which there is only a main verb followed by optional adverb phrases. The technical name of the type of verb that can stand alone in the verb phrase and function as the entire predicate is **intransitive.** The sentence type gets its name from the intransitive verb that is its distinguishing feature.

By extending the branches of the phrase marker, we get a representation of the constituent structure of sentences with intransitive verbs like the following:

(6)

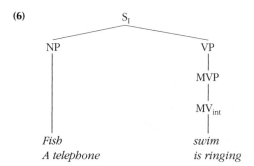

Fish   swim
A telephone   is ringing

The symbol S_I means "Sentence Type I," and MV with the subscript $_{int}$ means "intransitive main verb." Notice that there is no mention of adverb phrases in this tree. Adverb phrases are optional in Types I, III, IV, and V; their presence or absence does not distinguish one of these four types from another. For example, omitting *loudly* from *Jan snores loudly* does not change the structural type of the sentence; *Jan snores* still contains an intransitive verb. Similarly, *The customer complained* and *The customer complained persistently* both contain intransitive verbs, as do *Carla must have enrolled* and *Carla must have enrolled rather early.* (In Type II sentences, as we will see, one adverbial complement indicating place or time is required, but a variety of adverbial modifiers may occur optionally in all five sentences.)

In Chapter 6 we used phrase structure trees to clarify visually for you the relationships between the auxiliary (containing TENSE, MODAL, HAVE, and BE) and the main verb. Beginning in Chapter 7, we will be focusing on the structure of the entire predicate, which consists of the main verb phrase and its complements. Remember, as you read this chapter, that any combination of elements from the auxiliary may precede the main verb in the sentences we are discussing without affecting the basic structure of the predicate. Whether the verb in sentence (6) is *swim, are swimming,* or *must have swum,* for example, makes no difference in the basic sentence type of the predicate. Consequently, in order that students can concentrate visually on the verb complements—the topic of this chapter—we will branch only to the MVP and not to its parts. It is the main verb itself, and not its tense or aspect, that determines the sentence type.

In drawing trees for the sentence prototypes, we will include only essential constituents of the structural formulas. Remember that one or more adverbial modifiers can occur in the predicates of any of the five basic sentence types. In the discussion that follows each sentence type, we show how optional adverb phrases are added to the tree or formula.

A linear method of representing the constituent structure of sentence types is by means of the **structural formulas** just referred to, in which the sentence constituents are arranged in the same order as they occur in the basic form of the sentence. The structural formula for prototypical Type I sentences (like the ones displayed in the phrase marker above) is the following:

(7) $S_I = NP + MV_{int}$

A telephone + is ringing.

The formula says that Type I sentences consist of a noun phrase subject (in this case, *a telephone*) followed by an intransitive verb predicate (*is ringing*). Intransitive verbs can also have one or more **adverbial modifiers,** like *loudly*, *persistently*, and *rather early* in the examples at the beginning of this section. Adverbial modifiers of the verb add information about how, when, where, why, or how much something happened. Adverbs are the prototypical modifiers of verbs, but as we saw in Chapter 6, a variety of phrases and clauses may also function as adverbial modifiers, supplying the same sorts of additional meaning to the verb.

To draw a Reed-Kellogg diagram of the structures in (6), put the subject noun and the main verb phrase on a horizontal line bisected by a vertical line. Modifiers go on a line slanting away from the word they modify. Thus, the determiner *a* goes on a line slanting away from *telephone:*

(8)

| Fish | swim | | telephone | is ringing |

In representing the constituent structure of sentences that contain optional adverbial modifiers, we simply add an adverb phrase (ADVP) branch to the tree in the predicate or an optional ADVP to the structural formula. A structural formula for the same sentence, showing the optional adverbial phrase in parentheses, would look like this:

(9) $S_I = NP + MV_{int} + (ADVP)$

The phrase marker of *Jan snores loudly* would be:

(10)
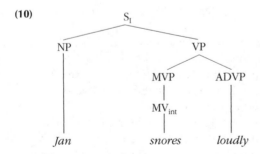

You can read the sentence directly from the phrase marker: *Jan* is the noun phrase subject; *snores* is the intransitive main verb; *loudly* is an adverb phrase; and together, *snores loudly* constitutes the entire predicate verb phrase.

Loudly is considered an **adverb phrase of manner** ($ADVP_{man}$) because it adds information about the way or manner in which the action represented by the verb is carried out. As we will see when we look at Type II verbs, **adverb phrases of time** ($ADVP_{tm}$), like *soon* and *now*, and **adverb phrases of place** ($ADVP_{pl}$), like *here* and *there,* sometimes behave somewhat differently in sentences than do adverbs of manner, so we will include a subscript to remind you each time which kind of adverb is being used. In a Reed-Kellogg diagram, the adverb *loudly* would appear on a line slanted away from the verb it modifies:

(11)

Prepositional phrases (PREPP), like *to the manager* in *The customer complained to the manager,* frequently function adverbially in a sentence in the same way that adverbs do, and they, too, can express information of time, place, or manner. A prepositional phrase is a form consisting of a preposition (such as *in, on, under, with, to, through, between, at,* and others) followed by a noun phrase (like *the manager* in the example above). The noun phrase following the preposition functions as the *object* of the preposition. Some examples of other prepositional phrases are *on Mondays, under the table, with great speed, through the night, between innings,* and *at the movies.*

When prepositional phrases function adverbially, you might find it helpful to think of them as having been substituted for an adverb. For example, the prepositional phrase in *Sarah shoots **with exceptional accuracy*** has the same function as the adverb modifier in *Sarah shoots **very accurately*** and occupies the same position in the sentence. There is, in fact, a phrase structure rule that specifies that any kind of adverbial constituent of a sentence can be a prepositional phrase:

(12)   ADVP $\longrightarrow$ PREPP

In the phrase structure rule in (12), ADVP represents a ***function,*** and PREPP represents one of the ***forms*** that can fulfill that function. As we have seen, other forms, such as simple adverbs or subordinate clauses, can also fulfill the adverb phrase function. A prepositional phrase is a form that can serve other functions, as well. Prepositional phrases are widely used as adjectival modifiers, as is the case in *My complaint **to the manager** got immediate results.*

The phrase marker for a sentence with a prepositional phrase functioning as an adverbial modifier would be:

(13)

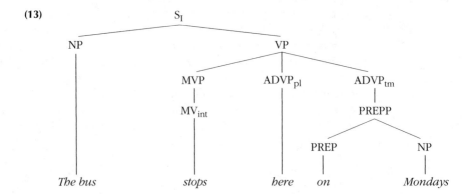

In order to focus on structural details more important for learning to distinguish among sentence types, we usually abbreviate the adverbial prepositional phrase part of the phrase marker by simply showing the words of the prepositional phrase directly beneath ADVP.

The abbreviated phrase marker would look like this:

(14)

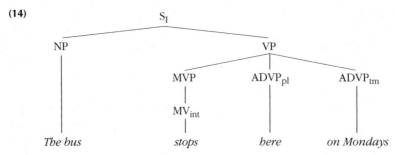

A related form that frequently functions as an adverbial modifier is a noun phrase without a preceding preposition:

(15)   The bus stops here *each Monday.*
Hans called *three times.*

In these examples, the noun phrases *each Monday* and *three times* function as adverbial modifiers, the equivalent of adverbs of time like *soon* or *often*. A complete phrase marker would represent such adverbial noun phrases like this:

(16)

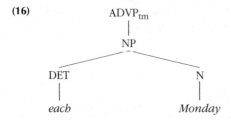

RULES OF THUMB
Tests for Identifying Type I Sentences
Intransitive Verb

1. You can test whether a verb is intransitive by dividing the predicate into phrases. If all the phrases except the main verb phrase are optional adverbial modifiers, then the verb is intransitive.
2. If you can substitute a prototypical adverb (like *here*, *then*, or *slowly*) for the phrase, it is an adverbial phrase.

Figure 7.1

However, as in the case of adverbial prepositional phrases, we can abbreviate the structure of adverbial noun phrases as:

(17) ADVP_{tm}

each Monday

Remember, from Chapter 5, the diagramming of the prepositional phrase? In a Reed-Kellogg diagram, the preposition goes on a line slanting away from the word it modifies—in this case, the verb *stops:*

(18)

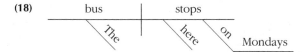

When there is no preposition, a blank line slants downward toward the noun phrase used as an adverbial modifier:

(19)

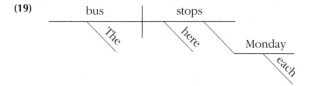

The Rules of Thumb in Figure 7.1 and the Summary in Figure 7.2 can help you to identify Type I sentences.

▇ *EXERCISE 7.2*

First, divide the following sentences into subject noun phrases and predicate verb phrases. Then label the main verb phrases, noun phrases, adjective

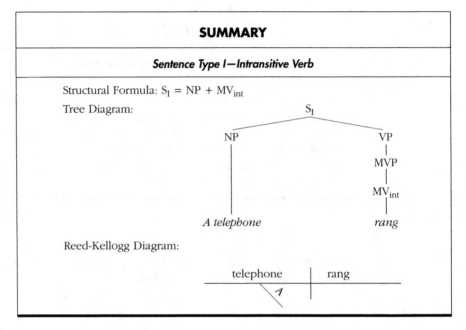

SUMMARY
Sentence Type I—Intransitive Verb

Structural Formula: $S_I = NP + MV_{int}$

Tree Diagram:

Reed-Kellogg Diagram:

Figure 7.2

phrases, and adverb phrases you find in the predicates. Finally, indicate which sentences are examples of the intransitive Type I pattern and which are not examples of the pattern.

EXAMPLE

Vera's instructor brought doughnuts to class today.

Subject	**Predicate**			
Vera's instructor	*brought*	*doughnuts*	*to class*	*today*
NP	*MVP*	*NP*	*ADVP*	*ADVP*
Not Type I	(Can you figure out why?)			

1. The weather changed suddenly this morning.
2. A sudden storm arrived without much warning.
3. We were just leaving for a picnic at the lake.
4. We went back inside the house instead.
5. We waited inside for an hour or so.
6. After that, we changed our plans.
7. We would have our picnic at home in the dining room.
8. After lunch, we remained in the house all afternoon.

■ *EXERCISE 7.3*

> Draw a phrase marker and a Reed-Kellogg diagram to show the structure of each of the Type I sentences below. In drawing phrase markers for this exercise, ignore the auxiliary portion of the main verb phrase, as we have done in our discussion above.
>
> 1. Several cookies remained on the child's plate.
> 2. The chocolate cookies had disappeared.
> 3. The ice cream sandwiches melted rapidly.
> 4. The gingerbread man fell to the floor.

▬ TYPES II, III, AND IV—LINKING (COPULAR) VERBS ▬

Type II—The Verb *Be* Requiring Adverbs of Time or Place

Look at the following examples:

(20)

Jesse	is outside.
Her job interviews	were yesterday.
Cheryl's notebook	must have been on the desk.
The reception	will be at noon.

If you divide these sentences into their constituents, you will see that they all contain a noun phrase subject, a main verb *be,* and an obligatory adverb phrase. That is, *Jesse is outside* can't be shortened to **Jesse is.* The adverb *outside* is essential. (The forms of *be,* as you recall, are *am, is, are, was, were, be, being,* and *been.*)

In Type II sentences, a form of the linking verb *be* requires an **adverbial complement** that completes the predicate and expresses place or time, like *outside* (ADVP$_{pl}$) or *yesterday* (ADVP$_{tm}$). Such complements refer to the place or time of the *subject,* not of the *verb.* Contrast the following:

(21) a. The train departs at noon.

b. The reception will be at noon.

In (21a), *at noon* tells the time of the action represented by the verb (departure). In (21b), *at noon* tells the time of the reception (expressed by the subject). Because *be* links the subject with its adverbial complement, it is called a **linking** (or **copular**) verb.

Type II sentences can be represented with a phrase marker like this one:

(22)

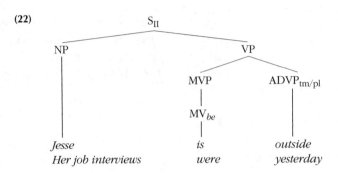

The adverb phrase symbol *ADVP* is written with a subscript $_{tm/pl}$ to indicate that it must be an adverbial constituent expressing either time or place. If the adverbial is one of place (*outside,* for instance), it would simply be labeled $ADVP_{pl}$. If the adverbial constituent is one of time (*yesterday*), the label would be $ADVP_{tm}$.

The structural formula for Type II sentences is:

(23) $S_{II} = NP + MV_{be} + ADVP_{tm/pl}$

Jesse + is + outside.

Her job interviews + were + yesterday.

The Reed-Kellogg diagram for Type II sentences is:

(24)

Adverb phrases of place and time include such adverbs as *inside, upstairs, here, away, nearby, then, now, today, tomorrow.* Prepositional phrases of time (*in the evening*) or place (*at the post office*) and noun phrases (*next week, Sunday*) can also function adverbially. For example, in Type II sentences like the following, a prepositional phrase of time or place, instead of a simple adverb, follows the verb and functions as an adverb phrase, the first one of place and the second one of time.

(25)   Cheryl's notebook   must have been *on the desk.*

The reception   will be *at noon.*

A Type II sentence with a prepositional phrase following the linking verb *be* looks like this when displayed in a phrase marker:

(26)

The Reed-Kellogg diagram would be:

(27)

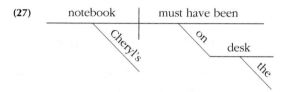

If the linking verb *be* is followed by a noun phrase functioning adverbially, the sentence has a phrase marker tree like this one:

(28)

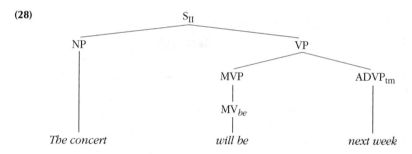

The Reed-Kellogg diagram for the same sentence is:

(29)

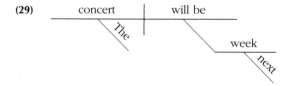

In the Type II sentence *The money was in my wallet all along,* which of the adverbial phrases is the required adverbial complement, and which is an optional adverbial modifier? To decide which phrase is necessary,

---

RULES OF THUMB

Tests for Identifying Type II Sentences

Linking Verb *Be* with Adverbials of Time or Place

1. Is the main verb a form of *be?* If the answer is yes, apply the next test.
2. Is the form of *be* followed by an adverbial phrase that expresses location or time? If the answer is yes, the sentence is Type II.

Figure 7.3

try omitting first one (**The money was all along*) and then the other (*The money was in my wallet*).

You can use the Rules of Thumb in Figure 7.3 and the Summary in Figure 7.4 to help you to recognize Type II sentences.

SUMMARY

Sentence Type II—Linking Verb Be with Adverbial of Time or Place

Structural Formula: S_{II} = NP + MV_{be} + $ADVP_{tm/pl}$

Tree Diagram:

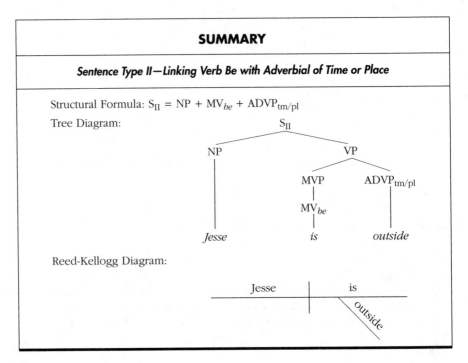

Reed-Kellogg Diagram:

Figure 7.4

> Draw a phrase marker and a Reed-Kellogg diagram for each of the following sentences. Notice that not all of them are Type II.

1. The crowds were hurrying toward the theater.
2. The performance began at 7:30 on Friday.
3. The actors had been in costume for two hours.
4. This production plays every night during the week.

Peripheral Cases—Intransitive Verbs

All of the examples of Type II sentences given so far involve the verb *be* and are clearly distinct from the examples of Type I sentences that we provided earlier. However, it is not difficult to think of sentences that seem to resemble Type I in some respects and Type II in others.

We have characterized the prototypical Type I verbs as intransitive verbs, for which an adverbial modifier is optional. However, a number of verbs are not quite so self-sufficient. These verbs are like intransitive verbs in that they are followed only by adverb phrases; however, they are not as able to stand alone as the intransitives we have described above as belonging to Type I. They are more like the *be* verbs of Type II. Notice in the sentences below that the adverbial is required:

(30)	Cheryl's notebook	must have been lying	on the desk.
	Her job interviews	took place	yesterday.
	Edward	lives	in Cincinnati.

The verb in the first example is intransitive; however, the adverb of place following it is obligatory, not optional. Omitting it results in a sentence that sounds unnatural: *?Cheryl's notebook must have been lying.* The remaining examples are more problematic. Although we can think of contexts in which a speaker might say *Her interviews took place* or *Edward lives,* such verbs usually require an adverb of time or place to complete their meaning.

In grammatical descriptions, sentence types are defined on the basis of prototype sentences, those that clearly fit a pattern without complication or ambiguity. For atypical sentences, linguists decide which group they are *most* like and assign them accordingly. In deciding whether to treat the sentences above as Type I or Type II (or some other type), we have to consider which pattern they most closely resemble, as they don't fit into any category perfectly. Because their verbs are incomplete by themselves and their complements are adverbial, like those required by the intransitive *be* verbs of Type II, the evidence suggests that we consider them a subclass of intransitives closely related to the *be* verbs of Type II, for which an adverbial complement is necessary rather than optional.

Type III—The Linking Verb Type with Adjectival Subject Complement

Study the following examples:

(31) Sheila   is beautiful.
His parties   were very lavish.
Bill   is becoming friendly.
Your uncle   has seemed happy in the past.

Notice that the predicate in each sentence contains an adjective phrase following the main verb, which may or may not be a form of *be*. In Type III sentences, the verb is unable to stand alone as a complete predicate but requires an adjective phrase following it: in prototypical sentences, either an adjective (like *beautiful*) or an adjective with an intensifier or qualifier (like *very lavish*). The adjective phrase follows the verb and describes the noun phrase functioning as subject (as *very lavish* describes *his parties*). Again, because the verbs serve to join or link the subject to the descriptive word or phrase in the predicate, they are called *linking* verbs (or in some scholarly grammars, *copulative* verbs). The adjective phrase that follows them functions as an adjectival **subject complement.** (Some grammars also use the term **predicate adjective** for this function.) One meaning of the word *complement,* as we have seen above, is "something that completes." The adjective phrase that functions as a subject complement in Type III sentences is required; it completes the predicate while providing descriptive information about the subject.

The phrase marker representation of Type III sentences looks like this:

(32)

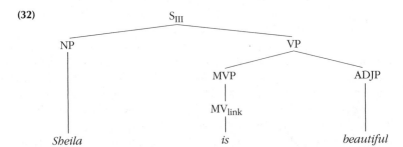

The symbol *MV* with a subscript *link* stands for a linking verb, *is,* in (32), and *ADJP* refers to the adjective phrase *beautiful* that functions as the subject complement.

The structural formula for Type III sentences is the following:

(33) S_{III} = NP + MV_{link} + ADJP
Bill + is becoming + friendly.

In the Reed-Kellogg diagram for Type III sentences, we encounter a new convention: a slanting line above the horizontal. It appears in the predicate and points back toward a noun the predicate adjective modifies. In (33) the predicate adjective modifies (tells something about) the subject; the diagram looks like this:

(34)

One important linking verb is *be* in its various forms. In fact, the linking function of Type III verbs can be seen most clearly in the forms of *be*. These come closest to playing a completely neutral, linking role in the sentence, simply joining the subject to its subject complement without adding much additional meaning, other than grammatical meaning such as tense. Other linking verbs (like *is becoming* and *seemed* in the example sentences) perform the same linking function as *be* but add their own individual meanings to the sentence.

The verbs of *sense* are frequently used as linking verbs, as in the following examples:

(35)   The milk *tastes* sweet.

Your corsage *smells* wonderful.

Bill *sounds* hoarse today.

His cashmere sweater *feels* silky.

Pat *looked* surprised after her victory.

Notice that adverb phrases (like *today* and *after her victory* in the examples above) are entirely optional in this sentence pattern. Their presence or absence does not change the basic sentence pattern of verb plus adjectival complement.

The adjectival complement in Type III sentences may or may not contain an adjective. Compare the following sentences:

(36)   a. He looked *weary*.

b. He looked *as though he had been up all night*.

c. He looked *like a zombie*.

All three sentences in (36) contain an example of *look* used as a linking verb. *Weary* is a prototypical adjectival subject complement. To understand the second and third sentences as exemplifying the same structure, it helps to perceive that *as though he had been up all night* and *like a zombie* are possible paraphrases of *weary*. Because they can substitute for an adjective in this sentence, they are functioning as adjective phrases. The form of the constituent in (36b) is a dependent clause and in (36c), a prepositional phrase. However, their functions are exactly the same as the adjective *weary*, for which they can be substituted.

By trying to replace the longer constituent with a single adjective and then evaluating the results, you are employing a *substitution test,* the method used by linguists seeking the best possible explanation of the data. In the example above, the analysis of *as though he had been up all night* and *like a zombie* as adjectival subject complements best explains the equivalent function of different forms.

Another alternative form that Type III sentences occasionally take is as follows:

(37)   Fred seems to be angry.

Here, the structure following the linking verb *seems* is the infinitive phrase *to be angry,* discussed in Chapter 11. Notice that *to be angry* can be replaced by the adjective *angry:*

(38)   Fred seems angry.
          Fred is angry.

As we did in the case of the examples in (36), we can apply the substitution test in this way to demonstrate that *to be angry* and *angry* are equivalent, both functioning as adjectival subject complements.

Sometimes the same verb can be either intransitive or linking, as the following sentences with the verb *grow* illustrate:

(39)   Eddie grew *listless* during the summer. (Type III)
          Eddie grew *slowly* during the summer. (Type I)

Notice that *listless* describes the subject, *Eddie* (the sentence can be paraphrased *Eddie was listless*). *Slowly,* on the other hand, is an adverb of manner, modifying the verb *grew* by indicating *how* Eddie grew.

RULES OF THUMB

Tests for Identifying Type III Sentences

Linking Verb with Adjectival Subject Complement

1. Is the main verb followed by an adjective phrase that refers back to and describes the subject? If the answer is yes, the sentence is Type III. For example, in the sentence *Pat looks great*, the adjective *great* describes *Pat*.
2. If the main verb in the sentence is not already a form of *be*, can the verb be replaced with a form of *be* without a major change in the meaning of the sentence? If the answer is yes, the sentence is probably Type III. For example, *His cashmere sweater feels silky* can be changed to *His cashmere sweater is silky* without greatly altering its meaning.
3. Is it among the most important linking verbs: *appear, become, seem, grow, prove, remain, turn, feel, look, smell, taste, sound?*

Figure 7.5

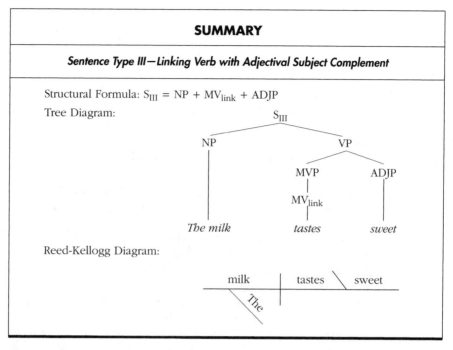

SUMMARY

Sentence Type III—Linking Verb with Adjectival Subject Complement

Structural Formula: $S_{III} = NP + MV_{link} + ADJP$

Tree Diagram:

Reed-Kellogg Diagram:

Figure 7.6

To help yourself in recognizing Type III sentences—linking verb with adjectival subject complement—follow the Rules of Thumb in Figure 7.5 and review the Summary in Figure 7.6.

■ *EXERCISE 7.5*

Draw a phrase marker for each of the following sentences. Not all are Type III.

1. The audience listened quietly in the auditorium.
2. A few people sat upstairs in the balcony.
3. The audience was restless toward the end.
4. The speech lasted too long.

WHAT'S THE USAGE? *Adjectives and Adverbs*

As a general rule, adjectives modify nouns and adverbs modify verbs. As a result, we expect adverbs to follow verbs as complements and modifiers. As you will see in our discussion of sentence patterns, this is usually the case. However, complicating the pattern is a relatively small number of verbs in English that are followed by adjective complements.

Speakers must in some way remind themselves that Type III sentences are exceptions to the rule that verbs are usually followed by adverbs. In careful usage, most speakers monitor their speech to preserve the distinction prescribed for formal speech and writing:

(40)   a. You sang *well.*   (***Type I—Adverbial modifier***)
         b. I feel *bad* about that. (***Type III—Adjectival complement***)

Many speakers maintain the distinction in all contexts. However, in informal situations, you may hear the inverse of these:

(41)   a. You sang *good.*   (***Type ?—Adjectival modifier***)
         b. I feel *badly* about that. (***Type ?—Adverbial complement***)

The verb in (41a) is intransitive (Type I), even though the modifier used is adjectival, and in (41b) it is linking (Type III), even though its complement is adverbial. We have no difficulty interpreting the two sentences, even though they do not conform to the usage prescribed by contemporary handbooks. Many speakers of English—often people in positions of power and authority—look on both (41a) and (41b) as errors of usage. Both are interpreted as nonstandard, (41b) as a hypercorrection, a failed attempt to conform to standard usage.

In your own class, you will probably find some students who are quite sensitive to the distinction between adjectives and adverbs and who flinch when it is not observed. Others may maintain the distinction in writing but not in speech. Still others may be unaware of the differences in usage discussed here.

What do linguists do to describe a situation like this? They simply note the regional and social distribution patterns for the use of adjectives in Type I sentences or adverbs in Type III and record current tendencies in dictionaries and handbooks of usage.

■ *USAGE EXERCISE 7.6*_____

For the examples below, identify the verb type (intransitive or linking) and select the adverbial or adjectival form that would be appropriate in formal usage.

1. The judges are speaking very (**quiet/quietly**) together.
2. Most of the casseroles look really (**good/well**).
3. The contestants remained (**quiet/quietly**) during the judging.
4. Morrie hopes the judging goes (**quick/quickly**), before his shepherd's pie collapses.
5. Julie's rattlesnake casserole entry did not do very (**good/well**) last year.
6. She felt (**miserable/miserably**) when the judges refused to taste it.

Type IV—The Linking Verb Type with Nominal Subject Complement

Analyze these sentences, focusing on the verbs and the phrase types in the predicates:

(42) Those men   are brutes.
The auction   was a success.
Our office   is becoming a jungle.
My three sisters   remained friends afterwards.

These sentences, like those of Type III, contain verbs that link the subject with a subject complement in the predicate, but in Type IV sentences, the linking verb is followed by a *nominal* constituent—that is, a noun phrase functioning as the subject complement. (*Nominal* means "functioning as a noun.") The noun or noun phrase that follows a linking verb in Type IV sentences always has the same **referent** as the subject—that is, it always refers to the same person, place, or thing as the subject noun phrase. For instance, the linking verb *are* in (42) is followed by the noun *brutes,* which is functioning as a subject complement. Both the subject *those men* and the subject complement *brutes* have the same referent. They refer to the same people, and *brutes* describes or characterizes *those men.*

Some grammars call nominal subject complements (like *brutes*) **predicate nominatives** because in languages like Spanish and German, these nouns occur in the same case (the nominative) as the subject noun. The terms *predicate adjective* and *predicate nominative* are useful in English for distinguishing adjectival subject complements in Type III sentences from nominal subject complements in Type IV sentences.

Type IV sentences can be represented by a phrase marker in the following way:

(43)

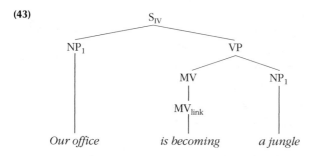

The structural formula for Type IV sentences is the following:

(44) $S_{IV} = NP_1 + MV_{link} + NP_1$

Our office + is becoming + a jungle.

Notice that two noun phrases occur in this pattern, one before and one following the verb. By placing the subscript $_1$ on both NP symbols, we show that they refer to the same person or thing. The Reed-Kellogg diagram for Type IV looks exactly like the one for Type III, except that in this case a noun, rather than an adjective, appears on the horizontal line following the verb:

(45)

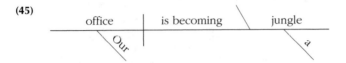

■ *EXERCISE 7.7*_____

To identify noun phrases by number (subscript), divide the sentence into phrases and call the first noun phrase you encounter (the subject) NP_1. Inspect the next noun phrase to see if it refers to the same thing as the subject. If it does, it is also NP_1. If it names something new, it is NP_2. Continue through the sentence, indexing each noun phrase constituent with a new number if it has a new referent or with the same number as the preceding one if it renames it.

Divide each of the following sentences into its constituent phrases and number the noun phrases consecutively, ignoring any, including those in prepositional phrases, that are part of adjective or adverb phrases. Which of the sentences contains a second NP_1? Does any contain an NP_2? Does any contain an NP_3? One has been done for you.

EXAMPLE

The frog became a prince before the astonished audience.

The frog [NP_1] became [MVP] a prince [NP_1] before the astonished audience [ADVP]

1. The National Hurricane Center starts the year with a list of 21 possible storm names.
2. It gives storms names that are easily remembered.
3. The Center has six sets of storm names.
4. Its alphabetically arranged lists include no names beginning with *q, u, x, y,* or *z.*
5. The Center uses each list of names every six years in rotation.
6. It permanently retires the name of a storm that causes widespread damage and deaths.
7. In 2005, it called the sixteenth storm "Katrina."
8. The National Hurricane Center has replaced "Katrina" in its list of names.

Type IV sentences can frequently be paraphrased in terms of classification. For example, *Carlos is an outstanding student* might be expressed as *Carlos can be **classified as** an outstanding student.* The nominal subject complement (*an outstanding student*) is the class or category into which the subject noun phrase (*Carlos*) falls.

Some of the linking verbs that occur in Type III sentences (for example, the forms of *be* and verbs such as *become, seem, remain*) also occur in the Type IV pattern. Compare the following:

(46)   a. Jan seemed a complete fool.   (Type IV)

        b. Jan seemed foolish.   (Type III)

        c. Jan seemed like a fool.   (Type III)

In (46a), *seemed* is followed by NP_1 (*a complete fool*), which refers to the subject, *Jan*. In (46b) and (46c), *foolish* and *like a fool* function as adjectival subject complements characterizing the subject.

Standard American English marks habitual action in Type II sentences by adding adverbial expressions of time, as in *He is usually at home.* As we have seen in Chapter 2, African American Vernacular English uses the invariant, uninflected *be*, also called "habitual *be*," for the same purpose, as in *He be at home* (meaning that he is usually at home). When *be* occurs in the present tense with no habitual action implied, AAVE can omit the main copular verb *be* entirely, simply juxtaposing the subject and its adverb, as in *He at school.* In the same way, the linking verb *be* can be omitted in AAVE: *He all right.* Similar omissions occur in Arabic, Russian, Hungarian, and Hebrew, all of which seem to feel no need for a copular verb at all.

The Rules of Thumb in Figure 7.7 will provide you with some tests to help you recognize Type IV sentences. Also review the Summary in Figure 7.8.

RULES OF THUMB

Tests for Type IV Sentences

Linking Verb with Nominal Subject Complement

---

1. Is the main verb a form of *be* or one of the other linking verbs (most commonly *become* or *remain*)? If the answer is yes, the sentence may be Type IV, and you should apply additional tests.

2. Is the verb followed by a noun or noun phrase that refers to the same person, place, or thing as the subject NP? If the answer is yes, then the sentence is probably Type IV.

3. Can the sentence be paraphrased with *may be classified as* in place of the verb? If the answer is yes, then the sentence is probably Type IV.

Figure 7.7

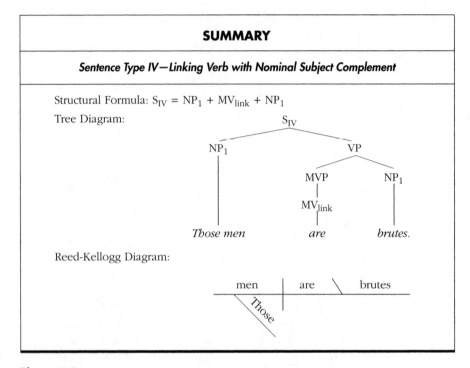

SUMMARY

Sentence Type IV—Linking Verb with Nominal Subject Complement

---

Structural Formula: $S_{IV} = NP_1 + MV_{link} + NP_1$

Tree Diagram:

Reed-Kellogg Diagram:

Figure 7.8

EXERCISE 7.8

Draw a phrase marker and a Reed-Kellogg diagram for each of the following sentences.

1. The cliff seemed a formidable obstacle.
2. The boy was an inexperienced climber.
3. The trail ran along a ledge.
4. The return trip would be a frightening one.

EXERCISE 7.9

Divide each of the following sentences into its subject noun phrase and predicate verb phrase. Label the sentence constituents: noun phrases, main verb phrases, adjective phrases, and adverb phrases. Underline constituents functioning as subject complements, either nominal or adjectival. Give the structural formula for each sentence, placing optional constituents in parentheses. Not all are Type IV.

EXAMPLE

That old car is an absolute wreck.

Subject	**Predicate**	
That old car	*is*	*an absolute wreck*
NP	MVP	NP

$S_{IV} = NP_1 \text{ [subject]} + Mv_{link} + NP_1 \text{ [subject complement]}$

1. The Grand Canyon has become a "must see" to many people.
2. Hiking down and back had been our family's goal for years.
3. Our first glimpse of the Canyon was a thrill to everyone.
4. The trip looks fairly simple from the top of the Canyon.
5. The climb back to the top, however, is a steep one.
6. Most of the family remained at the top during our hike down and back.
7. Flying over the Canyon in a small plane would have been easier.
8. It would also have been a much more expensive trip.

WHAT'S THE USAGE? *It is I Versus It is me*

The term *predicate nominative* serves as a reminder that when a pronoun occurs as a subject complement, formal usage requires the subject case—that is, the nominative case:

(47) It was *I* who volunteered to write the report.

The use of *It was I* illustrates a prescriptive rule that has largely disappeared in spoken standard American English. Speakers at all social levels say *It was me*, although many carry around with them vestiges of the rule, saying, for example, *This is she* on the telephone—a relatively formal situation where one is often speaking with strangers—but *I knew it was her all along* when speaking informally about a murder mystery. Handbooks on usage have generally stopped prescribing the use of the subject (nominative) pronoun in this context.

TYPE V—THE TRANSITIVE TYPE

Look at the following examples:

(48) John   hit Bill.
Three minnows   were nibbling her toes.
Cherry pie   enlivens any meal.
The man   had bought a cake for dinner.

These prototypical Type V sentences are different from each of the preceding four types that we have studied. As an introduction to Type V sentences, answer the questions in the following exercise.

■ *EXERCISE 7.10*_____

As we have seen, intransitive verbs in Type I sentences require no complements. Linking verbs in Type II, III, and IV sentences have complements that refer in some way to the subject of the sentence. These four verb types contrast with transitive verbs (Type V) in ways illustrated by the sentences below. Compare the verb complements in all five types and answer the questions about them.

a. Jenny purred. (intransitive verb, Type I)
b. Our neighbor's pet is outdoors constantly. (Linking verb, Type II)
c. The tomcat seemed very friendly. (Linking verb, Type III)
d. The smallest kitten became a family member. (Linking verb, Type IV)
e. Our neighbor's dog chased the cat outdoors. (Transitive verb, Type V)

1. What is true of Type I main verbs that is not true of Type V?
2. What is the difference between the role *outdoors* plays in (b) and (e) above?
3. How do Type III verb complements differ from those of Type V?
4. What is the difference between the role of the second noun phrase in (d) and (e) above?
5. What is the distinguishing feature of Type V sentences?

Verbs in Type V sentences require a noun phrase complement that refers to something or someone other than that to which the subject noun phrase refers. None of the other sentence types have this characteristic.

The second noun phrase (NP₂) in Type V sentences functions as a **direct object.** Verbs like *hit* and *nibbled* that are followed by noun phrases like *Bill* and *her toes* functioning as direct objects are called **transitive** verbs, from which Type V sentences derive their name.

The structure of sentences containing transitive verbs can be represented by the phrase marker that follows:

(49)

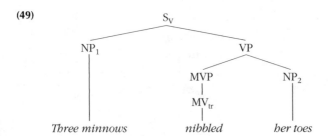

The structural formula for Type V sentences is the following:

(50) $S_V = NP_1 + MV_{tr} + NP_2$

Cherry pie + enlivens + any meal.

Transitive verbs, such as *nibbled* and *enlivens,* are represented by the symbol *MV* with the subscript $_{tr}$ for *transitive*. Notice that the first NP—*three minnows* in (49) and *cherry pie* in (50)—which functions as subject of the sentence, is identified in the phrase marker and in the formula with a subscript $_1$ to distinguish it from the second NP—*her toes* and *any meal* in the same examples—which functions as the direct object and is labeled with a subscript $_2$. The different subscripts mean that the first NP and the second NP have separate referents—that is, they name different persons, places, or things. If, in a position directly following the verb, a sentence contains a second noun phrase with a referent different from that of the subject noun phrase, you can be sure that the verb is transitive.

The Reed-Kellogg diagram for Type V sentences involves another convention, a vertical line following the verb that comes just to, but does not cross, the horizontal:

(51)

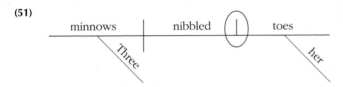

In counting noun phrases, label only those that are sentence constituents. What seems to be an NP_2 might be the object of a preposition, as in this example:

(52)   *Fred* [NP_1] fell on *his head*.

His head is not functioning as the direct object of *fell;* rather, it is the object of the preposition *on*. The verb *fell* is intransitive, not transitive, in this Type I sentence followed by an optional adverb phrase *(on his head)*.

If a predicate contains more than two noun phrases, the second noun phrase may or may not be a direct object. For example, (53) has three noun phrases with three different referents:

(53)   *Ms. Clark* [NP_1] gave *Evy* [NP_2] *the essay assignment* [NP_3].

In (53), NP_3, *the essay assignment,* is the direct object of the transitive verb *gave*. The noun phrase Evy is functioning as an **indirect object,** a structure we discuss in Chapter 8. If a sentence contains only two noun phrases—the second of which (a) immediately follows the verb and (b) has a referent different from the subject noun phrase—you are safe in analyzing it as a direct object.

RULES OF THUMB

Tests for Type V Sentences

Transitive Verb

---

1. Are the subject NP the actor, the verb an action, and the object NP the "receiver" of the action? If the answer is yes (as in *John hit Bill*, where *hitting* is an action, *John* performs the action, and *Bill* receives the action), then the sentence is probably Type V.

2. To find the direct object, ask *who?* or *what?* after the subject noun phrase and verb: *John saw who/what?* If the answer does not rename the subject, it should be the direct object.

Figure 7.9

Further analysis is required to identify direct object noun phrases in other contexts. We will discuss multiple object noun phrases in more detail below.

Traditional grammars have suggested the Rules of Thumb in Figure 7.9 to help with identifying Type V sentences and direct objects.

■ *EXERCISE 7.11*

Divide each of the following sentences into its subject noun phrase and predicate verb phrase. Label the sentence constituents: noun phrases, main verb phrases, adjective phrases, and adverb phrases. Identify the sentence type, and underline constituents functioning as direct objects.

EXAMPLE

Tourists in Yellowstone Park occasionally see grizzly bears near camp sites.

Subject	Predicate			
Tourists in Yellowstone Park	*see*	*grizzly bears*	*occasionally*	*near camp sites*
NP	*MVP*	*NP*	*ADVP*	*ADVP*

$S_V = NP_1 + MVP_{tr} + NP_2 \text{ [direct object]} + (ADVP)$

1. An angry bear can be a terrifying sight.
2. A human without a gun is helpless against a grizzly bear.
3. Thousands of grizzly bears once roamed the Rocky Mountains.
4. Gradually, the bears lost much of their habitat to waves of settlers.
5. Over time, the grizzly population diminished to a few thousand within the U.S.
6. Since 1975, the Endangered Species Act has protected the bears in the West.

7. The population of grizzlies in Yellowstone Park has tripled since then.

8. The government may remove grizzlies from the endangered species list.

■ *EXERCISE 7.12*_____

> Draw a phrase marker and a Reed-Kellogg diagram for each of the following sentences, numbering the noun phrases in each tree.

1. Our friends saved three good box seats for us.
2. Our team ran quickly onto the field.
3. The crowd delivered a loud, enthusiastic ovation.
4. The quarterback threw a completed 30-yard pass.
5. The defending team tackled the runner with unnecessary roughness.
6. The umpire's call was really no surprise.
7. The mood was grim on the opposing team's bench.
8. Our band was loudly playing our special fight song for us.

Transitive Verbs with Reflexive and Reciprocal Direct Objects

Compare the following two sentences:

(54)   a. Elmer cut *the apple* with a Swiss Army knife.

        b. Elmer cut *himself* with a Swiss Army knife.

The first example is easy to identify as a Type V sentence containing a transitive verb, but what about the second? If we assign subscripts to the noun phrases, is *himself* in (54b) NP_1 or NP_2? It clearly refers to the same person as the subject, but *cut* is a transitive verb in both instances. The form of the pronoun that ordinary should occur in the direct object position is *him*, as in *The knife cut him*.

The **reflexive pronoun** *himself* signals that this is an *exceptional* instance of a direct object that refers back to the subject. We understand the meaning and structure of this sentence by analyzing it in terms of the prototype transitive sentences: *Himself,* even though it renames the subject, occupies the NP_2 position of the direct object of a transitive verb. Other reflexive pronouns that can function as direct objects in this same way are *myself, yourself, herself, itself, ourselves, yourselves,* and *themselves.*

Another case in which the direct object may have the same referent as the subject is exemplified in the following sentences:

(55)   The doctors respected *each other.*

        My friends and I phone *one another* regularly.

The **reciprocal pronouns** *each other* and *one another* function much like the reflexive pronouns to signal a direct object relationship to the verb, referring back to plural subjects that have the same referents.

Transitive Verbs with Object Complements

A few transitive verbs allow their direct objects to be followed by an **object complement.** To understand the nature of object complementation, try the following exercise.

■ *EXERCISE 7.13*_____

> Complete each of the following sentences by adding at the end an adjective phrase or noun phrase that refers to NP₂ and seems necessary to complete the sentence. Be sure that the phrase you supply refers to NP₂ and not to the main verb. Then identify the phrase you have supplied as NP or ADJP.
>
> **EXAMPLE**
>
> Cheryl considered Carl's bean soup _____*salty*_____.   (ADJP)
>
> 1. I have always thought e-mail _____.
> 2. Maria's new computer made her _____.
> 3. Too much spam is driving people _____.
> 4. Louis keeps his password _____.
> 5. She found your Web site _____.
> 6. George called Google _____.

The examples in (56) illustrate two kinds of object complements.

(56)   The students elected *Mary* [direct object] *president* [object complement].

Wool socks will keep *your feet* [direct object] *very warm* [object complement].

In these two sentences, object complements follow and complete the sense of the direct objects *Mary* and *your feet*. Object complements may be nominal, like the noun phrase *president,* or adjectival, like the adjective phrase *very warm*. In sentences like these, the object complement contains the meaning *Mary was president* and *your feet will be very warm*. Other transitive verbs— such as *consider, find, have, like, prefer, think, appoint, call, name, declare, get, make,* and *want*—allow their direct objects to be followed by a descriptive object complement.

These are all Type V verbs and are followed by a direct object (an NP₂). When an object complement occurs, the pattern of the predicate is one of those given below:

(57)   a. $MV_{tr} + NP_2 + NP_2$

b. $MV_{tr} + NP_2 + ADJP$

If the object complement is a nominal, its referent is the direct object (much as the predicate nominative refers back to the subject in Type III sentences). Since it has the same referent as the direct object, it, too, is NP_2, as in (57a). If the object complement is an adjective, then the pattern is that given in (57b).

One way of visualizing the relationship between direct objects and their complements is to express the relationship between them in terms of Type III and IV verbs. For example, it is possible to paraphrase the relationship between the direct object and the object complements in the two sentences in (58):

(58)   They left *the house* (NP_2) *messy* (ADJP).

They left *the house* (NP_2) *a complete mess* (NP_2).

by using the Type III and IV sentences in (59):

(59)   *The house* (NP_1) was *messy* (ADJP).   (Type III)

The house (NP_1) was *a complete mess* (NP_1). (Type IV)

Tree diagrams of the sentences in (58) may help you visualize the relationships between the direct object *the house* and its complements *messy* in (60a) and *a complete mess* in (60b):

(60)   a. Adjectival Object Complement

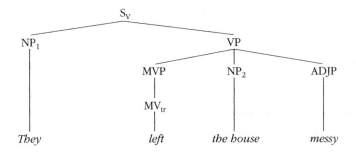

b. Nominal Object Complement

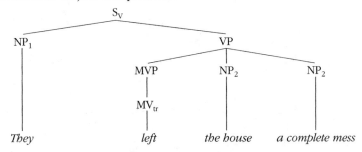

Reed-Kellogg diagrams of object complements separate the direct object and the object complement with a line slanting back toward the direct object, as in (61):

(61)   a. Adjectival Object Complement

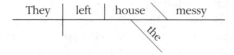

b. Nominal Object Complement

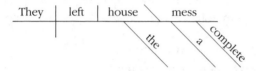

 EXERCISE 7.14_____

Identify any object complements in the following sentences, and decide whether they are functioning adjectivally or nominally. It may help you to identify the object complements if you try inserting the phrase *to be* between the direct object (the NP₂) and what you think is an object complement:

EXAMPLE

The judges declared the Hollyfield High team the winners.

The judges declared the Hollyfield High team *[**direct object**] (to be)* the winners *[**nominal object complement**]*.

1. Cy called the dinner inedible.
2. Madeline considered it a great success.
3. She always serves the food too cold.
4. She likes her pasta overcooked.
5. She made the sauce too salty.
6. Cy left the dessert on his plate.

Distinguishing Between Transitive and Linking Verb Sentence Types

Notice how the trees of prototypical Type IV and Type V sentences resemble each other:

(62)   Type IV:

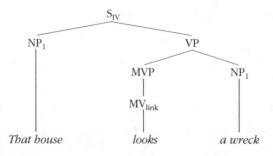

Type V:

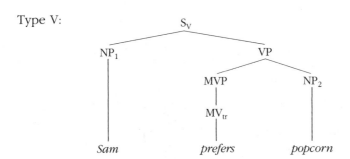

Both have two noun phrases, one functioning as subject and the other as a verb complement in the predicate. The most easily recognized feature that distinguishes them, however, is the fact that in Type IV sentences, the two noun phrases have the same referent (both are symbolized with NP_1), whereas in Type V sentences, the noun phrases have different referents (as is reflected in the different subscripts on the NP symbols).

Reed-Kellogg diagrams provide a visual reminder of the differences between linking verbs (Type IV) and transitive verbs (Type V) (see also Figure 7.10). The diagonal line used in the diagram of linking verb predicates slants back toward the subject, which the nominal subject complement renames. In contrast, the vertical line in the diagram of transitive verb predicates separates the direct object, with its own referent, from what has come before:

(63) Linking verb, Type IV:

RULES OF THUMB
Distinguishing Between Type IV and Type V Sentences Linking Verbs and Transitive Verbs
1. Is the verb followed by a nominal subject complement, that is, a noun phrase that refers to the same person, place, or thing as the subject noun phrase? If so, then the sentence is Type IV. **2.** Is the verb followed by a direct object, a noun phrase that has a referent different from that of the subject noun phrase? If so, the sentence is Type V.

Figure 7.10

Transitive verb, Type V:

Sam	prefers	popcorn

Verbs That Function in More Than One Sentence Type

Many English verbs can function in the predicate of more than a single sentence type. Examine these examples.

(64) Tomatoes grow well here.   Intransitive verb (Type I)
       Will grows restless during speeches.   Linking verb (Type III)
       Our neighbors grow tomatoes.   Transitive verb (Type V)

The examples in (64) illustrate three uses of the verb *grow*. The transitive and intransitive versions draw on the literal meaning of the verb. As a linking verb, it is used figuratively and means "to become."

(65) Josh goes to Paris in June.   Intransitive verb (Type I)
       Josh goes slightly crazy in July.   Linking verb (Type III)
       Then Lucy goes, "I don't think so."   Transitive verb (Type V)

Here *go* refers to the act of traveling in the intransitive sentence. As a linking verb, it is used metaphorically and means "to become." As a transitive, it means "says." The differences between intransitive and transitive uses of a verb do not necessarily involve a difference of meaning, however. Contrast these examples:

(66) The ball rolled slowly away.   Intransitive verb (Type I)
       The child rolled the ball slowly.   Transitive verb (Type V)

In the first sentence, the verb is used intransitively. *The ball* is the subject, and there is no other noun phrase. In the second sentence, the noun phrase *the ball* follows the verb and has a referent different from the subject noun phrase, *the child*. *The ball* is NP$_2$ and is functioning as the direct object of *rolled*.

Verbs like *roll,* which can be both transitive and intransitive, are common in English. In the sentences below, *cook* and *sell* are similar examples. You will be able to think of others.

(67) Tony is cooking the beans.
       The beans are cooking.
       Shelly sells Buicks.
       The Buicks are selling rapidly.

A characteristic of these contrasting usages is that when such verbs are used transitively in Type V sentences, their subjects are typically *agents,* actors that cause the action represented by the verb. Thus, for example, the child *causes*

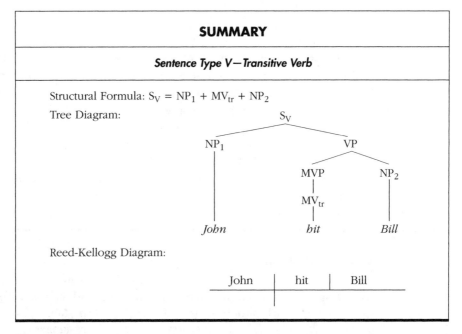

SUMMARY

Sentence Type V—Transitive Verb

Structural Formula: $S_V = NP_1 + MV_{tr} + NP_2$

Tree Diagram:

Reed-Kellogg Diagram:

Figure 7.11

the ball to roll, Tony *causes* the beans to cook, and so on. Used intransitively, the same verbs have subjects that are not agents. Instead of acting or causing the action of cooking, the beans simply undergo the cooking process; the ball rolls, but it does not cause the rolling. Figure 7.11 summarizes the characteristics of Type V sentences.

■ **EXERCISE 7.15**

The sentences in this exercise include some sentence constituents that are longer and more complex than those that occurred in our prototype examples. In each sentence, first separate and label the subject noun phrase and the predicate verb phrase. Then divide each predicate into its main constituents, labeling noun phrases, main verb phrases, adjective phrases, and adverb phrases. Give the structural formula for each sentence.

EXAMPLE

Many of this country's poorest immigrants have become extremely successful citizens whose contributions to the nation have benefited us all.

Subject | **Predicate**

Many of this country's poorest immigrants | *have become*
NP_1 | *MVP*

extremely successful citizens whose contributions have benefited us all.
NP_1

$S_{IV} = NP_1 \text{ [subject]} + MVP_{link} + NP_1 \text{ [subject complement]}$

1. The magnificent 25-pound Thanksgiving turkey that Ina had roasted with loving care slipped from the meat platter onto the floor before all the assembled guests.
2. After the telephone had rung six times, Harold's younger brother, who had dreamed of this moment for years, picked up the receiver without any intention of speaking into it.
3. After kissing Sleeping Beauty, the handsome young prince suddenly became a toad again.
4. One of our neighbors must own that dilapidated automobile with the crushed roof that has been sitting in front of the house for the last six weeks.
5. The old oak tree with an enormous lightning scar running down its northern side appears healthier than many of the unscarred trees in the same area.
6. An alarming-looking person from the Internal Revenue Service is at the door.

WHAT'S THE USAGE? *Comma Splices*

Although we are not conscious of sentence patterns as we use language, we expect subjects to come first, verbs to come second, complements to come third, and optional modifiers to come last. In interpreting what other people say or write, we use this expectation as a guide in assigning meaning to each segment of an utterance. If something occurs that interferes with that expectation, we usually mark it in some way to call attention to its irrelevance to the sentence pattern. Say the following out loud:

(68) a. Yes is not a suitable answer.
b. Yes, the ground is dry.

Notice that you paused after the *yes* in (68b), calling attention to the fact that it is not the anticipated subject. Commas (and pauses) are used to separate any phrases that are not part of the sentence pattern.

In writing, a single comma can mark off extra material that comes at the beginning or at the end of the sentence. (Example: *Without a moment's hesitation, the manager began cleaning up the spilled catsup.*) Within the sentence, however, commas must mark both the beginning and end of information that interrupts the subject-verb-complement pattern, signaling that what follows is neither subject, main verb phrase, nor complement. (Example: *Our whole class, with the possible exception of the nerd who sits in the front, surely failed the midterm.*) A lone comma that interrupts the sequence is traditionally called a **comma splice** (or **comma fault**). (Example: **Our whole class with a single exception, failed the midterm.*)

In speech, your tacit knowledge of sentence patterns is obvious in your intuitive use of pauses to mark off unnecessary information. People who read and write a great deal acquire that same intuitive sense of where to use commas. Until you have that intuitive sense, you can use a focal knowledge of sentence patterns to help guide you. The rule for using commas within a sentence is summarized in Figure 7.12.

RULES OF THUMB

Avoiding Comma Faults

1. Never insert a lone comma between the subject and predicate or between the main verb and its complement(s).
2. Use two commas to set off anything that interrupts the subject and predicate or the verb and its complement(s).

Figure 7.12

■ *EXERCISE 7.16*_____

Using the following verbs, create sentences of as many different types as you can, as we did in (64) and (65) above: *read, give, smell, roll, look, lay, turn.*

SUMMARY

Simple English sentences have four basic positions that define their structure: the subject position, the main verb position, the position filled by a required object or complement, and the position that can be filled by one or more adverbial modifiers. Figure 7.13 differentiates five types of English sentences in terms of the constituents that occupy each of these four positions in proto-type sentences. (The $\emptyset$ in position 3 of sentence Type I is called a *null;* it indicates that this position is empty in sentences containing intransitive verbs.)

SUMMARY

Five Basic English Sentence Types

Type	Position			
	1	2	3	4
I	NP	MV_{int}	$\emptyset$	(ADVP)
II	NP	MV_{be}	$ADVP_{tm/pl}$	(ADVP)
III	NP	MV_{link}	ADJP	(ADVP)
IV	NP_1	MV_{link}	NP_1	(ADVP)
V	NP_1	MV_{tr}	NP_2	(ADVP)

Figure 7.13

The Five Basic Sentence Types
Type I—Intransitive Verb

Structural Formula: NP + MV$_{int}$ + (ADVP)

Phrase Marker:

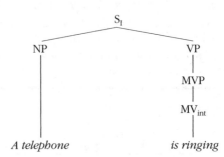

Reed-Kellogg Diagram:

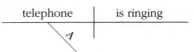

Type II—Linking Verb Be with Adverbial of Time or Place

Structural Formula: NP + MV$_{be}$ + ADVP$_{tm/pl}$

Phrase Marker:

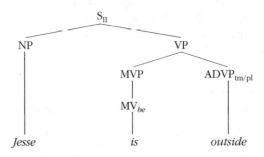

Reed-Kellogg Diagram:

Type III—Linking Verb with Adjectival Subject Complement

Structural Formula: NP + MV$_{link}$ + ADJP

Phrase Marker:

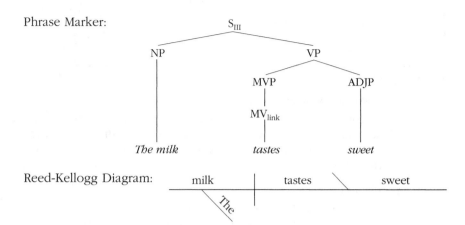

Reed-Kellogg Diagram:

Type IV—Linking Verb with Nominal Subject Complement

Structural Formula: NP_1 + MV_{link} + NP_1

Phrase Marker:

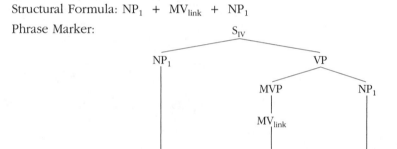

Reed-Kellogg Diagram:

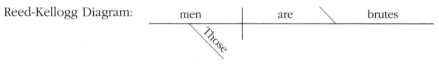

Type V—Transitive Verb

Structural Formula: NP_1 + MV_{tr} + NP_2

Phrase Marker:

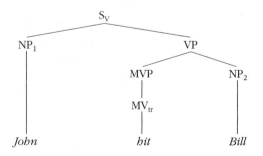

Reed-Kellogg Diagram:

| John | hit | Bill |

REVIEW EXERCISES

Recognizing Sentence Patterns

Divide each of the following sentences into its constituents and give the structural formula of each. Then represent the structure of each sentence using a tree diagram and a Reed-Kellogg diagram. An example has been done for you.

EXAMPLE

Sampson became rather bratty yesterday.

$S_{III} = NP_1$ *[subject]* $+ MVP_{link} + ADJP$ *[subject complement]*

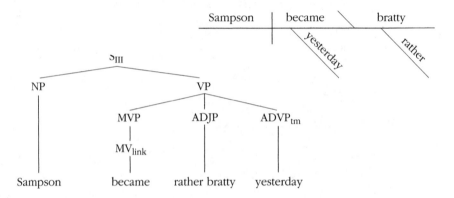

1. Margaret appeared unusually happy yesterday.
2. His laundered shirts are in the third drawer.
3. Adeline has become a municipal judge.
4. The employment agency offered some good vocational advice.
5. Good students study conscientiously.
6. The next-door neighbors arrived early.
7. The detective's search turned up several useful clues.
8. The exit is under the back stairs.

Practical Applications: Creating Sentence Patterns

Follow the directions below to generate sentences using the specified main verbs. You may use any combination of tense and aspect (present, past, perfect, or progressive), and you may use additional adverb phrases if you want.

1. Write a sentence containing *be* as a copular verb followed by an adverb phrase of time.

2. Write a sentence containing *taste* as a linking verb followed by an adjective phrase subject complement.

3. Write a sentence containing *speak* as an intransitive verb followed by an adverb phrase.

4. Write a sentence containing *look* as an intransitive verb followed by an adverbial prepositional phrase starting with the preposition *over*.

5. Write a sentence containing the verb and particle combination *look over* as a transitive verb followed by a direct object.

6. Write a sentence containing *like* as a transitive verb followed by a direct object and an adjective phrase object complement.

7. Write a sentence containing *be* as a linking verb followed by an noun phrase subject complement.

8. Write a sentence containing *name* as a transitive verb followed by a direct object and a noun phrase object complement.

KEY TERMS

adverb phrase of manner	reciprocal pronoun
adverb phrase of place	referent
adverb phrase of time	reflexive pronoun
adverbial complement	structural formula
adverbial modifier	subject
comma splice	subject complement
complement	predicate adjective
direct object	predicate nominative
indirect object	verb phrase
modifier	verb types
noun phrase	intransitive
object complement	linking, copular
predicate	transitive

Basic Sentence 8
Transformations

CHAPTER PREVIEW

One sentence can be transformed into another in English to emphasize information, to ask questions, to issue commands, or to deny that something is so. Because words may be added, deleted, or moved about by transformations, it sometimes becomes difficult to see the basic sentence types underlying transformed sentences. In this chapter, we help you analyze the relationship between basic sentences and transformed variants of them.

CHAPTER GOALS

At the end of this chapter, you should be able to

- understand the *transformational* process.

- distinguish among *transitive, intransitive,* and *linking verbs* in sentences that have undergone transformations.

- distinguish among *subject complements, direct objects, indirect objects,* and *object complements.*

- recognize *passive* sentences and convert them into *active* sentences.

- recognize the underlying pattern of sentences that have undergone the *passive interrogative, negative,* and *imperative transformations.*

If we spoke and wrote using only sentences that correspond to the five basic types in Chapter 7, our language performance would not only be childlike in its simplicity but also boringly repetitive. However, English provides us with the means for combining these five patterns into a richly infinite variety of longer, more complex sentences, capable of expressing intricate relationships between ideas, attitudes toward what is being discussed, and subtle differences in emphasis—the forms of expression that we take for granted in our speech and writing.

THE INDIRECT OBJECT TRANSFORMATION

Our ability to move constituents helps to explain sentence variety. Consider these examples:

(1) a. Maria gave a gift *to George.*

b. The bank sent a letter *to my father.*

c. Carol picked some flowers *for her cousin.*

Each of these three sentences contains a transitive verb and belongs to the Type V pattern, and each has a prepositional phrase, with *to* or *for* following the direct object. In each case, the prepositional phrase functions as an adverbial modifier of the verb. In each case, what is expressed in an adverbial prepositional phrase can be conveyed in another way. Examine these three related examples:

(2) a. Maria gave *George* a gift.

b. The bank sent *my father* a letter.

c. Carol picked *her cousin* some flowers.

The sentences in (2) have the same basic meaning as their counterparts in (1), but the pattern seems to have changed. The original NP_1 + MV_{tr} + NP_2 + ADVP sequence has been replaced with one in which the transitive verb is followed by two noun phrases. Its pattern is NP_1 + MV_{tr} + NP_2, followed by a third noun phrase, NP_3. In each sentence in (2), the preposition that was in the adverbial modifier in (1) has disappeared and the noun phrase that had functioned as the object of the preposition now occupies a place immediately following the verb, the position usually occupied by a direct object. In (1a), for instance, *a gift* is NP_2 and *George* is the object of the preposition *to*. In the corresponding sentence, (2a), the preposition *to* is gone; *George* now occupies the NP_2 position just after the verb; and *a gift* is now NP_3.

In the sentences of (2), each of the verbs appears to have two objects: a **direct object** (which has been moved out of its usual place following the transitive verb and is now NP_3) and an **indirect object** (the first noun phrase following the transitive verb, NP_2). For brevity, we symbolize the direct object function with the letters DOBJ and the indirect object function with IOBJ in the following:

(3) Structural Formula—

Type V Transitive Verb Sentences with an Indirect Object

NP$_1$	+	V$_{tr}$	+	NP$_2$	+	NP$_3$
				IOBJ		*DOBJ*

a. Maria   gave   George   a gift.

b. The bank   sent   my father   a letter.

c. Carol   picked   her cousin   some flowers.

Notice that in our structural formula for transitive verb sentences with two objects, because the indirect object and the direct object have different referents from the subject and from each other, each noun phrase has a different subscript: NP$_1$, NP$_2$, NP$_3$. It will be helpful to you, when you analyze sentence patterns, to remember that any time you have a sentence containing a constituent NP$_2$, the verb is transitive. If there is no other NP constituent of the verb phrase, NP$_2$ is the direct object. When you have both NP$_2$ and NP$_3$, the verb is still transitive, but the sentence contains an indirect object. Now NP$_2$ is the *indirect* object, and NP$_3$ is the *direct* object. Because there is no inflection available in English to differentiate the two kinds of objects, speakers rely on their position to signal which is which.

Traditional grammars sometimes tried to define indirect objects in terms of meaning as "the recipient of the direct object" or "that to whom or for whom the action is performed." Today, linguists would say that the indirect object is usually the "recipient" or "beneficiary" of the action. It may help you to remember to ask *what* to identify the direct object and *to whom* or *for whom* for the indirect object. For example, the answer to the question ***What*** *did Maria give George?* is the direct object, *a gift*. The answer to the question ***To whom*** *did Maria give a gift?* is the indirect object, *George*.

The relationship between transitive sentences with an indirect object and those that express the same basic meaning by means of a prepositional phrase with *to* or *for* can be described with the indirect object transformation. It includes two steps, one of *movement* and one of *deletion*. As it applies to our first three examples in this section, we can express it simply, as summarized in Figure 8.1.

SUMMARY

Indirect Object Transformation

---

1. Move the object of the preposition *to* or *for* to a position immediately following a transitive verb.
2. Delete the preposition *to* or *for*.

Figure 8.1

Applied step by step, you can visualize the transformational relationship in this way:

(4)   Maria gave a gift to George.
      ↓ (Move the object of the preposition to follow the verb.)
      Maria gave *George* a gift to _____.

      ↓ (Delete the preposition.)
      Maria gave George a gift.

The sentence with which we began can be represented with a phrase marker like example (5):

(5)   Type V Transitive Verb Sentence with Direct Object and Adverbial Phrase

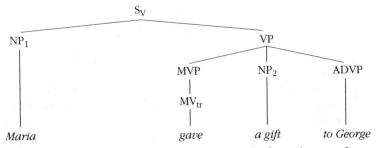

The sentence with an indirect object that results from the transformation is analyzed in example (6).

(6)   Type V Transitive Verb Sentence with Direct and Indirect Objects

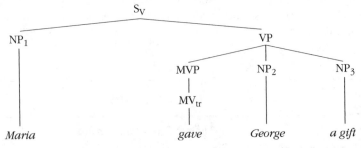

Notice that we have renumbered the noun phrases in this tree in order to clarify the new relationship between *George* and *a gift*.

Example (7) shows the Reed-Kellogg diagram for *Maria gave a gift to George:*

(7) Type V Transitive Verb Sentence with Direct Object and Adverbial Phrase

The diagram of *Maria gave George a gift* in (8) is identical to (7) except that the preposition *to* (which has been deleted by the IOBJ transformation) does not appear.

(8) Type V Transitive Verb Sentence with Direct and Indirect Objects

Traditional hints can be useful for recognizing and analyzing transitive verb sentences with indirect objects. If you continue to have trouble deciding which noun phrase is the direct and which the indirect object of a verb, it may help to remember that the indirect object can be expressed as an adverbial phrase, and adverbials are usually not essential to the verbs they modify. As a rule, even if you remove them, the verb continues to describe the same action. Thus, Willard is performing the same basic action in *Willard drove his car* and *Willard drove his car carefully*.

The same is true if you eliminate indirect objects. If you remove the indirect object from a sentence, the basic action of the verb remains constant.

(9) The army sent him [NP /IOBJ] an announcement [NP /DOBJ].

If you remove NP$_2$ (*him*), the action described in (9) remains unaffected:

(10) The army sent an announcement.

However, if you remove NP$_3$ (*an announcement*), as in (11), the action described changes:

(11) ?The army sent him.

Removing the direct object changes the meaning of the sentence.

Indirect Objects and Object Complements

In the discussion of transitive verbs in Chapter 7, we pointed out two situations in which a transitive verb can be followed by two noun phrases. One involves an indirect object (12a) and the other, an object complement (12b).

(12)   a. Edwin bought Eleanor a jewel. (NP$_1$ + MV$_{tr}$ + NP$_2$ + NP$_3$)

b. Edwin considered Eleanor a jewel. (NP$_1$ + MV$_{tr}$ + NP$_2$ + NP$_2$)

In (12a), *Eleanor* is the indirect object and *a jewel,* the direct object. It is derived from *Edwin bought a jewel for Eleanor.* In (12b), *Eleanor* is the direct object and *a jewel,* which also refers to Eleanor, is the object complement.

Reed-Kellogg diagrams of the two sentences may make the difference clearer to you. Example (13) diagrams example (12a), with its indirect object.

(13)   Edwin bought Eleanor a jewel.

The Reed-Kellogg diagram in (14) shows the relationship between the direct object, *Eleanor,* and its object complement, *a jewel,* by separating them with a diagonal line above the main horizontal line. The diagonal slants toward the direct object, reminding you that the object complement refers to the direct object: .

(14)   Edwin considered Eleanor a jewel.

| Edwin | considered | Eleanor | jewel |

Figure 8.2 reviews the tests you can apply to recognize and analyze indirect objects.

■ *EXERCISE 8.1*

Some of the following transitive verb sentences have indirect objects, while others do not. Transform any indirect objects you find into appropriate *to* or *for* prepositional phrases. Transform any *to* and *for* prepositional phrases into indirect objects, if possible. Note that not all sentences can be transformed in this way. An example has been done for you.

EXAMPLE

Coach McCall kicked <u>Francis</u> [IO] <u>the soccer ball</u> [DO]. Type V
Coach McCall kicked the soccer ball to Francis.

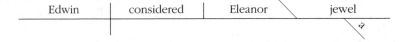

1. Santa brought lots of toys to their children last year.

2. His parents bought Max a new iPod with lots of memory.

3. Max offered his old iPod to his brother Austin.

4. His parents gave Austin a new game for his Game Boy.

5. Her godparents sent Edie a new princess outfit.

6. Her mother sends the godparents an invitation to Christmas dinner every year.

7. She also invited some foreign students to dinner.

8. Max usually sets the table for his mother.

RULES OF THUMB		
Recognizing Indirect Objects		
Use these tests to recognize and analyze transitive verb sentences with indirect objects:		
1. Is the verb followed by two noun phrases, each with a referent distinct from the other and from the subject?	If yes, the first noun phrase following the verb is probably an indirect object and the second noun phrase is a direct object.	*Maria [NP$_1$/Subj] sent George [NP$_2$/IO] a gift [NP$_3$/DO]*
2. Can the suspected indirect object noun phrase be made part of a prepositional phrase with *to* or *for* and moved to the end of the sentence?	If yes, then that noun phrase is an indirect object.	*Maria [NP$_1$/Subj] sent a gift [NP$_2$/DO] to George [Obj of Prep]*
3. Does the verb followed by two noun phrases include as part of its meaning the action of giving? Is the suspected indirect object the "recipient of the direct object" or "that to whom or for whom the action is performed"?	If yes, then that noun phrase is likely to be an indirect object.	*Maria [NP$_1$/Subj] "gave" George [NP$_2$/IO] a gift [NP$_3$/DO]*
4. If you remove the suspected indirect object from the sentence, does the meaning of the verb phrase remain about the same?	If yes, you have confirming evidence that the noun phrase is an indirect object.	*Maria sent George a gift = Maria sent a gift.*

Figure 8.2

■ *PRACTICAL APPLICATIONS EXERCISE 8.2* _____

Look at each version of the sentences you created in Exercise 8.1. Which versions sound better to you? Can you see any reasons for preferring one version to another? To help you decide, consider this: The sentence that has undergone the indirect object transformation [NP_1 + MV_{tr} + NP_2 + NP_3] has fewer words (an advantage). However, it has the indirect object as NP_2, where we expect to find the direct object. So when the indirect object has been moved to immediately follow the verb, we may find the sentence momentarily confusing (a disadvantage). You may see these competing advantages outweighing one another in the sentences above. In the example sentence, one might initially think the coach kicked Francis, not the ball, and, consequently, one might prefer the untransformed version.

========= *THE PASSIVE TRANSFORMATION* =========

Because the subject of the sentence often is an actor, or **agent,** performing the action of the verb, traditional grammars use the term **active** or **active voice** to describe the verbs in the basic Type V Transitive Verb sentences that we have considered so far.

(15)   John hit Bill.

A dog chews up my newspaper every day.

The clerk thanked my mother.

Study the following examples, which contain the same information arranged in a different order:

(16)   Bill was hit by John.

My newspaper is chewed up by a dog every day.

My mother was thanked by the clerk.

Traditional grammars call the verbs in sentences like those in (16) **passive** or **passive voice,** perhaps because in each one the subject of the sentence may be thought of as passively undergoing the action of the verb. Such sentences deemphasize the importance of the performer of the action. In them, the original subject (the actor noun phrase) is moved into an adverbial prepositional phrase (becoming the object of the preposition *by*). As a consequence, it is no longer a sentence constituent. In other words, it is not a subject or complement of the verb; it has become an optional adverbial modifier.

To put it another way, in the passive sentences, the speaker is not talking about the actor. The topic or focus has shifted to the direct or indirect object. Thus, the first sentence below is about Monica; the second is about the pie:

(17)   Monica ate the pie.

↓

The pie was eaten by Monica.

To these valid observations, we can add specific grammatical description using our transformational tools. However, first try out your independent analytical skills by doing Exercise 8.3.

▬ *EXERCISE 8.3*

Look again at example (17). See if you can identify what changes are necessary to transform an active sentence into a passive one. If you were asked to teach a group of Martians how to construct passive sentences in English, what steps would you have them perform?

In order to describe exactly how an active verb like *ate* becomes passive (*was eaten*), you need to recall the underlying pattern of the main verb phrase. In Chapter 6, we summarized the structure of all active main verb phrases as consisting of an auxiliary followed by the main verb, and we divided the auxiliary (AUX) into four components:

(18)   AUX = TENSE + (MODAL) + (PERFECT) + (PROGRESSIVE)
$$\begin{bmatrix} \text{present} \\ \text{or past} \end{bmatrix} \qquad \text{[HAVE + \{-en\}]} \qquad \text{[BE + \{-ing\}]}$$

First, let's analyze the underlying pattern of *Monica ate the pie:*

(19)   Type V Transitive Verb Sentence, Active Voice

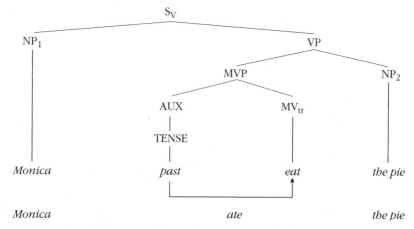

Keep in mind that in talking about active and passive sentences, we are talking about *systematic relationships* between pairs of sentences. To describe that relationship in terms of a series of transformational steps is to employ a valuable process metaphor for describing that relationship very explicitly. We suggest three such steps in moving from an active Type V sentence to its passive counterpart:

1. The subject, *Monica,* moves to a position at the end of the sentence, and the preposition, *by,* is inserted preceding it. The original subject thus becomes the object of the preposition, *by.*

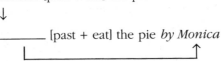

Monica [past + eat] the pie

↓

_____ [past + eat] the pie *by Monica*

2. The original direct object, *the pie,* moves from its slot following the verb to the beginning of the sentence, where it becomes the new subject.

↓

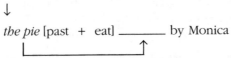

the pie [past + eat] _____ by Monica

3. The passive form of the verb is created by adding the passive marker BE + {-en} to the AUX, immediately preceding the main verb.

The pie [past + *BE + {-en}* + eat] by Monica

↓

The pie was eaten by Monica.

As a result of these changes, BE immediately follows the past-tense marker in the passive sentence; it incorporates the past morpheme, becoming *was.* Because *eat* immediately follows the past-participle marker, it occurs in its past-participle form, *eaten.*

A tree diagram of the passive sentence looks like the following:

(20) Type V Transitive Verb Sentence, Passive Voice

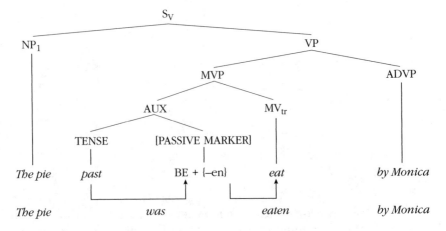

Any verb that appears in the same form as *was eaten*—that is, any verb that has an AUX containing BE followed by the past participle (represented as the morpheme {-en} but most often realized as a *d* or *ed* ending)—is in the passive voice. Add these labels to your working vocabulary of grammatical terms. Remember the **passive marker** (BE + {-en}) together with other terms describing the forms of verbs: *present tense* ({-s}), *past tense* ({-d}), *perfect aspect* (HAVE + {-en}), and *progressive aspect* (BE + {-ing}).

Passive sentences deemphasize the importance of the performer of the action by removing it from the agent slot, but they change neither the basic meaning conveyed nor the basic sentence type. Notice that the underlying relationship between the verb and the two noun phrases that have been rearranged remains unchanged in the sentences above. *Monica* is still the agent performing the action, and *the pie* is still the object undergoing the action named by the verb. Passive sentences, like the active ones from which they are derived, are Type V sentences. Only transitive verbs in Type V sentences can become passive.

Passive sentences also occur without the prepositional phrase at the end. The examples used above can all have their "*by*-phrases" deleted. They are still recognizable as passives because they contain the passive marker BE + {-en}:

(21) Bill was hit.

Every day, my newspaper is chewed up.

My mother was thanked.

The pie was eaten.

If moving the actor from subject position to object of the preposition *by* seems to reduce its prominence in the sentence, then surely deleting the actor altogether carries that reduction as far as it can go!

■ *EXERCISE 8.4*

Each of the items below appeared either in an advertisement or in the news. For each, first, find the passive verb phrases. Then, for class discussion, consider what might be the purposes and effects of using the passive voice and removing the agent/actor in each.

1. Please call regarding your 35mm camera we have on hold for you. Your product has been paid for. You must attend a solar seminar and be a homeowner to be eligible.

2. Reflective home addresses will be painted on the curbs along your street tomorrow. Your home will be included only with your permission. It is strongly recommended that you take advantage of this opportunity to have your home address professionally painted in large, easy-to-see REFLECTIVE numbers on the

curb in front of your house. This <u>service is provided</u> to assure you that in an emergency situation, Police, Fire Dept., and Paramedic personnel can find your home with a minimum amount of delay....Your cost for this service is only $5.00.

3. Martha Stewart <u>is said</u> to be searching for someone to succeed her as chief executive, according to people who <u>have been briefed</u> on the search.

4. In the recipe for chocolate-covered pretzels on page 70 of the December issue, 1 cup lukewarm water <u>was inadvertently omitted</u>.

5. In the recipe for Southwestern Turkey Chili, the 1/2 cup ground cumin <u>should be changed</u> to 2-1/2 tablespoons and the 2 cups dried black beans <u>should be changed</u> to 3/4 cup.

6. Soft vodka, <u>made from</u> the pure glacial waters of the River Neva....

7. The family <u>was notified</u> several weeks ago by a New York hospital that an unidentified patient might be their son, who <u>had not been seen</u> since September 11. Telephone calls <u>were placed</u>. Photos <u>were exchanged</u>. A match <u>was made</u>.

Direct and Indirect Objects

Some active sentences can be transformed into two different passive sentences. Look at these examples:

(22)   Diane gave Pablo some flowers.

↓

Some flowers were given [to] Pablo   (Direct object becomes subject)
by Diane.

or

Pablo was given some flowers by Diane.   (Indirect object becomes subject)

When a Type V sentence in the active voice includes both a direct object (*some flowers*) and an indirect object (*Pablo*), then either the direct or the indirect object can be moved to subject position to form a passive sentence.

SUMMARY
Passive Transformation
1. Move the subject noun phrase to the end of the sentence; insert *by* in front of it.
2. Move either the direct or the indirect object noun phrase to the beginning of the sentence.
3. Insert BE + {-en} into the AUX immediately before the main verb.
4. Optional: Delete the prepositional phrase beginning with *by*.

Figure 8.3

The sentence relationships we have observed thus far can be summarized as the **passive transformation** in Figure 8.3.

■ *EXERCISE 8.5* _____

A. The first four sentences below are in the active voice. Convert each into the passive, keeping the same tense (present or past) and aspect (if perfect or progressive).

　1. Several people presented a proposal for casual dress on Fridays to Mr. Snorf.

　2. Mr. Snorf has passed the proposal on to his boss, Ms. Larrabee.

　3. Ms. Larrabee is taking the proposal "under advisement."

　4. We had heard nothing from her since then.
　　　Nothing had been heard from her since then.

B. The next six sentences are in the passive voice. Convert each into the active, keeping the same tense (present or past) and aspect (if perfect or progressive).

　5. As a result, business suits are still expected for both men and women.
　　　Businesses all over town have adopted Casual Fridays.

　6. However, Casual Fridays have been adopted by businesses all over town.

　7. A pair of jeans can be seen with a suit jacket in the office on Friday.
　　　You can see

　8. So far, nothing is being said about the relaxed dress code.

　9. The responsibility for enforcing formal business dress during working hours was not given to anyone.

　10. Perhaps a second proposal will be prepared for Mr. Snorf.

■ *PRACTICAL APPLICATIONS EXERCISE 8.6* _____

It is often said that passive sentences are more difficult to understand than active ones. Compare the two versions of each sentence in Exercise 8.5 and see if any passive version is more easily understood than its active counterpart.

WHAT'S THE USAGE?　*Uses and Misuses of the Passive*

Note the differences between these two sentences:

(23)　Active:　　An anarchist threw the bomb.

　　　Passive:　　The bomb was thrown by an anarchist.

Although the passive transformation accounts for all of the syntactic differences between the two versions (the reversal in position of subject and direct object, the presence of *by* in the passive, and change in the form of the verb), the difference in focus is also important. The two sentences say the same thing, but when the "doer" of the action (the agent) is replaced in subject position by the receiver or result of the action, the topic of the sentence changes. The first sentence is about an anarchist; the second is about a bomb.

There are good reasons why most students, at some point in their academic careers, have been cautioned against using the passive. In the first place, when sentence constituents are moved out of their customary positions, the resulting sentences become slightly more difficult to understand, if only because the reader must reconstruct the basic, underlying relationships. This is especially true of passives. (In fact, the ability to understand passives is relatively late in developing; very young children, hearing the sentence *John was hit by George,* will assume that John did the hitting.) Mastering the art of writing clearly means, in part, avoiding sentence forms that make writing more difficult to understand.

In the second place, making a sentence passive, as we have seen, changes the focus of the sentence. Experienced writers use passives deliberately when they want to deemphasize the actor or to talk about the object. Inexperienced student writers sometimes use passive sentences inappropriately, when the actor is really the element being discussed. The following example illustrates what can go wrong in using the passive:

(24)   People have criticized the town council for lack of concern with the appearance of our city. But look at what they have achieved in the past few weeks. Sidewalks have been repaired on Valley Avenue. Trees have been planted along the median strip of Ocean Boulevard. Attractive new street lights have been installed in front of the library. And flowers have been planted in the borders at City Park.

Because the subject of the first sentence (*people*) is an indefinite and, hence, unimportant word that could be omitted, this sentence is a good candidate for the passive voice. As the sentence stands, it misleads the reader into thinking that the paragraph is about *people* rather than the *town council.* Furthermore, *they,* in the second sentence, is ambiguous. It could refer either to the people or to the council. The remaining sentences have been made passive, and their agents have been deleted. Yet these sentences are presumably meant to illustrate the activity of the town council. Removing the actor not only weakens the assertions; it also leaves ambiguous who performed the actions to which these sentences refer. As an argument, the paragraph lacks the force of the following, in which the active/passive voices have been reversed:

(25)   The town council has been criticized for lack of concern with the appearance of our city, but look at what they have achieved in the past few weeks. They have repaired sidewalks on Valley Avenue. They have planted trees along the median strip of Ocean Boulevard. They have installed attractive new street lights in front of the library. And they have planted flowers in the borders at City Park.

In the revision, the focus is clearly on the town council, a focus emphasized even more forcefully by the repetition of *they* in each of the four active sentences stating what they have done.

There is a third reason for avoiding passives: They contain more words than active sentences. Compare the wordiness of the two versions of the following sentences:

(26) a. Millions of dollars are wasted by defense industries each year. (10 words)

Defense industries waste millions of dollars each year. (8)

b. This can be finished today if some time is contributed by all of us. (14)

We can finish this today if all of us contribute some time. (12)

c. Food will be donated by a caterer, tables will be lent to us by a rental agency, and dishes will be provided by members of the club. (27)

d. A caterer will donate food, a rental agency will lend us tables, and members of the club will provide dishes. (20)

Though most English handbooks caution student writers against using the passive voice, it must be good for something because speakers of English, including professional writers, keep right on using it. To see why, look at the sentences below, in which the underlying subject (the performer of the action) has been deleted. Turning these back into the active form reveals why the writer or speaker might have preferred the passive version in each instance.

(27) a. A new house is being built down the street.

Someone is building a new house down the street.

b. Third-grade students were asked to bring canned goods for the earthquake victims.

The teachers asked third-grade students to bring canned goods for the earthquake victims.

c. Our refrigerator has just been repaired.

A repairman has just repaired our refrigerator.

d. Three ingredients were inadvertently omitted from the cheesecake recipe printed in yesterday's *Times*.

A former food editor inadvertently omitted three ingredients from the cheesecake recipe printed in yesterday's *Times*.

As you will have seen in the sentences above, sometimes the "doer" of the action is deleted because (1) it is unknown, (2) it is so obvious that it is not worth stating, (3) it would repeat a phrase already in the sentence, or (4) it might embarrass someone if the subject were expressed.

Another reason for using the passive is that we may want to focus interest on the direct object of the verb:

(28)   Thirty thousand telegrams were received by the White House on Friday.

Our car radio has been stolen again.

Phrasing these in the active voice would change the topic of the sentence and decrease the emphasis in each case on the consequences of the action named.

The passive can also be used to increase the coherence of a sentence, making connections between ideas clear to the reader. The subject of any sentence contains what is considered to be old information—something known both to the speaker and to the hearer; the predicate presents new information about the subject. The passive transformation can move old information out of the predicate and into the subject slot so that the new can appear at the end:

(29)   Once numbering in the millions, Australia's koala population has dwindled to about 400,000 as fur hunters [have taken] their toll. *Today the koala is threatened by disease, road accidents and a steady shrinking of the eucalyptus forests, where the animal lives and feeds.*
(Time, 17 September, 1990)

Notice that adverb movement has enabled the writer to set the time at the very beginning of the sentence; the passive transformation has moved the old information (the koala population, discussed in the preceding sentence) into the subject position, where it provides a transition from the earlier sentence. As a result, the new information (dangers to the koala) can be placed at the end, where we expect new information to occur.

Nevertheless, advertisers and journalists sometimes use agent deletion unscrupulously to imply that the agent is either a substantial group of people (30a) or someone of importance (30b):

(30)   a. Our mouthwash is preferred over all other brands.

b. The president is said to be contemplating an increase in taxes.

In typical "bureaucratese," the overly complex and often mystifying style used in the impersonal communications of large organizations, statements may rely on the passive voice to hide responsibility or escape blame:

(31)   Although some mistakes may have been made, the public is hereby assured that normal standards of quality service and confidentiality have now been reinstituted.

Who made the mistakes? Who is assuring the public? Who is reinstituting normal standards? The writer of this thoroughly passive statement covers up accountability by avoiding any mention of who is responsible.

■ *USAGE EXERCISE 8.7* _____

> In editing your writing, scrutinize all of the passive constructions to be sure that they have a function that justifies their use. Rewrite the following passive sentences as actives. Where no "doer" is included in the sentence, supply a "dummy" subject, like *someone, we,* or *they.* Decide for each whether the active or the passive would be preferable, and be prepared to discuss why you have chosen one form or the other. Not all of the examples are clear cut. You may decide that the active would be better in one context and the passive in another. An example has been done for you.
>
> **EXAMPLE**
>
> The list is expected to grow.
>
> *Someone expects the list to grow.*
>
> 1. Bacteria on the lab instruments were killed by radiation.
> 2. Most students prefer a challenging final exam.
> 3. Three viciously satirical cartoons were drawn by an anonymous critic.
> 4. They were asking people going through the security checkpoint at the airport to remove their shoes yesterday.
> 5. The existence of Bigfoot has been confirmed recently, according to the *Weekly Worldwide News.*
> 6. Proof of the existence of the Loch Ness Monster is eagerly being awaited.
> 7. Professor Withery is still hoping for a call from the Nobel Prize committee.
> 8. The Red Cross has taught our class first aid techniques, including CPR and the Heimlich Maneuver.

■ *EXERCISE 8.8* _____

> A reporter spoke this sentence on the *NewsHour with Jim Lehrer.* "What had that money been being spent on?" Can you figure out the AUX sequence underlying it? What is the active sentence from which it is derived?

Review: The Varieties of Be

Understanding how the auxiliary BE works in passive verb phrases, you are now in a good position to review all of the uses of this most unusual English verb. Through the accidents of history, the verb *be* not only has more forms than any other English verb—*am, is, are, was, were, be, being,* and *been*— but also a greater variety of grammatical functions.

Be *as a main verb*—Three of the five sentence types allow or require the linking verb *be* as the main verb:

(32)   Type II: Jesse *is* outside.

        Type III: The sky *is* cloudy.

        Type IV: Those men *are* brutes.

Be *as an auxiliary verb in the progressive aspect*—In this function, *be* always precedes a present participle, a verb with the {-ing} suffix:

(33)   Jerry *is planting* vegetables.

        present + BE + {-ing} + plant

        Monica *was eating* the pie.

        past + BE + {-ing} + eat

In some instances, as we have pointed out elsewhere, the present participle has been used so often that it has become an adjective, thus creating confusion for students who have difficulty differentiating the adjective from the participle. As forms they are identical, both ending in {-ing}. But compare the following examples:

(34)   Professor Cornwall *is boring.*

        Professor Cornwall *is boring* his students again today.

        Edwina *is entertaining.*

        Edwina *is entertaining* visitors from abroad.

In the first of each pair above, *boring* and *entertaining* are adjectives. Each of them fits the adjective frame sentence (*The boring professor is very boring*), and each can be compared (*Edwina is more entertaining than Eleanor*). However, *boring* and *entertaining* in the second of each pair of sentences are transitive verbs that can undergo the passive transformation: *His students are being bored again today by Professor Cornwall* and *Visitors from abroad are being entertained by Edwina.* By comparing how they function in context, we can determine which is an adjective and which is a present participle functioning as part of a main verb phrase in the progressive aspect.

Be *as an auxiliary in the passive voice*—In this function, as we have seen, *be* always precedes a past-participle form of the main verb:

(35) The pie *was eaten* by Monica.

past + BE + {-en} + eat

Our pet iguana *is adored* by everyone.

present + BE + {-en} + adore

*"Existential" **be**—*In this case, *be* is the approximate equivalent of *exist*. Examples like the following are relatively rare:

(36) Let it be!
(The Beatles)

Let there be light!
(Biblical book of Genesis)

To be, or not to be: that is the question....
(Hamlet)

Similar to these "existential" cases of *be* are sentences beginning with *there,* such as these:

(37) There are three marbles under your chair.

There is some broken glass underfoot.

■ *EXERCISE 8.9*

Identify which of the four functions (main verb, progressive auxiliary, passive auxiliary, existential) is illustrated with each *be* in the following sentences. When *be* is the main verb, identify the sentence type and whether the complement is an adverb phrase, an adjective phrase, or a noun phrase.

1. Scholarship application forms are on a table in the Office of Student Affairs.
2. The Founders' Scholarship is more valuable than any other.
3. Therefore, it is the most coveted scholarship that is offered by the university.
4. Some are special scholarships for students whose parents are alumni of the university.
5. Other scholarships are available only to students whose surname is Fitzgerald.
6. Scholarship award applications are being accepted all week.

■ *OTHER TRANSFORMATIONS* ■

As we pointed out at the beginning of this chapter, without the transformations that enable us to combine sentences of the five basic types, our ability to communicate would be severely hampered. We would be incapable of expressing many of the everyday essentials. For example, there would be:

no questions	*Is Betty there? Where is she?*
no commands	*Take out the trash!*
no exclamations	*What a mistake I made!*
no negatives	*Phil didn't buy the carpet.*
no passive sentences	*Jill was stung by a wasp.*

Nor would there be many other forms of expression that we take for granted in our use of English. In short, we could not communicate effectively or efficiently if our language made possible only those kinds of sentences we have thus far discussed.

In fact, we do create sentences with an incredibly rich and complex array of structures, including all of the kinds above. Sentences of the five basic types that we examined earlier are limited. They are all *positive,* although we often use *negative* sentences to express our ideas. The basic types are all *declarative* sentences, the kind that make statements. Yet we use language for other essential purposes as well. For example, we need *imperative* sentences to issue commands and *interrogative* sentences to ask questions. The variety of sentence structures that make up our language goes far beyond the patterns that we proposed as a starting point for increasing your understanding of English syntax. As an introduction to the discussion that follows, try doing Exercise 8.10.

■ *EXERCISE 8.10*

Consider each pair of sentences below. First, what, if any, is the difference in meaning between the two members of each pair? Then, what grammatically signals that difference in meaning?

1. a. Ally dressed up as Tinker Bell on Halloween.

    b. Ally did not dress up as Tinker Bell on Halloween.

2. a. Max had eaten all his candy by the next day.

    b. Had Max eaten all his candy by the next day?

3. a. You show me your costume.

    b. Show me your costume!

4. a. Amanda saved the best candy for her.

    b. Amanda saved the best candy for herself.

■ *NEGATIVE SENTENCES* ■

For every **positive sentence,** like *Webster will check the dictionary,* there is a possible parallel **negative sentence,** like *Webster will not check the diction-*

ary. One obvious difference between the two sentences is the presence of the word *not,* but exactly where and how is this constituent introduced into the sentence? As we examine the relationships among a variety of positive and negative sentences, we will discover a systematic pattern that can be described transformationally.

Negative Sentences with Auxiliary Verbs

If we considered only sentences with auxiliary verbs, our description of where to insert *not* would seem simple. Consider these examples (in which the downward-pointing arrows can be read as "is transformed into"):

(38)   Peter *will* arrive early.

↓

Peter *will* **not** (*won't*) arrive early.

Frances *has* finished her homework.

↓

Frances *has* **not** (*hasn't*) finished her homework.

Fred *is* painting his room white.

↓

Fred *is* **not** (*isn't*) painting his room white.

In each of these sentences, the negative word *not* appears after the auxiliary verb: after *will* in the first example, after *has* in the second, and after *is* in the third. (The auxiliaries plus *not* can usually be contracted, as indicated by the optional contracted forms in parentheses.)

We might say, then, that in English, we create negative sentences from positive ones by inserting the word *not* after the auxiliary verb. What happens when there is more than one auxiliary verb? Look at the examples below:

(39)   Jan *should have been* driving your car.

↓

Jan *should* **not** (*shouldn't*) *have been* driving your car.

Edward *has been* telephoning us regularly.

↓

Edward *has* **not** (*hasn't*) *been* telephoning us regularly.

In the first example, with the sequence *should have been,* the *not* appears after the modal *should,* and in the second, which contains both *has* and *been,* the *not* appears after *has.* No matter what combination of auxiliary verbs appears in a sentence, the negative marker *not* appears after the first one.

Negative Sentences with *Be*

A description of negative sentences in which the main verb is a form of *be* also appears to be uncomplicated, as you can see from these examples:

(40)   Betty *is* here.
↓

Betty *is* **not** (*isn't*) here.

Harold's old stereo *was* powerful.
↓

Harold's old stereo *was* **not** (*wasn't*) powerful.

The negative word *not* appears directly after the *be* verb in each example. The main verb *be* is, in fact, the only main verb in American English that behaves like an auxiliary in transformations, as we will see throughout this chapter.

Negative Sentences Without Auxiliary Verbs or *Be*

Consider these examples of sentences that have no auxiliary verbs and in which the main verb is not *be:*

(41)   a. Scott *thinks* deeply.

Scott **does not** (*doesn't*) *think* deeply.

b. The bank *remained* open after 5:00 P.M.

The bank **did not** *remain* open after 5:00 P.M.

The contrast between positive and negative sentences in these two examples differs somewhat from the earlier ones. In addition to the inclusion of the negative indicator *not,* these versions contain an inflected form of the helping verb *do.*

To form a negative sentence in English, we must have an auxiliary verb or a main verb *be* after which to place the word *not,* and if neither is present, a **substitute auxiliary verb (do)** must be used. *Not* is inserted after *do,* just as it would have been after any other auxiliary verb or *be.* The addition of *do* doesn't bring any new meaning to the sentence; for this reason, the auxiliary verb *do* is sometimes called the **dummy auxiliary.**

However, notice what happens grammatically: Tense is signaled by the form that *do* takes in the negative sentences rather than by the form of the main verb, as it was in the positive sentences. *Thinks* has the singular present-tense suffix {-s} in the positive version of (41a), but *does* signals the present tense in the corresponding negative sentence. Similarly, *remained* has the past-tense suffix {-ed} in the positive version of (41b), while *did* indicates the past-tense form in its negative version.

The main verb phrase formula in Chapter 6 did not include the auxiliary *do* because we do not use it as a helping verb in simple, declarative sentences. It appears only in sentences that have undergone some kind of transformation. When it is inserted, however, it behaves in ways similar to the other auxiliaries. Like the auxiliaries HAVE and BE, it becomes the carrier of tense; like modal verbs, it is followed by the base form of the main verb. Sentences with the auxiliary *do* inserted are, in fact, exactly parallel to sentences with other auxiliary verbs: *Not* is inserted after the first auxiliary (which is *do* when no other auxiliary is present).

We can express the positive/negative relationships we have observed thus far with a two-step **negative transformation** that enables us to start with a positive sentence and derive a negative one from it. As summarized in Figure 8.4, this transformation describes the relationship between the simplest pairs of positive and negative sentences in English. (As we have done with HAVE and BE, we will capitalize the auxiliary DO in main verb phrase formulas, in order to differentiate it from the ordinary verb *do,* which occurs in sentences such as *We do our homework after school in the afternoon.*)

The requirement that an auxiliary be present in an interrogative or negative sentence is difficult for many speakers learning English as a second language (ESL). Native speakers automatically learn to supply DO when necessary, but ESL students may require extra instruction on where DO should be added to questions and negative sentences.

SUMMARY

Negative Transformation

1. In a positive sentence, if there is no auxiliary verb or *be,* insert DO as an auxiliary verb.
2. Insert *not* after the first auxiliary verb or *be* in the positive sentence.

Figure 8.4

■ *EXERCISE 8.11* _____

> Convert each of the following positive sentences into its negative coun-
> terpart. Indicate whether you are inserting the negative word *not* after the
> substitute auxiliary DO, after another auxiliary, or after *be* as a main verb.
>
> 1. The year 2004 was one of the most violent hurricane seasons ever.
> 2. The storms of 2005 have challenged its records.
> 3. Global warming might be to blame for the upsurge in hurricane activity.
> 4. Greenhouse gases raise the temperature of Earth's atmosphere.
> 5. The Gulf of Mexico had a warmer temperature than usual in 2005.
> 6. The strength of Hurricanes Katrina and Rita was drawn from the warm water in the Gulf.
> 7. Global warming always accompanies increased hurricane activity.
> 8. There have been many quiet storm seasons during the period of rising global temperature.

Analyzing the Substitute Auxiliary DO

In order to understand clearly how the auxiliary DO works in negative sentences (as well as in other kinds of sentences, which we will study later), we
must recall the underlying structure of the verb phrase that we studied in
Chapter 6. Remember the pattern?

(42)

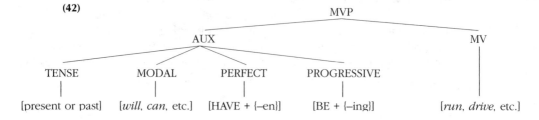

If we analyze one of our earlier examples (*Jan should have been driving your
car*) according to this pattern, the result (with the auxiliary bracketed) is:

(43) Jan + [present + should + HAVE + {-en} + BE + {-ing}] + drive + your car.

The negative transformation inserts *not* after the first auxiliary, giving us:

(44) Jan + [present + should + *not* + HAVE + {-en} + BE + {-ing}] + drive + your car.
↓

Jan should not have been driving your car.

Compare this analysis with what happens when the positive sentence has neither an auxiliary verb nor a main verb *be,* again drawing on an earlier example, *The bank remained open after 5:00 P.M.* In the positive version of the sentence, TENSE inflects the main verb *remain* that directly follows it, giving us the past-tense form *remained.*

Because this sentence has no auxiliary verb or *be,* the negative transformation requires that we insert the auxiliary DO. Because only TENSE (past) exists as an element of the auxiliary, we must insert DO immediately after TENSE in the underlying structure.

(45)   The bank + [past + *DO*] + remain + open + after 5:00 P.M.

Then we insert *not* after the newly inserted DO and incorporate past tense into DO.

(46)   The bank + [past + *DO* + *not*] + remain + open + after 5:00 P.M.
↓

The bank *did not* remain open after 5:00 P.M.

The dummy auxiliary DO, though it adds no meaning, is inserted to play the role of auxiliary when there is neither an auxiliary verb nor a main verb *be.* It carries out the grammatical functions of the auxiliary in a negative sentence—it signals tense and number—but it has no other independent meaning.

Diagramming Negative Sentences

Phrase markers place *not* under AUX, reflecting the fact that it becomes part of the verb phrase. For example, the phrase marker tree in (47) for the sentence *Egbert had not been snoring* represents its structure prior to transformations.

(47)

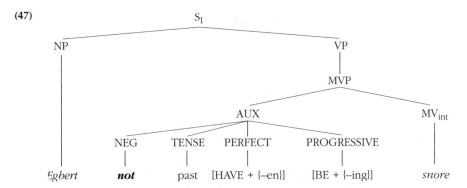

The phrase marker in (48) reflects the structure of the sentence after TENSE and the other verb inflections have been incorporated into the appropriate verbs and *not* has been moved to its position after the first auxiliary.

(48)

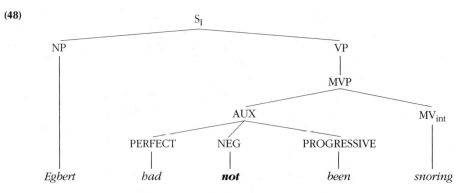

Reed-Kellogg diagrams do not reflect the underlying structure of negative sentences as phrase markers do. As exemplified in (49), *not* is treated as an adverbial modifier of the verb and placed on a diagonal line descending from the main horizontal.

(49)

▪ *EXERCISE 8.12*

Rewrite each of the following negative sentences, showing the underlying structure of the main verb phrase, which will contain *not* and some combination of the following elements:

[TENSE + (MODAL) + (HAVE + {-en}) + (BE + {-ing})] + main verb

or

[TENSE + DO] + main verb

EXAMPLES

My cat isn't eating well.

*My cat **[present + BE + not + {-ing} + eat]** well.*

My instructor doesn't consider me a bad student.

*My instructor **[present + DO + not + consider]** me a bad student.*

1. Ellie has not finished her English homework yet.
2. She did not understand the discussion of the negative transformation.
3. She had not asked anyone to explain it to her.
4. Julie is not working on her English homework right now.
5. Julie's problem is not sentence transformations.
6. She does not know how to do her math assignment.

7. Marty cannot figure out the underlying structure of sentence #15.

8. He has not yet had time to work it out.

WHAT'S THE USAGE?   *Double Negatives*

We have other ways of negating sentences in English. We can use prefixes like *in-* or *un-,* or we can change the indefinite pronouns *some* and *any* to *no* and *none:*

(50)   a. Her apologies were sincere.

Her apologies were insincere.

b. He is treating them kindly.

He is treating them unkindly.

c. He blamed somebody for the accident.

He blamed nobody for the accident.

d. The dog ate some of the cat food.

The dog ate none of the cat food.

If *not* is added to the negative versions of these sentences, the result has two negative signals:

(51)   a. Her apologies were not insincere.

b. He is not treating them unkindly.

c. He didn't blame nobody.

d. The dog didn't eat none of the cat food.

Notice that two negatives equal a positive in (51a) and (51b). These two examples illustrate a use of double negatives common in standard English. Their meaning is the equivalent of the positive versions in (50a) and (50b). The effect is different for (51c) and (51d), which contain *nobody* and *none.* Double negatives like these are avoided by speakers of standard English, even though they are common in other dialects. Double, and even triple, negation can be used for emphasis (*I don't never want none of that!*), but generally the double negative is just an alternative, nonstandard way of negating sentences in English.

Double and triple negatives are produced by a set of rules slightly different from those we have described. As we have pointed out, English rules permit double negation of adjectives and adverbs (*not uncertain, not unlikely*). When preceded by *not,* such words are interpreted as positive. Otherwise, standard English permits only one element of a sentence to be negated: either indefinites, such as *some* or *any,* or the first auxiliary verb. Nonstandard dialects have the same range of negatable words, but they permit more than one negative element per sentence. For example, the manager of the Grand Old Opry is said to have told the young Elvis Presley in 1954, "You ain't goin' nowhere, son." Such usage cannot be called *ungrammatical*. Sentences like *He didn't have none* and *You ain't goin' nowhere* are spoken and understood by native speakers of English, but they are produced by English grammatical rules different from those that produce standard English negation. Although such double negatives are stigmatized today, in earlier periods they were used by speakers of standard English for extra emphasis on the negative.

INTERROGATIVE SENTENCES

Sentences of the five basic types are all **declarative**—they make statements. In contrast, **interrogative sentences** ask questions. Two kinds of interrogative sentences are most important. The first kind is called the **yes/no question** because it seeks a yes or no answer:

(52)   Did someone eat the last piece of cake?

Example (52) tests the truth of an assertion that someone may have eaten the last piece of cake, and the appropriate answer is yes or no.

A second type is the ***wh*-question,** called that because it begins with one of the interrogative words, almost all of which start with the letters *wh-*. The *wh*-question assumes the truth of a statement and asks the listener to supply missing information about it.

(53)   Who ate the last piece of cake?

Example (53) accepts as a given that someone ate the last piece of cake and asks the listener to supply missing information—in this case, who did it.

Yes/No Questions

Exercise 8.13 asks you to explore the relationship of statements and yes/no questions.

■ *EXERCISE 8.13*

Here are some examples of statements with parallel yes/no questions (those asking for a simple confirmation). See if you can describe the steps involved in transforming one into the other.

1. The network could have rerun *The West Wing* again.
   Could the network have rerun *The West Wing* again?
2. Barbara has been reading the book.
   Has Barbara been reading the book?

3. Their new car is sitting in the driveway.
   Is their new car sitting in the driveway?

4. Twain is Jim's favorite author.
   Is Twain Jim's favorite author?

5. Bill turned off his computer.
   Did Bill turn off his computer?

In the first three examples, a yes/no question is formed by moving the first auxiliary verb to the front of the sentence:

(54) *Could* the network _____ *have* rerun *The West Wing* again?

Has Barbara _____ *been* reading the book?

Is their new car _____ sitting in the driveway?

In the fourth example, the yes/no question is formed by moving the main verb *be* to the front of the sentence.

(55) *Is* Twain _____ Jim's favorite author?

In each sentence, the auxiliary moved signals tense in the yes/no question. If there is no auxiliary verb or *be,* as is true in (56), the auxiliary DO appears at the beginning of the question where we would expect a regular auxiliary verb or *be.* When DO is inserted as an auxiliary, it inflects to show past tense, in contrast to the corresponding declarative sentence, in which *turned* is the signaler of tense.

(56) Bill *turned* off his computer.
      ↓
      Did Bill turn off his computer?

This pattern of contrasts is parallel to those that we observed in forming negative sentences from positive ones. Making yes/no questions from declarative sentences moves the first auxiliary or *be* to the front of the sentence. When neither an auxiliary verb nor *be* is present in the declarative sentence, then DO is introduced as a substitute auxiliary and becomes the carrier of tense. It is moved to the front of the sentence to create the inversion used in English to signal questions.

<table>
<tr><td colspan="1">SUMMARY</td></tr>
</table>

SUMMARY
YES/NO Question Transformation
1. In a declarative sentence, if there is no auxiliary verb or *be*, insert DO as an auxiliary verb. **2.** Move the first auxiliary verb or *be* to the front of the sentence.

Figure 8.5

These sentence relationships can be summarized in transformational form with the **yes/no question transformation** shown in Figure 8.5.

Diagramming Yes/No Questions

Phrase marker trees can represent the structures of sentences before and after the yes/no question transformation applies. Before the transformation, the phrase marker for the sentence *Has Barbara been reading the book?* includes in its AUX a YES/NO Q (yes/no question) node, as in example (57). The YES/NO Q node in the auxiliary symbolizes that this sentence structure underlies a yes/ no question; in every other way, it is identical to the declarative sentence *Barbara has been reading the book.*

(57)

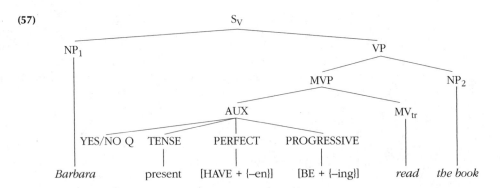

After the yes/no question transformation applies, the first auxiliary—HAVE, in this case—moves to the front of the phrase marker:

(58)

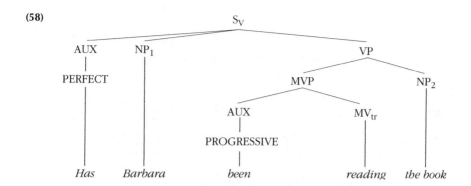

Reed-Kellogg diagrams present yes/no questions in the forms of the statements underlying them. The question analyzed with a phrase marker in example (58) is represented with a Reed-Kellogg diagram in example (59).

(59)

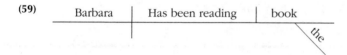

Notice that *Has* is capitalized in the Reed-Kellogg diagram to indicate that it is the first word in the sentence.

Negative Yes/No Questions

We often find it useful to combine two or more transformations in a single sentence. Look, for example, at how a simple assertion can be transformed into a variety of different sentences:

(60)   He opened his presents early.
　　↓

Did he open his presents early?　　　　　　　(question)
or

He didn't open his presents early.　　　　　　(negative)
or

Didn't he open his presents early?　　　　　　(negative question)

■ EXERCISE 8.14

Transform the following sentences first into positive yes/no questions and then into negative ones. One has been done for you.

EXAMPLE

The gardener should mow the grass every Thursday.

Should the gardener mow the grass every Thursday? (positive)

Shouldn't the gardener mow the grass every Thursday? (negative)

1. The airport traffic was quite heavy this morning.
2. We wanted to use the curbside check-in.
3. Most of the passengers were carrying electronic tickets.
4. I should have printed out a boarding pass at home.
5. The plane from Houston landed three minutes ago.
6. We can carry on this piece of luggage.
7. The other luggage will be checked through to New York.
8. Jill always wants to have the window seat.

Wh-Questions

In the transformations we have considered so far, the pattern of sentences remains fairly clear, even after additions, deletions, substitutions, and rearrangements have taken place. The situation becomes more complex with *wh*-questions. As a result of this transformation, parts of the predicate move to the beginning of the sentence, sometimes obscuring the underlying pattern.

Wh-questions differ from yes/no questions in two ways: (1) they ask for missing information rather than a simple confirmation or denial of information supplied in the question; and (2) they begin with an **interrogative word (*wh*-word).** The most common interrogative words are *who, whom, what, when, where, why, how, which,* and *whose*—words used to stand for information that the speaker presumably does not have.

Look at these examples of *wh*-questions:

(61)   a. Who played the solo?

       b. What will the judge decide?

       c. Where has Dan gone?

       d. When is the first exchange student arriving?

       e. Why are the police on the corner?

       f. Whom did the committee invite?

In each case, the interrogative word stands for the information that the question seeks.

Understanding this relationship makes it easy to determine the grammatical function of the interrogative word in the *wh*-question. First, answer the question, substituting the indefinite pronoun *someone* for the interrogative word *who*. Then analyze the grammatical function of *someone* in the answer. For example, if the answer to (62a) is (62b)—

(62) a. Who played the solo?

b. Someone played the solo.

then *someone* occupies the place of the *wh*-word and functions as subject of the declarative sentence that answers the question. Knowing that *someone* is the subject of the declarative sentence allows you to conclude that, in the corresponding *wh*-question *Who played the solo?,* the word *who* also functions as the subject.

With *wh*-questions that begin with interrogative words other than *who* or *whom,* you can use indefinite expressions (like *something, somewhere, at some time, for some reason,* and so on) to stand for the information the *wh*-question is seeking. Our second example, *What will the judge decide?* thus has an answer of *The judge will decide* **something.** Because questions move constituents around in the sentence, the role of the *wh*-word in the question version of the sentence is not as clear as is the role of *something* in the answer: Both are direct objects.

Figure 8.6 is a list of the *wh*-words used to ask for various kinds of information.

SUMMARY	
Interrogative (Wh-) Words	
What person?	*Who/whom*
What nonhuman thing?	*What*
Which person or thing?	*Which, What* (as determiners)
What place?	*Where*
For what reason?	*Why*
At what time?	*When*
In what manner?	*How*

Figure 8.6

We can use the transformational process that described the relationship between yes/no questions and declarative sentences to describe the **wh-question transformation,** but we will need to modify it. The first step of the yes/no question transformation inserts DO if there is no auxiliary or main verb *be*. As the question forms of the sentences above show, however, this is not quite the case with *wh*-questions. When the unknown is the subject, DO is not required. The first step in transforming declarative sentences into *wh*-questions, then, is to insert the auxiliary DO if the constituent representing the unknown information (an indefinite expression like *someone* or *something* in the following examples) is not the subject of the sentence and if there is no auxiliary or main verb *be*. The second step is to move the first auxiliary or main verb, if there is no auxiliary, to the front of the sentence.

(63) **Step 1:** Insert DO if required; move first auxiliary, or the main verb if there is no auxiliary, to the front of the sentence.
    a. Someone played the solo.
      ↓

      played someone ——————— the solo
        ↑_____|

    b. The judge will decide something.
      ↓

      will the judge——————— decide something
        ↑_____|

    c. Dan has gone somewhere.
      ↓

      has Dan ——————— gone somewhere
        ↑_____|

    d. The first exchange student is arriving sometime.
      ↓

      is the first exchange student ——————— arriving sometime
        ↑_____|

    e. The police are on the corner for some reason.
      ↓

      are the police ——————— on the corner for some reason.
        ↑_____|

    f. The committee invited someone.
      ↓

      The committee *did* invite someone
      ↓

g. *did* the committee _____ invite someone

If we stopped at this point, we would have yes/no questions in all but the first example. However, the *wh*-question transformation adds a substitution step. In order to ask for specific information, it replaces the indefinite expression (*someone, something, somewhere,* etc.) with the appropriate interrogative word. The substitution step affects the sentences above as follows:

(64) **Step 2:** Substitute the appropriate *wh*-word.

a. played ~~someone~~ *who* the solo

b. will the judge decide ~~something~~ *what*

c. has Dan gone ~~somewhere~~ *where*

d. is the first exchange student arriving ~~sometime~~ *when*

e. are the police on the corner ~~for some reason~~ *why*

f. did the committee invite ~~someone~~ *whom*

Finally, the *wh*-question transformation moves the interrogative word to the beginning of the sentence.

(65) **Step 3:** Move the *wh*-word to the front of the sentence.

a. *Who* played _____ the solo?

b. *What* will the judge decide _____?

c. *Where* has Dan gone _____?

d. *When* is the first exchange student arriving _____?

e. *Why* are the police on the corner _____?

f. *Whom* did the committee invite _____?

We have summarized our description of the relationship between declarative sentences and *wh*-questions as the *wh*-question transformation in Figure 8.7.

SUMMARY

Wh-Question Transformation

1. If the unknown is not the subject and if there is no auxiliary verb or *be,* insert DO as an auxiliary verb.

2. Move the first auxiliary verb or the main verb, if there is no auxiliary verb, to the front of the sentence.

3. Substitute an appropriate interrogative word for the constituent representing unknown information.

4. Move the interrogative word to the front of the sentence.

Figure 8.7

EXERCISE 8.15

Following the steps outlined in Figure 8.7, rewrite each of the following sentences as a *wh*-question. (In each sentence, an italicized indefinite word or phrase represents the unknown information.) An example has been done for you.

EXAMPLE

She saw *something* scurrying across the yard.

What did she see scurrying across the yard?

1. Josie ran out of the garden *for some reason.*
2. *Something* was crawling on her arm.
3. She left her trowel lying *somewhere* in the rose bed.
4. *At some time* she got up enough nerve to return to her gardening.
5. She looked *everywhere* for her trowel.
6. *For some reason* she couldn't find it anywhere.
7. *Someone* had put her trowel back into the shed.
8. She finished planting the tulip bulbs *in some way.*

Diagramming Wh-Questions

As represented in phrase marker trees, the underlying structure of *wh*-questions includes both a WH-Q (*wh*-question) in the AUX and an indefinite word or phrase representing the unknown information being requested. For example, before any steps of the *wh*-question transformation have been applied, the question *Whom did the committee invite?* has the structure represented in (66):

(66)

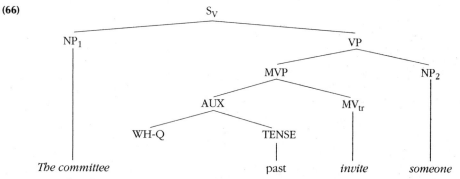

After the *wh*-question transformation has been applied, the phrase marker tree for the same sentence would look like this:

(67)

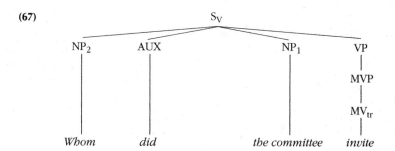

Wh-questions are represented with Reed-Kellogg diagrams as if they were statements, as in (68):

(68)

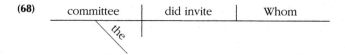

Interrogative Determiners

If you create *wh*-questions corresponding to the following declarative sentences, in which the italicized indefinite words stand for unknown information—

(69) a. Barbara wore *someone's* coat.

b. Barbara wore *some* coat.

your sentences are likely to be those in (70). Note that two possible versions (70b) and (70c) can be derived from (69b).

(70) a. Whose coat did Barbara wear?

b. Which coat did Barbara wear?

c. What coat did Barbara wear?

If you were to apply the steps of the *wh*-question transformation literally to the two declarative sentences, the results would be ungrammatical, as the transformation simply moves the *wh*-word to the beginning:

(71)   a. **Whose* did Barbara wear _____ coat? (Move the *wh*-word)

     b. **Which* did Barbara wear _____ coat?

     c. **What* did Barbara wear _____ coat?

What accounts for these ill-formed sentences? In each of these *wh*-questions, the interrogative word functions as a determiner preceding the noun *coat,* and moving it to the beginning separates the determiner from its noun.

One way to modify the transformation so that it accounts for these sentences is to specify, as part of the rule, that the entire constituent containing an unknown must move to the front of the sentence in the *wh*-question transformation. This would result in the following possible questions based upon (69):

(72)   a. *Whose coat* did Barbara wear _____?

     b. *Which coat* did Barbara wear _____?

     c. *What coat* did Barbara wear _____?

WHAT'S THE USAGE?   *Ending a Sentence with a Preposition*
What happens when the unknown is the object of a preposition?
Following the steps above, create a *wh*-question corresponding to the following declarative sentence, substituting an interrogative *wh*-word for the indefinite pronoun (*something*), which represents unknown information. Don't read on until you have created the question.

(73)   Keith polished his car with something.

Converting this into a *wh*-question leads to two possible results:

(74)   a. What did Keith polish his car with?
     b. With what did Keith polish his car?

Which version of (74) sounds better to you? If someone learning English as a second language asked you to describe the difference between the two, what would you say? Are they equally acceptable?

You may remember hearing at some point the prescriptive rule that you should never end a sentence with a preposition, and yet probably most speakers of American English are more likely to say (74a) than (74b) and would find *With what did Keith polish his car?* appropriate only in formal situations.

Now, before reading on, create a *wh*-question from the following sentence, converting *someone* into an appropriate *wh*-word. How many versions can you get?

(75)   Carol went with someone.

The *wh*-questions corresponding to (75) have an additional option associated with them. Are these the questions you created?

(76)   a. Who did Carol go with?

   b. Whom did Carol go with?

   c. With whom did Carol go?

▓ USAGE EXERCISE 8.16

Which of the alternatives in (76) would you prefer personally? Which one sounds most natural to you? Which one sounds more correct? Would your choice be determined by a grammatical "rule," by the context in which you are speaking or writing, or by both? If context is important, what situational factors would determine your choice? As both *who* and *whom* function in these sentences as the object of the preposition *with*, why does the subject form *who* in the first alternative sound acceptable to most Americans?

In the preceding section, one of the alternatives you considered was a choice between *who* and *whom*. The same decision confronts the speaker or writer when the interrogative word functions as a direct or indirect object. Consider the following examples:

(77)   Carolyn invited someone to the dance.
   ↓

Who/Whom did Carolyn invite to the dance?

Which alternative would you choose? Are both *who* and *whom* possible for you? Does one sound more correct or natural to you? In a later chapter, we have more to say about the choice between *who* and *whom;* meanwhile, try the following exercise to see what your own usage attitudes are.

▉ USAGE EXERCISE 8.17

Do you know the traditional rule for the use of *who* and *whom?* If you're not sure, check a writer's handbook or usage guide. If a scholar from abroad asked you to describe how Americans actually use *who* and *whom,* as opposed to how handbooks say we *should* use them, how would you describe the pattern? What factors of grammar and context (especially formality) play a role in determining which form is used? Which of the following alternatives would you choose? On what grounds would you base your decision?

Who/Whom did you say is calling?

▉ EXERCISE 8.18

Identify the function of the *wh*-word in each of the sentences below, and identify the pattern of the sentence containing the *wh*-word. It may help to follow the steps suggested in the example that has been done for you.

EXAMPLE
Which book did you leave on the train?

1. Answer the question, using an indefinite.
   *You left **some** book on the train.*
2. Identify the role played by the indefinite word.
   Determiner—***Some*** *book* (parallel to ***a*** *book*)
3. Identify the sentence type of the answer. (It will be the same as that of the question.)

You [NP₁ – subject] left [MVₜᵣ] some book [NP₂ – direct object] on the train [ADVP].
Which is a determiner; *some* replaces *which* in the answer.
The sentence has a transitive main verb. (Sentence Type V)

1. Who has the largest collection of Pokemon cards?
2. Since what year has Devon been collecting them?
3. How many years ago did Pokemon cards first appear?
4. Where do the kids usually get their cards?
5. Which boy is proudest of his own collection?
6. Why does Margie keep her Pokemon cards in that shoe box?

7. What card is the most valuable one in her collection?

8. What could she sell her most valuable cards for?

IMPERATIVE SENTENCES

As we have seen, transformations of basic sentences permit speakers to use language for a variety of purposes. Three major ones are asserting that something is or is not true, asking for information from another person, or getting someone to do something. We have looked at variations of the first two (declaratives and questions). One remains: commands.

Imperative sentences—like *Finish your soup!* and *Sit down!*—give commands and issue orders in a blunt way compared to the various other methods the language offers for making requests more politely (such as *Would you like to be seated?*). Traditional grammars describe imperative sentences as having *you* as an "understood" subject. The transformational analysis of imperatives in relation to the basic sentence types confirms this intuition.

Consider the following examples:

(78)   You walk faster.

↓

Walk faster!

You give her your ice cream.

↓

Give her your ice cream!

These pairs of examples would lead to a simple transformational description of the relationship between declarative sentences (which make a statement) and imperative ones (which issue a command): Delete the subject *you*. Yet sentences with *be* as a main verb suggest that our analysis needs to be a bit more complex.

Try transforming the following sentences into commands by simply deleting *you*.

(79)   You are here.

You are quiet.

You are a candidate.

The results are ungrammatical.

(80)   *Are here!

*Are quiet!

*Are a candidate!

No one issues orders that way. Correct imperative sentences would be:

SUMMARY

Imperative Transformation

---

1. Delete the subject *you* from a declarative sentence that contains no auxiliary verbs.
2. Delete TENSE from the AUX, leaving the base form of the verb.

Figure 8.8

(81)   Be here!

Be quiet!

Be a candidate!

How exactly are these imperatives related to their declarative counterparts?

Look again at the three grammatically well-formed imperatives with *be* in (81). The verb in each of them is in the base form, uninflected for either present or past tense. If we look back at our first two examples in this section, *walk* and *give* in the imperative sentences are also uninflected base forms. (The sentences from which we derived them have present-tense verbs that agree with second-person *you* as subject, so they, too, lack any tense suffix and look exactly like base forms.)

To derive all imperatives in the same way, we need to ensure that the imperative verbs are in the base form, not inflected for tense. Including that constraint, the **imperative transformation** summarized in Figure 8.8 describes succinctly the relationship between the simplest declarative sentences and their corresponding imperatives. By viewing imperative sentences (*Put out your cigar!*) transformationally, you can see how a deletion transformation accounts for the traditional notion that such sentences have an "understood" *you* as subject.

Verbs in Imperative Sentences

In the underlying structure of all verb phrases, TENSE, the first constituent of the verb phrase, converts the following verb (except for modals) from the base form to a form marked for present or past tense. The imperative transformation tells us to delete TENSE from the underlying structure of the verb phrase in order to ensure that the verb remains in the base form. Representing this structural change and the *you* deletion by means of tree diagrams displays graphically the relationship between declarative and imperative sentences:

(82)

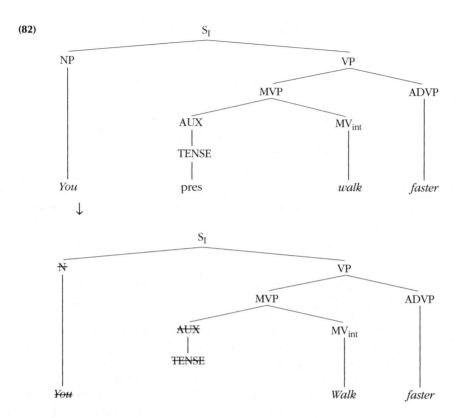

Diagramming Imperative Sentences

Example (82) illustrates how a phrase marker tree depicts the structure of an imperative sentence, revealing the presence of the "understood" *you* as underlying subject. Understanding how this deletion transformation works prepares you to understand why Reed-Kellogg diagrams traditionally marked with an *x* the "absent" subject of imperatives, as illustrated in example (83):

(83)

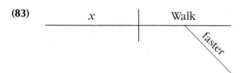

▓ ***EXERCISE 8.19***_____

Examine the following imperative sentences:

Behave yourself!

Control yourself!

Pick yourself up!

How can you explain the presence of the reflexive object in each of these sentences?

Hint: Remember what happens in Type V declarative sentences when the direct object refers to the same person as the subject:

I hit myself.

John washed himself.

They embarrassed themselves.

The reflexive object agrees in person and number with the subject. What do the reflexive objects in the imperative sentences agree with?

SUMMARY

In this chapter we have looked at two kinds of transformations. The first (indirect object, passive) resulted in sentences with the same meaning as the original, but with a change of focus or style. The second set of transformations involved those that change the meaning of a basic sentence (in our discussion, those that change assertions to negatives, questions, and commands). In addition, by examining the negative, interrogative, and imperative transformations, we have seen the systematic way in which English makes use of the substitute auxiliary DO as a signaler of tense. Each transformation proceeds by a series of steps that move, delete, insert, and substitute constituents in order to relate the simple prototypical model sentences to other sentences of greater variety and complexity.

REVIEW EXERCISES

Creating Transformations

A. Use transformations (negative, yes/no question, and negative + yes/no question combinations) to create as many variations based on the following sentences as you can.

B. Try creating a *wh*-question for each sentence below by treating the italicized constituent as if it were an unknown element and turning it into a *wh*-word.

C. Try performing the indirect object transformation on each sentence below. Which version do you prefer?

D. Try performing the passive transformation on each sentence below. Which version do you prefer?

1. *You* should visit the National Yo-Yo Museum in Chico, California.
2. Bob gave *his small hairy buffalo nickel* to the Wooden Nickel Museum in San Antonio.
3. The Museum of Jurassic Technology in Culver City, California, has *amusing* exhibits.
4. The Toaster Museum *recently* moved from Oregon to Virginia.
5. *Betty* will show the Squished Penny Museum in Washington, D.C., to her niece.
6. The British Lawnmower Museum in Lancashire opens *in the morning.*
7. The Post Mark Museum in Bellevue, Ohio, provides education about postmarks to *everyone interested.*
8. The Museum of Coathangers is a virtual museum *on the Internet.*

Sentence Patterns

Undo the transformations that the sentences below have undergone. Then identify the sentence verb type and sentence pattern of each. An example has been done for you.

EXAMPLE

When will you leave on your trip to Japan?

You will leave on your trip to Japan <u>sometime</u>.

You [NP₁ – subject] + will leave [MVP] on your trip to Japan [ADVP] sometime [ADVP].

Intransitive verb (Sentence Type I)

1. A Grand Challenge of Robots is sponsored by the Defense Department in October each year.
2. How do the robots navigate without the help of human controllers?
3. The robots are directed along a long, tortuous route by sophisticated computers.
4. The first hurdle in the competition is usually a tough two-mile qualifying course.
5. Last year 15 robot competitors participated in the million-dollar challenge.
6. The prize money was not won by any of the participants.
7. Isn't everyone excited about the two-million-dollar prize available this year?
8. What time is the competition on Saturday?

KEY TERMS

active voice
agent
declarative sentence
grammatical transformation
   imperative transformation
   indirect object transformation
   negative transformation
   passive transformation
   wh-question transformation
   yes/no question transformation
imperative sentence

indirect object
interrogative sentence
interrogative word (*wh*-word)
negative sentence
passive marker
passive verb
positive sentence
substitute auxiliary verb DO
   (dummy auxiliary)
wh-question
yes/no question

Finite Verb Clauses, Part I

9

ADVERBIAL
AND ADJECTIVAL CLAUSES

CHAPTER PREVIEW

In this chapter, we look at the differences between independent and dependent clauses and at sentences containing both. Dependent clauses, which may be nominal, adverbial, or adjectival, are introduced by words that mark them as dependent: either subordinating conjunctions or relatives (discussed in this chapter) or interrogatives or the complementizer that (discussed in Chapter 10).

CHAPTER GOALS

At the end of this chapter, you should be able to

- Distinguish among *simple, compound,* and *complex* sentences.

- Distinguish between *dependent* and *independent* clauses.

- Distinguish between *subordinate* and *relative* dependent clauses.

- Identify whether a dependent clause is functioning as an *adverbial* or *adjectival modifier.*

- Recognize a relative clause as either *restrictive* or *nonrestrictive.*

A *clause* is traditionally defined as "a string of words containing both a subject and a predicate." Sentences corresponding to the five basic patterns we discussed in Chapter 7 each contain a single prototypical clause with just one subject and one predicate. For that reason, they are called *simple sentences.* But sentences can include more than a single clause. Each of the following three examples contains two or more clauses; before reading on, mark each clause that you see. (You might want to review the five basic patterns at this point in order to help you recognize the clauses in the sentences to be analyzed in this chapter.)

(1)   a. I would appreciate it if you would remove your left foot from my toe.

b. After I paid for a new tire for your car, I certainly couldn't respond generously when you asked me for a loan.

c. Arlo rented comedy videos whenever he felt anxious about an exam.

In example (1a), *I would appreciate it* is one clause, and *you would remove your left foot from my toe* is a second. How can you tell? The key is to recognize the subject and predicate in each clause: *I* is the subject of the first clause, and *would appreciate it* is its predicate; *you* is the subject of the second clause, and *would remove your left foot from my toe* is its predicate.

Example (1b) includes three clauses: first, *I* (subject) *paid for a new tire for your car* (predicate); second, *I* (subject) *certainly couldn't respond generously* (predicate); and third, *you* (subject) *asked me for a loan* (predicate).

Example (1c) contains two clauses: *Arlo* is the subject of the first, and *rented comedy videos* is its predicate; *he* is the subject of the second, and *felt anxious about an exam* is its predicate.

As you can see from analyzing these sentences, *clause* and *sentence* do not always refer to the same thing. Some sentences contain more than one clause, and some clauses are not independent sentences. The following sentence, to take another example, contains two complete clauses, *he bought a new car* and *his old VW had stopped running:*

(2)   He bought a new car because his old VW had stopped running.

If the subordinator, *because,* is removed, either of the two clauses can stand alone as a sentence. But when they are combined in the single version given above, the second clause loses its independent status. The word *because* subordinates it to, or makes it dependent on, the **main clause.** Thus, example (2) is a single sentence containing two clauses; the dependent clause supplies material that explains something about the main (or independent) one:

(3)   a. He bought a new car.   (independent clause)

b. because his old VW had stopped running.   (dependent clause)

Both clauses are *finite*—that is, each contains a **finite verb,** a verb that is inflected to show tense. In (3a), the verb *bought* is in the past tense; in (3b), the auxiliary *had* is in the past tense; *stopped* has a past perfect inflection. However, the verb *running* is not a finite verb because its *-ing* inflection does not signal tense, either present or past.

To put it another way, in terms of our discussion in Chapter 6, a finite verb is one that occurs as part of a complete main verb phrase (MVP) containing:

(4) TENSE + (HAVE + {-en}) + (BE + {-ing}) + (BE + {-en}) + MAIN VERB

The verbs *bought* and *had stopped* in (3) are finite because they can be analyzed into main verb phrases as follows:

(5) *bought* = TENSE$_{[past]}$ + buy

had stopped = TENSE$_{[past]}$ + HAVE + {-en} + stop

In contrast to *bought* and *had stopped, running* is not a finite verb. Although it has an inflection (*-ing*), it lacks the rest of its auxiliary support (TENSE + BE). It is the present participle form of a verb used as though it were a noun (the direct object of *stopped*). Nonfinite verb phrases are those that contain no TENSE inflection (infinitives, participial phrases, and gerunds, for instance). Because they are extremely important in English as modifiers and complements, we will discuss them fully in Chapters 11 and 12.

We have identified *He bought a new car* as an **independent clause** because it can stand alone as a sentence. *Because his old VW had stopped running* is also a clause—it, too, contains a subject and a finite verb—but because it cannot stand alone as a sentence, it is considered a **dependent clause.**

You may wonder how we know which clause is dependent on the other. In this particular example, one clue is in the kind of information each supplies. The main clause tells *what* happened: *He bought a new car.* The dependent clause tells *why* it happened: *because his old VW had stopped running.* Notice, too, that when we reverse the order of the two clauses, the subordinator can follow along with the clause it precedes:

(6) He bought a new car because his old VW had stopped running.

Because his old VW had stopped running, he bought a new car.

Even when we invert the clauses, *because* remains tied to *his old VW had stopped running,* marking it as a dependent clause. In this chapter, we look at dependent clauses that function adverbially and adjectivally, showing how you can recognize them and how they are used within sentences.

SENTENCE VARIETIES

In connected discourse—that is, either in an extended conversation or in writing—the sentences that follow one another are usually related in some way. The speaker arranges them in a logical order to make it easier for the hearer to understand what is being said. Arranging sentences to follow one another is one of the ways we have of suggesting the relationships between ideas, but syntax, the internal organization of a sentence, provides us with others, including a variety of methods by which we attach one *proposition* (or statement of an idea) to another, connecting them with words that explicitly mark the nature of their relationship. To tap your own knowledge of this feature of English, rewrite the brief paragraph in Exercise 9.1. Notice the kinds of changes and additions you made to improve the style of the passage.

■ *EXERCISE 9.1* _____

> Without omitting details or changing the meaning, rewrite the paragraph below, getting rid of as many of the short sentences as possible.
>
> Josephina had finished her homework. Josephina logged on to her computer. The computer was in her bedroom. She tapped out an e-mail message to Maria. She stared at the screen. She toyed with her earring. She filed her nails. Josephina missed Maria. Maria had moved from Pomona to Reno only two days ago. Josephina and Maria had been best friends since childhood. Josephina and Maria had been constant companions since childhood.

Each of the sentences in the original version of the passage in Exercise 9.1 is a **simple sentence,** containing just one clause and one proposition. Notice that merely placing one simple sentence after another can be stylistically effective, as it is in the example that follows. The use of simple sentences adds emphasis and creates drama. Josephine's boredom and impatience are evident in the short, simple sentences describing her actions:

(7) She stared at the screen. She toyed with her earring. She filed her nails.

When too many short simple sentences are strung together, however, readers may become bored with the pattern. Even more important, logical connections between sentences are left implicit, and the readers must deduce them—or simply guess at what they are. One of the resources available for joining two simple sentences and thereby signaling how they are related is to use a coordinating conjunction. When we do so, each of the two halves remains an independent clause, and the resulting form is the **compound** of two simple sentences, as in (8), in which *so* is a coordinating conjunction.

(8) Josephina had finished her homework, so she logged on to her computer.

Two sentences can also be joined by using a *subordinating conjunction.* In this case, one sentence is said to be *embedded* within (placed inside of) the other; that is, one sentence becomes an adverb phrase within the other. The resulting form contains one independent clause and one dependent clause.

Such a sentence is called a **complex sentence.** The subordinator allows the speaker to specify exactly what the relationship is between the two clauses and to identify which one is embedded within the other. In the following, for example, *after* marks the second clause as dependent upon the first.

(9)   Josephina logged on to her computer after she had finished her homework.

Notice that, because it is functioning as an adverbial modifier, the subordinate clause in example (9), *after she had finished her homework*, can be moved to the beginning of the sentence:

(10)   After she had finished her homework, Josephina logged on to her computer.

In this way, the complex sentence in example (9) clearly contrasts with the compound sentence in example (8), in which the clause containing the coordinating conjunction cannot be moved:

(11)   *So Josephina logged on to her computer, she had finished her homework.

Another way of combining sentences is to combine a dependent clause with one or both of the sentence halves in a compound sentence, thus producing a form, such as the following example, which is **compound-complex:**

(12)   While she stared at the screen, she toyed with her earring, and then she filed her nails.

Example (12) is compound because it contains two independent clauses (*she toyed with her earring* and *then she filed her nails*) and complex because it also contains a dependent clause (*while she stared at the screen*).

The focus of this chapter is on complex sentences, those containing at least one independent clause and one dependent one. We discuss the methods used in English to place finite clauses within one another, beginning with prototypical dependent clauses that serve adverbial and adjectival functions. In the next chapter, we examine nominal clauses and consider ways of distinguishing among the three types.

A summary of the four sentence varieties is provided in Figure 9.1.

▦ *EXERCISE 9.2*

In order to familiarize yourself with the difference between independent and dependent clauses, identify each clause in the sentences below and decide whether each is independent or dependent. Remember that every structure containing a finite verb (a verb inflected for tense) constitutes a clause. An example has been done for you.

SUMMARY	
Sentence Varieties	
Simple sentence	A sentence containing one independent clause: one subject and one predicate.
Compound sentence	Two or more simple sentences joined by a coordinating conjunction.
Complex sentence	A sentence containing at least two clauses: one independent and one or more dependent.
Compound-complex sentence	A sentence containing two or more independent clauses and at least one dependent clause.

Figure 9.1

EXAMPLE

The astronomers were curious because their instruments had detected an anomaly.

The astronomers were curious = independent clause [past + be]

because their instruments had detected an anomaly = dependent clause
[past + HAVE + {-en} + detect]

1. Before packing her suitcase, Fern made a list. — *Simple sentences* [handwritten annotation: adverbial phrase]
2. There would be a pool at her hotel, so she would need a bathing suit. *compound*
3. She had forgotten suntan lotion when she went to the store. *dependent clause* [handwritten annotation: complex sentence]
4. In addition, she needed a pair of flip-flops so that she could walk on the beach comfortably. *dependent*
5. She added suntan lotion and flip-flops to her shopping list. *Simple sentence*
6. When she had packed everything, she closed her suitcase. *complex sentence*
7. After she had locked the suitcase, she could not remember the things that she had packed. *complex*
8. By the time her plane left, she had remembered several forgotten items, and she had decided to purchase them at her destination. *Compound - complex*

■ *EXERCISE 9.3* _____

Classify each of the sentences in Exercise 9.2 as simple, compound, complex, or compound-complex. In the example, *The astronomers were curi-*

ous because their instruments had detected an anomaly is a complex sentence: It contains an independent and a dependent clause.

SUBORDINATE CLAUSES

In Chapter 5, we identified a class of structure words as *subordinating conjunctions:* words that join two clauses, making one of them dependent on (or subordinate to) the other. Most but not all of the clauses formed by these conjunctions are **adverbial clauses.** They furnish the kind of information usually supplied by simple adverbs. In the examples that follow, the subordinate clause is italicized. Notice that each is a finite clause containing a subject and an inflected verb phrase:

(13)   Time   He always puts the papers in the garage *after he has read them.*

                   When the concert ended, the audience cheered.

       Place   The squad car pulled up *where a crowd had gathered.*

                   Where Gregorio's grandfather lived, everyone grew soybeans.

       Manner   The members of the audience remained seated, *as though they expected an encore.*

                   Mattie felt conspicuous on the stage, *as if everyone were watching her.*

       Cause   The clocks are slow *because the power was off last night.*

                   Because the turkey isn't fully cooked yet, dinner will be delayed.

       Condition He decided to stay an extra day, *although his money was running low.*

                   If they don't repair this properly, I won't pay for it.

As is true of adverbs in general, most adverbial clauses can be moved about in their sentences. Movement results not only in stylistic variety but also in a change in emphasis. Notice how the focus shifts when the clause is moved in the two versions of the same sentence below:

(14)   a. I will pay for the damage *because the accident was my fault.*

       b. *Because the accident was my fault,* I will pay for the damage.

There is nothing wrong with either version. The natural order of (14a) focuses on the speaker's willingness to pay for the damage. Moving the dependent clause to the beginning, as in (14b), not only focuses on who was at fault but also allows the statement to unfold in a chronological progression, cause first and effect second, giving the sentence a logical order you may prefer.

    Grammarians sometimes use the terms *dependent clause* and *subordinate clause* interchangeably; in this text, however, we use **subordinate clause** to refer exclusively to a dependent clause beginning with a subordinating conjunction. Thus, in our usage, a subordinate clause is one among several kinds of dependent clauses and can be recognized because it begins with one of the subordinators.

■ *EXERCISE 9.4*

Combine the sentences in each set below using subordinating conjunctions. (You may wish to consult the list of them in Chapter 5, Figure 5.12.) Try creating as many versions as possible by using a variety of subordinating conjunctions for each and by moving the dependent clause about in the sentence.

1. *Because* Children did poorly on the soccer field.
   Parents or coaches sometimes shouted insults at them.
2. Last year 30 parents and coaches clashed on a soccer field. *after*
   An adult tried to pick a fight with a teenager from the opposing team.
3. Some adults have been unsportsmanlike. *as a result*
   Managers of a youth soccer league in California have instituted "Silent Soccer."
4. The team may be doing poorly. *because*
   Parents and coaches cannot utter any sounds during a game this season.
5. A team member doesn't clear the ball fast enough. *therefore*
   The coach can only throw his arms into the air.
6. Someone has done well. *now*
   Adults can clap their hands.
7. Children score goals. *so that*
   Their parents can jump up and down.
8. One "Soccer Mom" doesn't want to watch. *because*
   The games seem like practice games., *therefore*
   She cannot shout encouragement.

Because a useful test for identifying some subordinate clauses is to see if the clause can be replaced by a single adverb of similar meaning, it will be useful for you to review the tests for adverbs summarized in Figure 4.5. A subordinate clause expressing time can often be replaced by an adverb like *then*:

(15)   He always puts the papers in the garage *after he has read them*.

        He always puts the papers in the garage *then*.

Similarly, a subordinate clause expressing place can be replaced by *there:*

(16) The squad car pulled up *where a crowd had gathered*.

The squad car pulled up *there*.

Although it's difficult to think of a single adverb to substitute for a subordinate clause expressing cause, the adverbial prepositional phrase *for some reason* can often serve as an easy-to-remember test replacement:

(17) *Because the turkey isn't fully cooked yet,* dinner will be delayed.

For some reason, dinner will be delayed.

However, no easy substitution test works for subordinate clauses functioning adverbially to express manner or condition, such as those illustrated above in example (13).

Another test that can help in recognizing subordinate clauses is that sometimes the sentence containing the clause can be transformed into a *wh*-question by substituting *how, when, where,* or *why* for the dependent clause. It's easy to see how this works for clauses expressing time, place, and cause:

(18) *When the concert ended*, the audience cheered.

When did the audience cheer?

Where Gregorio's grandfather lived, everyone grew soybeans.

Where did everyone grow soybeans?

The clocks are slow *because the power was off last night*.

Why are the clocks slow?

Mark rides a horse *as if he had been born in the saddle*.

How does Mark ride a horse?

As in the last example above, *how* can sometimes replace a subordinate clause expressing manner. However, like the adverb substitution test, the *wh*-question test won't work for every subordinate clause.

As we move forward in our discussion and look at other kinds of clauses, you may find it difficult to decide whether clauses are functioning in ways similar to adverbs, adjectives, or nouns. Use the tests in Figure 9.2 to help you identify adverbial clauses. Be sure, first of all, that the string of words you are analyzing is a dependent clause—that is, be sure that it consists of both a subject and a predicate containing a finite verb but that it is not an independent sentence. Then use the tests to see if it is adverbial. If a clause passes one of the first three tests, it is probably adverbial; if it passes all of them, it is a prototypical adverbial clause. We included the adverb test frame because

SUMMARY	
Adverbial Subordinate Clauses	
Form	A dependent clause introduced by a subordinator: *although, because, since,* and others (see Chapter 5, Figure 5.12)
Clause Function	An adverbial modifier
Punctuation	1. Punctuation is rarely required if the clause comes at the end of the sentence. 2. The clause is usually set off by commas if moved to the beginning or to somewhere within the sentence.
Tests	1. Some adverbial clauses can appear either at the beginning or at the end of the sentence. 2. The sentence containing the clause can sometimes be transformed into a *wh*-question by substituting *how, when, where,* or *why* for the dependent clause. 3. A single adverb can sometimes substitute for the dependent clause. 4. The clause can fit into the adverb test frame: *The man told his story _____.*

Figure 9.2

you will find it useful in locating phrases capable of occupying adverbial positions. As you will see in our later discussion, however, some clauses can function as either adjectivals or adverbials.

The dependent clause in example (2) above—*He bought a new car* **because his old VW had stopped running**—passes only three of the adverbial tests. The two clauses can be reversed:

(19) *Because his old VW had stopped running,* he bought a new car.

A question can be created from the sentence by substituting an adverbial *wh*-word for the entire dependent clause:

(20) *Why* did he buy a new car?

And finally, the clause appears in the adverb slot of its own sentence (the position following the complete sentence in the adverb test frame):

(21)　He bought a new car _____.

>carefully.
>
>thoughtfully.
>
>because his old VW had stopped running.

It fails the substitution test because you cannot substitute for it a single adverb that supplies the same kind of information as that furnished by the clause. (You can, however, replace the dependent clause with the adverbial phrase *for some reason*.)

■ *EXERCISE 9.5*

Use the four tests in Figure 9.2 to decide which italicized clauses in the complex sentences below are adverbial and which are not. Notice how many tests each clause passes.

1. A ridge *that lies between San Clemente Island and the mainland of California* is situated 1,086 feet below the surface. *adjectival*
2. Californians head for that undersea ridge *whenever they have time for game fishing.* *adverbial*
3. A warm-water current *that flows against the submerged mountains* sends nutrients upward, creating a concentrated feeding ground for marlin. ~~adverbial~~ *adjectival*
4. The Balboa Angling Club sponsors a Master Angler's Billfish (Marlin) Tournament each September, *to which big-game fishing clubs are invited.* *adjectival*
5. *After they pick their spot,* they wait for the 6:00 A.M. start before dropping their lines. *adverbial*
6. *While the boat moves along at seven knots,* five rods ride in sockets set into the stern. " "
7. *Although the fleet of contestants can catch 20 marlin in a day,* all fish must be released afterwards. *adverbial*
8. The winner gets a trophy *that identifies him or her as Master Angler of the Year.* *adjectival relative*

Diagramming Subordinate Clauses

Phrase markers and Reed-Kellogg diagrams can each help to make clear the structure of complex sentences with subordinate clauses. Both kinds of diagrams reflect the fact that complex sentences include at least one independent clause and one dependent clause. A phrase marker for a complex sentence will include an *S* symbol for each clause, as you can see in example (22), a graphic analysis of the sentence *Joan grimaced noticeably when Eric began his speech*. (In order to focus attention on the relationship between the clauses rather than on their internal structure, we will not show the structure of the Auxiliary in this or the following phrase markers.)

The uppermost S in example (22) represents the independent (main) clause *Joan grimaced*. The second S represents the subordinate clause *when Eric began his speech*. Notice that the second S and, to its left, SUB CONJ (for subordinating conjunction) are immediately below the symbol ADVP. That part of the phrase marker tells us that an adverb phrase (ADVP) here consists of a subordinating conjunction (*when*) followed by a clause (*Eric began his speech*).

(22)

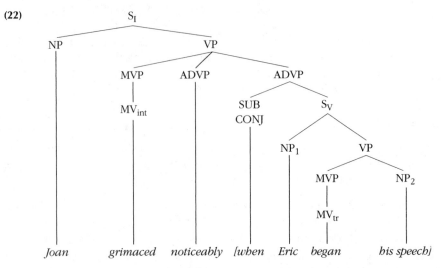

Even when an adverbial subordinate clause has been moved from its basic position at the end of the sentence to another position, the phrase marker reflects the underlying, more basic structure. For example, the sentence *Because Joan frowned at him, Eric sat down before his time ran out* includes two subordinate clauses, *because Joan frowned at him* and *before his time ran out*. Although the second of these has been moved to the beginning of the sentence, the phrase marker in (23) shows the grammatical relationships within the sentence prior to that movement.

(23)

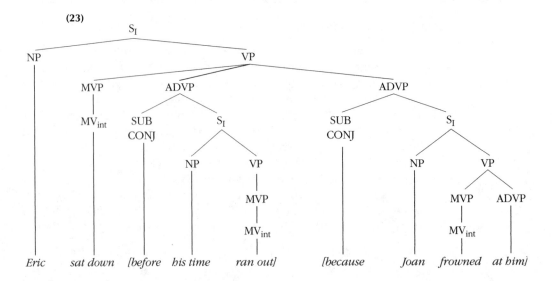

Reed-Kellogg diagrams allow us to show these same grammatical structures in another way:

(24)

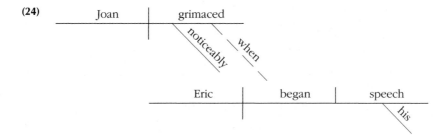

The main clause and the subordinate clause are analyzed in separate Reed-Kellogg frameworks that are linked by a broken line connecting their verbs. The subordinating conjunction is written on the broken line. This same pattern of analysis is followed when the sentence includes more than one subordinate clause.

(25)

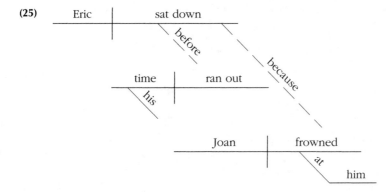

■ *EXERCISE 9.6*

Analyze each of the following sentences using a phrase marker and a Reed-Kellogg diagram.

1. Don's kitchen was a complete mess because Bill had cooked. *adverbial*
2. Robin opened the oven door before the soufflé was ready. *adv.*
3. Robin's mother felt rather sheepish after Bill complained.
4. Robin eats too fast unless his mother nudges him gently.

Subordinate Clauses That Can Function Adverbially or Adjectivally

In our discussion of subordinate clauses, all of the examples we used were adverbial modifiers, which is the usual function of clauses formed by subordinating conjunctions. To refresh your memory, the following sentence contains a prototypical subordinate clause, one that passes all four adverbial tests.

(26)   He had an appointment with the instructor *after our math class met last week.*

   a. *After our math class met last week,* he had an appointment with the instructor.

   b. He had an appointment with the instructor *then.*

   c. *When* did he have an appointment with the instructor?

   d. The man told his story *after our math class met last week.*

The same subordinate clause occurs in the following sentence, but it is not adverbial in function. Although it fits the adverb frame sentence, as is shown by (26d) above, it fails the other three adverbial tests. It cannot move to the beginning of the sentence; an adverb cannot be substituted for it; and a *wh-*question cannot be made from it.

(27)   He saw our instructor the day *after our math class met last week.*

   a. **After our math class met last week,* he saw our instructor the day.

   b. **He saw our instructor the day *then.*

   c. **When* did he see our instructor the day?

The subordinate clause in (27), in fact, is a required modifier, telling which day is meant. Without it, the sentence is incomplete (**He saw our instructor the day*). Thus, although (26) and (27) both contain identical clauses introduced by the subordinator *after,* the first is adverbial in function and the second is adjectival, modifying a noun phrase (*the day*).

   To further clarify for yourself the difference between the function of the clause *after our math class met last week* in (26) and in (27), examine Reed-Kellogg diagrams of these two sentences. Functioning adverbially, as it does in (26), the clause is connected in the diagram by a broken line to the verb *had,* which it modifies, in the main clause:

(28)

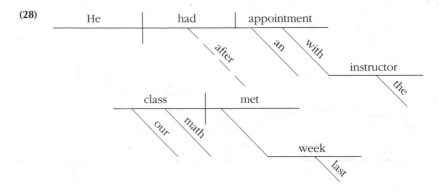

In contrast, when the clause functions as an adjectival modifier of *day*, as it does in (27), the diagram connects it to *day:*

(29)

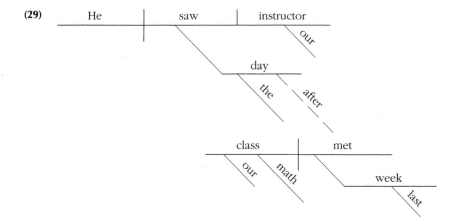

RELATIVE CLAUSES

Another set of dependent clauses includes those introduced either by *relative pronouns* (*who, whom, whose, which, that*) or by *relative adverbs* (*when, where, why*). **Relative clauses** are always **adjectival** in function: They modify nouns and are constituents of noun phrases. The nouns they modify (their antecedents) precede them.

(30) a. They have never met those people *who own the house on the corner.*

b. Our plane landed at Gatwick, *which is an airport south of London.*

c. We want to get rid of the bookshelf *that Uncle George gave us.*

In each sentence of (30), the italicized relative clause functions as an adjectival modifier of the preceding noun headword. In (30a) the clause tells which people; in (30b) it adds information about the location of Gatwick airport; and in (30c) it specifies which bookshelf is being discussed. In each case, the relative clause is a part of the noun phrase containing its antecedent (the noun it modifies). The entire phrase, *those people who own the house on the corner*, is the direct object of *met* in (30a). Similarly, the phrase *Gatwick, which is an airport south of London* is the object of the preposition *at* in (30b); and *the bookshelf that Uncle George gave us* is the object of the preposition *of* in (30c).

At first, relative clauses may not really seem like clauses to you. Unlike subordinate clauses, which can become independent if you delete the subordinating conjunction, relative clauses cannot stand alone as independent sentences either with or without their relative pronouns, as the following examples illustrate. Note, however, that each of the (a) versions is a complete clause containing a subject (*who, which,* and *Uncle George,* respectively) and a finite (inflected) verb:

(31)   a. *Who own the house on the corner
~~Who~~ *Own the house on the corner

b. *Which is an airport south of London
~~Which~~ *Is an airport south of London

c. *That Uncle George gave us
~~That~~ *Uncle George gave us

   Like subordinating conjunctions, **relative pronouns** join dependent clauses to main clauses, but unlike subordinators, relative pronouns play an important grammatical role in the clause of which they are a part. If you remember
that the relative pronoun stands in place of a noun phrase in its own clause,
it should be clearer to you that relative clauses have a complete subject and
a complete predicate. In the versions below, we have restored the noun phrases replaced by relative pronouns in (30).

(32)   a. [Those people] own the house on the corner.

b. [Gatwick] is an airport south of London.

c. Uncle George gave us [the bookshelf].

Thus, if you replace relative pronouns with the nouns they stand for, as we
have done in (32), the structure of the clause is easier to see.
   A sentence containing an embedded relative clause results when two clauses are combined, each of which contains the same noun or noun phrase. The
first step is the substitution of a relative pronoun for the second instance of
the repeated noun phrase:

(33)   a. They have never met *those people* + *Those people* own the house
on the corner
↓
They have never met *those people* + ~~*those people*~~ *who* own the house on
the corner.   └_____↑

b. Our plane landed at *Gatwick* + *Gatwick* is an airport south of London
↓
Our plane landed at *Gatwick* + ~~Gatwick~~ *which* is an airport south of
London.   └_____↑

c. We want to get rid of *the bookshelf* + Uncle George gave us
the bookshelf
↓
We want to get rid of *the bookshelf* + Uncle George gave us
~~the bookshelf~~ *that*.
└_____↑

The second step in the creation of relative clauses moves the relative pronoun to a position at the beginning of its clause. In the first two examples above, because the pronoun is the subject of its clause, it already occurs at the beginning. In (33c), however, it must be moved:

(34)   We want to get rid of *the bookshelf* +

_____ Uncle George gave us *that*

↓   ↑_____|

We want to get rid of *the bookshelf that* Uncle George gave us.

▓ *EXERCISE 9.7*_____

Combine each of the following pairs of sentences into a single sentence by turning one of them into a relative clause. If you are able to create more than one version, decide which you prefer. An example has been done for you.

EXAMPLE

William was eager to meet Sally's Uncle Ned.
Sally's Uncle Ned sold BMWs.

> a. *William was eager to meet Sally's Uncle Ned, who sold BMWs.*
>
> b. *Sally's Uncle Ned, whom William was eager to meet, sold BMWs.*

Version (a) focuses attention on William, while version (b) places the focus on Sally's Uncle Ned.

1. Wimbledon is the oldest championship tournament in tennis.
   Wimbledon is the third Grand Slam event of the year.

2. The tournament lasts for two weeks.
   The tournament is the only Grand Slam played on grass courts.

3. No matches are scheduled for "Middle Sunday." *which is*
   "~~Middle Sunday" is~~ considered a day of rest.

4. A committee evaluates applicants. *that*
   ~~Applicants~~ wish to play at Wimbledon.

5. An applicant has a sufficiently high world ranking.
   An applicant is directly admitted to the tournament.

6. An applicant does not have a high enough world ranking.
   An applicant may be admitted as a "wild card."

7. Other applicants may also participate in the tournament.
   Other applicants win in preliminary qualifying matches.
   Qualifying matches are held a week before Wimbledon.

8. The Main Court seats 14,000 spectators.
   The Main Court contains the Royal Box.
   Members of the Royal Family can watch the matches from the box.

Relative Clauses Within Prepositional Phrases

Relative clauses are adjectival; in other words, they modify a noun or noun phrase in the main clause that occurs, as well, in the underlying form of the relative clause. As we have seen, the relative clause immediately follows the noun it modifies, with the relative pronoun usually appearing as the first word in its own clause. In all of the examples we have looked at so far, the repeated noun phrase—the one that becomes the relative pronoun—has been either a subject, an object, or a determiner (a possessive noun) in its own sentence.

(35) It is easier to push today's manual lawn mowers, *which* usually weigh 20 pounds less than earlier models.

Which is the SUBJECT: [*Manual lawn mowers*] usually weigh…less…
                           (which)

The government cannot prohibit the expression of ideas *that* it finds offensive.

That is the DIRECT OBJECT: The government finds [*ideas*] offensive.
                                   (that)

The election victory went to Markley, whose quiet manner pleased the voters.

Whose is a DETERMINER: [*Markley's*] quiet manner…
                            (whose)

The repeated noun phrase can also occur as the object of a preposition. If it does, either the preposition or the relative pronoun may come first:

(36) The committee asked him many questions + he had no answers *to the questions*
      ↓
      The committee asked him many questions + he had no answer *to which*
      ↓

The committee asked him many questions *to which* he had no answers.

or

The committee asked him many questions *which* he had no answers *to*.

Traditional grammarians argued that prepositions should never come at the ends of sentences, but the fact is that they often do, even in standard written English. The first version (*many questions to which he had no answers*) is probably a little easier to understand than the second, where the preposition is separated from its pronoun (*many questions which he had no answer to*). However, both versions occur in standard English.

In example (36), you can see clearly that the relative pronoun *which* has two functions: It is the object of the preposition *to* within the relative clause, and it refers to the noun *questions* (its antecedent) outside of the relative clause. All relative pronouns have similar dual roles: They have specific grammatical functions within the relative clause (subject, object, determiner); and they refer to an antecedent outside of the relative clause.

Diagramming Relative Clauses

Phrase markers for sentences that include relative clauses show clearly the structure of the relative clause by representing it in the form of the sentence from which it is derived. Look at the following example of a phrase marker analysis of the sentence *The mosquitoes that live in North Dakota can recognize an out-of-state tourist instantly*.

(37)

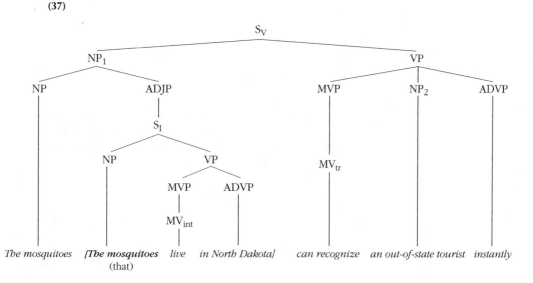

Notice in particular how the phrase marker represents a relative clause as being a clause (a sentence Type I, in this case) within a noun phrase: from NP_1 branches lead to the NP *the mosquitoes* and to an adjective phrase (ADJP) consisting of the sentence (S_1) *the mosquitoes live in North Dakota,* showing that the relative clause is part of a larger noun phrase.

Reed-Kellogg diagrams do not show as much of the underlying structure of relative clauses as phrase markers do; the relative clause is represented in its own sentence diagram, but the relative pronoun appears in its appropriate position, not the underlying noun phrase that it has replaced. A broken line links the relative pronoun with the noun phrase to which it refers.

(38)

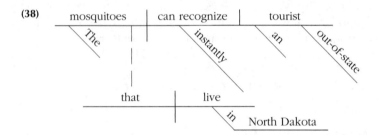

In *Mike never eats the lunches that his mother packs for him,* the relative pronoun *that* is the direct object and stands for *lunches* in the relative clause. In the Reed-Kellogg diagram, it appears in the object slot of its clause, with a broken line connecting it to the noun it modifies:

(39)

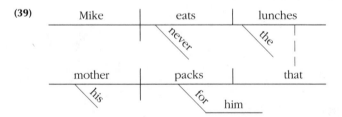

When the relative pronoun is a determiner, it stands for a possessive noun. For instance, in *Professor Snorf sometimes embarrasses students whose homework is turned in late, whose* is a determiner replacing the possessive in *students' homework.* In the diagram, a broken line connects it to its antecedent, *students:*

(40)

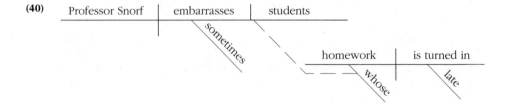

When the relative pronoun is located within a prepositional phrase—as it is in the sentence *Lorry's father loves his garage, in which he builds lifelike models of prehistoric animals*—a phrase marker (41) and a Reed-Kellogg diagram (42) each reflect that grammatical structure. The phrase marker shows the entire nominal that the relative pronoun replaces:

(41)

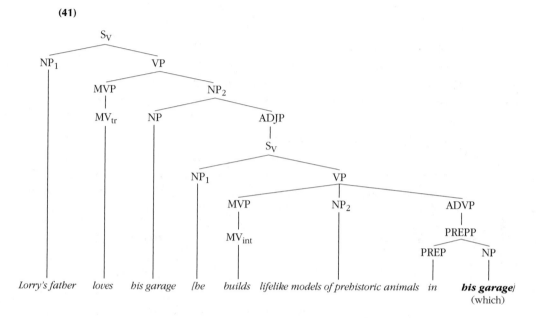

After the substitution of *which* for *his garage,* a movement transformation would apply to the sentence structure analyzed in (41), shifting the prepositional phrase *in which* to the beginning of the relative clause to produce the sequence *in which he builds.*

The Reed-Kellogg diagram, again, shows the relative pronoun connected to its antecedent with a broken line:

(42)

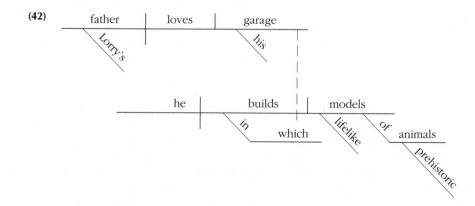

■ *EXERCISE 9.8*

> Show your analysis of each of the following sentences using a phrase marker and a Reed-Kellogg diagram.

1. Police officers fined an 83-year-old Australian woman who uses a walking stick 30 dollars.
2. They objected because she crossed the road too slowly.
3. She was slightly amused by the ticket that the police gave her.
4. The community in which she lives was outraged by the fine.
5. The police, who were surprised by the public outcry, have withdrawn the fine.

WHAT'S THE USAGE?   *Who/Whom*

According to traditional usage guides, when the human relative pronoun functions as the object of a verb or a preposition, it takes the form *whom*. However, speakers of English have, in fact, three options in forming a relative clause from the underlying clauses of (43):

(43) Those are *the people* + the house belongs to *the people*
      ↓

   a. Those are the people *to whom* the house belongs.
      or

   b. Those are the people *whom* the house belongs *to*.
      or

   c. Those are the people *who* the house belongs *to*.

These are listed in decreasing order of acceptability according to the traditions of formal written English. Usually, the first version is considered the best example of standard English usage. The pronoun *whom* is in the objective case because it is the object of the preposition *to*. In (43a) *whom* appears directly after its preposition. The second has been less accepted in formal writing, possibly because the preposition is separated from its object pronoun *whom*, occurring instead at the end of the sentence. Consequently, it may be a little harder to understand. The third is probably still the least acceptable because *who* is the form of the relative used in subject positions: in this sentence *who* is the object of the preposition *to*, so the form should logically be *whom*.

   In some sentences, it can seem difficult to decide whether to use *who* or *whom*. If you ever feel uncertain about which form is correct, your uncomfortable feeling is evidence that change is underway in this detail of American English. To what extent does your use of *who* and *whom* follow the pattern we have described in the previous paragraph?

   Traditionally and still in most formal usage, *who* functions as subject and *whom* as object—direct object, indirect object, or object of a preposition—although in informal situations, *who* is used by most people most of the time.

When you wish to be formally correct but are unsure which form to use, try turning the relative clause into a sentence, replacing the relative pronoun with the noun phrase for which it stands. Then analyze the grammatical function of that noun phrase. Alternatively, substitute an ordinary pronoun for the relative in the reconstituted sentence. Compare the following examples:

(44)   a. She is [the engineer] ***who/whom*** *I worked with.*
↓
I worked *with **who/whom?***
↓
I worked *with the engineer.*
or
I worked *with her.*   (Object pronoun is appropriate; therefore, *whom* is correct)

   (**not** *I worked *with she.*)

   b. She is [the engineer] ***who/whom*** *I met yesterday.*
↓
I met ***who/whom*** *yesterday?*
↓
I met *the engineer.*
or
I met *her.*   (Object pronoun is appropriate; therefore, *whom* is correct)

   (**not** *I met *she.*)

   c. She is the [engineer] ***who/whom*** *I believe completed the project.*
↓
I believe ***who/whom*** completed the project?
↓
I believe *the engineer* completed the project.
or
I believe *she* completed the project.   (Subject pronoun is appropriate; therefore, *who* is correct)

   (**not** *I believe *her* completed the project.)

If you substitute the antecedent (*the engineer* in these three examples) for the relative pronoun and turn the relative clause into a sentence, as we have done in the versions above, you can usually determine quickly the grammatical function that the relative plays. In the first two sentences, *whom* is the correct form because within the relative clause, the relative pronoun functions as object—of the preposition *with* in (44a) and of the verb *met* in (44b). In (44c), *who* is the correct form because within the relative clause, the relative pronoun functions as the subject of the verb *completed*. The words *I believe* don't change that relationship, even though it may seem at first that the relative pronoun could be the object of *believe*. In all three versions, substituting the pronouns *she* and *her* effectively confirms which form of the relative pronoun is appropriate.

   It is important to reemphasize that the form of the relative pronoun, *who* or *whom*, is determined by its own grammatical role within the relative clause, not by the grammatical function of its antecedent within the larger sentence. Thus, in example (45), the correct form of the relative pronoun is *whom* because within the relative clause, *whom* is the object of *with;* the fact that the noun phrase *the engineer,* the antecedent to which *whom* refers, functions as subject of the sentence does not affect the form of the relative pronoun.

(45) The engineer ***who/whom*** *I worked with* completed the drawings.

In (46), on the other hand, *who* is the correct form because the relative pronoun functions as subject of the relative clause. That its antecedent, *the designer,* functions as direct object of *met* in the sentence does not affect the form of the relative pronoun.

(46) I met the designer ***who/whom*** *called you.*

As an alternative, you can sometimes avoid deciding between *who* and *whom* by deleting the relative pronoun:

(47) She is the engineer I worked with.

She is the engineer I met.

In these cases, *I worked with* and *I met* are still relative clauses, even though the relative pronouns have been deleted.

The Omission of Relative Pronouns

In discussing problems of deciding between *who* and *whom,* we pointed out that one way to avoid a wrong choice is to omit the relative pronoun entirely, leaving the rest of the clause in place:

(48) That is the man *whom* my son works for.

↓

That is the man my son works for.

Be sure to notice that (48) is still considered to contain a relative clause: *my son works for.*

It can be difficult to identify relative clauses when the relative pronoun is missing. Compare the following versions of the same sentence:

(49) Will Rogers never met a man *whom he didn't like.*

Will Rogers never met a man *he didn't like.*

The computer *that you ordered* is extremely expensive.

The computer *you ordered* is extremely expensive.

No one believed the story *that he told* about being given a ride in a spaceship.

No one believed the story *he told* about being given a ride in a spaceship.

There is little difference in acceptability between the two versions of these sentences. Some people prefer the first because it is more explicit. Others prefer the second because it contains fewer words. Studies have shown that the versions without the relative pronoun are more difficult to understand. Even though they have fewer words, the missing relative pronoun would have provided significant information about the relationships between the independent clause and the relative clause. What is essential for the student of grammar is to recognize that both versions contain relative clauses, even though no relative pronoun is present in the second versions.

A phrase marker representing the structure of a relative clause with the relative pronoun deleted shows the constituent for which the deleted relative pronoun or adverb substituted, but you can indicate the deletion by striking out the deleted constituent, as in example (50).

(50)

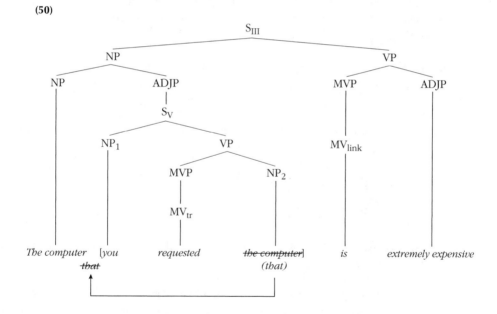

A Reed-Kellogg diagram shows the relationship of the relative clause to its antecedent (the noun phrase it modifies). However, it includes only those words present in the surface structure of the sentence; therefore, it does not really show the underlying structure of the relative clause prior to deleting the relative pronoun. Instead, it uses an *x* to represent the deleted relative pronoun in the slot where that constituent would have been. Example (51) illustrates this:

(51)

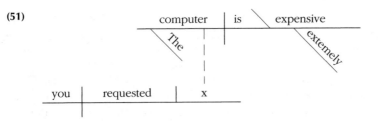

Relative Adverbs

Relative clauses can also be introduced by **relative adverbs** expressing either time (*when*), place (*where*), or reason (*why*). A relative adverb functions just like a relative pronoun: It refers to a preceding noun phrase, and it introduces a relative clause that modifies that noun. The only difference between a relative pronoun and a relative adverb is that the relative pronoun substitutes for a repetition of the antecedent noun or pronoun, while the relative adverb substitutes for an adverbial modifier (typically a prepositional phrase), which contains the repeated noun. Both kinds of clauses are adjectival, as the following examples illustrate:

(52) a. This is the house + I was talking about *the house*
  ↓
  This is the house + I was talking about *that*
  ↓
  This is the house *that* I was talking about. (relative pronoun)

 b. This is the house + Elvis lived *in the house*
  ↓
  This is the house + Elvis lived *where*
  ↓
  This is the house *where* Elvis lived. (relative adverb)

In each case, the relative clause identifies which house is being referred to; hence, both are adjectival clauses (noun modifiers).

To see how relative adverbs originate, compare the following sets of sentences. In each, an adverbial constituent (italicized) in the clause that will be transformed into a relative clause becomes a relative adverb in the (b) version and moves to the beginning of its clause in the (c) version.

(53) a. Name a day + You will have some free time *on some day*
  ↓

 b. Name a day + you will have some free time *when*
  ↓

 c. Name a day *when* you will have some free time.
   ↑_____|

In (53), the relative adverb *when* replaces the adverbial phrase *on some day* to create the relative clause *when you will have some free time; when* refers to the noun *day,* which the entire relative clause modifies adjectivally.

(54) a. Is this the place + We left the dog *someplace*
  ↓

b. Is this the place + we left the dog *where*
  ↓

c. Is this the place *where* we left the dog?
  ↑_____|

The relative adverb *where* in (54) replaces the adverbial modifier *someplace* in the clause *we left the dog someplace* to produce *where we left the dog,* a relative clause that functions as an adjectival modifier of the noun *place* in (54c).

(55) a. There is no reason + We shouldn't eat this cake *for some reason*
  ↓

b. There is no reason + we shouldn't eat this cake *why*
  ↓

c. There is no reason *why* we shouldn't eat this cake.
  ↑_____|

In a pattern similar to the earlier examples, here the relative adverb *why* replaces the adverbial phrase *for some reason* in (55a) and then moves to the front of its clause, where it immediately follows its antecedent, *reason,* the noun that the relative clause beginning with *why* modifies.

Relative adverbs, like relative pronouns, can sometimes be deleted from relative clauses. For instance, we can delete the relative adverb *why* from example (55c):

(56) There is no reason we shouldn't eat this cake.

Nevertheless, *we shouldn't eat this cake* remains a relative clause, adjectivally modifying *reason.*

Phrase markers and diagrams of relative clauses beginning with relative adverbs confirm the adverbial function of the relative adverb within its own clause: *Where, when,* and *why* will always be part of an adverbial phrase within the relative clause, as example (57) illustrates with the sentence *During the summer, my parents went back to the park where they first met.*

You can see from the phrase marker that the relative adverb replaces an adverbial constituent within its own clause: *Where* replaces *in the park,* which modifies the verb *met.* However, the entire relative clause, represented in the phrase marker by *they met first in the park,* [*where*], serves as an adjectival modifier of the noun phrase *the park* in the main clause, *my parents went back during the summer to the park.*

(57)

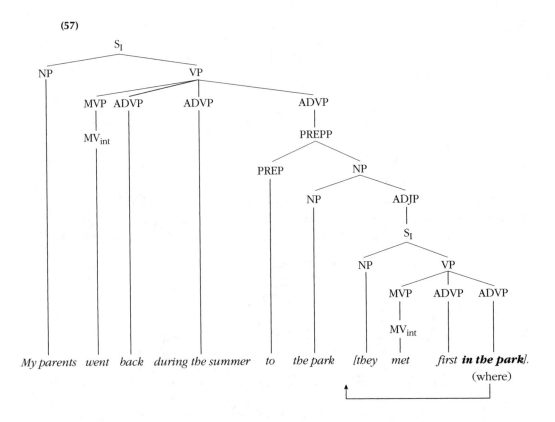

Example (58) analyzes the same sentence with a Reed-Kellogg diagram. Notice once again how the relative adverb *where* modifies the verb *met* within the relative clause (*where they met*), while the entire relative clause functions adjectivally as a modifier of *park* within the main clause.

(58)

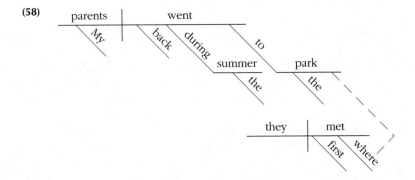

Relative Clauses Contrasted with Adverbial Subordinate Clauses

Because *when* and *where* can be either relative adverbs or subordinating conjunctions, you may momentarily become confused about the difference between a relative clause and a subordinate clause. For example, the relative clause and the adverbial subordinate clause in the examples below both begin with *when* and look identical if taken out of the sentences in which they occur.

(59) a. Gabriel anticipated a time + (relative clause)
when he could forget the army.

b. Gabriel relaxed thoroughly + (adverbial subordinate clause)
when he could forget the army.

We know that *when* is a relative adverb in (59a) because it refers to the preceding noun *time.* The relative clause *when he could forget the army* modifies *time,* telling which time Gabriel longed for.

In contrast, the subordinate clause *when he could forget the army* in (59b) begins with the subordinator *when,* and the entire clause functions as an adverbial modifier of the verb *relaxed,* telling when Gabriel could relax thoroughly. The clause it introduces does not have the function of a relative clause: There is no preceding noun that it modifies. Furthermore, this clause passes all four of the tests for adverbial subordinate clauses (Figure 9.2).

1. It can be moved: **When he could forget the army,** *Gabriel relaxed thoroughly.*

2. It can become the basis of a *wh*-question: *When did Gabriel relax thoroughly?*

3. An adverb can substitute for it: *Gabriel relaxed thoroughly* **then.**

4. It fits the adverb frame sentence.

Although the relative clause in (59a) also seems to fit the frame, it fails the other three tests.

Diagramming (59a) and (59b) helps to reinforce the distinction between the function of the clauses in the two sentences. The broken line linking the relative adverb *when* and the noun *time* in (60) signals the adjectival function of the relative clause.

(60)

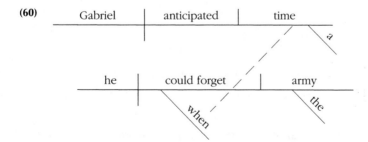

In (61), the subordinator *when* is written on a broken line linking the verb *relaxed* in the main clause with the verb *could forget* in the subordinate clause, which indicates the adverbial function of the subordinate clause.

SUMMARY	
Relative Clauses	
Form	1. A dependent clause introduced by a relative pronoun or relative adverb: *who, whose, whom, which, that, where, when,* or *why.* 2. The relative pronoun or adverb is a constituent of the clause it introduces.
Clause function	An adjectival modifier of the noun or noun phrase that immediately precedes the relative clause.
Punctuation	See Figure 9.4

Figure 9.3

(61)

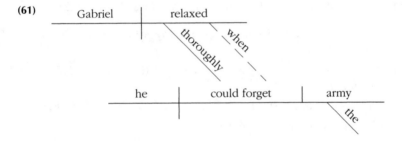

See Figure 9.3 for a summary of the characteristics of relative clauses.

■ *EXERCISE 9.9*

For each of the following sentences, find the relative pronoun or adverb, and give the constituent for which it substitutes. An example has been done for you.

EXAMPLE

The canoe that we just painted is sinking next to the dock.

that = *the canoe [We just painted the canoe.]*

1. A new Bio-Optic Organized Knowledge device that has been named "BOOK" has been introduced.[1]

2. BOOK, which has no electric circuits to be switched on, represents a breakthrough in technology.

3. It is small enough to be used by someone who is sitting in an armchair.

4. Manufacturers are able to double BOOK's information density by using Opaque Paper Technology (OPT), which allows them to print on both sides of a sheet of paper.

5. Pages that have been scanned optically by the reader need only be flicked by a finger to get to the next page.

6. Many BOOKs have an "index" feature that allows readers to find the exact location of any bit of information.

7. BOOK has an optional "BOOKmark" accessory that allows you to open BOOK at exactly the place where you quit reading before.

8. Readers who want to write notes in the margins of BOOK can use accessories that are called "Portable Erasable Nib Criptic Intercommunication Language Styluses" (PENCILS).

Restrictive and Nonrestrictive Relative Clauses

The purpose of most relative clauses is to provide specific identification for a noun. In (62), for example, the relative clause *who leave work at 5:00* tells exactly which commuters suffer traffic jams. In other words, it *restricts* the possible people to whom the word *commuters* may refer in this instance.

(62)   The commuters at Boeing who leave work at 5:00 suffer terrible traffic jams.

Such a sentence implies that there are *some* commuters at Boeing who leave work at other times and that they may not suffer terrible traffic jams. Compare (62) with (63).

(63)   The commuters at Boeing, who leave work at 5:00, suffer terrible traffic jams.

According to (63), *all* of the commuters at Boeing leave work at 5:00, and *all* of them suffer terrible traffic jams.

Relative clauses that help to identify specific referents are said to be **restrictive.** The relative clause in (62) is restrictive because it tells us precisely which commuters at Boeing are being referred to: the ones who leave work at 5:00. Relative clauses that simply supply additional information about a referent that is already precisely identified are said to be **nonrestrictive.** The relative clause in (63) is nonrestrictive because the sentence is referring to *all* the commuters at Boeing; the information in the relative clause, that the commuters leave work at 5:00, does not in this case help to define which commuters are being discussed. The commas surrounding the nonrestrictive relative clause in (63) signal that it is nonessential information.

Compare the following pairs of examples, which include relative clauses. In each case, the restrictive relative clause identifies the noun it modifies; the nonrestrictive relative clause adds information about the noun it modifies, but it doesn't uniquely identify it. If the restrictive relative clause is removed from each of the sentences that follow, the meaning of the main clause changes. But if the nonrestrictive relative clause is removed, the meaning of the main clause remains the same.

(64)

Restrictive	Have you seen the cathedral *in which Beckett was murdered?*
	Have you seen the cathedral? (The meaning changes; the restrictive relative clause is necessary for knowing which cathedral is meant.)
Nonrestrictive	Have you seen Canterbury Cathedral, *in which Beckett was murdered?*
	Have you seen Canterbury Cathedral? (The meaning is unchanged; the nonrestrictive relative clause adds information, but the proper name of the famous English church is all that is necessary for identifying which cathedral is being referred to.)
Restrictive	The house *that settlers built in 1842* was destroyed by Hurricane Hugo.
	The house was destroyed by Hurricane Hugo. (The meaning changes; the house is not identified without the restrictive relative clause.)
Nonrestrictive	Whittington House, *which settlers built in 1842,* was destroyed by Hurricane Hugo.
	Whittington House was destroyed by Hurricane Hugo. (The meaning is unchanged; because the house is distinguished from all others by its proper name, the relative clause doesn't help to identify it but just gives additional information about it.)
Restrictive	The woman *who was prime minister longer than anyone else in the twentieth century* made enormous changes in England.
	The woman made enormous changes in England. (The woman is not identified; the restrictive clause tells you just which woman is meant.)
Nonrestrictive	Margaret Thatcher, *who was prime minister longer than anyone else in the twentieth century*, made enormous changes in England.

Margaret Thatcher made enormous changes in England. (The meaning is unchanged; *Margaret Thatcher* already identifies just one woman; the nonrestrictive modifier adds information about how long she was Prime Minister but isn't needed to tell you which Margaret Thatcher is being discussed.)

Restrictive

The book *that has been on the best-seller list for 126 weeks* has made a lot of money for its publisher.

The book has made a lot of money for its publisher. (The book is not identified; the restrictive relative clause is necessary to distinguish the particular book referred to from all other books.)

Nonrestrictive

My friend Edna's first novel, *which has been on the best-seller list for 126 weeks,* has made a lot of money for its publisher.

My friend Edna's first novel has made a lot of money for its publisher. (The meaning is unchanged by the deletion of the nonrestrictive clause; *my friend Edna's first novel* doesn't rely on the clause to identify which novel is meant.)

The distinction between restrictive and nonrestrictive relative clauses becomes important when you must punctuate sentences containing them. As you see in the examples above, restrictive relative clauses are not separated from the rest of the sentence by commas; they provide information essential to the identification of the noun phrase they modify. In contrast, nonrestrictive relative clauses are set off by commas from the rest of the material in the sentence because they do not contribute the information you need for identifying the noun phrase they modify. In the case of nonrestrictive relative clauses, the commas function like parentheses, setting off material that adds to what the sentence communicates but that is not necessary for identifying the noun phrase that the relative clause modifies.

When a relative clause modifies a proper noun, like *Margaret Thatcher* in *Margaret Thatcher, who was prime minister longer than anyone else in the twentieth century,* the clause is almost always nonrestrictive because a proper noun usually identifies a specific person, place, or thing that doesn't need a restrictive clause to identify it. But if the proper noun doesn't label something unique, then a restrictive relative clause modifying it might be possible, as in example (65):

(65) Are you the Luis Valdez *who was in the senior class play in 1969?*

This sentence allows for the possibility of more than one person named *Luis Valdez*. The restrictive relative clause following the name makes clear which *Luis Valdez* the speaker means.

When a relative clause modifies a common noun with only one possible referent, the clause is most likely nonrestrictive:

(66)   Fred's mother, whose meatloaf was barely edible, cooked everything with lard.

In (66), the noun phrase *Fred's mother* can probably have only one referent; the relative clause *whose meatloaf was barely edible* says something about *Fred's mother* but doesn't tell which mother is being referred to, as Fred most likely has only one mother.

The speaker or writer knows whether a relative clause is restrictive (identifying the noun it modifies) or nonrestrictive (providing extra information about a noun already specifically identified). Intonation (pauses surrounding the nonrestrictive clause) or punctuation (commas replacing the pauses) help the listener or reader decide which kind of clause was intended. Compare the following:

(67)   a. The depositors who lost their life savings filed claims against the bank.

b. The depositors, who lost their life savings, filed claims against the bank.

The (a) version suggests that some depositors did not lose their life savings; only those who did are filing claims. The (b) version implies that all depositors lost their savings and all are filing claims. Punctuating relative clauses correctly is important because it helps readers to understand the intent of the writer (see Figure 9.4).

■ *EXERCISE 9.10*

The sentences in this exercise contain both adverbial clauses and relative (adjectival) clauses. Underline each adverbial and relative clause, label it, and punctuate it correctly. (Remember that restrictive relative clauses occur without punctuation; nonrestrictive relative clauses are set off from the rest of the sentence by commas.)

1. In the 1950s young people who were racing hot rods on Kern County's rural roads became a dangerous problem.
2. With the sheriff's help, the kids formed a nonprofit group that arranged legal drag races on a taxiway of the town's little-used airport.
3. Three generations of local families have gathered to watch the races at the runway on which the young people race.
4. The racers have paid the Inyokern Airport $1,000 per racing day, which allowed them to schedule drag races several times a year.
5. Although some drivers reached speeds of 200 mph, other homemade dragsters merely sputtered down the quarter-mile track.
6. Because Californians are known to love fast cars, the National Hot Rod Association is headquartered there.
7. After 51 years, the FAA has threatened the airfield's federal funding unless they stop non-aviation activities at the field.
8. If the young people cannot race on the airport runway, most fear a rise in the illegal street racing that prompted the track's founding in the first place.

SUMMARY	
Contrast Between Restrictive and Nonrestrictive Relative Clauses	

Restrictive Relative Clauses

How Used	Required to specifically identify the noun it modifies.
Markers	Any of the relative pronouns or relative adverbs: *who, whom, whose, which, that, when, where, why* Hint: If the relative pronoun can be deleted, the clause is restrictive. Hint: The relative pronoun *that* occurs only in restrictive relative clauses.
Punctuation	No commas because the relative clause provides essential information.
Examples	*The people **who own that barking dog** are away on vacation.* *The book **[that] I ordered for you** hasn't come in yet.*

Nonrestrictive Relative Clauses

How Used	Gives additional information about a noun already specifically identified.
Markers	The relative pronouns and adverbs *who, whom, whose, which, when, where* Hint: The relative pronoun can't be deleted from a nonrestrictive clause.
Punctuation	Set off by commas in writing, or by distinguishing pauses in speech.
Examples	*The Mullens, **who own that barking dog,** are away on vacation.* *Madame Bovary, **which I ordered for you,** hasn't come in yet.*

Figure 9.4

SUMMARY

Clauses are sequences of words made up of noun phrase subjects and verb phrase predicates. The main verb of the predicate is said to be finite because it is inflected for tense. Clauses that can stand alone as sentences are independent. Those that have subjects and predicates but cannot stand alone are dependent; they function as a constituent in some other clause. Sentences that are made up of a single independent clause are called simple sentences. When coordinating conjunctions join two or more independent clauses, the result is a compound sentence. When a dependent clause is combined with an independent one, the result is a complex sentence. In Chapter 9, we looked at two kinds of dependent clauses: those beginning with subordinating conjunctions and those beginning with relative pronouns and relative adverbs. Subordinate clauses usually function adverbially; they modify verbs, adverbs, adjectives, or complete sentences. Relative clauses are adjectival; they modify nouns and are constituents of noun phrases. In Chapter 10, we look at dependent clauses that can substitute for noun phrases: nominal clauses.

REVIEW EXERCISES

Distinguishing between Simple, Compound, and Complex Sentences

Decide whether each of the sentences below is simple, compound, complex, or compound-complex.

1. Because he established a stable, independent central government, Henry II was one of the most effective of English monarchs.
2. Richard I, who was known as "Richard the Lion-Hearted," spent only six months of his ten-year reign in England. *complex*
3. According to some historians, King John neither achieved the crown honorably, nor did he hold it with honor. *compound* *complex*
4. Henry IV invaded England while Richard II was fighting in Ireland.
5. Richard III was the last of the Plantagenet dynasty, which had ruled England since 1154, and he was the last English king to die on the battlefield. *compound complex*
6. The importance of the reign of Henry VIII is overshadowed by the story of his six wives. *simple*
7. Mary I's first act, which threw England into a period of religious persecution, was to repeal the Protestant legislation of her brother, Edward VI. *complex*
8. Elizabeth I, who was the last of the Tudor monarchs, had a terrible temper, but, as a ruler, she was able to maintain calm and peace. *relative adj* *compound complex*

Identifying Dependent Clause Types

This exercise tests your ability to identify dependent clauses and distinguish between adverbial subordinate clauses and adjectival relative clauses. In the sentences below, identify all of the dependent clauses and specify whether each is adverbial or adjectival. If you believe a clause is adverbial, see how many of the four tests for adverbial modifiers listed in Figure 9.2 that it satisfies. If you believe a clause is adjectival, identify the noun phrase it modifies. Some sentences contain more than one dependent clause.

An alligator that was presumably dumped illegally in Lake Machado in
Los Angeles has been named "Reggie." Someone probably brought Reggie
home from the South as a pet and decided to get rid of him when he
grew to be 10 feet long. After it had paid a Colorado alligator hunter $800
a day for a couple of fruitless days, the city hired a team of experts from
Gatorland in Florida to continue the hunt. The Gatorland team cruised
the lake in a motorized pontoon boat, from which they hoped to spot
Reggie. After he saw Lake Machado, which he characterized as nothing but
a mud hole, a Hurricane Katrina evacuee from New Orleans promised to
track the alligator back to his lair, where he planned to shine a flashlight
into Reggie's eyes before capturing him. When a wrangler catches an
alligator in Louisiana, he keeps the tail for himself and sells the hide. It
would be different in California. After the city took Reggie alive, it wanted
to offer him to the Los Angeles Zoo. Months after Reggie was first spotted,
he was still eluding capture in Lake Machado.

Restrictive/Nonrestrictive Relative Clauses

Identify each relative clause in the sentences that follow as either restrictive
or nonrestrictive and then punctuate each sentence correctly.

1. People who have a DSL connection are likely to be online for many
   hours every day.
2. Internet surfers need software with which they can zap spam, viruses,
   ads, and cookies.
3. I have software on my computer that will block adware programs which
   use cookies to track computer activities.
4. My antivirus program blocks worms and viruses that can make my computer crash.
5. My e-mail provider has a setting that blocks spam which is unsolicited
   junk mail.
6. The Internet firewall program that I use keeps hackers from identifying
   me.
7. I also have a spyware program that looks for programs on my computer
   that track my actions online.
8. Just in case the spyware program misses a dangerous program, I have
   other spyware software that I occasionally run.

Form and Function of Subordinate Clauses

Select the best answer to the questions about the following passage:

In a study *of the relationship between low-calorie eating and health,* scientists worked with 48 Labrador retrievers *that were from seven litters.* Dogs
were paired with siblings, one dog in each pair receiving all the food *it*
wanted; the other dog received 25 percent fewer calories than its sibling.

relative clause

Labrador retrievers who were raised on a low-calorie diet lived longer and had fewer health problems than their litter-mates. The study suggested that *if you cut down on your dog's treats,* you might add two years to its life.

sub. clause

1. FORM: Decide whether each of the five italicized phrases from the passag above is a subordinate (adverbial) clause, a prepositional phrase, or a relative clause.

2. FUNCTION: Decide whether each of the italicized phrases from the passage above is an adverbial modifier or an adjectival modifier.

KEY TERMS

clause functions
  adjectival clause
  adverbial clause
dependent clauses
  relative clause
  subordinate clause
finite verb
independent clause
main clause
relative clause types

nonrestrictive relative clause
restrictive relative clause
relative adverb
relative pronoun
sentence types
  complex sentence
  compound sentence
  compound-complex sentence
  simple sentence

ENDNOTE

1. The concept of the Bio-Optic Organized Knowledge device has been attributed to Isaac Asimov. Reports of its development are widely circulated on the Internet.

Finite Verb Clauses, Part II

10

NOMINAL CLAUSES

CHAPTER PREVIEW

In this chapter, we complete our discussion of dependent clauses by analyzing nominal clauses: those which can substitute for nouns or phrases. Nominal clauses are introduced by words that mark them as dependent: either the complementizer that or an interrogative word (introduced in Chapter 5).

CHAPTER GOALS

At the end of this chapter, you should be able to

- Recognize *that*-clauses and identify their *functions*.
- Distinguish between *that* as a *demonstrative pronoun*, a *relative pronoun*, and a *complementizer*.
- Recognize whether a dependent clause is functioning as a *nominal*, an *adjectival*, or an *adverbial* clause.
- Distinguish *appositive noun phrases* and *clauses*.
- Identify *interrogative* clauses.

THAT-*CLAUSES*

The first type of nominal clause is introduced by the complementizer *that*:

(1) *That it will rain tomorrow* seems absolutely certain.

People forget *that even grammarians get the blues*.

323

The good news is *that Joey won the pie-eating contest.*

Notice that each of these clauses occupies a position in the sentence that is normally filled by a noun or noun phrase and that each can be replaced by the pronoun *it* or *something:*

(2)   *It/something* (subject) seems certain.

People forget *it/something*   (direct object).

The good news is *something*   (subject complement).

In nominal clauses, *that* is called a **complementizer:** a word that creates a dependent clause that can substitute for a noun phrase sentence constituent. The resulting *that*-clause functions as a complement, a constituent that helps to *complete* the sentence. The complementizer *that* plays no role within its clause, nor does it contribute any information. Notice that if you remove the complementizer, what remains can stand alone as an independent clause:

(3)   *That the soccer game ended in a tie* surprised no one.

~~that~~ The soccer game ended in a tie.

Our professor told us *that there will be no exam next week.*

~~that~~ There will be no exam next week.

All *that* does is connect two clauses, putting one inside the other at a position usually occupied by a noun or other nominal constituent.

Direct quotations can be transformed into indirect ones by using a *that*-clause:

(4)   The teacher announced, *"Everyone earned an A on the midterm exam."*

The teacher announced *that everyone earned an A on the midterm exam.*

In direct quotations, or **direct discourse,** the exact words of the quotation are used and surrounded by quotation marks. Direct discourse has pronouns appropriate to the speaker and verb tenses appropriate to the situation. When direct discourse is converted into **indirect discourse,** pronouns and tenses frequently have to be changed:

(5)   Catherine said, "I don't want to intrude."

Catherine said *that she didn't want to intrude.*

Although *I* is appropriate in the direct quotation of what someone said, when reporting indirectly someone else's speech, the speaker or writer must change the pronoun. Similarly, the verb in the direct quotation is in the present tense the speaker would have used; in the reported speech, as the situation described occurred in the past, the verb must be changed to the past tense. If a present-tense verb in the direct quotation refers to future or ongoing time, as in (6):

(6)   She said, "I plan to be the first woman to land on Mars."

the speaker may use either present or past tense, as in (7):

(7)   She said that she *plans* to be the first woman to land on Mars.
She said that she *planned* to be the first woman to land on Mars.

If the verb in the direct quote is already in the past tense, the changes can become quite complex:

(8)   The operator said, "The phones were working yesterday."
The operator said *that the phones had been working the day before.*

Native speakers adjust their speech without conscious effort when using indirect discourse of this kind, while learners of English as a second language face the challenge of gradually mastering these complex but systematic patterns. For our purposes, it is important to recognize that both direct and indirect quotations are nominal clauses that function as the direct objects of verbs of saying.

Figure 10.1 summarizes contrasts between direct and indirect discourse. You may prefer to ignore the examples of interrogative clauses at this point; we discuss them in more detail below.

▨ *EXERCISE 10.1*

In each sentence below, create a *that*-clause as a substitute for the italicized pronoun. Then identify the role the clause plays in the larger sentence. An example has been done for you.

EXAMPLE

Marie prefers *something*.
*Marie prefers **that you not drum your fingers on the table.**   (direct object)*

1. Walter said *something*.
2. *Something* seemed suspicious to me.
3. The truth is *something*.
4. Before waiting another half hour on this corner, I think *something*.
5. Judith thought *something* when her cell phone began to ring during dinner.
6. Because of the storm, everyone believed *something*.

SUMMARY	
Contrasts Between Direct and Indirect Discourse	
Direct Discourse	
How Used	Gives exact words spoken by someone.
Markers	Word order and verb tenses are the same as they would have been when the words were originally said.
Punctuation	Quotation marks surround and appropriate end punctuation follows words spoken by someone. First word capitalized.
Examples	*Marie said, "We won't have time to see the second show."* *He asked, "How long has it been since this piano was tuned?"*
Indirect Discourse	
How Used	Reports the essence of what someone said.
Markers	Word order and verb tenses often differ from what they would have been when the words were originally said. Introduced by an interrogative word (*who, what, why,* etc.) or an optional *that*.
Punctuation	No punctuation used to set off from the rest of the sentence.
Examples	*Marie said **[that] we wouldn't have time to see the second show.*** *He asked **how long it has been since our piano was tuned.***

Figure 10.1

Differences Between Relative Clauses and Nominal *That*-Clauses

Students sometimes confuse nominal *that*-clauses with relative clauses introduced by the relative pronoun *that*. Several useful differences can help you distinguish between sentences like the following. Don't try to memorize these differences. Instead, work through them slowly, trying to get a feel for the difference between the two kinds of clauses. Before going on, be sure you understand each one.

(9)   a. **Nominal *That*-Clause**

You know *that I don't want to read that book.*

You know *something/it.*   (Pronoun can substitute for the clause.)

~~that~~ I don't want to read that book. (Deleting *that* leaves a complete clause.)

b. **Adjectival Relative Clause**

The oranges *that we bought today* are sour.

　*The oranges *something* are sour.　(Pronoun can't substitute for the clause.)

　~~that~~ *We bought today.　(Deleting *that* leaves an incomplete clause.)

c. **Adjectival Relative Clause**

He assigned a book *that I don't want to read.*

　*He assigned a book *something*.　(Pronoun can't substitute for the clause.)

　~~that~~ I don't want to read.　(Deleting *that* changes the meaning of the clause.)

First, because it occupies a noun position in the sentence, you can substitute a pronoun (*something*) for the entire nominal *that*-clause, as in (9a). However, because the relative clause is adjectival, you cannot substitute a pronoun for it, as you see in (9b) and (9c). Second, if the complementizer *that* is deleted, the part of the clause that remains can stand alone as an independent clause, as in (9a). The relative pronoun is part of its clause; if it is removed, either the clause is incomplete, as in (9b), or its meaning changes, as in (9c).

There are two other differences that you can demonstrate to yourself. Because relative clauses are adjectival, they follow a noun that they modify: *oranges* in (9b) and *book* in (9c). *That*-clauses may or may not follow a noun, but if they do, they do not modify its meaning in any way. In *Richard told his instructor that he didn't want to read that book, that he didn't want to read that book* follows but does not modify the noun *instructor*.

In addition, relative clauses are modifiers; if they are removed, an entire sentence remains.

(10)　He assigned a book ~~that I don't want to read~~
　　　↓
　　　He assigned a book.

That-clauses are sentence constituents; removing them leaves an incomplete sentence:

(11)　You know ~~that I don't want to read that book~~
　　　↓
　　　*You know.

You know is a phrase often used alone, but it is incomplete. One must know *something*.

Refer to Figure 10.2 for a summary of the characteristics of *that*-clauses.

SUMMARY	
That-*Clauses*	
Form	1. A dependent clause introduced by the complementizer *that*. 2. *That* plays no role in the clause it introduces.
Clause function	Fills a noun phrase position in the sentence (subject, object, complement).
Punctuation	No punctuation required.
Test	1. If *that* is removed, a complete clause remains. 2. *It* or *something* can substitute for the entire *that* clause.

Figure 10.2

Appositive *That*-Clauses

We have seen that both relative and nominal clauses can begin with the word *that*. Keep in mind the distinctions between the two types of clauses that we pointed out above as you look at the borderline case in (12), and decide whether you would characterize the dependent clause as a relative clause or as a nominal *that*-clause:

(12)   Did you hear his comment *that there would be no need to pay the fine?*

The clause *that there would be no need to pay the fine* seems to modify *comment,* but is it a relative clause? Most linguists would say that it is not. Because *that* does not have any function within the dependent clause, and no repeated noun phrase can substitute for *that* in this instance, it is not a relative pronoun. Linguists classify the clause in (12) as a nominal *that*-clause. *That* can be deleted from the dependent clause in (12) without changing its meaning, as you can see in (13):

(13)   ~~that~~ There would be no need to pay the fine.

And the entire clause can substitute for the noun phrase *his comment* in (14):

(14)   Did you hear ~~his comment~~ that there would be no need to pay the fine?

In sentences like these, the nominal *that*-clause acts as an **appositive clause.** An appositive is traditionally defined as a noun phrase that renames another noun phrase, one that it usually follows immediately. Because an appositive renames a noun phrase, it can also replace that noun phrase, as example (14) illustrates. Note the italicized examples of appositives in the sentences below. Whether the appositive is a nominal clause or a simple noun phrase, it can be deleted, as in (15a), or it can substitute for the noun phrase it renames, as in (15b).

(15) a. Grocery shoppers doubted the *Inquirer* story *that outerspace aliens had kidnapped Elvis.* (The appositive is a nominal clause.)
Grocery shoppers doubted the *Inquirer* story.
Grocery shoppers doubted that outerspace aliens had kidnapped Elvis.

b. Grocery shoppers doubted the *Inquirer* story, *an outrageous report about Elvis.* (The appositive is a noun phrase but not a clause.)
Grocery shoppers doubted the *Inquirer* story.
Grocery shoppers doubted an outrageous report about Elvis.

Whether the constituent functioning as an appositive is a simple noun phrase or a clause, linguists account for its presence in the sentence transformationally by deriving it from a nominal subject complement in a relative clause. In the next section of this chapter, we explain exactly how appositives can be derived from reduced relative clauses.

Relative Clauses and Deletion Transformations: Appositives

We saw in Chapter 9 how a relative pronoun can sometimes be deleted from a relative clause without changing the meaning or function of the clause. Here is an example repeated from our discussion of relative clauses:

(16) a. That is the man *whom* my son works for.
↓

b. That is the man my son works for.

Deleting the relative pronoun is an example of a stylistic transformation that allows us to eliminate repetition or to shift emphasis without affecting the basic meaning of a sentence.

For stylistic purposes, we can sometimes delete more than the pronoun from a relative clause. For example, if the relative clause contains a verb form of *be* followed by a nominal subject complement—sentence Type IV (NP_1 + MV_{link} + NP_1)—sometimes both the subject relative pronoun and the *be* verb can be deleted, as in example (17):

(17)   a. Mr. Hillgard, *who was my biology teacher,* secretly studies Egyptian mortu-
           ary science.
           ↓

       b. Mr. Hillgard, ~~who was~~ my biology teacher, secretly studies Egyptian mortu-
          ary science.

What remains after these deletions is no longer a relative clause. The noun phrase *my biology teacher* that was functioning as subject complement in the relative clause *who was my biology teacher* in (17a) becomes an apposi-tive in relation to the noun phrase *Mr. Hillgard* in (17b). This happens because everything has been deleted *except* the subject complement, itself a noun phrase. Like other appositives, those derived from relative clauses can replace the noun phrases they follow, as example (18) illustrates.

(18)   ~~Mr. Hillgard~~, My biology teacher secretly studies Egyptian mortuary science.

In a Reed-Kellogg diagram, an appositive is placed directly after the noun phrase that it renames, with the headword of the appositive noun phrase in parentheses. The diagram visually illustrates the equality of the two nominals:

(19)

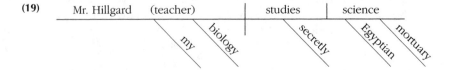

A phrase marker can show the entire clause structure from which the appositive is derived, as in example (20), where you find the whole relative clause *who was my biology teacher,* with an indication of which constituents will be deleted.

(20)

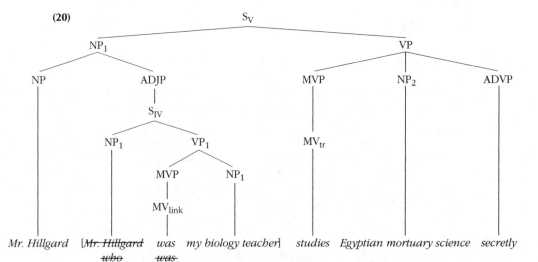

A phrase marker can also show the structure of the sentence with only the appositive noun phrase remaining from the original relative clause, as in example (21):

(21)

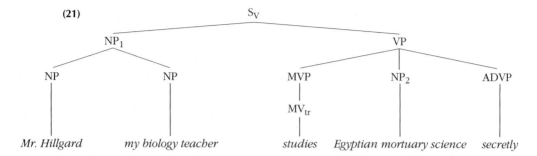

Because they are derived from relative clauses, which are adjectival modifiers in function, appositives might be thought of as being adjectival also. They certainly do add information about the noun phrase they rename. However, because they rename another noun phrase and because they can substitute for that noun phrase, appositives are considered nominal in function.

Like the relative clauses from which they are derived, appositives can be either restrictive or nonrestrictive, and they are punctuated appropriately to their status. For instance, in example (17a), the proper name *Mr. Hillgard* already uniquely identifies who is being referred to. Consequently, *who was my biology teacher* is nonrestrictive and is set off with commas. The appositive derived from it, *my biology teacher* in (17b), is also nonrestrictive and set off with commas. Most appositives are nonrestrictive.

A restrictive appositive provides information that is essential for identifying who or what is being renamed. Very often, restrictive appositives consist of proper names, as in example (22).

(22)   Eric's cousin *Gwendolyn* has the voice of an eight-year-old.

The implication of this sentence is that, in addition to Gwendolyn, Eric has other cousins who don't necessarily sound like young children; therefore, *Gwendolyn* is necessary for understanding which cousin is being referred to. Because it is restrictive, it is not set off with commas. Very short nonrestrictive appositives, like the name of a person in (22), are often not set off with commas in writing or by pauses in speech. In such cases, the writer or speaker relies on context to make the intended meaning clear.

Nonrestrictive appositives can sometimes be moved out of their basic position immediately following the noun phrase they rename. You might place an appositive at the beginning of a sentence, as in (23):

(23)   *An amazingly large child,* Goliath ＿＿＿＿＿＿＿ quickly dominated the

youth soccer league.

Certainly no friend of organized labor, Senator Beauregard Stevens _____

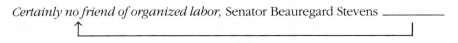

even refused to wear overalls labeled "Union Made."

Some brief appositives can be moved from a position following the subject noun phrase to the end of the sentence to give them special emphasis.

(24)   Commencement _____ finally arrived for the seniors, *a splendid day!*

The blasted slope of Mount St. Helens

_____ rose before the hikers, *a forbidding sight.*

Wherever an appositive has been moved, phrase markers and Reed-Kellogg diagrams represent them in their basic position, following the noun phrase they rename.

(25)

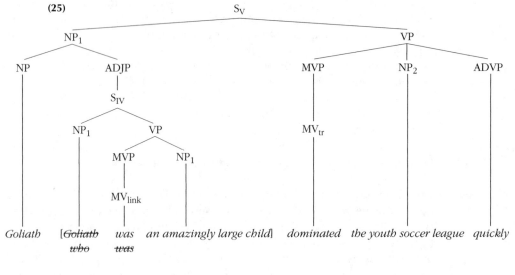

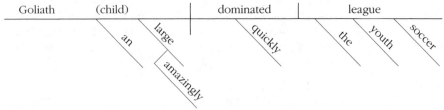

SUMMARY	
Functions of Nominal That-Clauses	
Subject	***That his license was revoked*** *shocked me.*
Direct object	*I hear **that the dance was a great success.***
Subject complement	*Her belief is **that most reported UFO sightings are genuine.***
Adjective complement	*I am astonished **that no one felt the tremor yesterday.***
Appositive	*Jennifer disputed the argument **that gravity waves are undetectable.***

Figure 10.3

When a direct object, such as the one in example (15), repeated here as example (26a), has a nominal *that*-clause functioning as an appositive, it, too, is derived from a nominal subject complement in a relative clause.

(26) a. Grocery shoppers doubted the *Inquirer* story *that outerspace aliens had kidnapped Elvis.*
       ↑

      b. Grocery shoppers doubted the *Inquirer story, which was that outerspace aliens had kidnapped Elvis.*

The deletion of the relative pronoun *which* and the linking verb *was* from the relative clause in (26b) leaves the nominal clause *that outerspace aliens had kidnapped Elvis* in (26a) as an appositive in relation to the noun phrase *the* Inquirer *story.*

Functions of Nominal *That*-Clauses

Figure 10.3 summarizes the grammatical roles nominal *that*-clauses can play.

■ *EXERCISE 10.2*

Look carefully at the dependent clause beginning with *that* in each of the following sentences. Decide whether it is a nominal clause or an adjectival relative clause. If you decide that it is a relative clause, identify the noun phrase that the clause modifies. If you decide it is a nominal clause, identify what specific nominal function the embedded clause plays in the sentence to which it belongs.

1. The "voice-over Internet protocol" (VOIP) that allows people to make free telephone calls is attracting more and more people.
2. VOIP means that people who have broadband connections can choose from a number of telephone providers.
3. An attractive feature of computer telephony is that you can take your computer phone wherever you go in the world.
4. In addition, your computer telephone number can be the same as the one that is in your home.
5. That a call home from anywhere in the world will be charged as a local call is attractive to business travelers. *nominal*
6. A fear that Internet telephone service will drive traditional telephone companies out of business is widespread. *nominal*
7. Some telephone companies want to block the new technology temporarily in hopes that it will fail. *nominal*
8. Others expect that they will be able to use the new technology in a way that will expand their own telephone services.

Diagramming Nominal *That*-Clauses

Remembering that nominal *that*-clauses occur in the functions and positions of noun phrases will help you in using diagrams to analyze sentences that include them. Consider, for example, a sentence with a *that*-clause functioning as direct object: *Francine declared that she detested pink shirts*. The phrase marker in example (27) places the *that-complementizer* (COMP) and its clause directly beneath the NP$_2$ in the direct object position:

(27)

In order to show that same dependent clause structure, Reed-Kellogg diagrams employ a platform that stands in the slot where the direct object would normally be placed, as you can see in example (28):

(28)

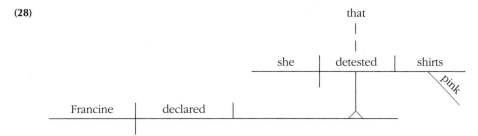

The complementizer *that* is connected to its clause with a broken line, reflecting that it has no role within the clause.

When a nominal *that*-clause functions as an appositive, as in the sentence *Maggie's parents retained their dream **that she would marry an ecologist,** a phrase marker shows the embedded sentence (*Their dream was that she would marry an ecologist*) underlying the appositive:

(29)

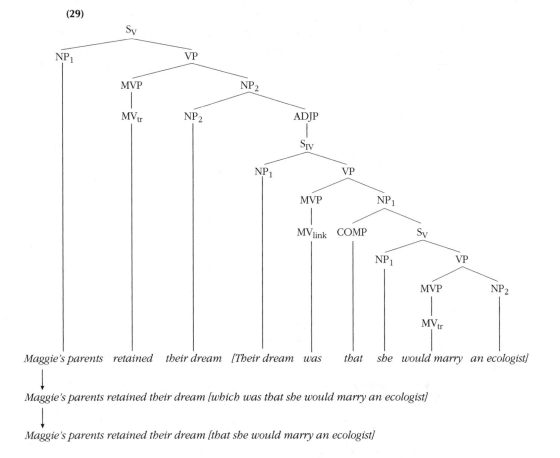

In a Reed-Kellogg diagram, parentheses surround the base of the platform for a nominal *that*-clause functioning as an appositive; the platform structure is placed immediately after the noun headword it renames (*dream*), as you can see in example (30):

(30)

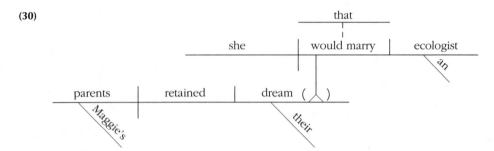

Compare the clausal appositives in the diagrams in (29) and (30) with the simple noun phrase appositives in (19) and (20), and you will see how the structure of appositives is similar in both cases.

Some adjectives (for example, *happy, glad, sad, angry, hurt, confident, doubtful, positive,* and others of similar meaning) and past participles functioning adjectivally (*disappointed, distressed, pleased,* and others) can take a nominal *that*-clause as a complement, as in *Florence seemed afraid **that we had insulted the mayor.*** A phrase marker analysis treats such **adjective complements** as NP constituents of an ADJP, as illustrated in example (31):

(31)

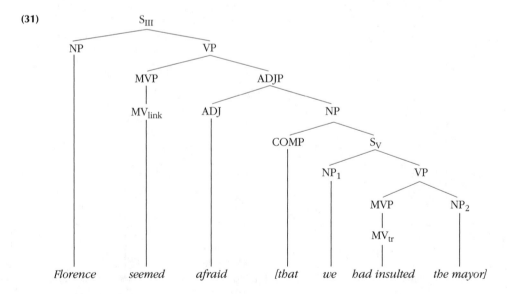

A Reed-Kellogg diagram traditionally treats such nominal *that*-clauses as if they were objects of a preposition:

(32)

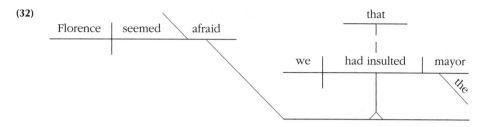

One way to understand the nominal function of these clausal complements of adjectives might be to change *seemed afraid* into *feared:*

(33)　Florence feared *that we had insulted the mayor.*

In (33), the nominal *that*-clause functions as direct object of *feared.* Another way to paraphrase the sentence in (32) so that you can better see the nominal nature of the dependent clause is to paraphrase it as an appositive. For example, we might paraphrase the sentence diagrammed in (32) as:

(34)　Florence seemed afraid of the fact *that we had insulted the mayor.*

In this sentence, *that we had insulted the mayor* has become an appositive of *the fact* without greatly changing the meaning.

■ *EXERCISE 10.3*

Analyze the following sentences by means of both phrase markers and Reed-Kellogg diagrams. Be alert to the subordinate (adverbial) and relative (adjectival) clauses that are included here along with nominal *that*-clauses.

1. A woman on a motorcycle reported that she had collided with a 250-pound bear.
2. An ambulance transported the woman to a hospital that treated her for a broken collarbone.
3. The California Highway Patrol officers said that the woman was going 50 to 65 mph when she hit the bear.
4. Officers believe that the shadows that occur in the late afternoon probably obscured the bear.
5. The report that the bear had fled the scene surprised no one.

━━━━━ *INTERROGATIVE CLAUSES* ━━━━━

A second kind of nominal clause is the dependent **interrogative clause,** one that usually involves a question, directed either to oneself or to another, about an unknown.

(35)   He asked *which car has a better service record.*

I wonder *who left that message on my machine.*

The movers asked *where they should put the piano.*

Interrogative clauses begin with the interrogative words *who, which, what, why, when, where,* and *how.* In addition to specifying what is unknown to the speaker or writer, interrogative words also play a grammatical role in their sentences, either as determiners (***which*** *car*), as pronouns (***who*** *left that message*), or as adverbs (***where*** *they should put the piano*).

Because the same structure words can function as relative pronouns, interrogative clauses may seem to resemble relative clauses. However, interrogative clauses function nominally, as noun phrase substitutes, in contrast to relative clauses, which are always adjectival. Carefully analyzing the function of the clause will enable you to distinguish confidently between interrogative and relative clauses, even when they seem superficially similar.

Interrogative clauses most commonly occur in direct or indirect questions. When you compare the direct and indirect versions below, you will notice that pronouns and verb tenses shift in the indirect question, just as they do in the nominal *that*-clauses used in indirect discourse.

(36)   He asked, "What time will you leave for work?"   (direct)

He asked *what time I would leave for work.*   (indirect)

Eleanor wondered, "Why has that bookshelf been moved?"   (direct)

Eleanor wondered *why that bookshelf had been moved.*   (indirect)

Some nominal clauses introduced by interrogative pronouns do not pose questions; they stand in place of an unknown or an indefinite. Look at the following:

(37)   Margaret bought *what we needed from the grocery store.*

Where Bigfoot regularly appeared was a secret known only to the local farmers.

Jim mostly worries about *how he can keep enough gas in his car.*

In all of these examples, the clause introduced by the *wh*-word occupies a noun slot in the sentence.

(38)   He asked [something]:   What time I would leave for work
                  Direct Object

Eleanor wondered [something]:   Why that bookshelf had been moved
                  Direct Object

SUMMARY	
Interrogative Clauses	
Form	1. A dependent clause introduced by an interrogative word: *what, who, whose, whom, which, where, when, why, how.* 2. The interrogative word plays a role in the dependent clause it introduces.
Clause function	Can fill noun phrase positions in the sentence (subject, object, complement, object of a preposition).
Punctuation	No punctuation required.
Test	1. The sentence containing the clause can be transformed into a *wh*-question by substituting *what* for the dependent clause. 2. *It* or *something* can substitute for the entire clause.

Figure 10.4

Margaret bought [something]:   What we needed from the grocery store
                    Direct Object

[Something] was known: Where Bigfoot regularly appeared
    Subject

Jim mostly worries about   How he can keep enough gas in his car
[something]:
*Object of
Preposition*

We summarize the basic features of dependent interrogative clauses in Figure 10.4 and examples of their functions in Figure 10.5.

EXERCISE 10.4

Because the interrogative words have the same form as relative pronouns, you may find the distinction between relative and interrogative clauses confusing. Locate the embedded clauses in each of the sentences below, and classify each as a relative (adjectival) or an interrogative (nominal) clause. If it is interrogative, identify the role the interrogative word plays in its clause and the role that the entire clause plays in the sentence. If the clause is a relative, identify the noun phrase it modifies.

SUMMARY	
Functions of Interrogative Clauses	
Subject of sentence	***What students need*** *is more parking spaces.*
Direct object	*Did you find* ***what you wanted*** *at the store?*
Subject complement	*That is* ***exactly why we wanted to leave.***
Object complement	*They found the film* ***just what they expected.***
Object of a preposition	*He is afraid of* ***where she will go.***
Indirect discourse (direct object)	*They asked* ***when dinner would be served.***

Figure 10.5

Some sentences may contain more than one dependent clause. An example has been done for you.

EXAMPLE

The ranger didn't know why the bear had returned.

Why (adverbial) the bear had returned =

Interrogative clause functioning as direct object

1. EBay, which has about 150 million registered users, has become a star of the World Wide Web.
2. It is the site where people can find anything from collectibles to automobiles.
3. What is most remarkable about eBay is what it offers to buyers and sellers throughout Europe.
4. EBay is trying to expand into China, which will probably be their biggest market in ten years.
5. Everyone wonders how eBay has come so far in such a short time.
6. More than 10,000 people gathered in San Jose in June to learn what has made eBay such a success.
7. The attendees toured the company headquarters, where they could see how large eBay has become.

8. Other online auction sites ask how they can attract as many buyers and sellers as those who use eBay.

Diagramming Interrogative Clauses

The graphic analysis of interrogative clauses with phrase markers and Reed-Kellogg diagrams closely resembles the analysis of nominal *that*-clauses, with minor differences reflecting contrasts between these two kinds of nominal clauses. Given the sentence *What the students said about Professor Dozoff didn't bother him,* you will notice that the phrase marker in example (39) rearranges the word order of the dependent clause to reflect the basic sentence pattern that underlies it. If you recall the question transformation, the interrogative words (*wh*-words), which represent an unknown, are moved to the beginning of the sentence to form questions. That is what has happened in sentences containing nominal interrogative clauses, as well. Therefore, *What the students said about Professor Dozoff* is assumed to derive from an underlying clause, *the students said [something] about Professor Dozoff.* It is this form that is represented in the phrase structure tree.

(39)

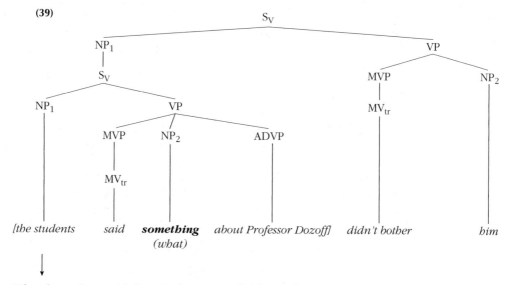

What the students said about Professor Dozoff didn't bother him

The Reed-Kellogg diagram of the same sentence in example (40) places the interrogative clause on a platform (familiar to you from diagramming *that*-clauses) in the subject position of the diagram because the dependent clause is functioning as subject of the sentence.

(40)

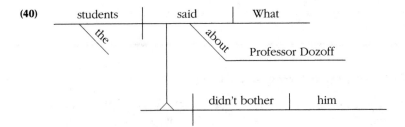

   Whether you use a phrase marker or a Reed-Kellogg diagram, the *wh*-word (or the pronoun or adverb from which it is derived) occupies a position reflecting its function within the dependent clause. In (39) and (40), *what* (or *something*) is in the direct object position within the clause *the students said something (what) about Professor Dozoff.*
   In the diagrams for *Deborah thought about how Boscoe smiled* in (41) and (42), *how* (or *somehow*) is placed appropriately for an adverbial modifier inside of the interrogative clause *how Boscoe smiled.* The entire dependent clause functions as object of the preposition *about.*

(41)

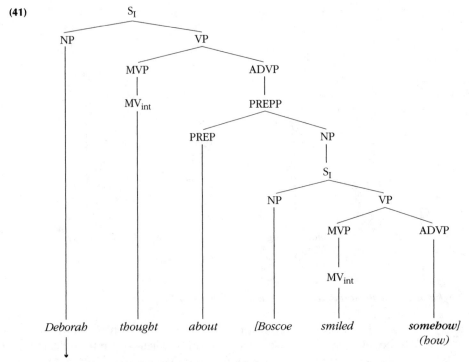

Deborah thought about how Boscoe smiled

(42)

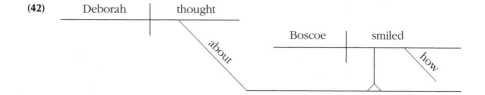

■ *EXERCISE 10.5*_____

> Analyze the following sentences using phrase markers and Reed-Kellogg diagrams. Be alert for several types of dependent clauses. Identify the kind of clause and its function in the sentence.
>
> 1. Sylvia asked where the tour guide was taking us next.
> 2. Henry wondered whose bags were still on the bus.
> 3. We had an argument about which group was going to the grotto.
> 4. How we would see the ruins in under an hour didn't worry Maggie.

■■■■■■■■■■ RHETORICAL PROBLEMS IN USING DEPENDENT CLAUSES ■

Grammar is a study of how we use the resources of the language to create sentences. *Rhetoric* is a study of how we use language to express and communicate ideas. As we have said, dependent clauses combine with independent ones to create complex sentences. *Complex* is, perhaps, a doubly appropriate word. Not only does it describe such sentences *grammatically* but it also describes them *rhetorically*. The more complicated the syntax of a sentence becomes, the more difficult it is to be certain that the sentence is communicating in a clear and straightforward way. In the sections that follow, we discuss some of the pitfalls associated with the use of dependent clauses.

WHAT'S THE USAGE?   *Using Dependent Clauses*

Because they are adverbial, subordinate clauses can move about in a sentence, appearing at the beginning, at the end, or even in the middle. In the sentence we have just written, the subordinate clause *because they are adverbial* could, all things being equal, appear first in the sentence (43a), after the subject (43b), after the modal or verb (43c), or at the end of the independent clause (43d):

(43)   a. *Because they are adverbial,* subordinate clauses can move about in a sentence.

b. Subordinate clauses, *because they are adverbial,* can move about in a sentence.

c. Subordinate clauses can, *because they are adverbial,* move about in a sentence.

d. Subordinate clauses can move about in a sentence *because they are adverbial.*

But all things are not equal in these examples. The order in which dependent and independent clauses occur affects the readability of a text. Psycholinguistic studies have found the (43d) is more easily processed by readers or hearers than (43b) or (43c). When you were studying writing, you may have been told to vary your sentence patterns by moving subordinate clauses to the beginning or middle spots in a sentence. The increase in sentence variety achieved by moving adverbial clauses around in a sentence may be counterbalanced by a decrease in readability. There are two rules that may help you decide when and whether to move an adverbial clause. The first is that if the subordinate clause states the *cause,* as it does in (43a), the sentence is likely to win both in readability and in variety. The second is that if dependent and independent clauses are arranged in temporal (chronological) order, they will be more easily processed by readers and hearers. Thus, (44a) is more easily understood than (44b):

(44)   a. *When I finish my homework,* I am going to the movies.

         b. I am going to the movies *when I finish my homework.*

WHAT'S THE USAGE?   *Punctuation of Dependent Clauses*
We have already seen that nonrestrictive relative clauses, because they provide nonessential information, are set off by commas.

(45)   Highway 101, *which has been closed for repairs,* reopens on Tuesday.
                                (nonrestrictive relative)

Pairs of commas may interrupt a sentence between constituents, as (45) illustrates. A *single* comma is never placed between the subject and the main verb or between the main verb and its objects or complements. When nominal clauses function as subjects, direct objects, subject complements, and objects of prepositions, they play essential roles in the sentence and are not set off from the rest of the sentence by commas.

(46)   Professor Windless said that we would review Chapter 11 before the exam.

         It is with adverbial subordinate clauses that punctuation problems most frequently arise. Usually, a subordinate clause is not set off with commas when it occurs in its normal adverbial position, at the end of a sentence.

(47)   That know-it-all friend of mine failed his driving test *because he forgot the hand signal for a right turn.*
         Get to the concert early *if you want a seat.*

However, when a subordinate clause contradicts the assertion of the main clause, commas are required, perhaps to help signal that contradiction:

(48) That know-it-all friend of mine failed his driving test, *even though he had passed the written one.*

You'll probably find a seat, *although you may have to sit in the back.*

Like adverbs, subordinate clauses can often be moved about in their sentences, and when they move out of the final position, they are set off by commas. We have not discovered many rules of English that have no exceptions, but there seem to be two for punctuating subordinate clauses when they have been moved out of sentence-final position.

Rule 1: When a subordinate clause begins a sentence, set it off with a comma.

Compare the following sentences with those in (47):

(49) *Because he forgot the hand signal for a right turn,* that know-it-all friend of mine failed his driving test.

If you want a seat, get to the concert early.

Rule 2: When a subordinate clause is placed in the middle of a sentence, set it off with parenthetical commas.

Compare (50) with (47) and (49):

(50) That know-it-all friend of mine, *because he forgot the hand signal for a right turn,* failed his driving test.

◼ USAGE EXERCISE 10.6

Combine each of the following pairs of clauses into single sentences using a subordinating conjunction that expresses the relationship between the two. Try two versions of each, one with the clause at the end and one with the clause moved either to the beginning or to the middle of the sentence. Punctuate each correctly, and be prepared to discuss the effectiveness of different versions. One has been done for you.

EXAMPLE

Willis felt like bowling. The moon was full.

Whenever the moon was full, Willis felt like bowling.

Willis felt like bowling whenever the moon was full.

1. Traffic ground to a halt. Two cars collided in the fast lane.
2. Velda's car had not moved for five minutes. She turned off her engine.
3. Ben got out his cell phone. He could call his office.

4. A tow truck drove along the side of the highway to the accident. Traffic still didn't move.

5. The automobiles finally began to move sometime. The drivers forgot their annoyance.

WHAT'S THE USAGE?   *Dependent Clauses as Sentence Fragments*

Because a dependent clause contains both a subject and a predicate, student writers sometimes confuse them with independent clauses, which are able to stand alone as sentences. A dependent clause, set off by a capital letter and a period as though it were an independent sentence, is called a **fragment** and is generally considered a serious error in writing.

If you have trouble recognizing fragments, two things may help. First, study the list of subordinators, reminding yourself that they create *dependent* clauses, clauses unable to stand alone as sentences. If you still have difficulty, try performing the question transformation on any clause about which you are uncertain. If you can create a yes/no sentence by moving an auxiliary verb (or *do*) to the beginning, you have verified that the structure is a sentence. If you cannot, it is not a sentence.

Consider the following:

(51)   Ellen got an A in physics. Because all of her experiments were done correctly and were turned in on time.

The first clause is an independent sentence; it can undergo the interrogative transformation:

(52)   Ellen got an A in physics.

Did Ellen get an A in physics?

The second clause in (51) is a fragment; because it is not an independent clause, it cannot undergo the transformation:

(53)   Because all of her experiments were done correctly and turned in on time.

*Were because all of her experiments done correctly and turned in on time?

Elliptical Dependent Clauses

Writers and speakers often delete parts of subordinate clauses, making them **elliptical,** or incomplete. Such structures can eliminate repetition, leaving concise, tightly organized statements:

(54)   a. *When plum pudding is properly stewed,*   (complete subordinate clause)
          plum pudding is delicious.
          ↓

       b. *When properly stewed,* plum pudding   (elliptical subordinate clause)
          is delicious.

          Although the report was hastily written,   (complete subordinate clause)
          the report was excellent.
          ↓

          Although hastily written, the report   (elliptical subordinate clause)
          was excellent.

English speakers interpret an elliptical subordinate clause as having the same subject as the main clause. When that rule is violated, the result is a *dangling modifier.* Such elliptical clauses are sometimes amusing and sometimes confusing:

(55)   a. *When properly stewed*, I like plum pudding.

       b. *Although hastily put together*, our team prepared an excellent report.

Example (55a) teases the reader with the possibility that the speaker must be stewed in order to like plum pudding. Example (55b) is ambiguous: Either the team or the report may have been hastily put together.

Notice that moving the elliptical clause to the end does not solve the problem. No matter where elliptical clauses occur, English speakers interpret them as having the same subjects as the main clause to which they are attached:

(56)   a. I like plum pudding *when properly stewed.*

       b. Our team prepared an excellent report *although hastily put together.*

Nominal Clauses   *The Omission of That*

As we have pointed out, you can often omit the initial complementizer in *that-*clauses. People are divided on which version they prefer. Each of the following is acceptable. The first is more explicit, but the second is more succinct.

(57)   a. I believe *that St. Augustine is the oldest city in the United States.*

       b. I believe *St. Augustine is the oldest city in the United States.*

Notice, first of all, that both versions are considered to contain nominal *that-*clauses, even though the complementizer has been deleted from the second one. In fact, sentences like (57b) sometimes trouble students who are trying to identify dependent and independent clauses. On first glance, the embedded clause (*St. Augustine is the oldest city in the United States*) appears to be more autonomous than the clause beginning *I believe.* Be sure you understand that the structure of (57b) is as follows:

(58)   Independent clause: I believe X.

           Dependent clause: [~~that~~] St. Augustine is the oldest city
                                         in the United States.

      Notice, too, that when you omit the complementizer *that,* you run the risk of creating a sentence that confuses the reader.

(59)   Some people doubted his stories about a solo trip up Mount Everest were true.

      Initially, the reader is likely to assume that *his stories about a solo trip up Mount Everest* is a direct object of *doubted.* In fact, it is the subject of the nominal clause *his stories about a solo trip up Mount Everest were true.* Retaining the complementizer *that* avoids the possibility of misreading:

(60)   Some people doubted *that* his stories about a solo trip up Mount Everest were true.

■ *USAGE EXERCISE 10.7*

Some of the sentences below are fragments and some are confusing because of dangling modifiers. Make any changes necessary to eliminate rhetorical problems.

1. Pierre sent in his symphony subscription check late. Although unhappy about his seat location, the orchestra would without a doubt play just as well without seeing him in the center of the front row.
2. Pierre's computer helped him to pass the time while waiting for the concert to start.
3. He can get two hours from his computer's battery when fully charged.
4. During the concerto, someone's cell phone began to ring. In spite of the warning broadcast before the performance.
5. After waiting in line to purchase a drink at the intermission, all of the tables were taken.
6. Many of the people sitting around Pierre were late returning to their seats. Despite the repeated warning bells that rang every two minutes.

SUMMARY

In Chapter 10, we looked at two kinds of nominal dependent clauses: (1) those beginning with the complementizer *that* and (2) those beginning with interrogative words. Such clauses can substitute for nouns or noun phrases in many positions within a sentence. A simple test helps identify a nominal clause. If you can substitute an indefinite pronoun (*something* or *someone*) for the entire clause, it is nominal.

REVIEW EXERCISES

Dependent Clauses Beginning with *That*

That can be the word introducing either a nominal clause or an adjectival relative clause. Identify the dependent clauses in the sentences below and identify the type of *that*-clause of each. If you believe the clause is nominal, identify the nominal function it plays in the sentence to which it belongs. If you think the clause is adjectival, identify the noun phrase the clause modifies. Remember, the introductory *that* may have been omitted from some of the clauses below. The clauses are still considered to be *that*-clauses or relative clauses, with or without the *that*. Some of the sentences contain more than one dependent clause. An example has been done for you.

EXAMPLE

That she is expected to work twelve hours this week seemed to confuse Edna.

The underlined clause is a nominal clause: subject of the sentence.

1. Because it has fared so well since its inception, most people have assumed that the euro is here to stay.
2. However, a euro that started the year at $1.35 had dropped to $1.22 by the end of summer. *relative only*
3. That the French and Dutch rejected the European Union's constitution *nominal* made economists take a second look.
4. Even after those referendums, the president of the European Central Bank dismissed the suggestion that a breakup of the European monetary union might occur. *nominal that clause*
5. Nevertheless, many Europeans are still rankled by the fact that inflated prices followed the switch to the euro. *nominal that*
6. In a recent poll, 56 percent of the Germans believed they would be better off with a return of the German mark.
7. An Italian welfare minister said his country would be better off if they went back to the lira.

8. The old lira used to be devalued when labor costs rose and industries feared that exports would cease to be competitive.

Other Dependent Clauses

Identify all of the dependent clauses in the following sentences and classify each as adverbial, adjectival, or nominal. If you believe a clause is adverbial, submit it to the adverbial tests in Chapter 9, Figure 9.2. If you believe it is adjectival, identify the noun it modifies. If you believe it is nominal, show that *it* or *something* can be substituted for it. Some sentences contain more than one dependent clause. An example has been done for you.

EXAMPLE

After the officer heard what the witnesses said, he charged the driver who hit my car.

After the officer heard what the witnesses said = adverbial (subordinate) clause. Passes all four tests.

what the witnesses said = nominal interrogative clause, direct object of <u>heard</u>

who hit my car = adjectival relative clause modifying <u>the driver</u>

1. Mountain lions, who have lived in the Americas for tens of thousands of years, face extinction due to the expansion of roads, housing, and commerce into the areas where they have traditionally roamed.
2. Cougar, catamount, panther, puma, and ghost cat are among the names they have been given.
3. A puma that lives in the Santa Monica Mountains in California gave birth to four cubs a couple of years ago.
4. What made the babies special was that they were the offspring of the last two known pumas in the Santa Monica Mountains.
5. The media, which included newspapers, television, and the Associated Press, moved in and began to report on the growth of the two male and two female baby pumas.
6. Baby pumas must learn where they can hide, in which dry stream beds they can find seeping water, and what constitutes a good hunting ground.
7. Before they are 18 months old, the mother puma will drive them away, forcing them out into the wilderness to find their own way.
8. The parents of the new cubs, who are known as Puma 1 and Puma 2, wear high-tech collars that show where they roam.
9. An investigation held 10 months before the birth of the cubs indicated that their father was attacking a rancher's goats.

10. After he learned that Puma 1 was the last known male in the mountains, the rancher, who had received permission to shoot the mountain lion, decided to let the permit expire.

11. The public rejoiced when they heard the news that four cubs had been born in the wild.

12. The bad news about the births is that the Santa Monica Mountains don't provide enough wild land to support six pumas.

13. Male mountain lions require about 150 square miles in which to roam and forage; females need only about 50 square miles.

14. The father puma, who was not around when the cubs are born, will not recognize his own offspring and may eventually kill one or more of them in a struggle over turf.

Subordinate Clauses—Form and Function

Identify the form and function of each italicized clause in the following passage. An example has been done for you.

EXAMPLE

Arnold had forgotten *that his driver's license would expire soon.*

Form–*That*-clause

Function–Nominal, direct object of *had forgotten.*

> *When a cat disappears,* owners fret and worry *that it will never return,* just as they would *if a child had disappeared. What people have used up until now to identify their pets* has been a collar tag or a tattoo. Both have limitations *that make them unsatisfactory in some situations.* Now veterinarians are recommending *that cats should be "microchipped."* A veterinarian implants a microchip *that is no bigger than a grain of rice* into the loose skin on the back of the cat's neck. The chip, *which contains an identifying numerical code,* can link a pet with its owner's name, address, and phone number. Many public agencies know *how to read the information on the microchip* and, thus, will be able to return the pet to its owner.

KEY TERMS

adjective complement
appositive
complementizer
direct discourse
elliptical clause
fragment

indirect discourse
nominal clauses
    appositive clause
    interrogative clause
    that-clause

Nonfinite Verb Phrases, Part I

11

INFINITIVE PHRASES

CHAPTER PREVIEW

In the next two chapters, we look at phrases containing infinitives, past participles, present participles, and gerunds, showing where they come from and what kinds of roles they play in sentences. Because infinitives, participles, and gerunds are verbs, they can have the same subjects, objects, complements, and modifiers they would have had in the clauses from which they are derived.

CHAPTER GOALS

At the end of this chapter, you should be able to

- Identify *infinitive phrases.*
- Recognize infinitives with or without *to* and those preceded by *for.*
- Distinguish between *infinitives* and *prepositional phrases.*
- Reconstitute the clauses underlying infinitive phrases.
- Recognize whether infinitive phrases are functioning as *adverbials, adjectivals,* or *nominals.*

When we discussed simple sentence types in Chapter 7, we described patterns in which sentence constituents, aside from the main verb phrase, contained no verbs. These included the following:

(1) **Noun phrases**—*his car, all of the houses*
Subjects, objects, subject complements, and object complements

Adjective phrases—*good, very happy*
Subject complements and object complements

Adverb phrases—*quite slowly, to the seashore*
Verb modifiers

In Chapters 9 and 10, we showed how it is possible to embed entire finite verb clauses within other clauses as nominal, adjectival, and adverbial constituents, thus creating complex sentences. The embedded clauses we discussed were *dependent clauses,* strings of words containing both a complete subject and predicate but made subordinate to another clause by either a subordinating conjunction, a relative pronoun or adverb, a complementizer such as *that,* or an interrogative word.

In this chapter, we consider how *partial clauses,* those that have had some constituents deleted, can be placed inside other clauses, where they function as the constituents of those clauses and of sentences. Consider the following examples, in which a phrase containing a verb has been embedded within a clause:

(2)   a. Kay hoped *to **arrive** before midnight.*
         b. She is looking for a book ***written** by Nabokov.*

The embedded verbs (bolded in these examples) are **nonfinite.** As a technical term, *nonfinite* means that these verbs are not preceded by TENSE; if participles, they are not accompanied by the other parts of the main verb phrase (TENSE and auxiliary verbs) that are obligatory, given their forms. For example, the time referred to in (2a) is in the past, so we might expect *arrive* to occur with some signal of past time; however, it stands alone, without TENSE or modal. If TENSE were present, the form would be *arrives;* if it were past, the form would be *arrived.*

Although no subjects precede *arrive* and *written* in (2), English speakers know from the context who was to arrive and who wrote the book. A way of representing the knowledge we have of unexpressed meaning in such phrases is to paraphrase the underlying clause and to show how that might be transformed grammatically into the phrase before us. For example, the meaning of (2a) can be paraphrased by using a *that*-clause to replace the phrase *to arrive before midnight:*

(3)   Kay hoped *that she would arrive before midnight.*

In (2b), *written* is a past participle, but it appears without either TENSE or the helping verb BE used to make it passive. However, both TENSE and BE are present in the relative clause that can paraphrase the last three words of (2b).

(4) She is looking for a book *that was written by Nabokov.*

Traditionally, the italicized structures in (2) are **nonfinite verb phrases** called *infinitive* and *participle phrases*. The information that we know about them—fully expressed in (3) and (4)—can be explained most clearly by describing (2a) and (2b) as containing **reduced clauses,** derived transformationally from complete clauses. To do this, we begin with the full information conveyed—a sentence like (3), for example—with a complete clause embedded within it, and describe grammatically how this might be transformed into (2a), in which parts of the clause have been erased but no information has been lost.

As we analyze infinitives and participles, remember that they can be created using any transitive, intransitive, or linking verb. Therefore, infinitives and participles can have whatever subjects, complements, and modifiers those verbs allow. Remember, too, that you analyze the patterns of infinitive and participle phrases just as you would analyze the patterns of the full clauses used to paraphrase them.

It may help you to perceive their form if you reconstruct the simple sentences underlying infinitives and participles before trying to identify the sentence types they represent. We show you how to do that with each kind of nonfinite verb phrase.

▬▬▬ *INFINITIVE PHRASES* ▬▬▬

The prototypical **infinitive phrase** in English is *to* plus a form of the verb that is unmarked for tense or number: *to do, to see, to have.* Notice that this form of the verb (called the *infinitive form*) is exactly the form under which you would find it listed in the dictionary. Although they are not marked for tense, infinitives may have subjects, objects, complements, and modifiers. Compare the following, in which the two clauses can be combined into two different structures. The first combination results in a full (although dependent) finite verb clause and the second, a reduced nonfinite infinitive phrase:

(5) a. I urge [something] + you should deliver this package on Friday
    deliver = [TENSE + MODAL_{[should]} + deliver]
    ↓
    I urge that you should deliver this package on Friday.

  b. I urge [something] + you should deliver this package on Friday
    deliver = [T̶E̶N̶S̶E̶ + M̶O̶D̶A̶L̶ + deliver]
    ↓
    I urge you to deliver this package on Friday.

The basic sentence pattern is the same for both the embedded clause and the infinitive phrase: Both contain the same subject (*you*), main verb (*deliver*), direct object (*this package*), and adverb of time (*on Friday*). However, TENSE and MODAL have been omitted from the main verb phrase of the nonfinite version—the infinitive.

Sometimes, the subject of an infinitive phrase is contained in an idiomatic phrase with *for*, as in example (6).

(6)   *For Lee to fix a flat tire* would be astonishing.

The idiom *for + [subject] + to + [infinitive]* (as in *for Lee to fix a flat tire*) is a formulaic way in which English reduces the structure of a clause to the structure of an infinitive phrase. In example (6), the sentence *Lee fixes a flat tire* has been transformed into the infinitive phrase ***for*** *Lee **to** fix a flat tire:* All the sentence constituents—the subject *Lee*, the verb *fix*, and the direct object *a flat tire*—are present in the infinitive phrase. The constituent that is absent is the main verb phrase element TENSE, which has been deleted in converting the verb from the finite main verb of a clause (*fixes*) to the nonfinite verb of the infinitive phrase (*to fix*).

When the subject of the infinitive is a pronoun, it occurs in the objective form. For example, *For **me** to fix a flat tire would be astonishing* is the idiomatic form (not **for **I** to fix a flat tire*).

(7)   Manuel wants ***me*** *to see the Canadian Rockies this summer.*
      ↑
      Manuel wants [something] + I see the Canadian Rockies this summer

In order to be brief and concise, a speaker can omit from an embedded nonfinite (reduced) clause any information that has already been provided elsewhere in the discourse. For example, the infinitive often appears with its subject deleted:

(8)   Manuel wants *to see the Canadian Rockies this summer.*
      ↑
      Manuel wants [something] + M̶a̶n̶u̶e̶l̶ to see the Canadian Rockies this summer.

In (7), because the subjects of *want* (***Manuel*** *wants*) and of *see* (***me*** *to see the Canadian Rockies*) are different, both have to be mentioned. In (8), however, *Manuel* is the subject of both *want* and *see the Canadian Rockies,* so he needs to be named only once. Similarly, in (9), the subject of both clauses is the indefinite *you,* so it is given only once.

(9)   *To be eligible for a student loan,* you must be a full-time student.
      ↑
      F̶o̶r̶ ̶y̶o̶u̶ to be eligible for a student loan, you must be a full-time student.

Omission of the subject is possible whenever the subject of the infinitive is the same as that of the main clause. If the subject of the infinitive and the subject of the main clause are different, then the subject of the infinitive shouldn't be deleted. Compare example (9) with example (10).

(10)   *For you to be eligible for a student loan,* your family must submit its income tax records.

If *for you* is deleted from (10), the meaning of the sentence changes. *To be eligible for a student loan, your family must submit its income tax records* is stating what is required for your *family* to be eligible for a student loan, not what is required for *you* to be eligible. If the subject of the infinitive is absent, we automatically assume that it is the same as the subject of the main clause.

Deletions occur because, in producing language, we appear to be responding to two competing imperatives: The first is to give information fully enough so that others can understand; the second is to give no more information than is necessary—to be as brief as possible. If we overload our speech with what our listeners already know, they stop listening.

The infinitive phrases we have looked at so far, with the exception of (9) and (10), have been nominal—that is, they have been capable of substituting for the indefinite pronoun *something*. In (9), *To be eligible for a student loan* serves as a sentence modifier, as does the introductory infinitive phrase in (10). Infinitive phrases can also function as adjectivals or adverbials:

(11)   His parents were skeptical about Jill's promise *to get all A's next semester.* (Adjectival: modifies *promise*)

They were running *to catch the train.* (Adverbial of reason: modifies *running*)

■ *EXERCISE 11.1*

Convert each of the following pairs of sentences into a single sentence containing an infinitive phrase. Brackets indicate where in the independent clause the infinitive phrase should be embedded. An example has been done for you.

EXAMPLE

[Something] can be boring + Someone eats alone

To eat alone can be boring.

1. Harry's dream is [something]. He will spend the year traveling in Europe.
2. [Something] is not easy. He will save enough money for the trip.
3. He plans [something]. He will fly to London first.
4. He will use the train under the English Channel [for some reason]. He will get to Paris.
5. His goal is [something]. He will see all the art museums in London and Paris.
6. [Something] would be ideal. He would be in the Alps during the winter.
7. He would stay there a few weeks [for some purpose]. He could go skiing.
8. I approve of Harry's plan [of some kind]. He would take a train [for some reason]. He would travel from Florence to Rome.

■ *EXERCISE 11.2*_____

> Look back at the infinitives you created in Exercise 11.1. Identify each as
> either nominal, adjectival, or adverbial, and give the function of each in its
> sentence.
>
> **EXAMPLE**
>
> *To eat alone* can be boring.
>
> *To eat alone* = nominal infinitive, subject of the sentence

Diagramming Infinitive Phrases

Diagrams help some students to visualize the role infinitives play in sentences.
Observe how the infinitive phrase is diagrammed when it is a subject.

(12)   *To ride without a helmet* is dangerous.

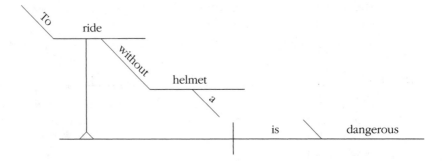

Notice that the function word *to* in the infinitive phrase is diagrammed as if
it were a preposition (which it really isn't, because it doesn't signal a relationship between a noun phrase object and another grammatical constituent).
The prepositional phrase *without a helmet* is shown as an adverbial modifier of *ride,* and the whole infinitive phrase structure is placed on a pedestal
in the position appropriate for its function—in this case, as subject of the
sentence.

The same pedestal structure is used when infinitive phrases function in
other ways—for example, as a direct object in example (13).

(13)   The officer wanted *me to show him my license.*

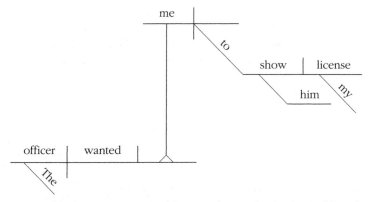

In the diagram, a vertical line intersects the horizontal line between *me* and the infinitive *to show,* indicating the subject/predicate relationship of these two constituents, which are part of an underlying sentence *I show him my license. Him* is diagrammed as the indirect object of *show* and *my license* as its direct object.

In contrast to Reed-Kellogg diagrams, which reflect the grammatical relationships in the spoken version of the sentence, phrase marker trees are particularly suited to revealing the sentence structures from which infinitive phrases are derived. Example (14) shows the structure underlying the sentence diagrammed above in (12), *To ride without a helmet is dangerous.* Grammatical transformations delete the subject of the infinitive (*someone*) and TENSE (shown by the deletion of the *-s* suffix on *ride*) and insert the infinitive marker *to.*

(14)

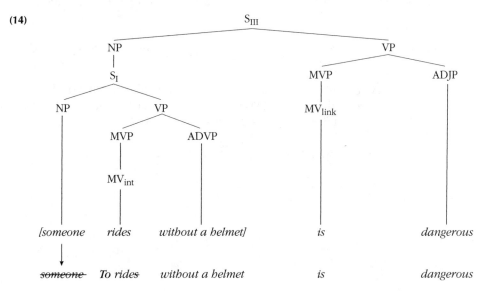

Similarly, the phrase marker in (15) reflects the underlying grammatical structure from which the infinitive phrase *me to show him my license* in (13) is derived. Transformations convert the subject form *I* to the object form *me* and the present tense *show* to the infinitive form *to show*.

(15)

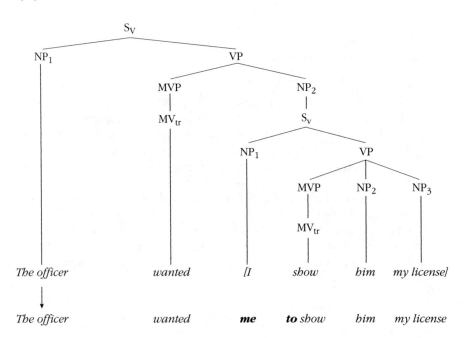

When infinitive phrases function adjectivally or adverbially, they are represented with a Reed-Kellogg structure similar to that used for prepositional phrase modifiers of nouns, as illustrated in (16).

(16)   a. Susan desperately sought an excuse *to explain her absence.*

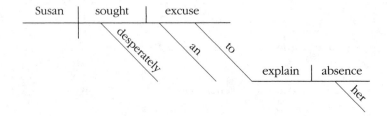

b. Keith smiled *to cover his embarrassment.*

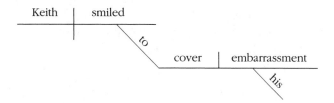

The same sentences analyzed with phrase structure trees look like this:

(17)

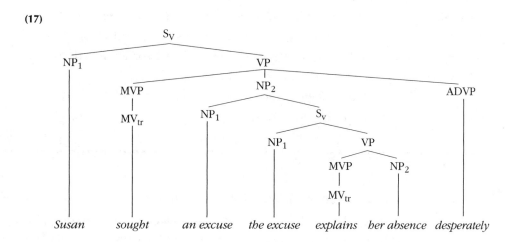

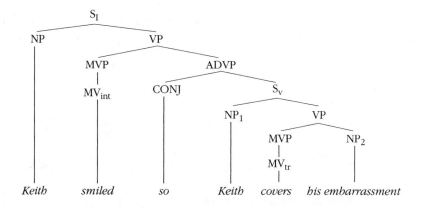

■ *EXERCISE 11.3* _____

In order to draw trees of infinitive phrases, you must first reconstruct the underlying clause from which the infinitive comes. For the sentences below, reconstruct the sentence underlying the infinitive phrase and identify its sentence type.

EXAMPLE

We wanted *to arrive late.*

We [NP₁] + *arrive* [Mv_INT] + *late* [ADVP_tm]. *Arrive* = Intransitive verb, Type I

1. Children like to look under rocks for worms and bugs.
2. As an adult, you might prefer to do something like bird-watching.
3. Observing birds in the wild gives you a chance to be a naturalist.
4. Even standard-sized binoculars will enable you to see birds in great detail.
5. Early morning is the best time to go bird-watching.
6. A field guide is useful to identify the birds that you see.
7. When you hear a bird call, use your binoculars to zero in on the bird.
8. If you see a red-crested hoodwinker, be sure to record it.

Clauses Embedded Within Infinitive Phrases

In the examples we have used, the infinitives all come from clauses that are simple sentences. However, it is also possible for a complex sentence to reduce and become an infinitive phrase. When this occurs, one of the dependent clauses will remain within the infinitive phrase. Because each verb in a sentence originates as the main verb of a clause, each has its own sentence pattern. In the examples below, we italicize the infinitive phrase, bold the embedded dependent clause, and show the predicate type for each verb:

(18)   The pilot attempted *to stop the airplane **before it rolled off the runway.***
        ↓

Main clause:

The pilot attempted *something.* $MV_{tr} + NP_2$ = Type V

Infinitive phrase:

to stop the airplane *sometime* $MV_{tr} + NP_2 + ADVP$ = Type V

Adverbial subordinate clause:

before it rolled off the runway $MV_{int} + ADVP_{pl}$ = Type I

To stop the airplane is the direct object of *attempted,* and *before it rolled off the runway* is an adverbial modifier of time within the infinitive phrase.

(19) They want *to believe **that the tax bill is a good one.***
↓

Main clause:

They want *something.* $MV_{tr} + NP_2$ = Type V

Infinitive phrase:

to believe *something* $MV_{tr} + NP_2$ = Type V

Nominal *that*-clause:

that the tax bill is a good one $MV_{link} + NP_1$ = Type IV

To believe that the tax bill is a good one is the direct object of *want* in the main clause; *that the tax bill is a good one* is the direct object of the infinitive *to believe.*

Passive Infinitives

An infinitive that is derived from a passive finite verb clause will itself be passive:

(20) a. I expect *that all the calamari will be eaten before 7:00.* (passive verb)
↓

b. I expect *all the calamari to be eaten before 7:00.* (passive infinitive)

You can verify that *to be eaten* is a passive infinitive in (20b) because it contains the passive marker [BE + {-en}]: *be eaten.* Remember that *eaten* is a transitive verb; in its active form, it will have a subject (an indefinite pronoun like *someone* or *they*) and a direct object *(all the calamari).* The active infinitive version is shown in (21b).

(21) a. I expect *they will eat all the calamari before 7:00.*
↓

b. I expect *them to eat all the calamari before 7:00.*

You may not have known how to state the rule, but you are able to recover the clauses underlying infinitive phrases because, when interpreting infinitives, you assume that the subject will be explicitly stated unless it is identical to the subject of the main clause. If the subject of the infinitive is *not* the subject of the main clause, then the subject of the infinitive must be included as part of the infinitive phrase. Some verbs require that *for* introduce infinitive phrase complements when the subject is included:

(22) a. I am hoping *for the school magazine to publish this poem.*
      b. It is time *for everyone to go home.*

Notice that *for* is required in these two sentences only if the subject is expressed. If no subject is included, *for* is omitted and the meaning changes.

(23) a. I am hoping *to publish this poem.*
      b. It is time *to go home.*

In (23a), we might assume that the subject of the infinitive is the same as the subject of the main clause, but we cannot make that assumption for (23b). Because *it* is an empty word filling the subject slot, there is nothing in the main clause to identify the subject of the infinitive; hearers presume that the subject is indefinite. The speaker could be saying that it is time for the speaker or for the hearer(s), or both, or people in general to go home. Whether or not *for* occurs as part of the infinitive construction seems to depend on the verb preceding the infinitive.

■ *EXERCISE 11.4* _____

Identify the subject of the infinitive verbs in the sentences below. Reconstruct the full underlying clause, if necessary. An example has been done for you.

EXAMPLE

The car began to give us trouble soon after we bought it.

The car *gave us trouble.*

1. Ig Nobel Prizes[1] go to people who deserve to be recognized for some unusual achievement.
2. In 1991, the Ig Nobel Committee voted to give the economics prize to Michael Milken, the father of the junk bond.
3. Another year, the economics prize went to an official who caused Orange County, California, to go bankrupt.
4. Part of the goal of the Ig Nobel Prize is to make people laugh.
5. A recent winner used magnets to levitate a frog.
6. Swedish scientists won when they created a study to show that chickens prefer beautiful humans to plain ones.

7. A three-country team of winners had chosen to study the effect of chewing-gum flavor on brain waves.

8. This year the committee decided to honor the man who invented karaoke.

Infinitives Without *To*

Occasionally, you will find it difficult to identify an infinitive because the initial *to* has been deleted.

(24)   a. Did you watch *him leave the package on the doorstep?*

b. All we did wrong was *lock the keys in the car.*

It is not too difficult to recognize (24a) as a reduced infinitive; its subject pronoun (*him*) is in the objective form, and its verb lacks the inflection that would be required for a third-person singular subject in the past tense (*he left the package*). In example (24b), no subject is expressed for the infinitive, and *lock* has the same form as it would have even if it were a present-tense verb with *we* as its subject. However, the infinitive marker *to* can be inserted to give the infinitive phrase its more familiar form: *All we did wrong was* **to lock the keys in the car.**

Both infinitive phrases can be paraphrased as unreduced clauses:

(25)   Did you watch [while] he left the package on the doorstep?

All we did wrong was [that] we locked the keys in the car.

To recognize the infinitive in the example below is even harder. What proofs can you think of to support the analysis of *perform* as an infinitive in (26a)? The subject pronoun (*you*) has no distinctive object form (a possible clue to infinitives), and the verb, with *you* as its subject, would not have an inflection in the present tense, as (26b) shows:

(26)   a. I'll watch you *perform* a magic trick.

b. I'll watch while you *perform* a magic trick.

There are two ways of affirming that *perform* in (26a) is an infinitive. You can change the subject of the infinitive (*you*) to a pronoun that has an object form;

(27)   I'll watch *her* perform a magic trick.

Alternatively, you can change the tense of the verb in the main clause to past tense. If *perform* also changes tense, as is the case in (28b), it is a main verb:

SUMMARY	
Infinitive Phrases	
1. Infinitive with subject	*We believe **him to be innocent.***
2. Infinitive without subject	*She wants **to be alone.***
3. Infinitive preceded by *for*	*They are eager **for him to win.***
4. Infinitive without *to*	*We heard **him open the door.*** Contrast: *We want **him to open the door.***

Figure 11.1

(28) a. I *watched* you *perform* a magic trick.   (infinitive phrase)
      b. I *watched* while you *performed* a magic trick.   (embedded clause)

If the pronoun functioning as subject of the suspected infinitive must be in the object form, as in (27), or if the tense doesn't change, as in (28a), the verb is an infinitive.

A Summary of the forms of infinitives is provided in Figure 11.1.

■ *EXERCISE 11.5*

Find the infinitive phrases in the sentences below and identify their subjects. In the example that has been done for you, notice that there are two finite verbs, *felt* and *died,* both inflected with the past-tense morpheme. A third verb, *shudder,* is uninflected (nonfinite). It is an infinitive with *to* omitted.

EXAMPLE

Ben felt the automobile shudder just before the engine died.

the automobile shudder = *infinitive phrase*
the automobile = *subject*

1. The invitations to the surprise party asked guests to arrive before 7:30 P.M.
2. John asked if it would be all right to bring a friend with him.
3. Ally asked Ellen to arrive a little early to help with the decorations.
4. The caterers wanted to have the kitchen and dining room to themselves.

5. People began to arrive at about 7:00 P.M.

6. While waiting for the guest of honor to arrive, people stood about chatting quietly.

7. Ally asked someone to be on the lookout from an upstairs window.

8. When they heard the doorbell ring, everyone was expected to be quiet.

FUNCTIONS OF INFINITIVE PHRASES

Infinitive constructions, like complete dependent clauses, can function adverbially, adjectivally, or nominally. Some of the tests used to identify the functions of dependent clauses in the preceding chapter can be used to identify the functions of infinitives.

Adverbial Infinitives

Do you remember the tests that enable you to verify that clauses are functioning adverbially? If you can (1) substitute an adverb for them, (2) create a question by substituting a *wh*-adverb (*where, why, when, how*) for them, or (3) move the clause about in its sentence, then it is usually functioning adverbially. The first, substituting an adverb, will not help you identify an **adverbial infinitive,** but asking a *wh*-question (using *why*) or attempting to move the infinitive phrase around in the sentence will. For example, you can support your hypothesis that the infinitive phrase in (29) is adverbial either by creating a *wh*-question from it or by moving the infinitive construction to the end.

(29)	*To do well in school,* you must study hard.	(Adverbial infinitive)
	a. *Why* must you study hard?	(Test #1—*Wh*-question)
	b. You must study hard *to do well in school.*	(Test #2—Movability)

An alternative to the *wh*-question test, and one that may provide confirming evidence that an infinitive phrase is functioning as an adverbial modifier, is to paraphrase the infinitive with the words *in order to:*

(30)	You must study hard *in order to do well in school.*	(Test #3—*In order to*)

If you try the same tests on the infinitives below, you will find that they pass one or more, demonstrating that they, too, are adverbial modifiers.

(31) a. Josh climbed to the top of the stands *to see more clearly.*

b. You must eat wisely *to remain truly healthy.*

Figure 11.2 summarizes the tests for identifying adverbial infinitive phrases.

SUMMARY	
Tests for Identifying Functions of Infinitive Phrases	
Adverbial	*Karen will need fifty pizzas **to feed this crowd.***
1. *Wh*-question using *why*	***Why** will Karen need fifty pizzas?*
2. Movability	***To feed this crowd,** Karen will need fifty pizzas.*
3. Paraphrase with *in order to*	*Karen will need fifty pizzas **in order to feed this crowd.***
Adjectival	*He is building a cupboard **to fit in that corner.***
1. Usually can be restated as a relative clause	*He is building a cupboard **that will fit in that corner.***
2. Modifies a noun that precedes it	*He is building **a cupboard** to fit in that corner.*
Nominal	*She wants **to ski in Austria during the holidays.***
1. Substitute *something* or *it* for the infinitive phrase	*She wants **something.***
2. *Wh*-question using *what*	***What** does she want?*

Figure 11.2

Adjectival Infinitives

Although there are no tests like those that verify adverbial function to support your identification of **adjectival infinitives,** it will help if you notice that they are like relative clauses in that they immediately follow the noun or noun phrase that they modify. In fact, they can often be restated as relative clauses, as has been done in the second versions below. The constituent modified is bolded.

(32) a. World War I was a war *to end all wars.*   (adjectival infinitive)
         ***a war** that will end all wars*   (Paraphrases as a relative clause; modifies *war*)

     b. Fred is looking in the kitchen for something *to eat.*   (adjectival infinitive)
         ***something** that he can eat*   (Paraphrases as a relative clause; modifies *something*)

c. A test doesn't always give you   (adjectival infinitive)
   an opportunity *to demonstrate*
   your true ability.
   an opportunity *in which you*   (Paraphrases as a relative can
   demonstrate your true ability   clause; modifies *opportunity*)

Like the relative clauses that express the same meaning, these adjectival infinitives are *restrictive* modifiers.

Nominal Infinitives

Nominal infinitives are the most common and are the easiest to recognize. As one simple test for infinitives functioning nominally, you can substitute a pronoun for the entire nominal infinitive construction. As a second test, you can create a *wh*-question using *what* in place of the infinitive:

(33) Rebecca doesn't like   (nominal infinitive)
          to fill glasses to the brim.
          Rebecca doesn't like *something.*   (Test #1—Pronoun substitution)
          What doesn't Rebecca like?   (Test #2—*Wh*-question)

Nominal infinitives can occur in many sentence positions:

(34) a. *To meet all those deadlines* will not be easy.   (subject)
          b. His devoutest wish is *to climb Mt. Everest.*   (subject complement)
          c. The team should try *to find a new manager.*   (direct object)
          d. Mimi always considered him   (object complement)
             to be her best friend.

The examples that follow show Reed-Kellogg diagrams containing an infinitive phrase functioning as a direct object (35a) and as an object complement (35b):

(35) a.

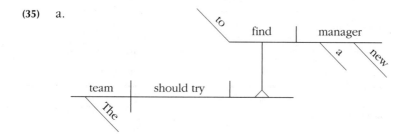

b.

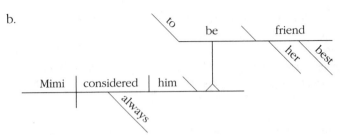

As we saw in the preceding chapter, some adjectives take nominal *that*-clauses as complements, as in (36).

(36)   The publisher is **certain** *that your book will become a best-seller.*

Those people are **happy** *that their dogs can run free.*

Nominal infinitives can serve as complements to many of the same adjectives. In (36), the adjective *certain* takes the nominal complement *that your book will become a best-seller,* and the adjective *happy* takes the complement *that their dogs can run free.* In (37), infinitive phrases take the role of nominal complement to *certain* and *happy.*

SUMMARY	
Functions of Infinitive Phrases	
Nominal Infinitives	
1. Subject of sentence	***To be an adolescent*** *can be difficult.*
2. Direct object	*She wants* ***to travel to the South Pacific.***
3. Subject complement	*My New Year's resolution is* ***to jog thirty miles every week.***
4. Object complement	*The court found him* ***to be competent.***
5. Adjective complement	*They were pleased* ***to see so many people in the audience.***
Adjectival Infinitives	
Noun modifier	*This is a good place* ***to begin the race.***
Adverbial Infinitives	
1. Sentence modifier	***To be honest,*** *I can't remember his name.*
2. Verb modifier	*She dieted* ***to lose weight.***

Figure 11.3

(37)   The publisher is ***certain*** *to publish your book.*

Those people are ***happy*** *for their dogs to run free.*

Figure 11.3 provides a Summary of the functions of infinitive phrases.

▥ *EXERCISE 11.6*_____

Identify the infinitive phrases in the sentences below and decide whether each is adverbial, adjectival, or nominal. If it is adverbial, note which tests support your analysis; if it is adjectival, give the noun modified and try paraphrasing it as a relative clause; and if it is nominal, write out the sentence containing the pronoun you have substituted for the infinitive construction, as illustrated in the example. Likewise, use tests in Figure 11.2 to support your analysis.

EXAMPLE

To become a veterinarian has been the dream of her childhood.

To become a veterinarian = *Nominal infinitive phrase; subject; something* can substitute for the phrase [***Something*** *has been the dream of her childhood*].

1. You will find it difficult to name a sport that has changed as dramatically in the last few years as girls' basketball.
2. In the 1970s, not many girls had an opportunity to play intramural basketball.
3. Because girls' games were held in the afternoon at first, not many people came to watch them play.
4. To play in tournaments before large crowds threw some of the girls off their game.
5. One great early player knew how to shoot, how to play under the net, and how to defend.
6. She was able to score more than 1,000 points in her first three years of high school basketball.
7. In her senior year, her hope was to cap her high school career with a statewide win for her team.
8. The high school athletic director forgot to send in an application for the girls' team to play in the state tournament.

━━━━━ DIFFERENCES BETWEEN INFINITIVES ━━━━━ AND PREPOSITIONAL PHRASES

Because *to* can be either an infinitive marker or a preposition, you may sometimes find it difficult to distinguish between infinitives and prepositional phrases. The difference should be clear if you remember that the base form of a verb follows the infinitive marker and a noun phrase follows the preposition.

(38) Juan plans *to enter college next fall.*   (infinitive phrase)
to + verb (*enter*)

(39) The letter was delivered *to the wrong office.*   (prepositional phrase)
to + noun phrase (*the wrong office*)

Because some words can be used as either nouns or verbs, you may encounter ambiguous constructions, especially in headlines, where structural clues are often omitted to achieve brevity:

(40) MOM LEAVES ESTATE TO MURDER DEFENDANT
([Little Rock] *Arkansas Gazette,* 15 June 1989)

The meaning of (40) depends on whether *murder* is a verb (from an underlying infinitive *to murder the defendant*) or a noun modifying *defendant,* the object of a preposition (*to the murder defendant*). Can you see the ambiguity of example (41)?

(41) LAWYER ACCUSED OF LYING TO FLY
(*Miami Herald,* 6 JULY 1988)

▬▬▬ *PERIPHERAL CASE—OUGHT TO* ▬▬▬

Not all structures are as clearly differentiated as those we have looked at above. Based on the discussion so far, how would you analyze *to sell his broken-down Ford* in the following sentences? Is it an infinitive phrase in both sentences? If so, how is it functioning?

(42) a. He tried *to sell his broken-down Ford.*
     He tried *something.*

  b. He ought *to sell his broken-down Ford.*
    *He ought *something.*

Notice, first of all, that *to sell his broken-down Ford* is a nominal infinitive in (42a) but not in (42b): You can substitute a pronoun (*it* or *something*) for the former but not the latter. In fact, you cannot substitute any single noun, verb, adjective, or adverb for *to sell his broken-down Ford* in (42b). It is not a constituent. Where can substitutions be made in this sentence? *Must* (or *might* or *should*) could be substituted for *ought to*, suggesting that *ought to* is a constituent: a phrasal modal verb. If this is true, *ought to* should fit into the modal slot of the main verb phrase:

(43) a. TENSE + MODAL_{[ought to]} + HAVE + {-en} + Verb_{[do]}
He ought to have done well on the test.

b. TENSE + MODAL_{[ought to]} + BE + {-ing} + Verb_{[do]}
He ought to be doing well on the test.

On the basis of similarities, then, the *to* phrase in (42a) is classified as an infinitive form and in (42b), it is not. *Ought to* is a two-word modal auxiliary, *ought* plus the particle *to*, with the approximate meaning of *should*.

SUMMARY

In Chapter 11, we introduced nonfinite verbs. Nonfinite verbs appear in phrases that result from the removal of TENSE and the auxiliaries from an original clause and the conversion of the main verb of that clause into forms that can function adverbially, adjectivally, or nominally. We have focused on one kind of nonfinite verb phrase, the infinitive phrase, and the adverbial, adjectival, and nominal roles it can play within sentences. Because infinitives remain verbs, they can have the same subjects, objects, complements, and modifiers that the verb would have in a main clause. We have, as well, suggested tests that may help you to differentiate the infinitive marker *to* from the preposition *to* and from the verb particle *to*.

REVIEW EXERCISES

Identifying Infinitive Phrases

This exercise tests your ability to recognize infinitive phrases and distinguish them from prepositional phrases. In the pasage below, identify the infinitive phrases, whether or not *to* is present. Some sentences contain more than one infinitive phrase; several include prepositional phrases beginning with *to*.

According to a report on *CBS News Sunday Morning,* dogs love to dance with humans. Now there are dog dancing competitions, where owners and their dogs are expected to dance together to tunes like "The Beer Barrel Polka." One competitor says she hasn't gone dancing with her husband for 36 years, but that her dog is always ready to dance. She says her friends think she must be a little bit crazy to go to dog dancing competitions. It has been difficult to promote dog dancing as a competitive sport. It is sometimes hard to get a hotel near an event because many hotels are unwilling to accept dogs. Although dogs can wear decorative collars and ankle bands in the competition, they are not allowed to wear hats, dresses, or coats. One organizer explained that they want to keep the events dignified. Some people who enjoy watching the dogs dance would like to see dog dancing become an Olympic sport.

Infinitive Phrase Structure and Function

Read the passage below and then select the best answer to each question:

Gamma ray bursts occur in the universe almost every day. Until a year ago, such explosions had been too rapid for scientists to detect. Before the launch of the Swift satellite into orbit, telescopes were unable to detect short-lived bursts. Now NASA's orbiting Swift satellite has spotted an exploding star 12.6 billion light years from Earth. Its explosion, 200 seconds long, took place 500 million years after the creation of the universe. These large explosions seem to be related to the creation of black holes. Scientists expect to learn more about the early life of stars by observing long-duration gamma ray explosions.

1. In *too rapid for scientists to detect,* what is *scientists to detect?*
   a.   an adjectival infinitive phrase
   b.   an adverbial infinitive phrase
   c.   a nominal infinitive phrase
   d.   an adverbial prepositional phrase

2. What proof(s) can you give to support your answer to #1?

3. What is the function of *too rapid for scientists to detect?*
   a.   an adverbial modifier
   b.   a direct object
   c.   a nominal subject complement
   d.   an adjectival subject complement

4. What is *into orbit?*
   a.   an adjectival infinitive phrase
   b.   an adverbial infinitive phrase
   c.   a nominal infinitive phrase
   d.   an adverbial prepositional phrase

5. What is *to the creation of black holes* in *to be related to the creation of black holes?*
   a.   an adjectival infinitive phrase
   b.   an adverbial infinitive phrase
   c.   a nominal infinitive phrase
   d.   an adverbial prepositional phrase

6. What is to *learn more about the early life of stars?*
   a.   an adjectival infinitive phrase

    b.   an adverbial infinitive phrase

    c.   a nominal infinitive phrase

    d.   an adverbial prepositional phrase

7. What proof(s) can you give to support your answer to #6?

Infinitive Phrase Functions

Using the tests in Figure 11.2 as a guide, identify the function of the italicized infinitive phrases in the sentences below.

1. After school, Mel's plan was *to play tag football with some friends.*
2. His parents expected him *to finish his homework* before he did anything else.
3. He hoped *to complete his homework* after the game.
4. When the game was over, several of his friends sat down *to talk.*
5. Mel's decision *to join them* was a mistake.
6. He was surprised *to discover that an hour had passed.*
7. *To arrive home before his parents* was uppermost in his mind as he hurried along the street.
8. As he turned the corner, he was upset *to see his father's car in the driveway.*

Analyzing Infinitive Phrase Structure

Reconstruct the sentences underlying the italicized infinitive phrases in the sentences above and then identify the constituents and the sentence pattern of each. An example has been done for you.

EXAMPLE

Job had never expected *to marry a neurosurgeon.*

Job [NP$_1$ – subject] would marry [MV$_{trans}$] a neurosurgeon [NP$_2$ – direct object].

Marry = Transitive verb, Type V

Practical Applications: Writing Infinitive Phrases

Follow the directions below to generate sentences from the italicized words with an infinitive phrase of your own choice. Try to identify the function of the infinitive phrase you have created.

1. Write a sentence about something you *might visit* in the future. Begin with "I would like...."
2. Write a sentence about what would be (or is) necessary if you are *to arrive* at school on time; begin with "In order to...."

3. Write a sentence about something you have decided *that you will do* after graduation; begin with "I have decided...."

4. Write a sentence about *why* you are taking this course; end the sentence with "in order to...."

5. Write a sentence about *what* your goal is after college; begin the sentence with "My goal is...."

6. Write a sentence on the pattern of #3 in the Exercise on Infinitive Phrase Functions above.

KEY TERMS

infinitive phrase   nonfinite verb
   adjectival infinitive phrase   nonfinite verb phrase
   adverbial infinitive phrase   reduced clause
   nominal infinitive phrase

ENDNOTE

1. The name of these prizes is apparently a pun based on *ignoble* and *Nobel Prize*.

Nonfinite Verb Phrases, Part II

12

PARTICIPLE AND GERUND PHRASES

CHAPTER PREVIEW

Like the infinitive phrases discussed in Chapter 11, participle phrases and gerund phrases contain nonfinite verbs and are derived from complete sentences containing subjects, objects, complements, and modifiers. Participle phrases can function adverbially or adjectivally; gerund phrases function as nominals.

CHAPTER GOALS

At the end of this chapter, you should be able to

- Distinguish between *present-participle* and *gerund* phrases.

- Recognize *past-participle* phrases.

- Distinguish between the adverbial and adjectival functions of *participle* phrases.

- Identify the nominal functions of *gerund* phrases.

- Recognize *dangling modifiers*.

PRESENT PARTICIPLE PHRASES

In Chapter 9, we saw that a clause containing a **present participle** could become an adverbial subordinate clause.

(1)   *While he was running for the bus,* he broke his foot.

That initial clause can retain its adverbial function after being reduced to an elliptical participle clause, as follows:

(2)   *While running for the bus,* he broke his foot.

Because the subordinating conjunction remains, this is still considered a reduced dependent clause.

  If the subordinator disappears, we are left with a **participle phrase,** which consists of a participle and, optionally, the subject or the complements (or both) of the verb from which it is derived.

(3)   *Running for the bus,* he broke his foot.

  Like infinitive phrases, participle phrases can have all of the constituents associated with the verbs underlying them—subjects, objects, complements, and modifiers.

(4)   *Suddenly feeling dizzy,* Jean sat down to rest.
  ↑

Jean suddenly felt dizzy.
  Jean = the underlying subject of *feeling*
  suddenly = adverb functioning as adverbial modifier of *feeling*
  dizzy = adjective functioning as subject complement (predicate adjective)

Fearing the worst, the ship's crew remained calm.
  ↑
The ship's crew feared the worst.
  The ship's crew = the underlying subject of *fearing the worst.*
  the worst = noun phrase functioning as direct object of *fearing*

His car being in the garage, Tom had to take a bus to the office.
  ↑
His car was in the garage.
  His car = the underlying subject of *being*
  in the garage = prepositional phrase functioning as adverbial complement
    of *being*

  Because dependent clauses are often nested within other dependent clauses, a participle phrase derived from a dependent clause may itself contain a dependent clause, as example (5) illustrates:

(5)   *Looking at the fish **that had been kept in the refrigerator all week,*** Fred lost his appetite.

a. *Looking at the fish* = participle phrase

> Fred = the underlying subject of *looking*
>
> *at the fish* = prepositional phrase, adverbial modifier of *looking*
>
> b. *that had been kept in the refrigerator all week* = relative clause modifying *fish*
>
> > *that* = relative pronoun functioning as subject of *had been kept*, renames *fish*
> >
> > *in the refrigerator* = prepositional phrase functioning as adverbial modifier of *had been kept*
> >
> > *all week* = noun phrase functioning as adverbial modifier of *had been kept*

■ *EXERCISE 12.1* _____

> Identify the participle phrases in the sentences below. Reconstruct the sentence underlying each participle phrase, label its constituents, and identify the verb type. An example has been done for you.

EXAMPLE

Expecting friendly dogs, the postman opened the gate.

The postman [NP₁-subject] expected [Mv_tr] friendly dogs [NP₂-direct object].

Expected = *transitive verb (Type V sentence)*

1. The butterfly, needing to operate independently, must forage for food and find a mate within a short cycle of life.
2. By responding to specific tastes and odors, females are able to locate host plants on which to lay their eggs.
3. Being innately attracted to specific colors, butterflies learn to associate nectar with color.
4. Some blossoms have marks on their petals, showing insects where to probe for nectar.
5. Other flowers change color as they age, indicating to the insects that they no longer contain nectar.
6. While subsisting almost entirely on the nectar they find in flowers, butterflies help pollinate the plants they visit.
7. Apparently recognizing landmarks, they eventually visit the same plants in the same sequence every day.
8. Once having been released from a net, butterflies remember to avoid that site entirely from then on.

Butterflies have been released from the net

> As is true of infinitive phrases, the subject of a participle phrase can be omitted only if it is the same as the subject of the main clause. In (6), the subject of both *repaired* and *let* is *Bill:*

(6) *Having repaired his fishing rod,* Bill confidently let the fish tug on his line.

↑

Bill having repaired his fishing rod, Bill confidently let the fish tug on his line.

Rather than repeat the same word (*Bill*) twice, we normally delete the first mention of *Bill,* as in (6).

When the main clause does *not* have the same subject as the participle phrase, a misunderstanding (sometimes humorous) can result if the actual subject of the participle is not mentioned, as in (7):

(7) Having repaired his fishing rod, the fish tugged on Bill's line.

The intended subject of *repaired* is *Bill,* but because *fish* is the subject of the main clause, it also seems to be the subject of *repaired,* clearly an absurdity in the real world. The participle phrase in this case is referred to as a **dangling modifier.** Although we may not always notice dangling modifiers in speech, they can be a distracting problem in writing. We discuss their cure in a What's the Usage? section later in this chapter.

Functions of Present Participle Phrases

Participle phrases can function as adverbial or adjectival modifiers. Tests used to identify the function of dependent clauses can be used to identify the function of participle phrases.

Adverbial Participle Phrases

Adverbial participles are relatively easy to spot because they occupy the same positions in sentences as do the full subordinate clauses from which they are derived. You can verify that a participle phrase is adverbial by using the tests for subordinate clauses: (1) substitution of an adverb, (2) formation of a *wh*-question using a *wh*-adverb, and (3) rearrangement. For instance, the example that follows passes all three tests:

(8) *Starting the engine,* Peter noticed a grinding sound.

    a. Peter noticed a grinding sound *then.*   (Test #1)

    b. *When* did Peter notice a grinding sound?   (Test #2)

    c. Peter, *starting the engine,* noticed a grinding sound.   (Test #3)

However, an adverbial participle phrase will not necessarily satisfy all three tests. A simple adverb cannot substitute for the adverbial of cause in (9), and the phrase is not easily moved. However, a *wh*-question can be made from the participle phrase:

(9) *Forgetting where our car was,* we systematically searched the parking lot.

Why did we systematically search the parking lot? (Test #2)

Adjectival Participle Phrases

Adjectival participles, which are reduced forms of relative clauses, are also easy to spot. Like the relative clauses from which they are derived, they immediately follow the noun they modify.

(10)   a. The people *watching the movie* stamped their feet.

    b. Do you know the man *driving that car?*

You can test whether participles are adjectival by trying to paraphrase them as relative clauses:

(11)   a. The people *who were watching the movie* stamped their feet.

    b. Do you know the man *who is driving that car?*

Diagramming Present Participle Phrases

Diagrams help some students to visualize the function of participle phrases. Observe how the adverbial participle phrase appears in a Reed-Kellogg diagram:

(12)   Turning the corner, we felt a sudden gust of wind.

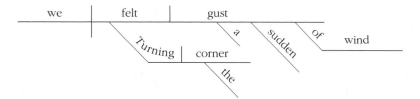

In the diagram, the structure containing the present participle is attached to the main subject/predicate line of the sentence at a point reflecting the function of the participle phrase modifier. The participle phrase is placed on a line like the one used for prepositions and their objects. The participle curves around, falling partly on the diagonal line and partly on the horizontal. Other components of the participle phrase, such as the direct object *corner* and its determiner *the,* are placed on or in relation to the horizontal line, just as they would be in diagramming a complete sentence or subordinate clause.

We analyzed the participle phrase in (12) as adverbial, placing it beneath the verb *felt,* because it can be paraphrased as an adverbial clause, as in (13).

(13) *As we were turning the corner,* we felt a sudden gust of wind.

You can verify that the clause in (13) is functioning adverbially by subjecting it to the adverb substitution test:

(14) *Then* we felt a sudden gust of wind.

the *wh*-question test:

(15) *When* did we feel a sudden gust of wind?

and the movability test:

(16) We felt a sudden gust of wind *as we were turning the corner.*

Phrase markers are most useful for representing the underlying sentence structure of present participle phrases. The phrase marker in example (17) illustrates the relationship between the main clause, *we felt a sudden gust of wind,* and the clause underlying the present participle phrase, *we were turning the corner.*

(17)

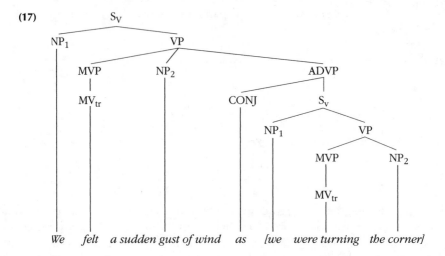

Grammatical transformations alter this underlying structure by deleting the conjunction, the subject *we,* and TENSE + AUX from the embedded sentence *we were turning the corner,* as in (17), and moving the remaining present participle phrase, *turning the corner,* to the beginning of the sentence.

SUMMARY	
Present Participle Phrases	
Present participle phrase with subordinating conjunction (elliptical clause)	***While eating dinner,*** *we discussed politics.*
Present participle phrase without subordinating conjunction	***Turning the corner,*** *we felt a sudden gust of wind.*
Present participle phrase with subject expressed	***Many students being sick that day,*** *the professor postponed the film.*

Figure 12.1

(18) We felt a sudden gust of wind [we were turning the corner].
 ↓
We felt a sudden gust of wind [~~we were~~ turning the corner].
 ↓
Turning the corner, we felt a sudden gust of wind.

Figure 12.1 provides a summary of the forms of present participle phrases.
    Diagrams can also help some students visualize the adjectival function of participle phrases.

(19) The people watching the movie stamped their feet.

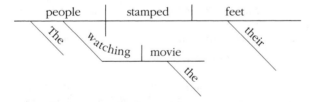

A phrase marker analysis, example (20), shows the subject-predicate structure underlying the participle phrase. It may help you see how adjectival participle phrases are created:

(20)

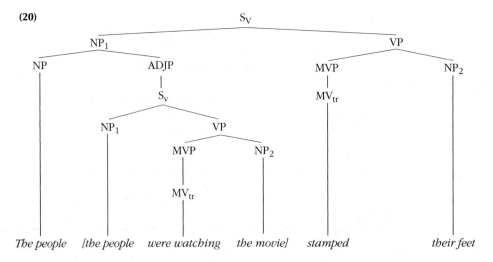

The people were watching the movie in example (20), shown again in (21a), will undergo the relative clause transformation to become *who were watching the movie* in (21b); deletion of *who* and *were* will leave the participle phrase *watching the movie* in (21c).

(21)   a. The people [the people were watching the movie] stamped their feet.
                    ↓

                            who

           b. The people [~~the people~~ were watching the movie] stamped their feet].
                    ↓

           c. The people [~~who were~~ watching the movie] stamped their feet.
                    ↓

           d. The people watching the movie stamped their feet.

Often, it is easy to identify the function of the participle phrase because it clearly refers to or adds information about either a verb or a noun.

(22)   a. *Moving to Vienna,* von Droheim scrupulously avoided all keyboard music.

           b. The harpsichord *standing in the corner* once belonged to von Droheim.

In example (22a), the phrase *moving to Vienna* tells *when* von Droheim avoided keyboard music; it is an adverbial modifier of *avoided.* In example (22b), the phrase *standing in the corner* is an adjectival modifer identifying *which* harpsichord is meant; it can be expanded into the relative clause from which it is derived, as in example (23).

(23)   The harpsichord *that is standing in the corner* once belonged to von Droheim.

■ *EXERCISE 12.2*

> Identify the present participle phrases in the sentences below and decide whether each is adverbial or adjectival. If adverbial, what tests from Figure 9.2 in Chapter 9 does the phrase pass? If adjectival, give the word it modifies and try to transform the phrase into a relative clause.

1. Listening to her iPod with her eyes closed, the receptionist failed to notice that there was a new visitor in the office. *adjectival*
2. The visitor, standing impatiently at her desk, cleared his throat loudly. *adj*
3. Suddenly realizing that he was there, the receptionist blushed and removed her earphone. *adj*
4. Some of the people waiting in the office smiled at her embarrassment. *adj*
5. Asking the visitor to be seated, the receptionist announced his name to her boss. *adj*
6. Taking out his Blackberry, the man decided to check his e-mail.
7. The others in the waiting room, growing bored, resumed what they had been doing.
8. The receptionist replaced her earphone, closing her eyes again.

In contrast to the clear cases above, the participle phrase in example (24) appears to be only distantly related, if at all, to any single constituent of its sentence.

(24) *Speaking of musical fetishes,* von Ribbentrop composed only for the sousaphone.

Speaking of musical fetishes doesn't modify *von Ribbentrop*—it was not von Ribbentrop who was speaking of music—nor does it modify *composed* or *sousaphone*. Instead, it seems to modify the whole sentence, referring in this case to the topic of conversation when the sentence was spoken. When a participle phrase functions in this way, it is called a **sentence modifier,** a function traditionally thought of as being adverbial.

Other kinds of adverbs and adverbial phrases can also function as sentence modifiers: adverbs, prepositional phrases, clauses, and infinitive phrases.

(25) *Honestly,* I can't imagine what she meant.   (adverb)

In my opinion, Fred is an excellent rumba dancer.   (prepositional phrase)

No matter what you say, he plans to vote against the amendment.   (clause)

To tell the truth, I found his moralistic lectures tiresome.   (infinitive phrase)

However, the distinction between an adverbial modifier of a verb and an adverbial sentence modifier is often a fine one; there may be no obvious

SUMMARY	
Functions of Present Participle Phrases	
Adverbial Participle Phrases	
Sentence modifier	***Considering how late it is,*** *we ought to go home.*
Verb modifier	***[After] hearing about the new assignment,*** *the students groaned.*
Adjectival Participle Phrases	
Noun modifier	*Those people **waiting for the bus** look tired.*

Figure 12.2

criteria to allow you to make a strong case for one analysis or the other. Thus, the distinction does not make a great deal of practical difference.

Like other adverbials, participle phrases can often be moved in the sentences they modify. They are usually set off by commas, wherever they occur in the sentence.

Figure 12.2 offers a summary of the functions of present participle phrases.

Differences Between Present Participles and Adjectives

Some present participles have occurred as noun modifiers so often and for so long that they have become adjectives. This is especially true of participles that express actions capable of existing in varying degrees. In Chapter 1, we pointed out that speakers of English will recognize that (26a) is permissible but that (26b) is not:

(26) a. The boring man is very boring.

b. *The snoring man is very snoring.

We accept (26a) because *boring* has become an adjective in English. Not only does it fit the adjective frame sentence, but it can also be compared (*more boring, most boring*). *Snoring* is not treated as an adjective, however; it is simply a participle. As such, it can modify a noun, but it fails all other adjective tests. It neither compares nor intensifies. Note that the same word may be an adjective in one sense or position and a participle in another:

(27) The static on that radio is ***annoying*** me. (participle)

*The static on that radio is very annoying me.

*The static on that radio is more annoying me than anything else.

The static on that radio is ***annoying*** *to me.* (adjective)

The static on that radio is very annoying to me.

The static on that radio is more annoying to me than anything else.

■ *EXERCISE 12.3*

In each of the sentences below, identify the italicized words as adjectives or participles. If you decide they are adjectives, list the adjective tests that they satisfy. An example has been done for you.

EXAMPLE

He warned us never to abandon a *smoking* campfire.

Smoking *is a participle. You cannot say* ****very smoking campfire*** *or* ****a more smoking campfire.***

1. The children *amusing* themselves quietly with paper cups and straws seemed to astonish their parents.
2. Martin didn't know what to do about a *dripping* sound that could be heard somewhere in the kitchen.
3. The old saying that you should let *sleeping* dogs lie has a *fascinating* source.
4. The *blaring* radio next door was *annoying* Josh, who was *trying* to study for a final exam.
5. The party hosts were *standing* at the door with *charming* smiles to welcome everyone.
6. To be frank, the Trick-or-Treaters found the life-sized mummy *standing* by Max's front door too *frightening*.
7. *Rising* inflation makes it difficult for middle-class families to maintain their standard of living.
8. An *alarming* message appeared on Ned's computer screen, *telling* him that he had made a fatal error.

■ *EXERCISE 12.4*

Locate all the infinitive phrases in the sentences in Exercise 12.3. Give the sentence constituents of the predicates and identify the verb type of each infinitive.

EXAMPLE

He warned us never to abandon a smoking campfire.

To abandon [MV$_{tr}$] a smoking campfire [NP$_2$–direct object] = transitive verb, Type V Sentence

GERUNDS

When a verb with the *-ing* inflection occupies a noun position, it is called a **gerund.** Like participles, gerunds can have all of the constituents associated with the sentences from which they are derived. They can have a subject, take an object, be followed by a complement, or be modified by an adverb phrase. In example (28), *giving* is a gerund, and *giving him a flu shot* is a **gerund phrase.**

(28)　　She didn't mind *giving him a flu shot.*

　　　　　↑

She didn't mind *something.*

She + TENSE + give + him + a flu shot.

　　giving him a flu shot = gerund phrase functioning as direct object of *mind*

　　She = the underlying subject of *giving*

　　him = pronoun functioning as indirect object of *giving*

　　a flu shot = noun phrase functioning as direct object of *giving*

In example (29), *being* is a gerund, and *being editor of the school paper last year* is a gerund phrase.

(29)　　He liked *being editor of the school paper last year.*

　　　　　↑

He liked *something.*

He + TENSE + BE + editor of the school paper + last year.

　　being editor of the school paper last year = gerund phrase functioning as direct object of *liked*

　　He = the underlying subject of *being*

　　editor of the school paper = noun phrase functioning as subject complement of *being*

　　last year = noun phrase functioning as adverbial modifier of *being*

Notice that, in both of these sentences, the subject of the clause underlying the gerund phrase is the same as the subject of the main clause—*she* in (28) and *he* in (29). If the subjects are different, both should be expressed, as in (30), where the gerund *considering* is the headword of the gerund phrase *his considering the play amusing.*

(30)　　*His considering the play amusing* surprised them.

　　　　　↑

Something surprised them.

He + TENSE + consider + the play + amusing.

　　His considering the play amusing = gerund phrase functioning as subject of *surprised*

　　　　his = possessive pronoun that identifies *he* as the underlying subject of *considering*

> *the play* = noun phrase functioning as direct object of *considering*
> *amusing* = present participle functioning as object complement of *the play*

WHAT'S THE USAGE? *Subjects of Gerunds*

When the subject of the gerund is expressed, its form has traditionally been possessive, as is the case in (30). Why the possessive? Gerunds are functioning as though they were nouns and their subjects function as determiners. As you will recall, when nouns and pronouns are used as determiners, they occur in the possessive form (*Shakespeare's* plays; *his* book). Usage seems to be changing on this in American English. Usage handbooks may still prescribe that the possessive be used in writing, as the following examples illustrate:

(31) a. Do you mind *my* speaking frankly to you?
      (*I* speak frankly.)

      b. She hated *Suzy's* calling every night.
      (*Suzy* called every night.)

In spoken English, however, one often hears the objective form of the pronoun and the unmarked form of the noun as the subject of a gerund:

(32) a. Do you mind *me* speaking frankly to you?

      b. She hated *Suzy* calling every night.

The sentences in (32) mean the same as those in (31). However, compare the two sentences in (33). Is the range of meanings the same for both?

(33) a. His parents find *Joey's* driving a little bit nerve-wracking.

      b. ?His parents find *Joey* driving a little bit nerve-wracking.

Functions of Gerunds and Gerund Phrases

Gerunds and gerund phrases function, like nouns and noun phrases, as subjects, objects, and complements of verbs, and objects of prepositions:

(34) *His immediately demanding your payment* showed his inexperience.
      (Gerund as Subject)

      Felicia's grandmother enjoys *riding a ten-speed bicycle.*
      (Gerund as Direct Object)

      Sherry's hobby was *saving ordinary coins in a tin can.*
      (Gerund as Subject Complement)

      Gerald can afford college by *regularly working two jobs.*
      (Gerund as Object of a Preposition)

In Reed-Kellogg diagrams, gerunds have a special line of their own. The gerund is curved above a step, as in the following example:

(35)   *His immediately demanding your payment* showed his inexperience.

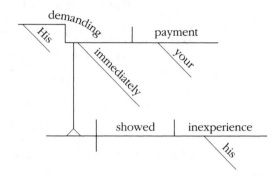

As we saw earlier with infinitives and present participles, phrase markers such as that in example (36) are especially useful for showing the underlying sentence structure of gerunds:

(36)

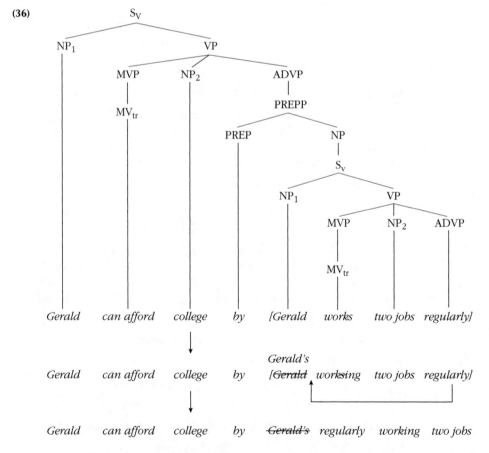

The clause *Gerald works two jobs regularly* that is embedded in example (36) underlies the gerund phrase *regularly working two jobs* that functions as object of the preposition *by* in example (34). In reducing the embedded clause to a gerund phrase, transformations delete TENSE and convert the verb into the gerund form. The subject *Gerald* becomes possessive. The adverb *regularly* moves to a position before the verb it modifies. Because the subject of the sentence and the subject of the gerund phrase are the same, the second mention of the subject (the possessive *Gerald's*) is deleted. If the two subjects are not the same, then both must be retained, as in (37), in which *Gerald* is the subject of the sentence and *his wife's* identifies the subject of the gerund *working*.

(37) Gerald can afford college by his wife's regularly working two jobs.

The tests for identifying gerunds and adverbial and adjectival participle phrases are presented in a summary in Figure 12.3.

SUMMARY	
Tests for Identifying Adverbial Participle Phrases	
*He tried to think carefully **while answering their questions.***	
1. Substitution of an adverb	*He tried to think carefully **then.***
2. *Wh*-question using a *wh*-adverb	***When** did he try to think carefully?*
3. Movability	***While answering their questions**, he tried to think carefully.*
Tests for Identifying Adjectival Participle Phrases	
*The static **coming from that radio** is annoying.*	
1. Usually can be restated as a relative clause.	*The static **that is coming from that radio** is annoying.*
2. Modifies a noun that precedes it.	*The **static** coming from that radio is annoying.*
Tests for Identifying Gerunds	
*She hates **waiting around for a repairman to show up.***	
1. Substitute *something* or *it* for the gerund phrase.	*She hates **something.***
2. *Wh*-question using *what*	***What** does she hate?*

Figure 12.3

Differences Between Gerunds and Present Participles

Notice the contrast in the pair of sentences below. If you try the tests given in Figure 12.3, you will see that the first contains a participle and the second, a gerund.

(38)   a. *Betty having told us that you were coming,* we weren't surprised.

b. We appreciated *Betty's having told us that you were coming.*

The embedded phrase in (38a) is an adverbial present participle construction, and its subject *(Betty)* is in the uninflected form. The embedded phrase in (38b) is a gerund, with the entire phrase functioning as the direct object of the verb *appreciated.* Its subject *(Betty's)* is a possessive form of the noun. The use of the possessive subject with a gerund helps clarify the difference between participle and gerund phrases; hence, the distinction is usually maintained in careful writing, although not always in speech.

The possibility that the same form may be either a gerund or a participle sometimes results in amusing headlines.

(39)   OWNERS RESPONSIBLE FOR BITING CANINES
(Tribune [New Albany, Indiana], 9 September 1985)

If *biting* modifies *canines,* it is an adjectival participle, and *canines* is the object of the preposition *for:*

(40)   responsible for + canines that bite

If *biting* itself is the object of the preposition *for,* it occupies a noun position and is a gerund:

(41)   responsible for + biting their canines

■ *EXERCISE 12.5*

The sentences below are ambiguous because the italicized words can be interpreted as either participles or gerunds. Explain the ambiguity by stating the meaning of the gerund version and of the participle version, as was done for (39) above.

1. CLINTON HONORS MISSING
   (The Arizona Republic, 19 November 2000)

2. AVOID DAMAGING TERMITES BY FOLLOWING SIMPLE RULES
   ([Appleton-Neenah-Menasha, Wisconsin] The Post Crescent, 18 May 2005)

3. DOUGHNUT HOLE, NUDE DANCING ON COUNCIL TABLE
   (Redlands [California] Daily Facts, 3 April 2000)

4. JUDGE DELAYS RULING ON PADDLING PRINCIPAL
   (The Indianapolis Star, 9 November 1996)

5. DISTRICT ATTORNEY DECLINES TO TRY SHOOTING SUSPECT
   ([New Orleans] The Times-Picayune, 30 November 2001)

6. IT'S TIME TO DEEP-SIX TODDLER GIVING HIGH-FIVES
   ([Syracuse, New York] The Post Standard, 3 February 2003)

■ *EXERCISE 12.6*

Identify the function of each participle or gerund construction in the sentences below as adverbial, adjectival, or nominal. If it is adverbial, list the adverbial tests it satisfies; if adjectival, identify the noun it modifies; and if nominal, show that *it* or *something* can substitute for the gerund phrase. An example has been done for you.

EXAMPLE

The family spent its vacation swimming in icy mountain lakes.

Adverbial participle: **swimming in icy mountain lakes;** *an adverb can substitute for the phrase (The family spent its vacation* **wisely***);* **how** *can substitute for it in a* **wh-***question (***How** *did the family spend its vacation?).*

1. I found sleeping during the storm difficult because of the banging shutters.
2. We tiptoed around so that we would not awaken the sleeping baby.
3. Eddie got his license without learning how to park the car.
4. Polly has spent a lot of time learning how to park the car.
5. We all like to watch Polly learning how to park the car.
6. Have you tried searching for a catcher's mitt on eBay?
7. Searching for the Picasso Museum, Helen paused to admire a rosebush blooming nearby.
8. You can find almost anything by searching with Google.

Differences Between Gerunds and Nouns

Gerunds appear in the noun positions of sentences, but because they are not really nouns, they cannot take noun inflections.

(42) *Eating* too many green apples made her sick.

*Eatings too many green apples

After functioning for a long time on the periphery of nounlike words, some gerunds have become true nouns. Consider the following:

(43) *The congressional meetings* lasted several hours.

SUMMARY	
Functions of Gerund Phrases	
1. Subject	***Electing him president*** *was our first mistake.*
2. Direct object	*They regret **buying that little sports car.***
3. Subject complement (predicate nominative)	*Eleanor's hobby is **collecting coins.***
4. Object of a preposition	*He supports himself by **working as a waiter after school.***

Figure 12.4

Meetings comes after a determiner and is plural. It has become a noun in English, at least when used in this sense. The same word can be a noun in one instance and a gerund in another, however. Notice the contrast in the following:

(44)   a. We held *the meeting* last week.

    b. They enjoy *meeting each other for lunch every Saturday.*

In (44a), *meeting* is a true noun. It is preceded by a determiner, it can be pluralized, and it can be modified by an adjective (*We held the final meetings last week*). In (44b), *meeting* fails the noun tests; it is a gerund.

Figure 12.4 lists the functions that gerunds and gerund phrases can serve.

Differences Between Gerunds and Participles

How do linguists decide unusual or borderline cases? They test difficult examples against various prototypical patterns and decide which pattern the case at hand most resembles. In the following examples, is *listening* a gerund or an adverbial participle?

(45)   a. *While listening to the concerto,* Marcia decided to study music.

    b. *After listening to the concerto,* Marcia decided to study music.

Listening is a participle in (45a), and the phrase is adverbial. It is a reduced form of the adverbial subordinate clause *While she was listening to the concerto.* *Listening* in (45b) has a different origin. It cannot be derived from *After she was listening to the concerto.* In fact, *after* is a preposition in (45b) and *listening to the concerto* is a gerund phrase that can be replaced by the pronoun *that.* In this, too, it contrasts with the participle form:

(46) a. After *that,* Marcia decided to study music.

    b. *While *that,* Marcia decided to study music.

    How would you identify the introductory phrase in (47)?

(47) *Listening to the concerto,* Marcia decided to study music.

Note that *listening to the concerto* cannot be a gerund phrase; no pronoun can substitute for it, but an adverb, such as *then,* can. Therefore, it must be a participle phrase.

Another test that often helps to distinguish participles from gerunds in borderline cases is the ability of gerunds, in some contexts, to accept a possessive noun or pronoun. Participles cannot be preceded by a possessive. Compare the following:

(48) a. *After reading her grandmother's will,* Shirley quit her job at the answering service.
    After her reading [of] her grandmother's will, Shirley... (The gerund *reading* can occur with a preceding possessive.)

    b. *While reading her grandmother's will,* Shirley thought about a trip to Europe.
    *While her reading [of] her grandmother's will, Shirley... (The participle *reading* cannot be preceded by a possessive.)

■ *EXERCISE 12.7*

In each of the following sentences, decide whether the italicized word is a noun, adjective, participle, or gerund. If you think it is a noun or adjective, list the noun or adjective tests it satisfies. If you think it is a gerund, write out the sentence containing a pronoun substituted for the gerund phrase. If you think it is a participle, identify its function (adjectival or adverbial), and explain the tests that confirm your hypothesis. An example has been done for you.

EXAMPLE

An *interesting* congressional *hearing* on health care will be held next week.

interesting = *adjective. It modifies **congressional hearing,** it can be preceded by **very,** and it can be compared.*

hearing = *noun. It is preceded by a determiner and can be pluralized.*

1. *Eradicating* invasive nonnative species has become a *pressing* item on the agenda of conservation biologists.

2. A common sewer rat (nicknamed Razza) was released on a deserted New Zealand island to test methods of *trapping* nonnative animals.

3. *Evading* capture despite his *wearing* of a radio collar, the rat eluded trackers for more than four months.

4. After *circling* the island for three days, the rat settled on one spot, *using* a small 2½-acre area for its home.

5. *Finding* it *puzzling* that they were unable to trap the rat, the scientists began *laying* twice as many traps as usual.

6. In the tenth week of the study, the battery in Razza's collar died, *leaving* the scientists clueless about his activities.

7. In the twelfth week, residents of an island 438 yards away reported *seeing* birds *behaving* strangely.

8. Six weeks later, *using* trained dogs to detect rodent scent, the scientists succeeded in *catching* Razza in a trap baited with penguin meat.

PAST PARTICIPLE PHRASES

Passive clauses containing **past participles** can also be reduced so that they become participle phrases.

(49)   a. *When they were awakened by the unusual noise,* the dogs began to bark.
↓

b. *When awakened by the unusual noise,* the dogs began to bark.

If you analyze the main verb phrase in the subordinate clause of (49a), you will notice that it contains the passive marker [BE + {-en}]:

(50)   were awakened = TENSE$_{[past]}$ + BE + {-en} + awaken

The sentence type of a past participle phrase may be difficult to analyze both because it is passive and because information has been deleted. To analyze the structure of such a past participle phrase, you must first transform the subordinate clause from which it is derived back into its active form:

(51)   *Restored by a good rest,* Cindy was
eager to enter another marathon.
↑   (By way of clause reduction)
After Cindy was restored by a
good rest, Cindy was eager to
enter another marathon.
↑   (By way of passive transformation)
After a good rest restored Cindy
+ Cindy was eager to enter
another marathon

Once the transformations have been reversed, as is shown in (51), it is easier to see that *restored by a good rest* comes from a Type V sentence in which *restored* is a transitive verb, *a good rest* is the subject, and *Cindy* is the direct object.

In addition to underlying subjects and objects, past participle phrases can include adverbial modifiers and object complements. *Very softly* is an adverb phrase functioning as an adverbial modifier of *spoken* in (52).

(52) *Although spoken very softly,* his words were picked up by the microphone.

In (53), *the best candidate for the job* is a noun phrase functioning as object complement.

(53) *Considered by everyone the best candidate for the job,* Eleanor felt confident during the interview.

You may find it difficult to identify object complements in past participle phrases because passivization separates the direct object (*Eleanor* in the sentence above) from the object complement (*the best candidate for the job*). Notice that the participle phrase in (53) is derived from the sentence in (54).

(54) *Everyone* considered Eleanor the best candidate for the job.

After you supply the missing subject (*everyone*) and make the sentence active, placing the direct object, *Eleanor,* in its normal position, you will see that the object complement, *the best candidate for the job,* also returns to its normal position following the direct object, where it is easier to recognize.

The types of past participle phrases are summarized in Figure 12.5.

SUMMARY	
Past Participle Phrases	
Past participle phrase with subordinating conjunction (elliptical clause)	***Although denied permission to leave the house,*** *Jim went to a movie.*
Past participle phrase without subordinating conjunction	***Properly furnished,*** *this house will look better.*

Figure 12.5

■ EXERCISE 12.8

Identify the subject of the nonfinite past participle constructions in the sentences below.

1. Determined to find a 24-pound turkey for Thanksgiving, Ben had gone to several markets.
2. When stuffed with chestnut dressing, the turkey was too heavy for Kelly to lift.
3. Timing the roasting of such a big bird filled with stuffing proved difficult.
4. Waiting in casseroles arranged on a table in the kitchen, most of the side dishes needed only to be reheated at the last minute.
5. The turkey, when finished roasting, would have to sit for 30 minutes before being carved.
6. During that time, the covered casseroles could be reheated in the oven.
7. Platters of oysters, opened by Ben, were in the refrigerator, ready to be served.
8. For dessert, someone had made a pumpkin cheesecake topped with whipped cream.

Functions of Past Participle Phrases

The examples of past participle phrases that we have discussed so far have functioned adverbially; they have all been reduced versions of subordinate clauses. Participle phrases can also result from the reduction of relative clauses.

(55)   The car *parked in front of our house* belongs to a neighbor.

The adjectival participle phrase identifies the car; it is derived from a relative clause that has a similar function.

(56)   The car *that is parked in front of our house* belongs to a neighbor.

Past participle phrases often have an adjectival function. They occur as modifiers that follow a noun, as modifying phrases that precede or follow the sentence, or as object complements, as in the following:

(57)   Roosevelt found a third of the nation *ill-housed, ill-clothed,* and *ill-fed.*

In (57), the past participle phrases *ill-housed, ill-clothed,* and *ill-fed* function adjectivally as complements describing the direct object *a third of the nation.*

Differences Between Adjectival and Adverbial Past Participles

Some linguists consider all past participle phrases to be functioning as adjectivals; others do not. Although *when overfed* seems to modify the noun *goose* in (58), consider the adverbial tests the past participle phrase fulfills:

(58)   The goose, *when overfed,* becomes even more succulent.

    a. The goose becomes even   (adverb substitution)
       more succulent *then.*

    b. *When* does the goose become even   (*Wh*-adverb question)
       more succulent?

    c. The goose becomes even more   (adverb movement)
       succulent *when overfed.*

Despite the information *when overfed* provides about the goose, the phrase behaves like an adverb. It does not identify or characterize a goose so much as it states a condition under which something is true. Contrast the behavior of the past participle phrase in (58) with that seen in (59):

(59)   Skydance, *beaten before the race began,* never got ahead of the pack.

    a. ?Skydance never got ahead of the pack _____.
       (No adverb substitute available)

    b. ?Why did Skydance never get ahead of the pack?
       (The answer is not *Beaten before the race began.*)

    c. ?Skydance never got ahead of the pack, *beaten before the race began.*
       (The participle phrase cannot be moved away from the noun it modifies.)

The reduced clause in (58) passes all three adverbial tests, but the one in (59) passes none of them. It does not seem to be adverbial. It is adjectival.

Restrictive and Nonrestrictive Participle Phrases

Because they are derived from relative clauses, participle phrases functioning adjectivally can be either restrictive or nonrestrictive. Look carefully at examples (60a) and (60b) and decide for yourself which one includes a restrictive participle phrase and which a nonrestrictive.

(60)   a. The lone Romulan warship, *crippled by photon torpedoes,* drifted slowly toward the asteroid.

    b. The Romulan warship *crippled by photon torpedoes* drifted slowly toward its undamaged sister ship.

If you concluded that the past participle phrase in example (60a), the one set off with commas, is nonrestrictive, you are correct. How could you tell? The fact that only one Romulan warship is referred to in (60a) means that the participle phrase modifier does not function to specify or restrict *which* warship is being referred to. It provides additional information not needed for uniquely identifying the warship under discussion. Furthermore, it is set off

SUMMARY	
Functions of Past Participle Phrases	
1. Postnoun modifier (adjectival)	*The car **parked behind the movie theater** belongs to an usher.*
2. Prenoun modifier (adjectival)	***Irrigated** fields produce most of our lettuce.*
3. Adjectival object complement	*The crowd saw them **trounced by their opponents.***
4. Pre- or postclause modifier (adverbial)	***When inflated,** the balloon measured six feet in diameter.*
5. Pre- or postclause modifier (ambiguous: adverbial or adjectival)	***Refused a place on the ticket,** Hubert decided to run as an Independent.*

Figure 12.6

with commas, just as nonrestrictive relative clauses are. Compare (60a) with (61), a paraphrase with a nonrestrictive relative clause replacing the participle phrase:

(61) The lone Romulan warship, *which had been crippled by photon torpedoes,* drifted slowly toward the asteroid.

In contrast, the participle phrase in (60b) is restrictive. It identifies which Romulan ship is being referred to, distinguishing it from another one, its undamaged sister ship. In this case, the modifier contains identifying information, and like the restrictive relative clause in (62), it is not set off with commas.

(62) The Romulan warship *that had been crippled by photon torpedoes* drifted slowly toward its undamaged sister ship.

Notice, however, that only a nonrestrictive participle phrase can be placed in front of the noun phrase it modifies, as in example (63).

(63) *Crippled by photon torpedoes,* the lone Romulan warship drifted slowly toward the asteroid.

If the restrictive modifier in (60b) is moved in front of the noun phrase it modifies, it becomes nonrestrictive in its meaning, as you can see in example (64).

(64)   *Crippled by photon torpedoes,* the Romulan warship drifted slowly toward its undamaged sister ship.

Figure 12.6 summarizes the functions performed by past-participle phrases.

■ *EXERCISE 12.9*

Identify present and past participle phrases functioning adjectivally in the following sentences, and decide whether each is restrictive or nonrestrictive.

1. Some owners find it difficult to exercise their Border Collies, a dog bred to herd sheep.
2. In order to burn off their collie's inbred love of running, many owners have started to throw Frisbees for their dogs to retrieve.
3. Promoted by local clubs, Frisbee retrieval has grown more prominent in recent years.
4. Frisbee Dogs, also called Disc Dogs, appear during the summer in parks and on beaches, as well as in TV advertising.
5. Thrilled by their dogs' skill at retrieving Frisbees, some owners decide to take them to the Southern Disc Dog Nationals in Atlanta.
6. Broken into two major divisions, Toss-and-Catch and Freestyle, the competition accepts all breeds.
7. In Freestyle, a timed and choreographed event, points are awarded to the dog and handler best blending their movements with each other and with music.
8. In both divisions, the dog is really chasing "sheep" flying eight feet in the air.

■ *EXERCISE 12.10*

Identify all the participle phrases in the sentences below and decide how they are functioning in the sentences of which they are part: as an adverbial modifier, an adjectival modifier, or a part of the main verb phrase. List the tests you have used to justify your answers. (Notice that some may be part of the main verb phrase.)

1. Located in the Valley of the Kings, King Tut's tomb was the best-preserved royal necropolis ever found in Egypt.
2. While hidden for 3,000 years, it had escaped tomb robbers, flooding, and vandals.
3. With the odds stacked against discovery, the area had been looted only twice before 1922.
4. Funerary objects brought to Thebes for safekeeping pointed to the existence of the tomb.

5. Other objects scattered throughout the area confirmed the belief that a tomb lay somewhere in the Valley of the Kings.

6. Financed by Lord Carnarvon, a team of men digging in the valley after World War I at first searched in vain.

7. Only in 1922 did they find the entrance to the tomb, still sealed with the royal stamp of Tutankhamen.

8. Finally excavated, the treasures of Tutankhamen were placed in the Cairo Museum.

Differences Between Past Participles and Adjectives

Many past participles have been used as noun modifiers for so long that they have become adjectives in English. Compare the past participle forms in (65). Both come from passive sentences.

(65) *Disturbed* by rumors, the committee decided to investigate the mail order company.

The paintings *offered* to the museum were auctioned off for 30 million dollars.

If you recall how we differentiated between adjectives and present participles (adjectives can be compared and can follow *very* in the adjective frame sentence), you will see that *disturbed* has become an adjective in English (*very disturbed; more disturbed than usual*), but *offered* has not (**very offered; *more offered than usual*). Contrast the results of the adjective test on each of the following. The same word can be an adjective in one construction but a past participle in another.

(66) *Informed* of her test results, Patrice decided to take the SATs again.

*More informed of her test results than others,...   (participle)

Informed on many subjects, Meredith is in demand as a speaker.

More informed on many subjects than some people,...   (adjective)

Even when, through usage, past participles have become peripheral adjectives, they often preserve their ability to appear with the modifiers and complements associated with them as main verbs. Thus, when used adjectivally, *disturbed* and *informed* can be qualified (*very disturbed/informed*) and compared (*more disturbed/informed*); both can keep the modifiers and complements associated with them as passive predicates.

■ *EXERCISE 12.11*_____

Decide whether the italicized words in each of the sentences below are participles or adjectives. Justify your answers by giving the adjective tests that each word passes or fails.

1. *Retired* seniors with enough money to live wherever they want often are choosing to live near their *beloved* alma maters.

2. Initially *attracted* by the intellectual life of the college community, they are also *pleased* with the opportunity to interact with younger people.

3. They are *interested* in taking classes, attending athletic events, and enjoying the cultural life *offered* by universities.

4. *Prompted* by research showing that *increased* mental activity helps ward off dementia, seniors are flocking to university towns across the country.

5. *College-affiliated* retirement communities, sometimes *underwritten* by the universities, have appeared in many college towns.

6. Colleges see *retired* seniors as a pool of *respected* mentors for younger students and, of course, as a pool of potential donors.

7. The intergenerational relationships *cultivated* between retirees and students enrich the university life for everyone.

8. In some cases, scholarships *donated* by seniors living nearby benefit *impoverished* students who otherwise could not afford college tuition.

Past participle phrases appear without the grammatical subjects that were included in the passive clauses from which they were derived. Consequently, readers and listeners must infer what the subjects were, basing their analysis on what occurs in the main clause. As is true of other nonfinite verbs, a past participle is interpreted as having the same subject as the main clause in which it is embedded. If it does not, the result is a **dangling participle:**

(67)   *Stored in the refrigerator,* we can keep oranges for six weeks.

The participle phrase in (67) is called *dangling* because it is not followed immediately by its intended subject, *oranges.* Separated from its underlying subject, it dangles. You can easily correct dangling participles by restoring the entire dependent clause from which the participle is derived:

(68)   When oranges are stored in the refrigerator, we can keep them for six weeks.

Alternatively, you can revise the main clause so that its subject is the same as that deleted from the participle phrase:

(69)   Stored in the refrigerator, oranges last for six weeks.

When we focus attention on dangling participles, it is easy to spot them and to recognize the unintended meanings they communicate.

(70)   Dangling: Trying hard to write my term paper, my baby sister kept disturbing me with her crying.

Revised: While I was trying hard to write my term paper, my baby sister kept disturbing me with her crying.

Dangling: When inflated with air, six people can ride on this raft.

Revised: When inflated with air, this raft can carry six people.

In speech, dangling participles usually go unnoticed. The speed of spoken language and the rich context of nonverbal cues that surrounds and supports the speaker's message can keep listeners from observing the unintended meanings that result from the dangling construction. However, in writing, dangling modifiers can be distracting. Because a number of structures can dangle, we discuss them in a separate section below.

WHAT'S THE USAGE?   *Dangling Modifiers*

A variety of considerations determine how a speaker will phrase any given message. On the one hand, the speaker's desire to be understood means that information should be provided fully. On the other hand, the hearer desires that the speaker not waste words. In fact, listeners may become impatient if a speaker is unnecessarily explicit. Each of the options available for eliminating redundancy costs something in clarity, requiring the hearer to supply information removed by the speaker. Compare the following sentences:

(71)   a. While John prepares Fred's dinner, John always has the television on.

b. While John prepares Fred's dinner, he always has the television on.

c. While he prepares Fred's dinner, John always has the television on.

d. While preparing Fred's dinner, John always has the television on.

(71a) is an example of a completely explicit utterance. However, because it repeats John's name twice, it is inefficient. Turning one of the mentions of *John* into a pronoun avoids that repetition, but doing so requires the hearer to think back through what has been said in order to identify who or what the pronoun refers to. In (71b), the reference is ambiguous; it could be either Fred or John who has the television on. In (71c), the pronoun precedes the noun it refers to. Although the sentence is not ambiguous, the hearer must wait for the second clause to have the referent of the pronoun made clear. In (71d), the subject of the verb *preparing* has been deleted and must be supplied by the hearer. English speakers can interpret clauses from which the subject has been removed because of the convention in English that says that the subject of the participle can be deleted only if it is the same as the subject of the main clause.

The following presents a possible problem of interpretation because it violates the convention governing subject deletion:

(72) While preparing Fred's dinner, John's television is always on.

The dangling participle phrase in (72), *while preparing Fred's dinner,* is one variety of *dangling modifier,* a nonfinite verb construction in which the underlying subject is not the same as the subject of the main clause. Even though dangling constructions may cause no confusion at all, there are two good reasons for trying to understand them. First, careful writers try to avoid writing sentences containing them because they place an unnecessary burden on the reader. Second, usage tests given to applicants to graduate schools, for teaching credentials, and for some jobs require the ability to recognize and correct them. Therefore, you would do well to learn the rule governing the deletion of the subject in nonfinite verb phrases and to master the ways of correcting danglers when they occur.

The subject of the nonfinite verb can be deleted only if it is the same as the subject of the verb in the main clause.

Subject Deletion Rule
Nonfinite Verb Phrases

Any phrase containing a nonfinite verb can dangle.

(73) Dangling infinitive

    a. Unable to start my car, my dog and I never arrived at the vet's office.

    b. To enjoy a safe day at the beach, suntan lotion is necessary.

Dangling present participle

    a. While mixing the martinis, the olives spilled all over the floor.

    b. Finishing their summaries of *Macbeth,* the teacher dismissed the students.

Dangling past participle

    a. While seated in the auditorium, music suddenly surrounded us.

    b. Fully loaded, I can't carry that suitcase.

Dangling modifiers like these can be eliminated by supplying the appropriate subject in either the embedded phrase or the main clause in accordance with the Subject Deletion Rule for Nonfinite Verb Phrases.

(74) For *dangling infinitives,* the best sentence usually results if you change the main clause:

a. Unable to start my car, I never arrived at the vet's office with my dog.

b. To enjoy a safe day at the beach, you should use suntan lotion.

For *dangling present participles,* you can usually change either the participle phrase or the main clause:
a. While Mr. Gordon was mixing the martinis, olives spilled all over the floor.
   While mixing the martinis, Mr. Gordon spilled olives all over the floor.
b. After the students finished their summaries of *Macbeth,* the teacher dismissed them.
   Finishing their summaries of *Macbeth,* the students were dismissed by the teacher.

For *dangling past participles,* you can usually change either the participle phrase or the main clause:
a. While we were seated in the auditorium, music suddenly surrounded us.
   While seated in the auditorium, we were suddenly surrounded by music.
b. When it is fully loaded, I can't carry that suitcase.
   ?Fully loaded, that suitcase cannot be carried by me.
   Better: Fully loaded, that suitcase is too heavy for me.

Correcting dangling modifiers is easy. Recognizing them is not. One reason is that they are extremely common in speech. We are used to hearing them, even on radio and television from speakers of standard English. As a consequence, they sound normal to us. They are less common in writing and in scripted broadcasts. If you wish to rid your writing of dangling modifiers, we suggest that you look carefully at modifying phrases containing nonfinite verbs, bearing in mind the rule for subject deletion given above. Figure 12.7 provides a Summary of the characteristics of dangling modifiers.

WHAT'S THE USAGE?   *Misplaced Modifiers*
Many nonfinite verb phrases can be moved about in sentences for stylistic effect. You may, however, unintentionally place a phrase in a position where it could modify more than one constituent of a sentence, creating a **misplaced modifier:**

(75)   They will rebuild the houses destroyed with stricter standards.

There are two verbs in this sentence, either of which could have the adverbial modifier *with stricter standards.* A first reading of the sentence may suggest that "stricter standards destroyed the houses." Logic forces the reader to reconsider and decide that they are going to *rebuild* with stricter standards. Correcting the sentence is not easy, because simply moving the phrase into position after the verb it modifies produces an awkward alternative:

(76)   ?They will rebuild with stricter standards the houses destroyed.

	SUMMARY
	Dangling Modifiers
Definition	Occurs when the deleted subject of an infinitive or a participle phrase is not the same as the subject of the main clause.
Examples	1. *To find shoes that fit properly, several stores may have to be visited.* 2. *While changing the oil in my Ferrari, two of my acrylic nails broke.* 3. *When completely folded, they put the laundry away.*
Correction	Either rearrange the main clause so that its subject is the same as the deleted subject, or supply the subject for the dangling verb form.
Examples	1. *To find shoes that fit properly, you may have to visit several stores.* 2. *While changing the oil in my Ferrari, I broke two of my acrylic nails.* *While I was changing the oil in my Ferrari, two of my acrylic nails broke.* 3. *When completely folded, the laundry was put away.* *When the laundry was completely folded, they put it away.*

Figure 12.7

It is for situations like this that we use some of the stylistic variants that we have looked at so far. Creating a passive and a relative clause solves the problems of reference in (75):

(77)   The houses that were destroyed will be rebuilt with stricter standards.

■ *USAGE EXERCISE 12.12*_____

Most of the sentences below were taken from television broadcasts. Identify and then correct the dangling and misplaced modifiers.

1. In addition to testing their blood pressure, cholesterol, and electrolytes, the horses are also weighed.

2. After struggling for over a year in pain and partial paralysis, the doctors told Roosevelt he would never walk again.

3. The government agreed to repave the roads with great reluctance.

4. Professor Baldwin hopes that, by teaching the causes of violence, her students will be better able to deal with violence.

5. Prior to being dismantled in the early part of this century, Southern California had a model transportation system.

6. Having traveled halfway across the Pacific, the green island of Hawaii was a welcome sight when Sharon Carpenter first glimpsed it.

7. Burned on the outside but juicy inside, Jeff Smith, the "Frugal Gourmet," gazed at the lamb roast on the grill.

■ *USAGE EXERCISE 12.13*

Rewrite the following headlines to remove the dangling or misplaced modifiers.

1. PEDESTRIAN HIT IMPROPERLY CROSSING SW 13TH NEAR UF
   (The Gainesville Sun, 14 December 2002)

2. AUTO TAG FEES TO AID ANIMALS SITTING IN BANK
   ([Fort Lauderdale, Florida] Sun-Sentinel, 7 December 1994)

3. GAME CANCELED AFTER KILE'S DEATH RESCHEDULED
   ([Charleston, Illinois] The Times Courier, 17 July 2002)

4. WARMEST WEEKEND AHEAD IN 6 MONTHS
   (Chicago Tribune, 14 March 2003)

5. FONDA SHARES STORY OF PHYSICAL STRUGGLES WITH MONTANA TEENS
   ([Tennessee] Johnson City Press, 15 February 2005)

6. BODY FOUND IN K.C. TIED TO 5 OTHERS
   ([Fox River Valley, Wisconsin] The Post Crescent, 5 September 2004)

7. BUSH BACKS WAR IN WEST VIRGINIA
   ([California] The Oakland Tribune, 5 June 2004)

8. DEMOCRAT PROMISES ALL AMERICANS ACCESS TO HEALTH CARE WHILE IN STATE
   ([Morgantown, West Virginia] Daily Athenaeum, 1 September 2004)

NOMINATIVE ABSOLUTES

Nominative absolutes are related to the nonfinite verb phrases studied in this chapter. They consist of a subject noun phrase followed by some part of the predicate: either a participle form of the main verb or a complement or modifier of the main verb. As we have seen, complements and modifiers may take almost any form. Consider the following italicized examples and the sentences from which they are derived. In each case, TENSE and a form of the verb *be*, either the auxiliary or the main verb, have been removed to create the absolute.

(78) *The year's work completed*, Santa lay down for a long rest.

The year's work was completed. (Type V passive sentence: *completed* = past participle)

His voice quavering, Charlie called, "Is anyone there?"
His voice was quavering. (Type I sentence: *quavering* = present participle)

Help nearby, the team climbed confidently to the top.
Help was nearby. (Type II sentence: *nearby* = adverb)

Jemika studied the painting, *her chin in her hand*.
Her chin was in her hand. (Type II sentence: *in her hand* = adverbial prepositional phrase)

The children waited in vain for the Great Pumpkin, *their faces forlorn*.
Their faces were forlorn. (Type III sentence: *forlorn* = predicate adjective)

His hands like ice, Morris was reluctant to greet the President.
His hands were like ice. (Type III sentence: *like ice* = predicate adjectival prepositional phrase)

Absentee ballots still to be counted, no winner has yet been announced.
Absentee ballots are still to be counted. (Passive infinitive of Type V sentence: *to be counted still* = infinitive phrase from *someone counts absentee ballots still*)

His computer a heap on the floor, Darren despaired of ever putting it back together again.
The computer was a heap on the floor. (Type IV sentence: *a heap on the floor* = predicate nominative)

Absolutes have traditionally been called nominative because the absolute construction begins with a noun phrase as its headword. Nevertheless, they function adverbially as sentence modifiers. Some, like (79a), explain reasons or conditions for the action described in the main clause; others, like (79b), describe the manner in which the action of the main clause is performed.

(79) a. *Her view blocked by the crowd*, Diane could not see the speaker.

b. *Her eyes shaded by her hand*, Diane watched the horses race around the track.

■ *EXERCISE 12.14*_____

> Absolutes occur primarily in writing, providing an economical way of highlighting some condition or detail of a scene. Identify the absolutes in the following sentences and try rewriting them as full clauses to see the effect the absolute has.

1. The bull charged and Romero waited for the charge, the muleta held low, sighting along the blade, his feet firm. (Ernest Hemingway, *The Sun Also Rises*)

2. When he looked around again the girl was standing up on the rushing board, her arms spread wide, her eyes lifted toward the moon. (D. H. Lawrence, "Winter Dreams")

3. I saw her across the room when I awoke, reading a newspaper, her glasses low across the bridge of her nose as she stared at the page intently. (Ralph Ellison, *Invisible Man*)

4. Alone in his rooms, Ned Beaumont walked the floor awhile, his face pinched, his eyes shiny. (Dashiell Hammett, *The Glass Key*)

5. It took a moment to register that these were the same human beings who had loitered around the pool back on the Island, looking silly in sunglasses and sunhats, noses smeared with suntan cream, and speaking a grossly inadequate Spanish to the maids. (Julia Alvarez, *How the Garcia Girls Lost Their Accents*)

SUMMARY

In Chapter 12, we continued our discussion of nonfinite verb phrases, concentrating on participles, which can function as adjectival and adverbial modifiers, and gerunds, which function only as nominals. Even though they are no longer main verbs in a clause, nonfinite verbs can keep the subjects, complements, objects, and modifiers that were part of the clauses in which they originated. If the rules governing the deletion of the subject of an infinitive or participle are violated, the result is a dangling modifier. Absolute constructions consist of a subject noun phrase followed by a partial predicate. Although traditionally called nominative, absolutes function adverbially as sentence modifiers.

REVIEW EXERCISES

Recognizing Participle and Gerund Phrases

Decide whether the italicized phrases in the sentences below are present participle, past participle, or gerund phrases.

1. *Never seen in Europe before Columbus arrived in the Indies,* rattlesnakes are indigenous to the Americas.
2. Seventy species, *ranging in size from 18 inches to 7 feet,* have been identified.
3. The rattle, *made of two to ten hollow interlocking segments,* is the snake's most distinctive feature.
4. When a rattlesnake vibrates its tail, separate segments *bouncing against one another* create a *rattling* sound.
5. Rattlers are generally peaceable, *striking only to capture rodents.*
6. *Unless cornered,* they flee when they are approached by humans.
7. Nevertheless, 8,000 people are bitten each year, sometimes as a result of *stepping on a rattlesnake.*
8. More than half of the bites result from *the human's trying to grab the snake.*

Form and Function of Phrases and Clauses

Identify the form and function of each italicized phrase or clause in the sentences below. Analyze sentences 1, 3, 5, and 7 with phrase markers and sentences 8, 10, 12, and 13 with Reed-Kellogg diagrams.

1. Two thieves struggled *to remove a Rembrandt from the silk-draped wall of the Gardner Museum.*
2. Two thieves struggled to remove a Rembrandt from the *silk-draped* wall of the Gardner Museum.
3. A high-pitched alarm, *warning guards that museum visitors were standing too close to pictures,* made the thieves stop abruptly.
4. A high-pitched alarm, warning guards *that museum visitors were standing too close to pictures,* made the thieves stop abruptly.
5. After *turning off the alarm,* the thieves completed what remains a record heist.
6. After turning off the alarm, the thieves completed *what remains a record heist.*

7. The paintings, *whose total value today would be $300 million,* disappeared with hardly a clue.

8. The alarm proved *to be the only deterrent to the thieves that night.*

9. The alarm proved to be the only deterrent *to the thieves that night.*

10. *When they investigated the theft,* police found that both guards were inexperienced.

11. When they investigated the theft, police found *that both guards were inexperienced.*

12. Another problem was *that one guard was stoned at the time of the theft.*

13. The paintings, *13 masterworks from the Gardner collection,* have never resurfaced.

Practical Applications: Modifiers

Find and correct any dangling or misplaced modifiers in the sentences below. Some of the sentences are correct as they stand.

1. Finding infinitive phrases easy to recognize, Gwen moved on to nominative absolutes.

2. Having spent too much time reviewing interrogative clauses, there was no time left for participle phrases.

3. A schedule is useful to be sure that everything is covered during your final review.

4. After studying grammar for a semester, some errors in your own writing should be clearer to you.

5. When marked and graded, the professor will return exams to the students.

Nonfinite Verb Phrases

Read the following paragraph and then select the best answer for each of the questions that follow it.

Researchers have found that dogs have from 10,000 to 100,000 times the sense of smell that humans have. Dogs can, for instance, detect bladder cancer by smelling urine samples. Some skin cancer survivors claim their dogs sniffed persistently at what turned out to be a cancerous mole, thus suggesting to their owners that something was wrong. Because dogs are sensitive to the smell of fear, some doctors use them to spot potential suicide victims.

1. What is *that dogs have from 10,000 to 100,000 times the sense of smell that humans have?*

a.	a nominal clause	d.	a main verb phrase
b.	an adjectival clause	e.	a participle phrase
c.	an adverbial clause		

2. What is *that humans have?*

a.	a nominal clause	d.	a main verb phrase
b.	an adjectival clause	e.	a participle phrase
c.	an adverbial clause		

3. What is *smelling urine samples?*

a.	a participle phrase	d.	a prepositional phrase
b.	a gerund phrase	e.	an adjective plus complements
c.	an infinitive phrase		

4. What is *their dogs sniffed persistently at what turned out to be a cancerous mole?*

a.	a nominal clause	d.	a main verb phrase
b.	an adjectival clause	e.	a participle phrase
c.	an adverbial clause		

5. What is *what turned out to be a cancerous mole?*

a.	a *that*-clause	d.	a prepositional phrase
b.	an interrogative clause	e.	a subordinate (adverbial) clause
c.	a relative clause		

6. What is *thus suggesting to their owners that something was wrong?*

a.	an adjectival participle phrase	d.	a prepositional phrase
b.	an adverbial participle phrase	e.	an infinitive phrase
c.	a nominal gerund phrase		

7. What is *that something was wrong?*

a.	a nominal clause	d.	a main verb phrase
b.	an adjectival clause	e.	a participle phrase
c.	an adverbial clause		

8. What is *to spot potential suicide victims?*

   a.   an adjectival participle phrase   d.   a prepositional phrase

   b.   an adverbial participle phrase   e.   an infinitive phrase

   c.   a nominal gerund phrase

KEY TERMS

dangling infinitive

dangling modifier

dangling participle

gerund

gerund phrase

misplaced modifier

nominative absolute

participle phrase

   adjectival participle phrase

   adverbial participle phrase

past participle

present participle

sentence modifier

Appendix
THE SOUNDS
OF AMERICAN ENGLISH

APPENDIX PREVIEW

In the Appendix we introduce a phonemic alphabet, in which each symbol represents a single sound and each sound is represented by just one symbol.

APPENDIX GOALS

At the end of this section, you should be able to

- Describe the human speech apparatus.

- Describe the production of English consonants and vowels and provide the *phonetic symbol* for each.

- Distinguish between *graphemes* and *phonemes*.

- Transcribe English words into the *International Phonetic Alphabet*.

- Read words written in the *International Phonetic Alphabet*.

- Understand *sound change*.

In order to represent accurately the differences among the dialects of speakers from different regions of the country or the different social groups discussed in Chapter 2, it is useful to have a way of referring to the *sounds* rather than the *spellings* of words. For some languages, the spelling system fits the standard pronunciation system well; it is possible to look at a word and, from the spelling, guess how it will be pronounced. English, unfortunately, is not one of those languages.

The solution to the problem of recording speech differences in writing is a **phonemic alphabet,** a system of writing in which there is one symbol for every significant sound of the language. A significant sound—one capable of signalling meaning—is called a **phoneme,** which means, roughly, "a systematic sound." For instance, the sound represented by the initial letter *s* in the word *sun* is a phoneme that helps to signal the meaning of that word. If we change it—for example, to the sound represented at the beginning of a word by the letter *r*—the entire meaning of the word is changed. *Run* is a completely different word from *sun,* a difference signaled by the change of a single phoneme.

Students are used to speaking of the letters of the alphabet, which linguists call **graphemes,** as though they referred directly to sounds, but many do not. Some letters are superfluous. We do not really need the letter *c,* for instance. It signals either the sound that can be spelled with the letter *s* (*cede, cesspool, century*) or the sound spelled by *k* (*cage, cost, picnic*). The letter *x* represents the two sounds spelled with *k* (or *ck*) and *s* (*tax* sounds the same as *tacks*). English spelling also uses **digraphs:** two graphemes or letters that represent only one sound, such as *wh, qu, ch, sh, th,* or the *ck* in *tacks.* To produce an alphabet containing just one symbol for each significant sound, linguists list the words of a language, searching for pairs (like *kit* and *bit*) that differ in only one sound. If the change in that sound produces a change in meaning, as it does in *kit* and *bit,* then the difference in sound must be signaling the difference in meaning.

CONSONANTS OF ENGLISH

Consider, for a moment, what letters would be needed to spell each of the following words if you used just one letter for each sound:

grim   rim   rib   kid   kit   wit   sit   slit   split

The alphabetic spelling system works to indicate pronunciation for all of these words, but linguists go one step farther in deciding whether each letter used in these words represents a sound that is *phonemic.* Each sound must not only be different from the others but it must also be used to signal a difference in *meaning* between two words. For example, *wit* and *kit* differ only in the initial sound; because the words refer to different things, that sound difference must be the signal we use to differentiate between them. If each word in the series above differs from an adjacent word both in meaning and by the presence or absence of a single sound, the sound that differentiates the two is said to be

phonemic, and the two words that are distinguished by the single sound are called a **minimal pair.**

Look for a moment at the pairs of words below. Each pair differs in only one sound, a sound that is used in our language to distinguish between them. They are, therefore, minimal pairs.

bit : pit	bit : big	hit : kit
bib : rib	fig : wig	sit : slit
rid : grid	rid : lid	rim : vim
sit : zit	tip : nip	zip : yip

As we have already seen, the minimal pair *bit* and *pit* proves that /b/ and /p/ are two different phonemes in English. *Bib* and *rib* show that /b/ and /r/ are different phonemes, and so forth. What we have done with the examples above is demonstrate that English uses sounds represented by the following letters to signal meaning: *b, d, f, g, h, k, l, m, n, p, r, s, t, v, w, y,* and *z.*

If you compare this list with our alphabet, you will find that we have included all of the consonants except four. It is not possible to demonstrate that *c, q,* or *x* represent phonemes in English. As we have seen, *c* and *x* are unnecessary because they represent sounds usually spelled with *k* and *s.* In a similar way, *q* is superfluous because it represents the two sounds that can be spelled with *k* and *w.* The only other letter not accounted for is *j.* The initial sound in words like *jig* cannot be represented by the simple letter *j* because we use a system based on the **International Phonetic Alphabet (IPA),** a set of common symbols used by linguists all over the world to represent sounds regardless of the language in which they occur. Symbols used in American linguistic phonemic notation differ slightly from the IPA. In the IPA, *j* represents a sound different from the one it signals in English spelling. So, in our phonemic alphabet, we must modify the letter to differentiate it from the IPA symbol. The device generally used is the placement of a wedge above the *j: ǰ.*

The phonemic alphabet we have created thus far is very much like our ordinary alphabet, but it is not yet complete. Certain sounds of English are not represented by the 17 consonants we have isolated above. Consider the following words:

wit : wish	wish : witch	wit : with
sin : sing	ether : either	composer : composure

These words present more complex problems. For a variety of historical reasons, single letters are not available to represent the final sounds in *wish, witch, with,* and *sing* or the medial (middle) consonant sounds in *ether, either,* or *composure.* Yet the pairs above demonstrate that each of the sounds is phonemic; it is capable of signaling a meaning difference in a pair of words differing only in that sound. Consequently, we need symbols to represent these sounds. The ones traditionally used for English are as follows:

š	s-wedge	for the final sound in *wish*
č	c-wedge	for the final sound in *witch*
ŋ	eng	for the final sound in *sing*
θ	theta	for the final sound in *wreath* and the middle sound in *ether*
ð	eth	for the middle sound of *either*
ž	z-wedge	for the middle sound in *composure*
ǰ	j-wedge	for the final sound of *wedge*

To indicate the difference between phonemic writing and alphabetic writing, it is customary to italicize words cited in their traditional spelling (*wish*) and to place between slashes (/ /) phonemes and phonemic representations of the pronunciations of words. The vowel used in most of the words above is written phonemically with a small capital ɪ, so that *wish* becomes /wɪš/.

Below, some of the examples we have used so far are written phonemically. Study them carefully to be sure that you understand what each symbol represents. Remember that there is no necessary correspondence between the number of phonemes and the number of letters used to spell words. In some cases, English uses a combination of letters to represent a single sound.

wit	/wɪt/	*sit*	/sɪt/
kid	/kɪd/	*slit*	/slɪt/
jig	/ǰɪg	*split*	/splɪt/
rid	/rɪd/	*grit*	/grɪt/
knit	/nɪt/	*with*	/wɪθ/
sing	/sɪŋ/	*witch*	/wɪč/

We have postponed writing *ether, either,* and *composure* phonemically because they require vowels that we have not yet discussed. We return to them in more detail later in this appendix.

Figure A.1 lists the symbols for the consonant phonemes of English. Those that are the same as the letters we ordinarily use are given first in their usual order. Those for which new symbols must be mastered are given at the end of the list.

<table>
<tr><td colspan="2" align="center">**SUMMARY**</td></tr>
<tr><td colspan="2" align="center">*Consonant Phonemes of English*</td></tr>
</table>

/b/	as pronounced at the beginning of *bit*
/d/	as pronounced at the beginning of *did*
/f/	as pronounced at the beginning of *fit*
/g/	as pronounced at the beginning of *give*
/h/	as pronounced at the beginning of *hit*
/k/	as pronounced at the beginning of *kit*
/l/	as pronounced at the beginning of *lit*
/m/	as pronounced at the beginning of *mitt*
/n/	as pronounced at the beginning of *knit*
/p/	as pronounced at the beginning of *pit*
/r/	as pronounced at the beginning of *rim*
/s/	as pronounced at the beginning of *sin*
/t/	as pronounced at the beginning of *tin*
/v/	as pronounced at the beginning of *vim*
/w/	as pronounced at the beginning of *wig*
/y/	as pronounced at the beginning of *yen*
/z/	as pronounced at the beginning of *zit*
/š/	as pronounced in the middle of *assure*
/ž/	as pronounced in the middle of *azure*
/θ/	as pronounced at the beginning of *thin*
/ð/	as pronounced in the beginning of *then*
/č/	as pronounced at the beginning of *chin*
/ǰ/	as pronounced at the beginning of *gin*
/ŋ/	as pronounced at the end of *sing*

Figure A.1

▨ EXERCISE A.1

Write the following words phonemically, using /ɪ/ and /o/ for the vowels called for. Notice that, in the spelling representations, some letters appear that are not pronounced.

EXAMPLES

pit   ____/pɪt/____

coach   ____/koč/____

1. coal	_____	9. minnow	_____
2. ditch	_____	10. fish	_____
3. width	_____	11. yolk	_____
4. grope	_____	12. host	_____
5. joke	_____	13. both	_____
6. win	_____	14. thick	_____
7. wing	_____	15. vote	_____
8. wink	_____	16. loathing	_____

ALLOPHONES

As we have seen, it is possible to write the consonants of English phonemically by adding seven symbols to our customary alphabet representations. We need additional symbols for vowels as well. There are only five letters for vowels in the alphabet, but our system uses 14 or 15 vowel sounds (depending on the speaker) and sound combinations to signal meaning.

The phoneme /ɪ/, used in the exercise above, is suggested as the appropriate symbol for the vowel in very different-sounding words: *witch, wish, win,* and *wing.* Your ear may tell you that the sound represented by /ɪ/ changes in each word as the consonant following it changes. Should that difference be reflected by the use of different symbols? Linguists have two choices here. They can either increase the number of symbols to increase the precision of the alphabet, or they can use the same symbol for different sounds, as long as no meaning change corresponds to the change in sound. As we have pointed out in describing consonants, linguists have chosen the latter course. The International Phonetic Alphabet provides methods of representing *all* of the variant sounds heard in any language, but so many symbols are involved and so many sound differences must be pinpointed that it becomes an inefficient way of recording language for general purposes.

While a **phonetic alphabet** may attempt to symbolize all of the detectable differences among sounds, a *phonemic* alphabet ignores differences that are not used to convey meaning differences. As we have seen, the differences between the initial consonants of *bit, pit, sit,* and *kit* correspond to differences in meaning between these four words—that is, by changing the initial consonant, we change the meaning of the word. Therefore, /b/, /p/, /s/, and /k/ are identified as separate phonemes for English. However, we cannot find a minimal pair differentiated by the slightly different /ɪ/ sounds above.

The ability to change meaning by changing a sound is crucial to phoneme identification. If meaning is *not* changed by a difference in sound, then that difference is not phonemic. To demonstrate for yourself such a nonphonemic difference in sound, try this experiment:

1. Cut or tear a narrow strip of scrap paper (not from the pages of this textbook!) about 1/2 inch by about 6 inches. Hold the strip of paper between two fingers so that the loose end hangs close to your lips.

2. Repeat several times the word *spin.* Does the paper move? If you're holding the paper close enough to your lips, you should see the paper move only slightly after the /p/ sound, if at all.

3. Keeping the paper in the same place, pronounce several times the word *pin.* What difference do you observe in the way the paper moves?

You should see the strip of paper move away from your lips after the /p/ of *pin* distinctly more than you did after the /p/ of *spin* because these two versions of /p/ are quite different. The /p/ of *pin* is called an *aspirated* /p/, meaning that it is accompanied by the puff of air that caused your strip of paper to move. The /p/ in *spin* is not accompanied by such an explosive puff of air.

Although in some languages this distinct difference between the two /p/ sounds is phonemic, in English, it is not. The difference never serves to distinguish meaning. In fact, whenever /p/ occurs in initial position in a word, it is accompanied by the puff of air; in other positions, the puff of air is minimal or absent. The aspirated and unaspirated /p/'s differ phonetically; there is a genuine physical difference between them. However, that difference is always predictable, tied to the differences in phonological environments. The sounds /p/, /t/, and /k/ are aspirated when they appear at the beginnings of syllables but not when they occur after an /s/. Because the phonetic difference between the two pronunciations of /p/ is completely predictable and never signals a meaning difference, we can represent both sounds with the same phonemic symbol. When a phoneme has variant pronunciations depending on its position in a word, the variants are called **allophones.**

To go back to our vowel examples, if our language had two words with the sequence *w sh,* one containing the vowel of *witch* and one the vowel of *wish,* and if there were a consistent difference of meaning associated with the use of the different vowels, then we would say that the difference between the two vowels is phonemic, and we would have to use a different symbol for each, even in *wish* and *witch*. However, it is impossible to find any pair of words in English where the change of /ɪ/ before the /š/ sound does not happen automatically, without a change of meaning. The change of consonants is sufficient to differentiate the minimal pair, and because the vowel difference results from the pronunciation of adjacent consonant sounds, the difference is completely predictable. Because the differences in vowel quality do not signal any meaning difference, we can use the same vowel symbol for both words, asserting that, even though the two vowel sounds differ slightly *phonetically,* they function in our language as members of the same *phoneme,* /ɪ/. Phonemic transcriptions that ignore allophonic differences, using a single symbol to represent all variants of a phoneme, are said to be *broad transcriptions.*

Slight **phonetic** differences between sounds become crucial in identifying vowel phonemes because we can hear the alteration of vowels caused by surrounding consonants much more clearly than we can hear the alteration of consonants brought about by the sounds before or after them. For example, if you say the words *ten* and *tenth,* you will notice that the /n/ has two quite different pronunciations. However, we are less aware of the phonetic differences between allophones of the same consonant phoneme and thus less troubled by them than we are by the phonetic differences among allophones of vowel phonemes.

In setting up a phonemic alphabet, linguists seek the most efficient method of representing the significant sounds of a language. The phonemic alphabet provides symbols for all of the phonemes of the language (the sounds used to convey meaning), but it does not represent every allophone of those phonemes (variants of phonemes that occur consistently in the language but are not used to change the meaning of words).

■ VOWELS OF ENGLISH ■

Consonants and vowels are considered different classes of sounds because they are produced differently. In creating **consonants,** we impede the flow of air from the lungs by bringing one part of the vocal tract (the parts of our body used in creating speech) into close proximity with another. For some consonants, we stop the flow of air by completely closing off the vocal tract at some point. For example, to pronounce the phoneme /b/, we momentarily cut off the flow of air by pressing the lips together. For others, we bring portions of the vocal tract close together and release them before they stop the sound, sometimes with vibration or friction. The phoneme /f/, for instance, involves the sound produced by the friction of air rushing through a narrow slit formed between the lower lip and the upper front teeth. Or we may use the presence or absence of voice to contrast consonants.

To feel the difference between **voiced** and **voiceless** sounds for yourself, place your fingers on your Adam's apple and produce first the sound of *f,* /f/. Sustain that sound for a few seconds. Now quickly switch to the sound of *v,*

SUMMARY						
Vowel Tongue Positions						
	Front		*Central*		*Back*	
High	beat	/i/			boot	/u/
	bit	/ɪ/			book	/u/
Mid	bait	/e/	but /ə/		boat	/o/
	bet	/ɛ/			bought	/ɔ/
Low	bat	/æ/			pot	/a/

Figure A.2

/v/. You should be able to feel very clearly the vibration that accompanies the sound of /v/, which is voiced, in contrast to the absence of such vibration with /f/, which is voiceless. *Voicing* is the result of moving air causing the vocal folds (or vocal cords) to vibrate within the larynx behind the cartilage of the Adam's apple. This vibration, your voice, is what you feel and hear when you sustain the sound of /v/.

The sound of the phoneme /v/ is a combination of voicing and friction created when the lower lip touches the upper teeth. Unlike /v/ and the other consonants, **vowels** do not involve blockage of the vocal tract or friction produced by its narrowing. In creating vowel sounds, we let the air flow out unimpeded while only the vocal folds vibrate, creating the kind of sound you hear when you say "ah." As a result, *all English vowels are voiced,* except when they are whispered.

To differentiate vowels, we change the shape of the mouth (a resonating chamber for speech) by rounding and unrounding our lips and by moving our tongue up and down or forward and back. Thus, vowels are said to be high, mid, or low (made with the highest point of the tongue high, in the middle, or low in the mouth) and front, central, or back (made with the tongue thrust forward, kept neutral, or pulled back). Try pronouncing slowly *beet* and *bat,* one after the other, and notice how the jaw drops when you say *bat*. The tongue, of course, also drops. Similarly, pronounce *beet* and *boot,* and see if you can feel the tongue pull forward and toward the upper teeth when you say *beet* and toward the back of the mouth when you say *boot*. These illustrate the difference between front and back vowels. As you pronounce the vowels from front to back, from *bait* to *but* to *boat,* you should be able to feel your lips rounding and your tongue pulling back. Finally, pronounce the words listed in Figure A.2 so that you can feel the contrasting tongue and lip positions associated with each vowel as you also become familiar with the symbols that represent the vowel phonemes.

English makes frequent use of an unstressed vowel in the second syllable of words like *horses, butter, bottle,* and *shorten.* This mid, central vowel is such an important feature of English that many linguists give it a separate symbol (/ə/) called **schwa,** even though no clear minimal pair justifies its phonemic status. Other linguists treat it as an allophone of the sound in *but,* as we do, and use the same symbol for the vowels in the two syllables of *mother* /məðər/. Beginning students are not entirely content with either arrangement. If the same symbol is used, the difference in pronunciation bothers them. The differences represented by the schwa are considerable, even in unaccented final syllables. (Compare the vowel in the last syllable of *horses* and of *bottle.*) If different symbols are used, students must learn a more complicated phonemic alphabet. As our wish in this discussion is to simplify the phonemic alphabet as much as possible, we use a single symbol for both the stressed and the unstressed forms of the vowel made in the middle of the mouth and occurring twice in *oven* /əvən/ and in *crumble* /krəmbəl/.

■ *EXERCISE A.2*_____

Observing your own pronunciation, write the following words phonemically to become more familiar with the vowel distinctions we have discussed so far. If you put the words into the context of sentences, you are more likely to pronounce them naturally (as you ordinarily do in informal speech) than you are if you try to transcribe them in isolation.

Because different people pronounce words differently, you may occasionally disagree with others on the pronunciation of a word.

1. pin	_____	9. creep	_____
2. lamp	_____	10. rustle	_____
3. wrote	_____	11. cough	_____
4. rot	_____	12. steeper	_____
5. steps	_____	13. could	_____
6. look	_____	14. fasten	_____
7. Luke	_____	15. preach	_____
8. mate	_____		

What we need to represent the sounds in the words given above, then, are 11 vowel symbols. In addition to these 11, English has, as well, three **diphthongs** (double vowel sounds), produced by beginning with the tongue placed for one vowel and ending with it placed for another. One of these diphthongs occurs in the word *line*. This vowel begins with the tongue in position for pronouncing /a/ and ends with it in position for /i/. We represent this diphthong by the symbol /ai/, as in /lain/. In contrast, the vowel of *loin* begins with the tongue in position for the open o of *bought*, represented by the symbol /ɔ/, before moving toward the position for /i/. This diphthong is symbolized with /ɔi/, as in /lɔin/. The third diphthong is the vowel sound in *pout*, for which the tongue starts out in position for /a/ and ends near the position for /u/. It is represented by /au/, as in /paut/.

Recall that we postponed writing *ether, either,* and *composure* phonemically because they require vowels that we had not yet discussed. We are now prepared to review the sounds in those words.

ether	/iθər/
either	/iðər/
composure	/kəmpožər/

The words below, written phonemically, illustrate the vowels used in words more complex than those we have looked at so far. Examine them, and be sure you understand the relationship between the sound and symbol in each case. Notice the differences between spelling and phonemic representation. Some letters represent no sound at all; some sounds have no apparent representation in the spelling (for example, there is a /y/ in *cue*); and some represent sounds not usually attributed to them (there is no /g/ sound in *wringer*). These transcriptions represent the sounds of rapid, naturally occurring speech. After you understand them, try the exercises that follow.

plough	: /p̌lau/	*cheeses*	: /čizəz/	*decorate*	: /dɛkəret/
rough	: /rəf/	*cue*	: /kyu/	*wringer*	: /rɪŋər/
through	: /θru/	*measure*	: /mɛžər/	*regional*	: /riǰənəl/
though	: /ðo/	*quiet*	: /kwaiət/	*school*	: /skul/
hiccough	: /hɪkəp/	*gratitude*	: /grætətud/	*I*	: /ai/

Figure A.3 lists each of the English vowel sounds and diphthongs, with an example given for each.

SUMMARY
Vowel Phonemes of English
Simple Vowels
/i/ the vowel sound in *beet* (written /bit/) /ɪ/ the vowel sound in *bit* (written /bɪt/) /e/ the vowel sound in *bait* (written /bet/) /ɛ/ the vowel sound in *bet* (written /bɛt/) /æ/ the vowel sound in *bat* (written /bæt/) /u/ the vowel sound in *boot* (written /but/) /ʊ/ the vowel sound in *put* (written /pʊt/) /o/ the vowel sound in *boat* (written /bot/) /ɔ/ the vowel sound in *bought* (written /bɔt/) /a/ the vowel sound in *cot* (written /kat/) /ə/ the vowel sounds in *butter* (written /bətər/)
Diphthongs
/ai/ the vowel sounds in *bite* (written /bait/) /ɔi/ the vowel sounds in *void* (written /vɔid/) /au/ the vowel sounds in *bout* (written /baut/)

Figure A.3

▨ *EXERCISE A.3*

Write each of the following words phonemically, paying special attention to those words containing diphthongs.

1. talk   _____   6. pencil   _____

2. pouch   _____   7. pine   _____

3. relax   _____   8. crowding _____

4. coy   _____   9. lightning _____

5. rider   _____   10. foil   _____

■ *EXERCISE A.4*

Write phonemically the sounds represented by the italicized letters in each of the following pairs of words.

1. lea*sh*, lie*ge*   _____ _____
2. ri*dge*, ri*ch*   _____ _____
3. mu*sh*, mu*ch*   _____ _____
4. sou*gh*t, sot   _____ _____
5. *ough*t, *ou*t   _____ _____
6. f*u*ll, f*oo*l   _____ _____
7. sh*i*ne, sh*ee*n   _____ _____
8. la*the*, pa*th*   _____ _____

9. p*u*t, p*u*tt   _____ _____
10. si*nn*er, si*nk*er   _____ _____
11. le*ss*er, le*ch*er   _____ _____
12. ri*ng*er, li*ng*er   _____ _____
13. pre*ss*ure, plea*s*ure   _____ _____
14. rou*ge*, rou*gh*   _____ _____
15. ba*tch*es, ba*dg*es   _____ _____

■ *EXERCISE A.5*

Write each of the following words phonemically. Remember that in the spelling representations, some letters appear that are not pronounced. Since different people pronounce words differently, you may occasionally disagree with others on the pronunciation of a word. In your own pronunciation, you may or may not find a difference between the last two words. When you compare your transcriptions, notice especially the places where we have used the schwa.

1. cute   _____
2. funnel   _____
3. prevent   _____
4. piano   _____
5. fireman   _____
6. gender   _____
7. ashes   _____
8. glazed   _____
9. challenge   _____
10. taxes   _____

11. rotate   _____
12. goodness   _____
13. bundle   _____
14. thigh   _____
15. leisure   _____
16. outrage   _____
17. joyous   _____
18. thy   _____
19. cot   _____
20. caught   _____

AMERICAN PRONUNCIATION

For some speakers of American English, *cot* and *caught* contain two different phonemes, and the change of sound from /a/ to /ɔ/ signals the difference in meaning between the two words. For others, the words are identical and can both be transcribed as /kat/. For such speakers, *cot* and *caught* are **homophones** (words having the same sound but different meanings) for which the context must supply the difference in meaning.

How can such a difference exist among speakers of a language? Because the distinction between these two sounds is rarely if ever the only available clue to meaning. Words containing /ɔ/ differ sufficiently in possible contexts from words containing /a/ so that it is very difficult to construct the kind of ambiguity that might be possible for pairs of sentences like the following, in which the difference between the two vowel phonemes communicates a significant difference in meaning.

(1)	a. He kissed the baby.	/kɪst/
	b. He cussed the baby.	/kəst/
(2)	a. She flagged the runner.	/flægd/
	b. She flogged the runner.	/flagd/

The difference between *pin* and *pen* (or *since* and *sense*) is not maintained in the speech of many Americans, especially among those living in the South, but Southern speakers maintain the distinction in others words (like *pit* and *pet*). Where American speakers maintain the differences between similar phonemes, such as between /ɪ/ and /ə/ and between /æ/ and /a/, they may be consciously or unconsciously motivated by the need to base meaning distinctions on those differences in sound. Where some Americans' pronunciation has merged what for other speakers are separate phonemes, such as /ɪ/ and /ɛ/ or /a/ and /ɔ/, making homophones of words like *pin* and *pen* or *cot* and *caught*, context must make clear which meaning is intended.

▓ EXERCISE A.6

Write phonemically each of the words that are listed below. Write each as you actually say it, not as you think it should be said, and compare your answers with others in your classroom. You may be surprised at how much variety there is among speakers of American English. You may, in fact, discover that you have more than one pronunciation of some of these. (Don't forget to use the schwa for unaccented syllables.)

1. wash _____
2. salmon _____
3. forehead _____
4. orange _____
5. length _____
6. almond _____
7. falcon _____
8. arctic _____
9. data _____
10. route _____

11. root _____
12. economic _____
13. interesting _____
14. humor _____
15. tomato _____
16. creek _____
17. rodeo _____
18. Missouri _____
19. newspaper_____
20. often _____

PRONUNCIATION AND SPELLING

Some languages in the world are written with alphabets that are almost phonemic—that is, each sound is represented by a different, single symbol. Learning to spell in such languages is much easier than is learning to spell in English. The fit between our alphabet and our sound system is notoriously bad. Why is this so?

For one thing, the sound system changed after we adopted the alphabet. If you have studied a European language, you have learned pronunciations for many of the letters of the alphabet that differ from our own. These are the pronunciations that at one time prevailed in English as well. For example, the first letter of the alphabets used in Europe is pronounced /a/ (as in *got*); in English, we say /e/ (as in *gate*); Europeans pronounce the second letter, *b*, as /be/; we pronounce it /bi/. The English pronunciation is the result of the Great Vowel Shift, a change in English pronunciation that occurred after our spelling system was established.

Another reason for the lack of fit between our pronunciation and our spelling system is that some sounds have disappeared from words, although the spelling has remained unchanged; *gnat, comb,* and *listen,* for example, were once pronounced with a sound for each letter. The same process of change is still going on; some sounds are in the process of disappearing right now. For many speakers of American English, words like *where, when,* and *whale* are pronounced the same as *ware, wen,* and *wail.* For others, they begin with an /h/: /hwɛr/, /hwɛn/, /hwɛl/. If you are in the second group, note that, although the spelling places the *w* first, you don't pronounce these words that way. According to the sound patterns of English, it is not possible to pronounce an initial /w/ followed by an /h/ because /h/ occurs only at the beginning of syllables.

Not only are sounds disappearing, but in some words, sounds that occur regularly in pronunciation are not represented in the spelling. *Cute* and *use,* for example, include the phoneme /y/—/kyut /, /yuz/—with no corresponding letter in the spelling.

Besides the problems caused by our fixed spelling system's not reflecting changes in pronunciation, another difficulty arises because we have adopted spellings along with vocabulary borrowed from all over the world. Look at the following examples, in which the same digraph represents three different sounds:

ch = /č/   *chill* (Native Germanic)
ch = /k/   *charisma* (Greek)
ch = /š/   *chauffeur* (French)

Such differences occur because the borrowed words entered English at different periods and from different languages. The new words were unaffected by the sound change that altered the pronunciation of older English words with the same spelling.

The opposite problem exists as well: One sound can be represented by many spellings because of different patterns of change or because of borrowing from languages with different spelling conventions. Consider a few of the alternative spellings of the /i/sound:

/i/ spelled *e*   *meter* (French)
/i/ spelled *ee*   *see* (Native Germanic)
/i/ spelled *ea*   *seat* (Native Germanic)
/i/ spelled *ei*   *ceiling* (Old French)
/i/ spelled *e_e*   *cede* (French)

Arguments in favor of spelling reform reappear regularly in the American press. One well-known advocate of such reform, George Bernard Shaw (1856–1950), insisted that, according to our spelling system, it would be possible for *fish* to be spelled *ghoti,* by using the *gh* at the end of the word *rough* to represent *f,* the *o* in *women* for /ɪ/, and the *ti* in words like *nation* for /š/. Shaw left a part of his fortune in a fund to be awarded to the person(s) devising the best phonemic alphabet for English, and although the prize was awarded, the alphabet that was proposed has not been adopted for general use.

Why not? First of all, switching to a new alphabet would, in one or two generations, make all of our existing literature impossible to read unless students learned both the new and the old writing systems. Great sums of money would be required to translate standard works into the new system. A certain amount of chaos would inevitably follow. In the second place, we would have to decide whose pronunciation to use as the basis of our spelling system. As you have seen in the exercises, not everyone pronounces words the same way. Should the first sound in *economics* be /i/ or /ɛ/? Should the vowel sound in *route* be /u/ or /au/? And what about those speakers who have two pronunciations: /u/ in *Route 66* and /au/ in *paper route?*

Most important, however, the discussion ignores the fact that there is a great deal of regularity to our spelling system, regularity that becomes even clearer if we know something of the language from which a word has been borrowed. In fact, students of the language lament that we would lose historical information evident in the spelling system we use. If, for example, a word begins with a /k/ sound spelled *ch,* we know that it comes from Greek. The system also provides a reminder of relationships between words. Although no /g/ is pronounced in *malign* and the second vowel sound is a diphthong /ai/, the spelling reminds us of its semantic tie to *malignant.* Such a transparent connection between pairs of related words contributes to the efficiency of our learning English vocabulary, even as it complicates our learning to spell. The more students know about the history of English, the more English spelling makes sense to them.

PHONICS AND PHONEMIC AWARENESS

The knowledge that spoken language is made up of several levels of discrete (separate) units is a crucial factor in children's learning to read. Indeed, children who do not develop **phonological awareness,** the ability to perceive the segmental nature sounds, do not learn to read well at all. **Phonemic awareness,** the ability to recognize the discrete sounds of spoken language (the phonemes) and to connect those sounds to letters and letter combinations (graphemes), is also essential. And, finally, research suggests that it is critical for children to be aware of syllables in order to become good readers.

Phonemic awareness is the core of **phonics,** a reading instructional strategy used both with native and second-language learners. Phonics not only addresses the complex rules of English spelling but emphasizes the relationship between the sounds of speech and the letters of the alphabet. Phonics is thus used to teach beginning readers how words can be divided into smaller units, called *syllables,* and how individual sounds are combined into words, so that *b-a-t* would be sounded out as the word *bat.* In recent years, phonemic awareness has been introduced into reading strategies, along with instruction in rules for converting sounds into spelling. The system of writing used in teaching phonics is different from the symbols we are using here, but the principle is the same: One letter is equivalent to one sound. The level of a learner's phonemic awareness can predict success or failure in learning to read.

It is hoped that those who acquire phonemic awareness become more familiar with the general notion that spoken words are made up of sound and, more specifically, that the basic building blocks of spoken words are the phonemes, not the letters.

SUMMARY

In order to represent the morphemes and words of English as they are pronounced, linguists use a system of phonemic symbols, one symbol for each distinctive sound. By learning to use a simple phonemic alphabet, you gain skills necessary for understanding important aspects of the system of English grammar.

REVIEW EXERCISES

Reading Phonemic Transcriptions

The following words are written in phonemic transcription. Write each in normal English spelling.

1. /slauč/ _____
2. /pɪŋk/ _____
3. /pul/ _____
4. /θɪmbəlz/ _____
5. /šekɪŋ/ _____
6. /səraundəd/ _____
7. /pɪčt/ _____
8. /nɔtəkəl/ _____
9. /fənɛtɪks/ _____
10. /ɛksplənešən/ _____

11. /waiz/ _____
12. /ɛksplen/ _____
13. /bičəz/ _____
14. /kaŋgrəs/ _____
15. /saikaləǰi/ *Psychology*
16. /nɔizəz/ _____
17. /skwikt/ *squeaked*
18. /səsid/ *succeed*
19. /faundešən/ *founda*
20. /tɛrəfaiŋ/ *terrifying*

KEY TERMS

allophone
consonant
digraph
diphthong
grapheme
homophone
International Phonetic Alphabet (IPA)
minimal pair
morpheme
phoneme

phonemic
phonemic alphabet
phonemic awareness
phonetic
phonetic alphabet
phonics
phonological awareness
schwa
voiced versus voiceless sounds
vowel

Glossary

Active voice—The form of the verb used when the actor or agent is the subject, and the goal or recipient is the direct object (*Our team won the game*). A verb phrase in the active voice does not contain BE + {-en}, the past participle form of the verb. (See **Passive voice.**)

Actor—The logical subject of a verb; the person or other animate being that performs the action of the verb (*Arle sings*). (See **Agent.**)

Adjectival—A word or phrase that functions as an adjective would in a predicate adjective or a noun-modifying role (*stone wall*). (See **Adjective phrase.**)

Adjectival clause—Usually a relative clause (*the book that I read*), but sometimes a subordinate clause (*the week after you left*).

Adjective—A form-class word; usually modifies a noun; can be compared (with *-er* or *more*) and can follow *very* (*taller, very tall*).

Adjective phrase—As a sentence constituent, an adjective (*feels lonely*) or any group of words that can substitute for an adjective (*feels like a motherless child*).

Adverb—A form-class word; frequently can move in its sentence; usually modifies verbs, adjectives, adverbs, or the whole sentence (*Time passed quickly*).

Adverb phrase—As a sentence constituent, an adverb (*moves slowly*) or any group of words that can substitute for an adverb (*moves like a snail*).

Adverbial—A word or phrase that functions as an adverb would, modifying verbs, adjectives, adverbs, or the whole sentence (*sharp as a tack; ran without stopping for breath*).

Adverbial clause—Usually a clause introduced by a subordinating conjunction (*He arrived after you left*).

Affix—A morpheme added to the beginning (prefix) or ending (suffix) of a word. (See **Prefix, Suffix.**)

African-American Vernacular English (AAVE)—Any of the nonstandard varieties of English spoken chiefly by African Americans and known colloquially as **Black English, Black English Vernacular,** or **Ebonics.** The latter is a blend of *ebony* "black" + *phonics* "the science of spoken sounds."

Agent—The initiator of an action named in a verb. The agent's relationship with the verb remains constant, whether the sentence is active (*Twyla threw the ball*) or passive (*The ball was thrown by Twyla*). (See **Actor.**)

Allomorph—A variant of a single morpheme (e.g., the past participle morpheme occurs in a variety of forms, including *have eaten* and *have walked*).

Allophone—The variant of a single phoneme (e.g., the [l] in *light* and *milk* are pronounced at different positions in the mouth, but are heard as being the same phoneme /l/).

Amelioration—The process by which a word loses its negative connotations and acquires positive ones. In Old English, *pretty* meant "cunning, sly." In Middle English, *nice* meant "foolish, stupid, wanton."

Antecedent—The noun or noun phrase that a pronoun refers to or stands for. *My old hat* is the antecedent of *it* in *There's my old hat; I thought it was lost.*

Appositive—A noun or noun phrase that immediately follows and renames another noun or noun phrase (*Mary Smith, a student at USC, spent the summer studying in Dijon*).

Aspect—The verbal category that is expressed in English by the progressive tense to indicate the duration (*he is/was walking*) and by the perfect tense to indicate the completion (*he has/had walked*) of an action.

Attributive adjective—An adjective that precedes and modifies a noun (*the small boy*). (See **Predicate adjective.**)

Auxiliary verb—A structure-class word used with a main verb to indicate tense, aspect, and mood (*have eaten, is eating, might eat*) and to form negatives (*didn't eat*) or questions (*Did you eat?*).

Base—The morpheme that contains the basic meaning of a word (also called a *root* or *stem*). A derivational affix can be attached to the base to create new words (*rebuild, government*); an inflectional morpheme can be attached to supply grammatical information (*rebuilding, governments*).

Beneficiary—The person who benefits from the action of a verb. (See **Recipient.**)

Binary—A feature of structural grammatical analysis that divides sentences and constituents into two parts (**S = NP + VP or NP = Det. + N,** etc.).

Black English Vernacular—(See African-American Vernacular English.)

Bound morpheme—A morpheme that cannot stand alone as a word (*{-ing}*).

Branch—A descending line in a phrase structure tree; the offshoot of a node.

Cardinal numbers—The numbers used for counting (*one, two, three*).

Case—The grammatical relationship of nouns and pronouns to other words in a sentence; sometimes signaled by inflections (e.g., the possessive forms of nouns and pronouns; the subject and object case forms of pronouns).

Casual speech—The informal use of language, as among friends. (See **Styles.**)

Clause—A sequence of words containing a subject and predicate; may be dependent or independent.

Comma splice—The improper use of a comma to join two independent clauses; also called **Comma fault.**

Comment—That part of the sentence that provides information about the topic or subject of the sentence. The predicate of a sentence. (See **Topic.**)

Common noun—A noun that names nonunique persons, places, or things (*tree, cat, car*).

Communicative competence—The ability to use a language appropriately in a variety of social and cultural circumstances.

Comparative—Degree expressed for adjectives and adverbs by using *more* or {-er}: (*more beautiful; happier*).

Complement—A word or phrase that completes the predicate, such as direct and indirect objects, subject complements, object complements (*Bill grew impatient; Bill grew roses*).

Complementizer *that*—*That* used to introduce a nominal clause (*I know that you didn't believe his story*).

Complex sentence—A sentence containing one independent clause and at least one dependent clause (*He insulted me* [ind. clause] *before he left the room* [dep. clause]).

Compound sentence—A sentence containing two or more independent clauses (*He insulted me* [ind. clause] *and then he left the room* [ind. clause]).

Compound-complex sentence—A sentence containing two or more independent clauses and at least one dependent clause (*He insulted me* [ind. clause] *before he left the room* [dep. clause], *and then he slammed the door* [ind. clause]).

Compounding—The creation of a word by combining two words (*sidewalk*).

Conditional—The verb form used to express uncertainty about an action. Conditionals are used to talk about possible or imaginary situations. In English, the conditional is generally indicated by a modal auxiliary verb (*They would if they could*).

Conjugation—The complete set of inflections of a verb.

Conjunction—A structure-class word that connects two or more words, phrases, or sentences. See **coordinating** or **subordinating conjunction** or **conjunctive adverb.**

Conjunctive adverb—An adverbial structureclass word that connects two independent clauses (e.g., *therefore, nevertheless*).

Connotation—The negative or positive associations implied by a word. *Sweat* has negative connotations; *perspire* has more neutral ones.

Consonant—A speech sound produced by obstructing the passage of air, either fully [p], or partially [f].

Constituent—One of the phrases that constitute (make up) the structure of a sentence (noun phrase, main verb phrase, adjective phrase, and adverb phrase); more generally, any unit that functions directly as part of a larger unit is a constituent of the larger unit (the noun *globe* in *the entire globe*).

Consultative style—The kind of language used in situations where adults interact with superiors or with people they do not know.

Content word—A form-class word (noun, verb, adjective, adverb).

Coordinating conjunction—A structure-class word that connects two words, phrases, or clauses that are considered equal (e.g., *and, or, nor*).

Copular verb—A verb like *be* used to link a subject with a predicate complement that either renames or in some way modifies the subject. The verb indicates either that the subject and predicate nominative are the same (*New York is a large city*), or that the subject has a certain property (*New York is exciting*).

Correlative conjunction—A two-word coordinating conjunction (e.g., *either... or; both ...and*).

Count noun—A noun that can be preceded by a number (*five books*).

Dangling modifier—A modifier that does not refer clearly to what it modifies, including dangling participles (***Before finishing lunch,*** *the bus left*) and dangling infinitives (***To avoid backstrain,*** *proper posture is essential for computer operators*).

Declarative sentence—A sentence that makes a statement.

Declension—The inflection of a noun or pronoun to indicate its number (*book/book**s***) or case (*he/him*).

Degree—The quality of an adjective or an adverb that permits it to be used in the comparative and superlative.

Demonstrative pronoun—The pronouns *this, these, that,* and *those.*

Dependent clause—A clause (a structure containing both a subject and predicate) that is unable to stand independently as a sentence (*We slept **until the sun rose;** the girl **whom he met***).

Derivation—The formation of words by adding prefixes and suffixes to existing words and bases (*react, active*).

Derivational morpheme—A morpheme that creates one word from another (*enrage, critical*).

Descriptive grammar—An analysis of the patterns of a language by the application of the principles of linguistics; in contrast to pre- scriptive grammar, descriptive grammar is characterized by generalizations based on observation and analysis of data rather than on opinion and belief.

Determiner—A word that precedes and modifies a noun, but is not an adjective or another noun; a structure-class word that can substitute for *a/an* or *the.* Determiners include articles, demonstratives, possessives, indefinites, and numbers.

Developmental errors—Errors made when learning a language based on the speaker's incorrect inference of grammatical rules. For example, in acquiring English, a learner may say *he goed* instead of *he went.*

Digraph—Two letters that represent a single speech sound (the *ph* in *graph* or the *ee* in *speech*).

Diphthong—A speech sound that begins with one vowel and glides into another within the same syllable (as in *oil* or *key*).

Direct discourse—The quotation of the exact words spoken by someone (*He asked, "**What time is it?** "*).

Direct object—A noun or noun phrase that completes the meaning of a transitive verb (*Someone bought **that yellow house***).

Dummy auxiliary—The auxiliary *do* used to form negative and interrogative sentences (*I **did** not read the assignment, **Did** you read the assignment?*).

Ellipsis—The omission of one or more elements from a grammatical construction.

Elliptical clause—A subordinate clause from which constituents, often the subject and an auxiliary verb, have been deleted (Full subordinate clause: ***Although she had finished with her project,*** *Linda still worried about its evaluation;* elliptical clause: ***Although finished with her project,*** *Linda still worried about its evaluation.*)

Etymology—The origin and linguistic development of a word.

Euphemism—The substitution of a neutral term for one considered to be offensive (*powder room, water closet, toilet* are all euphemisms).

Extension—The process by which the meaning of a word broadens to include more categories in its reference. *Bead* originally meant "prayer"; then it narrowed to "prayer bead." Finally it extended its reference to any small ball pierced for stringing.

Finite verb—The main verb of a clause, occurring last (after tense and auxiliaries) in the main verb phrase (*Sharon has **written** an essay*).

Form—Denotes the *part of speech* of a word or the makeup of a grammatical structure; often used in contrast with **function**. In *a rock wall, rock* is a noun in form, though it is adjectival in function, modifying the noun *wall.*

Form class—The set of words capable of changing form through the addition of inflectional and derivational morphemes; nouns, verbs, adjectives, adverbs. Form classes are also called *parts of speech.*

Formal style or usage—The language used in public speech, such as lectures, sermons, and political addresses, or in writing.

Fragment—A phrase or clause that is punctuated and capitalized as though it were a complete sentence, even though it is unable to stand alone as an independent clause. (*Going happily along the way.*) Also called **Sentence fragment.**

Frame sentence—A sentence with an empty slot in the position typically occupied by a member of a particular form class. Nouns occupy the empty slot in the frame sentence (*The*) _____ *seems all right.*

Free morpheme—A morpheme that can stand alone as a word.

Function—The role a word or phrase plays in a sentence. The noun phrase *a letter* has the *direct object* function in *Jerry wrote **a letter.***

Function word—A structure-class word, such as a determiner, conjunction, or preposition.

Gender—The classification of English nouns and pronouns as masculine (*he*), feminine (*she*), or neuter (*it*) based on the sex of the person or thing referred to or on the conventional assignment of sex to inanimate objects (e.g., ships have traditionally been referred to as feminine).

Generalization—See **Extension.**

Generic pronoun—The two personal pronouns that are used to refer to others without specifying the masculine or feminine gender of the person referred to (*you* and *they*).

Gerund—A verb having the {-ing} inflection and functioning as a nominal phrase (*He dislikes **biking***).

Gerund phrase—A gerund accompanied by the subject or the complements (or both) of the verb from which it is derived (*He dislikes **my biking alone in the mountains***).

Gradable adjective—An adjective that can occur with qualifiers (*rather **late**, very **late**, somewhat **late***). **Nongradable** adjectives cannot be compared (**somewhat **dead**, *more **double***).

Grammatical feature—A characteristic of a subclass of words that determines how they may be used. Nouns may have the feature *count* if they may be pluralized (*three oranges*) or *non-count* or *mass* if they cannot (**three electricities*).

Grammatical meaning—The kind of meaning conveyed by word order (*Dog bites man* versus *Man bites dog*) and other grammatical signals such as structure-class words (e.g., determiners, prepositions, auxiliaries, etc.).

Grammatical transformation—A systematic description of the relationship between syntactic structures (e.g., the active and passive forms of a sentence).

Grapheme—A letter of the alphabet.

Headword—The main word of a phrase, the one that others modify.

Helping verb—(See **Auxiliary verb.**)

Homophone—Two words that sound alike but have different meanings (*won* and *one*).

Hypercorrection—An attempt to be overly "correct" resulting in the production of language different from the standard (*between **Harlan and I*** instead of *between **Harlan and me***).

Idiolect—The language variety unique to a single speaker.

Immediate constituent (IC) analysis—A structuralist system of analyzing the structure of sentences and their parts.

Imperative—A command (*Keep the change!*).

Indefinite pronouns—Pronouns that have no specific referent (e.g., *some, any, several*).

Independent clause—A clause able to stand alone as a sentence (*Paula started the fire*).

Indirect discourse—The report (paraphrased) of what someone said (*He asked **what time it was***).

Indirect object—A noun phrase that can occur between a transitive verb and its direct object (*Mary gave **Carlos** a book*).

Infinitive—The unmarked base form of the verb usually preceded by the infinitive marker *to*.

Infinitive form—The unmarked base verb form used after a modal auxiliary (*can **see***); the form of the verb listed in a dictionary entry.

Infinitive phrase—An infinitive that includes the subject or the complements (or both) of the verb from which it is derived (*His family urged him **to apply for the post***).

Inflection—A change in form that signals the grammatical function of nouns, verbs, adjectives, adverbs, and pronouns (e.g., noun plurals, verb tenses).

Inflectional morpheme—A morpheme used to create a variant form of a word in order to signal grammatical information (e.g., the suffix {-ed} signals that a verb is past tense: *walk**ed***).

Informal style or usage—A speech style used in casual settings, as among friends, for example.

Intensifier—(See **Qualifier.**)

Interlanguage—The language form produced by speakers acquiring a second language that combines linguistic features from both their native and their new languages.

International Phonetic Alphabet—A set of common symbols used by linguists to represent accurately the sounds of any language in the world.

Interrogative—A question sentence.

Interrogative clause—A nominal dependent clause beginning with an interrogative word and usually involving a question, directed either to oneself or to another, about an unknown (*I wonder **who left that message on my machine***).

Interrogative word—The structure words used to begin questions; pronouns (*who, whom, whose, which, what,* etc.) and adverbs (*where, when, how,* and *why*).

Intransitive—A verb that has no complement or has an adverb as its complement; a verb in a Type I sentence (*The baby **is sleeping***).

Lexical meaning—The kind of meaning conveyed by words that name things or qualities or actions or events (*judgment, sad, slowly, walk*).

Lexicon—The complete stock of words known by any speaker; a speaker's "mental dictionary."

Linguistic competence—A speaker's knowledge of the phonology, morphology, syntax, and semantics of a particular language.

Linguistic insecurity—An anxious desire to be correct sometimes felt by speakers who believe their language does not always conform to Standard American English. (See **Hypercorrection.**)

Linking verb—A verb that is followed by an adjectival, adverbial, or nominal subject complement; a verb in a Type II, III, or IV sentence (*Edward **is** at school; Edward **looks** ill; Edward **remains** my best friend*).

Main clause—The independent clause in a complex sentence (***Paula started the campfire** after she set up the tent*).

Main verb—The verb that fills the last position in the main verb phrase (*should have been **finished***).

Main verb phrase—The sentence constituent containing tense, the auxiliaries, and the main verb.

Minimal pair—Pairs of words that differ in only one sound (***rat*** and ***cat***).

Misplaced modifier—A modifier so positioned that it is difficult to decide what it modifies (*Mildred went shopping for a dog **with a friend***).

Modal auxiliary—A structure-class word used with verbs (*can, could, will, would, shall, should, may, might,* and *must*).

Modifier—A word or phrase whose function is to give grammatical or lexical information about another word in the sentence (*Subtle* in *a **subtle** color*).

Mood—The classification of verbs according to whether they make a statement (**indicative**), utter a command (**imperative**), or express doubt or unlikelihood (**subjunctive**).

Morpheme—A sound or combination of sounds having a single meaning; the smallest unit of language that has meaning or serves a grammatical function; a morpheme can be a word (*elephant, pen*) or part of a word *(elephants* includes two morphemes—{elephant} and {plural}—as does *penned*—{pen} and {past tense}).

Morphology—The branch of grammar that studies the structure of words.

Narrowing—The process by which the meaning of a word becomes more specialized and includes fewer categories in its reference. *Hussy,* a variant of "house wife," narrowed to refer to strumpets and prostitutes.

Node—A point in the phrase structure tree diagram from which constituents branch off.

Nominal—A word, phrase, or clause that functions as a noun phrase but does not necessarily contain a noun (***Smoking** can be dangerous to your health*).

Nominal clause—Usually a *that*-clause or an interrogative clause.

Nominative—The case used in inflected languages to indicate the subject of a sentence. In English the nominative case is evident in the pronouns *I, he, she, we,* and *they,* as opposed to the object forms *me, him, her, us,* and *them.*

Nominative absolute—A sentence modifier consisting of a reduced clause from which AUX and *be* have been removed, leaving the subject noun phrase followed by a participle form of the main verb or a verb complement. (***His heart beating fast**, Joey waited to hear who had won the prize.*)

Noncount (mass) noun—A noun that ordinarily cannot be preceded by a number or the determiner *a/an* (e.g., *grass, indifference, warmth*).

Nonfinite verb—A verb without tense (an infinitive, participle, or gerund) that occurs other than in a main verb phrase and functions nominally, adjectivally, or adverbially (*He likes **to drive;** a **drinking** fountain; **drinking** and **driving** do not mix*).

Nonfinite verb phrase—A nonfinite verb that includes the subject or complements (or both) of the finite verb from which it is derived (***Lisa's accepting a position as a law clerk** pleased her grandmother*).

Nonrestrictive relative clause—A relative clause that is not essential to the identification of the noun phrase it modifies; set off with commas (*Geof's father, **who is in his eighties,** lives in New Mexico*).

Nonstandard—Pronunciation, vocabulary, or grammar that differs from what is in dictionaries and prescriptive handbooks; more generally, usage that violates community norms for written and spoken language appropriate for public discourse (*He **done** it instead of He **did** it*).

Noun—A form-class word; most nouns can be made plural or possessive; typically, nouns name entities or concrete or abstract things (e.g., *pencil, Fred, sincerity*).

Noun phrase—As a sentence constituent, a noun (***people***) or any group of words that can substitute for a noun (***People who live in glass houses*** *shouldn't throw stones*).

Number—The singular or plural state of nouns and pronouns.

Object case—The form of a pronoun used when it is the object of a verb or preposition (*No one saw **him** open the door for **us***).

Object complement—A noun phrase in the predicate that modifies the direct object (*We thought him **a fool/foolish***).

Ordinal number—Numbers used as determiners (*first, second, third*, etc.).

Participle—A verb ending with either the {-en} or the {-ing} morpheme and occurring as an adjectival or adverbial modifier or after the auxiliary HAVE or BE in a main verb phrase.

Participle phrase—A participle with the subject or the complements (or both) of the verb from which it is derived (***The family eating in the park*** *reminded me of home*).

Parts of speech—Four of the traditional parts of speech, **nouns, verbs, adjectives,** and **verbs,** constitute **form classes** because members of each class share the ability to change form through derivational and/or inflectional morphemes. Other traditional parts of speech include **structure words.**

Passive marker—The auxiliary combination BE + {-en} used to create the passive voice.

Passive transformation—The transformation that describes the relationship between active and passive sentences; see **Passive voice.**

Passive voice—The form of the verb used when the object of a transitive verb becomes its subject; it results from the movement of the subject into a prepositional phrase with *by,* the insertion of BE + {-en} into the main verb phrase before the main verb, and the movement of the direct or indirect object into the subject position (*Heat sapped our strength* becomes *Our strength was sapped by heat*).

Past participle—The form of the verb ending with the {-en} morpheme and able to be used in the sentence *I have always _____ (believed, forgotten) something.*

Past tense—The form of the verb expressing a past action (*ate*) or state (*was*) and containing the {-ed} morpheme.

Pejoration—The process by which a word degenerates, acquiring negative connotations over time. *Senile,* which once simply meant "aged," now means "exhibiting memory loss or mental impairment associated with aging."

Perfect verb forms—Verbs ending with a pastparticiple morpheme (*has eaten, has studied*).

Peripheral example—An example that shares some but not all of a category's characteristics. The word *diligence* is a peripheral example of a noun. It has two noun characteristics: It contains a noun-making morpheme (*-ence*) and it can fit in the frame sentence (*Diligence seems necessary*). However, it can neither pluralize (**diligences*) nor become possessive (**diligence's*) and when it stands alone it cannot be preceded by an article (**the/a diligence*).

Person—A grammatical category differentiating between speaker (**first person:** *I, we*) and either the one spoken to (**second person:** *you*) or others (**third person:** *he, she, it, they*).

Personal pronoun—The pronouns naming people and things (*I, you, we, it*, etc.).

Phoneme—A family of speech sounds that speakers of a language hear as being the same. For some speakers of English, the vowels in *cot* and *caught* are the same and, hence, a single phoneme. For others they are two different phonemes.

Phonemic alphabet—A system of writing in which there is one symbol for every significant sound in the language.

Phonemic awareness—The awareness that spoken words are made up of separate sounds. Training in phonemic awareness involves teaching techniques such as rhyming sounds or cutting syllables into smaller segments of sound.

Phonetic—A representation of the sounds of speech in which a distinct symbol designates each unique sound.

Phonetic alphabet—(See **International Phonetic Alphabet.**)

Phonics—A method of teaching reading and spelling based on familiarizing students with the phonemic interpretation of ordinary spelling. Phonics stresses the relationships between written letters and the spoken sounds represented by those letters.

Phonological awareness—The ability to deal explicitly and segmentally with phonemes.

Phrasal verb—A two-word verb made up of a verb plus a particle (***Look*** *it* ***up,*** **Try on** *the dress*).

Phrase—Word or words that functions as a unit within a sentence (noun phrase, adjective phrase, prepositional phrase, etc.). May be a single word.

Phrase marker—A transformationalist system of representing the hierarchical structure of the phrases making up a sentence; resembles an upside-down tree.

Plural—A grammatical feature enabling nouns and pronouns to express the difference between one and more than one (*car/cars*).

Possessive—A grammatical trait of nouns and pronouns generally expressing possession (*Mary's, his*).

Pragmatic competence—The ability to use language in interpersonal relationships, taking into account such complexities as social distance between speakers and indirectness required in a given situation.

Predicate—The second of two parts of the sentence; the verb plus its complements; usually an assertion predicated about the subject (*Brazil **won the 1994 World Cup***).

Predicate adjective—An adjective or adjective phrase that follows a linking verb and characterizes the subject in some way; an adjectival subject complement (*Jenny seems **happy***).

Predicate nominative—A noun or noun phrase that follows a linking verb and renames the subject; a nominal subject complement (*Jenny became **a pilot***).

Prefix—An affix attached to the beginning of a word to create a new word (*act/**en**act, tidy/**un**tidy*).

Preposition—A structure-class word that precedes a noun phrase functioning as its object; together, the preposition and its object form a unit that can modify form-class words; can be simple (*to, under, of*) or phrasal (*because of*).

Prepositional phrase—A preposition followed by a noun phrase functioning as its object (*up the street*).

Prescriptive grammar—In contrast to descriptive grammars based on linguistic observation and analysis, prescriptive grammar judges particular items of language usage as either "correct" or "incorrect," based on opinion and tradition dating in part from the eighteenth century; the regulative rules found in writer's handbooks and some textbooks.

Present participle—The form of the verb ending in -*ing* and able to be used in the sentence *They are _____ (that) right now.*

Present tense—The form of the verb expressing present time (*I **like**, he **likes***).

Principal parts of English verbs—The five forms most verbs can take: the base form (*eat*); the simple present tense (*eats*); the simple past tense (*ate*); the past participle (*eaten*); and the present participle (*eating*).

Progressive verb forms—Verbs ending with the present-participle morpheme -*ing* (*is **eating***).

Pronoun—A word that can substitute for a noun or noun phrase, such as the personal pronouns *he, she, it.*

Proper noun—A noun that names a specific person, place, or historical event (*Gandhi, Chicago, the Civil War*).

Prototypes—Members of a class having the most characteristics typical of that class; a prototype is a clear example.

Prototypical example—An example that belongs to a category because it shares all or most of the category's characteristics. An example of prototypical noun is the word *desk*. It can be pluralized (*desk**s***), it occurs with the possessive (*the desk**'s** top*), and it fits the frame sentence (*The desk seems all right*).

Pro-verb—A verb like *do* that can substitute for the second occurrence of another verb (*I **like** the play more than you **do***).

Qualifier (intensifier)—A structure-class word; precedes and indicates the degree of adjectives and adverbs (***very** long, **more** slowly*).

Question—A sentence used to elicit information (*What time is it?*).

Question word—A structure-class word used to name the item for which a question seeks identification. It is also called an **interrogative** or a ***wh*-word** because most question words in English start with *wh-* (*who, whom, whose, which, what, where, why, when,* and *how*).

Recipient—The person for whom or to whom the action of a verb is performed; the indirect object.

Reciprocal pronoun—The pronoun combinations *each other, one another.*

Reduced clause—The grammatical structure remaining when constituents (including tense and the auxiliaries) are removed from a clause (***While waiting for the train**,* which is derived from a full clause, *While I was waiting for the train*).

Reed-Kellogg diagram—A traditional system for diagramming sentences; devised in the nineteenth century by the American grammarians Brainerd Kellogg and Alonzo Reed.

Referent—The thing that a word names or refers to. (The referent of *cow* is a class of animals with specific characteristics.)

Reflexive pronoun—A pronoun ending in -*self* or -*selves*, such as *herself, themselves*.

Regional dialect—A form of speech associated with a geographic area or region.

Relative adverb—The adverbs *where, when,* and *why,* used to introduce relative clauses (*the place **where** you live*).

Relative clause—A clause that begins with a relative pronoun or relative adverb and modifies a noun or noun phrase that precedes it (*the boy **who lives here***).

Relative pronoun—The pronouns *who, whose, whom, that,* and *which,* used to introduce relative clauses (*the boy **who** lives here*).

Restrictive relative clause—A relative clause that identifies the referent of a noun or noun phrase that it modifies; not set off with commas (*A man **who is in his eighties** is an octogenarian*).

SAE—Standard American English refers to the variety of American English that is widely shared by middle class, urban, educated speakers and most closely resembles the written form of the language taught in schools.

Schwa—The symbol (ə) used to represent the mid-central neutral vowel in English, as in the final syllable of *sof**a**.* In our version of the phonemic alphabet, it also represents the vowel in *cut.*

Semantic change—The change in the meaning of a word or phrase over a period of time.

Semantic feature—Elements of meaning (like *human/nonhuman, animate/inanimate*) that affect how words can be combined.

Semantics—The study of the meaning of words, sentences, or other language forms.

Sentence—A word or group of words that usually consists of at least one subject and predicate.

Sentence modifier—A word, phrase, or clause functioning as an adverbial modifier of the whole sentence (***To be frank,** I have never answered the letter*).

Simple sentence—A sentence consisting of a single independent clause (*Joan flies gliders*).

Social dialect—A form of speech used by a group within a society characterized especially by the socioeconomic status, ethnicity, and/or gender of the speakers.

Sociolinguistic stratification—The distribution of linguistic variables into levels corresponding to social variables. The stratification continuum runs from the dialects of speakers without formal education, whose speech may contain a high degree of nonstandard forms, to the social dialect of educated, middle-class professionals, whose speech rarely contains nonstandard forms.

Specialization—See **Narrowing.**

Standard—Pronunciation, vocabulary, and grammar that conform to what is stated as being appropriate in dictionaries and prescriptive handbooks; more generally, usage that matches community norms for written and spoken language appropriate for public discourse.

Standard Spoken English—The relatively uniform variety of language spoken throughout the country and based on Standard Written English.

Standard Written English—The edited variety of language appropriate for use in writing. Also known as Standard Edited English.

Structural formula—In Transformational Generative Grammar, a statement of the sequence of obligatory constituents making up a sentence. For example, the formula S —> NP + VP states that a sentence (S) consists of a noun phrase (NP) followed by a verb phrase (VP).

Structure-class words—Words that occur in a single form and signal structural (grammatical) relationships within phrases, clauses, and sentences (e.g., determiners, auxiliaries, prepositions, etc.).

Style—Variation in language use based on the formality or informality of the social setting.

Style shifting—When the speaker adapts language use to the formality or informality of the situation (*Goodbye!* as opposed to *See ya!*).

Subject—The first of two parts of the sentence; usually the topic about which something is asserted (or predicated) (***Brazil** won the 1994 World Cup*).

Subject case—The form of a pronoun used when it is the subject of a clause or sentence.

Subject complement—The nominal or adjectival constituent that follows a linking verb (*Jenny seems **happy**; Jenny became **a pilot***).

Subjunctive—A verb form used mainly to express the speaker's attitude about the likelihood or factuality of a given situation. Traditionally, the subjunctive is used to describe an occurrence contrary to fact (*If only I **were** ten years younger*).

Subordinate clause—A dependent clause beginning with a subordinating conjunction; usually adverbial in function (*Tim began running **when he heard a noise***).

Subordinating conjunction—A structure-class word that makes one clause dependent upon another (e.g., *although, because*).

Suffix—An affix added to the end of a word, either to create a new word (*act/actor*) or to add grammatical information (*old/oldest*).

Superlative—Degree expressed for adjectives and adverbs by using *most* or {-est}: (***most** beautiful, happi**est***).

Syntax—The part of grammar dealing with the arrangement of words into phrases, clauses, and sentences.

Tag question—A question at the end of a statement that seeks the listener's agreement (*That was a good show, **wasn't it?***).

Textual competence—The ability to use language for a variety of purposes, such as stories, conversations, and letters.

That*-clause**—A dependent clause beginning with the expletive *that* and functioning nominally; *that* may be deleted (*I said **that I would pay;** I said **I would pay).

Third-person singular—The pronouns *he, she,* and *it* and nouns that they can replace; also used to refer to the form of the verb ("third person singular, present tense") that is used when such a noun or pronoun is the subject (*She **tries** it*).

Topic—The theme of the sentence; that about which the speaker wants to say something. (See **Comment.**)

Transfer errors—Errors made when acquiring a second language in which a speaker substitutes features of the native language in the new language (for example, an Italian speaker saying *He has cold* [Italian *Lui ha freddo*] for the English *He is cold*).

Transitive verb—A verb that has a direct object as its complement; a verb in a Type V sentence (*Betty **owns** that car*).

Underlying structure—The form of a sentence before any transformations have occurred. For example, *I want to eat* derives from two underlying sentences: *I + [present] + want + something* and *I + [present] + eat.*

Verb—A form-class word having an {-s} affix in the third-person singular (*He walk**s***) and an {-ing}

affix in the present participle form (*He is walk**ing***); typically, verbs designate actions, sensations, and states (*swim, feel, seem*).

Verb expansion rule—The formula that describes which tense and participle morphemes are affixed to the auxiliaries and verb of the main verb phrase.

Verb particle—A word or words that combine with a verb to create a phrasal verb (*put **over on**, think **through***).

Verb phrase—As a sentence constituent, a verb (***performed***) or any group of words that can substitute for a verb (***performed yesterday in the London Coliseum***).

Verbal—A word derived from or having characteristics similar to a verb.

Voice—An ability of verbs to express the relation between the subject and the action expressed by the verb. In the active voice, the subject is the agent who performs the action (*Birds eat insects*); in the passive voice, the subject receives the action of the verb (*Insects are eaten by birds*).

Voiced/Voiceless sounds—Sounds uttered with the vocal folds vibrating are voiced: ([b], [d], [g]). Sounds uttered without vibration of the vocal folds are voiceless: ([p], [t], [k]).

Vowel—A speech sound produced with a relatively free passage of breath flowing through the vocal cavity ([a], [e], [i], [o], and [u]). Vowels generally form the nucleus of syllables.

***Wh*-question**—A question that asks for specific information, as opposed to one that asks for a yes or no answer; typically, *wh*-questions begin with an interrogative word, such as *who, what, when, where, why,* or *how.*

***Wh*-word**—An interrogative word, usually beginning with *wh,* used to introduce questions.

Yes/no question—A question to which the answer is either yes or no (*Is it time to go?*).

Zero allomorph—An inflection on nouns or verbs presumed to be present although invisible. For example, in *three **sheep*** and *He **bit** a home run,* the plural of *sheep* and the past tense of *bit* are said to be realized as zeros.

Index